chocolate
CHOCOLATE

LISA YOCKELSON

PHOTOGRAPHY BY BEN FINK

WILEY

JOHN WILEY AND SONS, INC.

This book is printed on acid-free paper. ♾

Published by John Wiley & Sons, Inc., Hoboken, New Jersey
Published simultaneously in Canada

COVER AND INTERIOR DESIGN by Vertigo Design, NYC
COVER AND INTERIOR PHOTOGRAPHY by Ben Fink
BAKING FOR PHOTOGRAPHY by the author
PROP STYLING by the author with Ben Fink
CONCEPTUAL VISION PRESERVATION by Pamela Chirls, senior culinary editor, John Wiley & Sons, Inc.
COMPUTER TECHNICAL ASSISTANCE AND SUPPORT FOR THE AUTHOR by John George of CGI-AMS
All of the linens, silver, and china in the photographs are from the author's private collection.
The author and publisher extend grateful thanks to Frank Babb Randolph of Frank Babb Randolph Interior Design for the loan of wallpaper background materials for some of the photographs.
Comments about *ChocolateChocolate* may be forwarded to the author at fourstarbaking@earthlink.net.

LIBRARY OF CONGRESS CATALOGING-IN-PUBLICATION DATA

Yockelson, Lisa.
ChocolateChocolate / Lisa Yockelson.
p. cm.
ISBN-13 978-0-471-42807-7 (cloth)
ISBN-10 0-471-42807-8 (cloth)
1. Cookery (Chocolate) 2. Chocolate. I. Title: Chocolate chocolate. II. Title.
TX767.C5Y63 2005
641.6'374--dc22
2005001254

PRINTED IN CHINA

10 9 8 7 6 5 4 3 2 1

TO THE MEMORY OF MY GRANDPARENTS

Lillian Levy Yockelson

AND

Louis Yockelson

for the inspiration to reach far and long

Contents

With appreciation

THE VISION FOR *CHOCOLATECHOCOLATE* surely came from my late mother and paternal grandmother. In elementary school, while other children were baking in miniature ovens with doll-sized equipment, I baked right along with each of them in two separate, but equal, grown-up kitchens. A genuine love of and respect for the baking process was planted only to sprout years later in a literary context. This volume, then, honors their memory.

Pamela Chirls, my editor at Wiley for *Chocolate Chocolate* (and for *Baking by Flavor*), clearly recognized the value of documenting my work in chocolate-baking. With absolute devotion, determination, and thoughtful literary attention to every stage of its creation, Pam moved the process along to produce a portrait of my work in chocolate. All of this has been accomplished with a full editorial plate in addition to responsibilities at home, mothering twins Allix and Julia, and the youngest addition, Isabelle, who has grown up—adorably—along with this book. Simply stated, Pam is a dream editor and this book is distinguished by her commitment to it.

In addition to Pam, gracing every circumstance with his own brand of good taste and calming charm, is Mickey Choate, my literary agent at The Choate Agency in Pelham, New York. Who else would patiently listen to each and every development in the writing of *ChocolateChocolate;* take care of the business of publishing, track my recipes-in-progress; bake brownies, cupcakes, and sky-high layer cakes from the working manuscript; and be the intelligent voice at the other end of the telephone? Although *ChocolateChocolate* was fashioned with recipes and research that have long been a part of my baking studies, it is with his support that this work has flourished into the book you now hold in your hands.

The imprint of Ben Fink, the photographer for *ChocolateChocolate,* is represented on these pages as so much more than the craft of capturing baking-centered images. Although Ben is an artist whose work is set in a contemporary place in time, the perspective that he brings to each cake, cookie, or scone in *ChocolateChocolate* has a Renaissance-like feel to it. His understanding about my work grasped a certain poignancy, refined passion, and clean, romantic intensity. Through Ben's extraordinary range, I discovered an entirely new plane for the medium of chocolate.

As outstanding book designers, Alison Lew and Renata DeOliveira at Vertigo Design NYC, welcomed this project and conferred their imaginative stamp to it. As the author, I am spoiled by Vertigo's creative attention to the contents of this work. From the beginning, as we sat around a table exploring the conceptual elements and visual structure of this book, this design group has been a bright beacon of style.

At Wiley, an all-encompassing group of professionals embraced this project, and they are: Robert Garber, vice president and executive group publisher; Natalie Chapman, vice president and publisher; Claire Griffin, director of marketing; Todd Fries, senior marketing manager; Diana Cisek, director of production; Gypsy Lovett, associate director of publicity; Michele Sewell, culinary publicist; Jaime Harder, associate publicist; Michael Olivo, senior production editor; Paul Dinovo, associate director of creative services; Jeff Faust, art director; PJ Campbell, director of events; Anna Christensen, events coordinator; Anne Ficklen, executive editor; Kristi Hart, editor; Linda Ingroia, senior editor; Justin Schwartz, senior editor; Rachel Bartlett, assistant editor; Adam Kowit, assistant editor; Jessica DeSanta, editorial assistant; Jennifer Brennan, editorial assistant; and Christine DiComo, editorial assistant.

An author's work shares the collective influence of editors near and far, past and present, and my contributions to the literature of baking have been shaped by these editors, each notable in her own right: Patricia Brown, Susan Friedland, Darra Goldstein, Sheryl Julian, and Phyllis Richman.

John George, my talented computer technology and systems management expert (of CGI-AMS), has been instrumental in overseeing the structure that allowed me to work on this project from its beginning to its all-encompassing final manuscript (no small task). As well, John and his talented life partner Peter Maye (director of print production at Discovery Creative Resources within Discovery Communications) have been enthusiastic taste-testers of nearly every dessert in this book (no small task).

The ongoing expertise of Daniel Magruder at Voell Custom Kitchens in Arlington, Virginia; Frank Randolph of Frank Babb Randolph Interior Design; the wonderful group at Landscape Projects in Bethesda, Maryland; Eleni Louh and Tiana Marmaras at Yves Delorme; and all of the technical experts at the William F. Collins Company continue to make my home life both attractive and functional—for which, many thanks.

A bevy of friends and professionals—distinguished authors and food writers, equipment specialists, caterers, chefs and pastry chefs, critics, design and business experts, purveyors, and fine home bakers—continue to encourage me, and they are: Alison Arnett, Rose Levy Beranbaum, Larissa Berrios, Tish Boyle, Flo Braker (the godmother of *Baking by Flavor*, superb baker, and distinguished friend), Peter Brett, Warren Brown, Joan Burka, Marcel Desaulniers, Teresa Farney, Gail Forman, Susan Fussell, Stephanie Gorenflo and her daughter Claire Gorenflo, Alexandra Greeley, Carole Greenwood, Bruce Healy, proprietors Dan Adams and John Marshall of Highfield Dairy and Farm in Fulton County, Pennsylvania (the source for buying those beautiful Aracauna eggs at the FRESHFARM Market at Dupont Circle), Mindy Galke, Valerie Hill, Michèle Jacobs, Kate Jansen, Susan Lampton and David Michael Lampton, Carolyn Larson, Manuel J. Le Gourlay, David Lebovitz, Robert Lescher, Susan Lescher, Susannah Lescher, Quentin Looney, Susan Lindeborg, Jeanne McManus, Nancy Pollard, Susan Purdy, Peter Reinhart, Marie Romejko, Anna Saint John, Debra Samuels, Charles Santos, Terri Sapienza, Renee Schettler, Lisa Stark, Sylvia Thompson, Carole Walter, and Robert Wolke. And from Aunt Lisa to The Cupcake Kids—Alexander and Clara Choate, and Julia, Allix, and Isabelle Chirls—many thanks for your collective taste-testing of the little cakes, and one piece of baking advice: remember not to eat all of the sprinkles before you frost the cupcakes.

On a special note, Rose Levy Beranbaum, dear friend and author of the landmark book *The Cake Bible*, shares my intensity and reverence for the baking process. Her encouragement continues to be steadfast and sure, and her kindnesses are constant.

And to the memory of my family—my paternal great-grandmother Rebecca Levy, paternal grandparents Lillian Levy Yockelson and Louis Yockelson, parents Irene and Bernard Yockelson, and uncle Wilbert Yockelson—who adored all things delicious and beautiful. You would have loved this book. You are remembered.

A chocolate journal

FOR AS LONG AS I CAN REMEMBER, the flavor of chocolate has been an obsession, a craving, a calling. As an ingredient in baking, it lures me with the rich promise of putting a fork into something velvety, downy, buttery, and deeply moist. I believe that chocolate is a trophy flavor. Would any thinking person turn away a mighty chocolate cupcake covered in a frosting that repeats chocolate in dashing peaks and swirls? Or a luxurious chocolate waffle? (It may be a waffle, and it may be griddled in an iron, but to me it tastes like warm, almost-fudgy cake.) And what about an enormous cookie, all buttery and chewy, touched with brown sugar and stubby with chips or chunks of chocolate?

Chocolate is an elemental flavor. In a compelling way, its magnetic presence draws you into a recipe and, at a pivotal moment, into dessert. As a voluptuous ingredient, it attracts with every bite. What you bake with chocolate can be *romantic* and *indulgent* (an ultra-moist square of chocolate cake capped with a silky, handmade truffle), *sleek* (a towering panettone flecked with tiny chocolate chips), *fanciful* (individual Boston Cream Cakelettes, a collusion of vanilla cake, creamy filling, and chocolate glaze), *intense* (an endlessly buttery flourless chocolate cake), or *cozy* (a thick slice of birthday layer cake covered in waves of frosting). The depth, intensity, and utter range of a chocolate dessert is great and impressive.

This baking cookbook, *ChocolateChocolate,* is actually a written record—a kind of baking diary documented in a detailed way—of all the batters and doughs that I've stirred up in endless succession as I watched a mixing bowl revolve with a chocolatey mixture in it.

You will see that the extensive recipe section in this baking book is a departure from the usual organization by type of dessert. Instead of recipes grouped by category, such as cakes, cookies, pies, and so on, they are arranged by specific themes. The subject matter—arranged in such sections as "Brownie Style," "Mudslide," "Deep, Dark, and Bittersweet," "Chips and Chunks," and "Flourless and Almost-Flourless Chocolate Cakes"—reflects the way I approach baking, and that is by the design, development, and style of the recipe. The soul of this book is the result of my probing into the process of working with chocolate in batters and doughs.

THE ORGANIZATION OF *CHOCOLATECHOCOLATE*

ChocolateChocolate is divided into two parts.

The first part of this book introduces you to the hows and whys of using chocolate in baking recipes. The entire section is intended as a resource guide that illustrates how the flavor of chocolate can be orchestrated to forward its true intensity in what you bake.

The second part contains many voluptuous recipes that, taken together, compose a sweet tableau of my favorite chocolate doughs and batters. Each recipe is accompanied by a description, a procedure, and, as appropriate, an assortment of end notes: Style, Accent, Study, and Element. These comments and suggestions will show you how to expand on a recipe and provide you with insight into certain ingredients and techniques:

The *Style* section will give you the opportunity to elaborate on the basic recipe, offering variations that may suggest adding nuts, another type or form of chocolate, an extra condiment, or an accessory ingredient.

The *Accent* section explains how to cultivate and step up the chocolate flavor in a particular recipe.

The *Study* section explains a reason for using a particular method or technique, a special baking hint, an interesting note that has contributed to the evolution of a recipe, or advice from my research on the subject of baking with chocolate. For example, particular brands of bittersweet chocolate are suggested for certain sweets and appear in this note when a recipe features it.

The *Element* section proposes a way to use what you bake in one recipe as a fanciful addition or component to another dessert. For example, the Chocolate Fudge Sauce (page 376) or Bittersweet Chocolate Plate Sauce (page 390) can be used as an undercoating or topping for some of the single-layer chocolate cakes or tortes.

Along with recipes, and notes on technique, ingredients, and equipment, *ChocolateChocolate* also contains a number of informative charts. At a glance, the charts reveal a significant part of: my research in chocolate and the desserts that highlight it, and they are: a survey of chocolate available in its many forms, styles, and strengths; the path to understanding how chocolate relates to basic baking staples; the way to negotiate levels of chocolate intensity in a dessert; the nature of basic chocolate batters and doughs; a list that reveals all the premium butters that fare best in chocolate-based desserts; and the characteristics and functions of basic baking ingredients. At the end of the book, a freezing chart lists the recipes that can be frozen—baked or unbaked—for future use.

Baking with chocolate is a sweet and simple art that is rewarding and immediately accessible. *ChocolateChocolate* can be used in several ways: to find a recipe for a favorite dessert that's just packed with chocolate; to learn how chocolate behaves in the baking process; to gather information on the various types and intensities of chocolate and discover their many uses; and of course, to simply rejoice in what is surely the most luxurious of all flavors. When chocolate is combined with familiar baking staples, something miraculous happens: what you pull from the oven is irresistible, darkly alluring, astonishing. In its every essence and form, when it's chocolate, it dazzles and enchants. And isn't that divine?

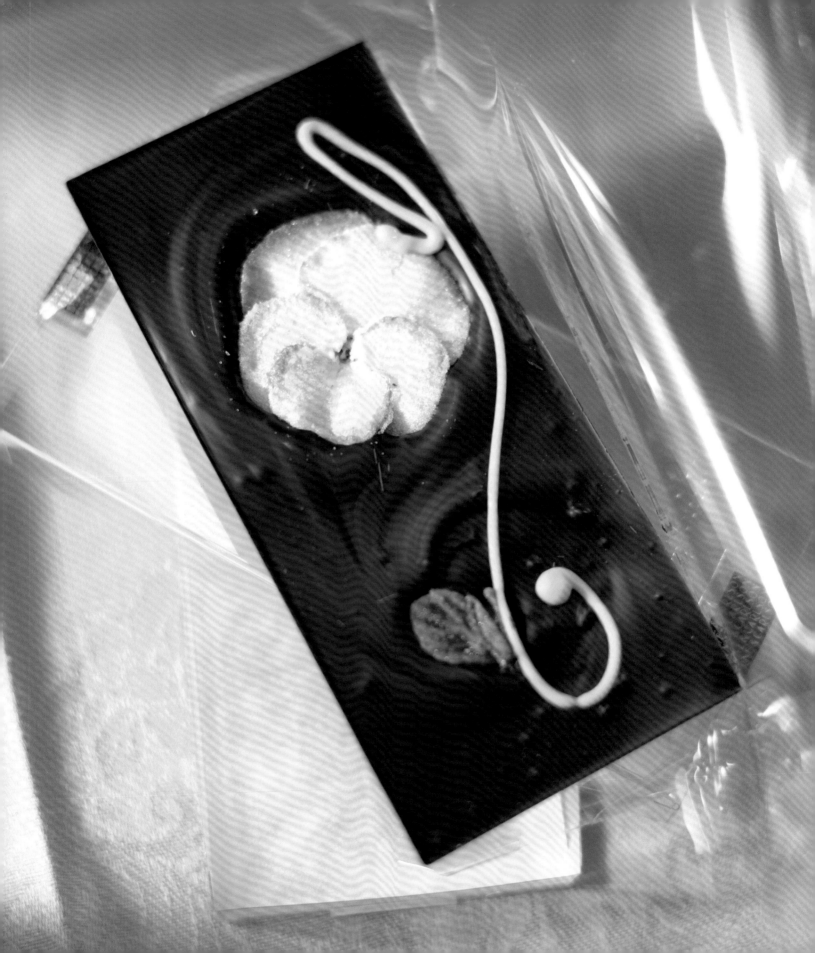

THE PROCESSING OF CHOCOLATE—from the tropical bean to the bar or block of chocolate you so lovingly unwrap—is important, for it develops two pivotal characteristics: taste and texture. The flavor and consistency of chocolate used in a batter, dough, frosting, filling, or sauce are the direct result of specific methods of cultivation and production.

THE CACAO, OR COCOA, tree (*Theobroma cacao, L.*), is tropical, flourishing in locations within a zone 20 degrees north and south of the equator. Cacao trees thrive in a humid environment. This evergreen tree is bred by seeding or grafting. Pods containing cocoa beans develop from insect-impregnated flowers. The pods, as they ripen, turn from a greenish red to a burnt orange hue and are removed by cutting them away from the trunk of the tree or from the more substantial branches to which they're attached. The pods are cut open to expose the beans; there are about 35 beans nestled in a pod. At this point, the beans, attached to a medial core called the placenta, are quite damp. The beans are composed of two components, the outer "shell" and an interior "nib."

After the oval-shaped beans are removed from the pods, they undergo a fermentation process to cultivate their flavor. When fermentation is completed, the beans are dried in their atmospheric surroundings, cleaned, and roasted to unlock all the wonderfully complex flavors. Next the beans are shelled or left unshelled, depending upon the roasting objective: the beans are either roasted whole or in shelled form. If the nibs themselves are to be roasted, the shells are removed first. The nibs are the essence of chocolate flavor; they are ground to produce the all-important chocolate liquor. The grinding process serves to cultivate the composition and taste of the chocolate. The resulting chocolate liquor is the purest rendering of the bean and is commonly known as unsweetened chocolate. (Unsweetened chocolate is also referred to as "baking chocolate" or "bitter chocolate," both dated terms given the current language that references premium chocolate.) Beyond producing chocolate liquor, the nibs are ground with a sweetener and occasionally with supplementary cocoa butter, lecithin (a plant-based emulsifier that helps to establish a creamy, satiny textural quality and good flowing capability), and/or a flavoring. Exactly what accompanies the nibs in the grinding process depends on the ultimate production requirement.

The ground mixture is then conched, a process by which the ingredients (chocolate liquor, plus an emulsifier, sweetener, fat, and/or flavoring) are combined and beaten for a continuous, and frequently extended, period of time. Through several phases, conching refines the chocolate by reducing its acidity in order to create a supple, creamy texture and develop the best flavor possible. The resulting chocolate—with its proper "flow," fully developed flavor, reduced bitterness, and velvety texture—is then tempered. The tempering process is essentially one of manipulating the temperature of melted chocolate so that, on cooling, it is shiny, firm, and shelf-stable. When chocolate is tempered correctly, it is lustrous, free of streaks, and breaks into pieces with a proper "crack" or "snap." Appropriately tempered chocolate has an almost crisp-sounding rupture to it when you break it apart in your hands. The same crisp crack is noticeable when you bite into a chocolate-dipped bonbon, or any piece of molded chocolate that is perfectly tempered. Tempered chocolate is then shaped and cast into blocks or bars.

A chocolate vocabulary

THE ESSENTIAL FORMS OF CHOCOLATE, designated as such by the presence of cocoa solids, are (1) *unsweetened;* (2) *semisweet* and *bittersweet* (under the umbrella designation of "sweet" chocolate); (3) *milk;* and (4) *cocoa powder.* About *white chocolate:* note that cocoa solids are not present in white chocolate, but there are specific requirements for ingredients in its production in order to identify it by that name. About *couverture:* couverture is the designation given to bittersweet, white, or milk chocolate that has been conched for a longer period of time and carries with it a significantly higher percentage of cocoa butter. Its peerless coating quality makes it ideal to use for dipping candy fillings or to mold into fancy chocolate embellishments for decorative work and centerpieces. Melted and used in doughs and batters, couverture chocolate contributes exceptional silkiness and moistness.

The Code of Federal Regulations (CFR) of the United States government has established precise standards to identify primary cacao-based products (21 CFR PART 163—CACAO PRODUCTS: Subpart A—General Provisions through Subpart B—Requirements for Specific Standardized Cacao Products). In the information below, note that when "sweeteners" is an element, documentation refers to it as "nutritive carbohydrate sweeteners." The sweetener in the range of chocolate represented here is sugar, and specifically in many types of chocolate I've worked with, cane sugar. Finally, a Standard of Identity for white chocolate has been installed and determined, and this has been in effect since January 1, 2004. Following is a review of the cacao-based products (all percentages are designated as "by weight of").

CACAO NIBS are designated as the "food" (see accordingly § 163.110 (a) *Description* (1), Code of Federal Regulations) resulting from the processing (curing, cleaning, drying, cracking) of cacao beans.

CHOCOLATE LIQUOR (UNSWEETENED CHOCOLATE) is the result of grinding the cocoa nibs. The chocolate liquor (unsweetened chocolate) is made up of a minimum of 50 percent cocoa butter ("cacao fat").

BOTH SEMISWEET AND BITTERSWEET CHOCOLATE are designated as "sweet chocolate" and contain a minimum of 35 percent chocolate liquor. ("Sweet" chocolate must have at least 15 percent chocolate liquor.) Other ingredients—sweetener, cocoa butter, emulsifier, spice, milk, cream, butter, and flavoring among them—may be added.

As you will see in the chart on page 5, A Baker's List of Chocolate, many premium boutique bittersweet or extra-bittersweet chocolate bars contain varying levels/amounts of cocoa and frequently feature the percentage content prominently on the label.

MILK CHOCOLATE contains a minimum of 10 percent chocolate liquor, a minimum of 3.39 percent milk fat, and a minimum of 12 percent milk solids, as well as such additions as sweetener, spice, cocoa butter, emulsifier, and flavoring.

BREAKFAST COCOA (COCOA POWDER) is the end result of the procedure of crushing/grinding into powder what remains after a certain amount of cocoa butter is pressed out from the ground nibs. A minimum of 22 percent cocoa butter ("fat") is present in breakfast cocoa. An alternate name for breakfast cocoa is "high fat cocoa." "Breakfast cocoa" and "high fat cocoa," the two specific identifications given to cocoa powder in formal documentation, are known to readers and cooks as simply "cocoa" or "unsweetened cocoa powder." Cocoa is available either alkalized (treated with an alkali to neutralize its acidity and called "Dutch-process" or "Dutched") and nonalkalized (also known as "natural" cocoa). In addition to an alkali, "breakfast cocoa" may also include spices and flavorings.

The recipes in *ChocolateChocolate* call for "unsweetened alkalized cocoa powder," for I prefer its flavor. Depending on the brand, the term "Dutch-processed" may or may not appear on the label. Some ingredient lists on the boxes or bags reveal that the cocoa powder has been treated with an alkali, or Dutch-processed.

WHITE CHOCOLATE, with its absence of cocoa solids, is required to consist of a minimum of 20 percent cocoa fat (butter), 14 percent milk solids, and 3.5 percent milk fat, in addition to a "nutritive carbohydrate sweetener" (not in excess of 55 percent). In addition to other ingredients, it may also contain butter, milk, emulsifier, and flavoring.

The overall code for cacao products cites detailed requirements, including descriptions and ingredients, and these serve to classify each one in detail. For further information regarding the Standard of Identity for cacao products and additional ancillary information, consult the following sections of in-depth primary source material in the Code of Federal Regulations (21 CFR PART 163—Cacao Products):

§ 163.110 on cacao nibs

§ 163.111 on chocolate liquor

§ 163.112 on breakfast cocoa

§ 163.113 on cocoa

§ 163.123 on sweet chocolate

§ 163.130 on milk chocolate

§ 163.124 on white chocolate

A wealth of chocolate

FOR THE CHOCOLATE-LOVING BAKER, there is a nearly boundless, and oftentimes daunting, assortment of chocolate available to use in the baking process. The chart, A Baker's List of Chocolate, classifies chocolate by its brand name, type, and quantity. Specific sources are identified, as applicable. While many forms and intensities of bittersweet, intense bittersweet, semisweet, milk, and white chocolate, in addition to cocoa powder and chocolate embellishments, are available to the cook, this list offers a selection of those chocolates most worthwhile to use in the baking process.

A baker's list of chocolate

Chips, chunks, wafers, buttons, and pistoles (pellets or wafers)

NAME	SOURCE AND TYPE	QUANTITY
WEISS KACINKOA BITTERSWEET CHOCOLATE 85% COCOA	*La Cuisine—The Cook's Resource* intense bittersweet pistoles (pellets)	8 ounces
WEISS EBENE BITTERSWEET CHOCOLATE 72% COCOA	*La Cuisine—The Cook's Resource* intense bittersweet pistoles (pellets)	8 ounces
WEISS ACARIGUA BITTERSWEET CHOCOLATE 70% COCOA	*La Cuisine—The Cook's Resource* bittersweet pistoles (pellets)	8 ounces
VALRHONA EXTRA AMER BITTERSWEET PISTOLES 67% CACAO	*La Cuisine—The Cook's Resource* bittersweet pistoles (pellets)	8 ounces
VALRHONA EXTRA BITTERSWEET PISTOLES 61% CACAO	*La Cuisine—The Cook's Resource* bittersweet pistoles (pellets)	8 ounces
MERKENS BITTERSWEET BUTTONS	*The Baker's Catalogue* bittersweet buttons	1 pound
MICHEL CLUIZEL ILHA TOMA 65% CACAO PISTOLES	*La Cuisine—The Cook's Resource* bittersweet pistoles (pellets)	8 ounces
GUITTARD BITTERSWEET ONYX WAFERS 72% CHOCOLATE LIQUOR	*The Baker's Catalogue* bittersweet wafers	1 pound
SCHOKINAG EXTREME DARK CHIPS 75% CHOCOLATE LIQUOR	*The Baker's Catalogue* extreme/intensely bittersweet chips	1 pound
SCHOKINAG BITTERSWEET CHIPS	*The Baker's Catalogue* bittersweet chips	1 pound
GHIRARDELLI DOUBLE CHOCOLATE CHIPS	bittersweet chips	11.5 ounces
NESTLÉ SEMI-SWEET MORSELS	semisweet chips	6 ounces; 12 ounces; 24 ounces
NESTLÉ MEGA MORSELS	large semisweet chips	11.5 ounces
GHIRARDELLI SEMI-SWEET CHOCOLATE CHIPS	semisweet chips	12 ounces

NAME	SOURCE AND TYPE	QUANTITY
NESTLÉ MINI MORSELS	miniature semisweet chips	12 ounces
BAKER'S SEMI-SWEET CHOCOLATE CHUNKS	semisweet chunks	12 ounces
CACAO BARRY CHOCOLATE CHIPS	*La Cuisine—The Cook's Resource* semisweet chips	1 pound
CACAO BARRY MINI CHIPS	*La Cuisine—The Cook's Resource* miniature semisweet chocolate chips	8 ounces
CACAO BARRY MICRO CHIPS	*La Cuisine—The Cook's Resource* ultra-tiny semisweet chips	8 ounces
MERKENS SEMISWEET CHOCOLATE CHIPS	*The Baker's Catalogue* semisweet chips	1 pound
VOSGES HAUT-CHOCOLAT BLACK PEARL CHIPS 55% CACAO COUVERTURE	ginger + Japanese wasabi + black sesame seeds + Belgian dark chocolate	4 ounces
SCHOKINAG SPECIAL EDITION SEMISWEET CHOCOLATE BAKING CHUNKS 50% COCOA	semisweet baking chunks	1 pound
SCHARFFEN BERGER BITTERSWEET CHOCOLATE CHUNKS	bittersweet chunks	8 ounces
CALLEBAUT SEMISWEET CHOCOLATE CHUNKS	*The Baker's Catalogue* semisweet chunks	1 pound
CANDY COATED MINI CHIPS	*The Baker's Catalogue* multi-colored-coated semisweet mini chips	8 ounces
NESTLÉ MILK CHOCOLATE MORSELS	milk chocolate chips	11.5 ounces
BAKER'S MILK CHOCOLATE BIG CHIPS	large milk chocolate chips	10 ounces
VOSGES HAUT-CHOCOLAT NAGA CHIPS 40% CACAO	sweet Indian curry + coconut + Belgian milk chocolate	4 ounces

NAME	SOURCE AND TYPE	QUANTITY
SCHOKINAG SPECIAL EDITION MILK CHOCOLATE BAKING CHUNKS 32% COCOA	milk chocolate baking chunks	1 pound
MICHEL CLUIZEL MILK CHOCOLATE 45% CACAO PISTOLES	*La Cuisine—The Cook's Resource* milk chocolate pistoles (pellets)	8 ounces
WEISS LAIT SUPREME MILK CHOCOLATE 39% CACAO	*La Cuisine—The Cook's Resource* milk chocolate pistoles (pellets)	8 ounces
GHIRARDELLI CLASSIC WHITE CHIPS	white baking chips	11 ounces
NESTLÉ PREMIER WHITE MORSELS	white baking chips	12 ounces
SCHOKINAG SPECIAL EDITION WHITE CHOCOLATE BAKING CHUNKS 28% COCOA BUTTER	white chocolate baking chunks	1 pound
VALRHONA IVOIRE WHITE CHOCOLATE PISTOLES	*La Cuisine—The Cook's Resource* white chocolate pistoles (pellets)	8 ounces
CALLEBAUT WHITE CHOCOLATE CHUNKS	*The Baker's Catalogue* white chocolate chunks	1 pound

bar, square, and block/chunk chocolate

NAME	SOURCE AND TYPE	QUANTITY
LINDT CHOCOLATE CRÉÉ À BERNE SWISS BITTERSWEET CHOCOLATE	bittersweet bar	3.5 ounces
LINDT EXCELLENCE SWISS BITTERSWEET CHOCOLATE	bittersweet bar	3.5 ounces
LINDT EXCELLENCE 70% COCOA EXTRA FINE DARK CHOCOLATE	bittersweet bar	3.5 ounces
CALLEBAUT BITTERSWEET CHOCOLATE	bittersweet block	17.5 ounces
SCHARFFEN BERGER BITTERSWEET CHOCOLATE 70% CACAO	bittersweet bar and block	3 ounces (bar); 9.7 ounces (block)

NAME	SOURCE AND TYPE	QUANTITY
SCHARFFEN BERGER DARK CHOCOLATE NIBBY BAR COCOA BEAN PIECES IN 62% CHOCOLATE	bittersweet bar	1 ounce
VALRHONA 70% BITTERSWEET COUVERTURE	*Dean & Deluca* bittersweet bulk/block/chunks	quantity varies by weight of packaged block/chunks
VALRHONA LE NOIR AMER CHOCOLAT NOIR DARK BITTERSWEET CHOCOLATE 71% CACAO	bittersweet bar	3.5 ounces
VALRHONA LE NOIR GASTRONOMIE CHOCOLAT NOIR BITTERSWEET CHOCOLATE 61% COCOA	bittersweet bar	8.75 ounces
VALRHONA GRAND CRU NOIR MANJARI GASTRONOMIE CHOCOLAT NOIR DARK CHOCOLATE 64% COCOA	*Dean & Deluca* dark chocolate bar/block	7.06 ounces
VALRHONA EQUATORIALE CHOCOLAT DE COUVERTURE NOIR DARK BITTERSWEET COUVERTURE 55% CACAO	bittersweet block/bar	14 ounces
VALRHONA GUANAJA DARK BITTER CHOCOLATE 70% COCOA	bittersweet bar	2.62 ounces
VALRHONA CARAÏBE DARK CHOCOLATE 66% COCOA	bittersweet bar	2.62 ounces
VALRHONA CARRÉ GUANAJA GRAND CRU DE CHOCOLAT NOIR AMER 70% COCOA	bittersweet bar	3.1 ounces
SCHOKINAG SPECIAL EDITION BITTERSWEET COUVERTURE 71% CACAO	bittersweet block/bar	1 pound
EL RAY BUCARE BITTERSWEET CHOCOLATE (CARENERO SUPERIOR) 58.5% COCOA	bittersweet block	14.1 ounces
CHARBONNEL ET WALKER DARK CHOCOLATE 55% COCOA	bittersweet bar	4.4 ounces
MICHEL CLUIZEL "HACIENDA CONCEPCION" CHOCOLAT AMER DARK CHOCOLATE 66% CACAO	bittersweet bar	3.5 ounces

NAME	SOURCE AND TYPE	QUANTITY
MICHEL CLUIZEL CHOCOLAT AMER DARK CHOCOLATE 60% CACAO	bittersweet bar	3.5 ounces
MICHEL CLUIZEL CHOCOLAT AMER BRUT BITTER CHOCOLATE 72% CACAO	bittersweet bar	3.5 ounces
MICHEL CLUIZEL CHOCOLAT AMER AU GRUÉ DE CACAO DARK CHOCOLATE WITH COCOA BEAN PIECES 60% CACAO	bittersweet bar	3.5 ounces
DOMORI SUR DEL LAGO CLASIFICADO COCOA ESTATE COUVERTURE 75% COCOA	*La Cuisine—The Cook's Resource* bittersweet block/chunks	8 ounces
DOMORI CARANERO SUPERIOR COCOA ESTATE COUVERTURE 75% COCOA	*La Cuisine—The Cook's Resource* bittersweet block/chunks	8 ounces
DOMORI BLEND NO1 GRAND BLEND DARK CHOCOLATE 78% MINIMUM CACAO	bittersweet bar	1.76 ounces
DOMORI BARRIQUE GRAND BLEND DARK CHOCOLATE 75% MINIMUM CACAO	bittersweet bar	1.76 ounces
DOMORI BREAK GRAND BLEND DARK CHOCOLATE 80% MINIMUM CACAO	bittersweet bar	1.76 ounces
BERNARD CASTELAIN ARTISAN CHOCOLATIER MACAÏBO CHOCOLAT NOIR 70% AMÉRIQUE DE SUD DARK CHOCOLATE 70%	bittersweet bar	3.5 ounces
CÔTE D'OR INTENSE NOIR DE NOIR BELGIAN DARK CHOCOLATE	bittersweet bar	3.52 ounces
LAKE CHAMPLAIN DARK CHOCOLATE	bittersweet bar	3 ounces
ENRIC ROVIRA RAJOLES CHOCOLATE NEGRO DARK CHOCOLATE 70% COCOA	bittersweet bar	3.5 ounces
GHIRARDELLI DARK CHOCOLATE	bittersweet bar	3 ounces
FRAN'S CHOCOLATES, LTD. NATURAL PREMIUM BAR 58.5% COCOA	bittersweet bar	¾ ounce

NAME	SOURCE AND TYPE	QUANTITY
FRAN'S CHOCOLATES, LTD. BUCARE CRUNCH PREMIUM DARK CHOCOLATE BARWITH CACAO NIBS 58.5% COCOA	bittersweet bar	2 ounces
SCHARFFEN BERGER semisweet 62% COCOA	semisweet block	9.7 ounces
BAKER'S GERMAN'S SWEET CHOCOLATE BAR	sweet chocolate bar	4 ounces
VALRHONA LE NOIR semisweet chocolate 56% CACAO	semisweet bar	3.5 ounces
VALRHONA 64% SEMISWEET COUVERTURE	*Dean & Deluca* bittersweet bulk/block/chunks weight of packaged	quantity varies by block/chunks
VALRHONA LE LACTE 40% CACAO MILK CHOCOLATE	milk chocolate bar	3.5 ounces
SCHARFFEN BERGER 41% CACAO	milk chocolate bar	3 ounces
VALRHONA EQUATORIALE LACTÉE CHOCOLAT DE COUVERTURE AU LAIT MILK CHOCOLATE COUVERTURE 35% CACAO	milk chocolate block	14 ounces
VALRHONA CARRÉ DE JIVARA GRAND CRU DE CHOCOLAT AU LAIT	milk chocolate bar	3.1 ounces
MICHEL CLUIZEL CHOCOLAT AU LAIT 33% COCOA	milk chocolate bar	1.05 ounces; 3.5 ounces
SCHOKINAG SPECIAL EDITION MILK CHOCOLATE BAR 38% CACAO	milk chocolate block/bar	1 pound
LINDT SWISS CLASSIC MILK CHOCOLATE	milk chocolate bar	3.5 ounces

NAME	SOURCE AND TYPE	QUANTITY
GHIRARDELLI MILK CHOCOLATE	milk chocolate bar	3 ounces
ENRIC ROVIRA RAJOLES chocolate con leche milk chocolate 40% cacao	milk chocolate bar	3.5 ounces
DOLPHIN CHOCOLAT au LAIT MILK CHOCOLATE	milk chocolate bar	2.47 ounces
LAKE CHAMPLAIN MILK CHOCOLATE	milk chocolate bar	3 ounces
CÔTE D'OR BELGIAN MILK CHOCOLATE CONFECTION	milk chocolate bar	5.29 ounce
VALRHONA WHITE GASTRONOMIE CHOCOLAT BLANC	white chocolate bar/block	7.06 ounces
EL REY ICOA WHITE CHOCOLATE VENEZUELAN SINGLE BEAN CARNERO SUPERIOR	*Sur La Table* white chocolate bar	2.8 ounces
NESTLÉ PREMIER white baking bars	white chocolate bars	6 ounces (three 2-ounce bars)
LINDT SWISS TABLETTE BLANCHE CONFECTIONERY BAR	white chocolate bar	3 ounces
SCHOKINAG SPECIAL EDITION WHITE CHOCOLATE BAR 28% cocoa butter	white chocolate block/bar	1 pound
VALRHONA white chocolate bulk chunks	*Dean & Deluca* white chocolate bulk/ block/chunks	quantity varies by weight of packaged block/chunks
VALRHONA IVOIRE white chocolate	*La Cuisine—The Cook's Resource* white chocolate bulk/ block/chunks	8 ounces

NAME	SOURCE AND TYPE	QUANTITY
BERNARD CASTELAIN ARTISAN CHOCOLATIER CHOCOLAT NOIR BITTER CHOCOLATE EXTREME 85% COCOA	intense bittersweet/ extra-bittersweet bar	3.5 ounces
MICHEL CLUIZEL CHOCOLAT GRAND AMER BITTER CHOCOLATE 85% CACAO	intense bittersweet / extra-bittersweet bar	1.05 ounces or 3.5 ounces
BAKER'S UNSWEETENED BAKING CHOCOLATE SQUARES	unsweetened squares individually wrapped	eight squares, 1-ounce square
SCHARFFEN BERGER UNSWEETENED CHOCOLATE 99% COCOA	unsweetened block	9.7 ounces
VALRHONA COCOA PATE EXTRA 100% UNSWEETENED CHOCOLATE	*La Cuisine—The Cook's Resource* unsweetened chocolate bulk block/chunks	8 ounces
GUITTARD'S UNSWEETENED BAKING CHOCOLATE	*The Baker's Catalogue* unsweetened disks	1 pound

cocoa powder

NAME	SOURCE AND TYPE	QUANTITY
CACAO BARRY EXTRA BRUT POUDRE DE CACAO	*La Cuisine—The Cook's Resource* alkalized	2.2 pounds
DROSTE COCOA	alkalized	8.8 ounces
DUTCH-PROCESS BLACK COCOA	*The Baker's Catalogue* alkalized	1 pound
DOUBLE DUTCH-PROCESS BLACK COCOA DUTCH PROCESS AND BLACK COCOA BLEND	*The Baker's Catalogue* alkalized	1 pound
BENSDORP COCOA	*Dean & Deluca* alkalized	12 ounces
SCHOKINAG SPECIAL EDITION COCOA POWDER 22/24% COCOA BUTTER CONTENT	alkalized	12 ounces
COCOA DE ZAAN	*La Cuisine—The Cook's Resource* alkalized	2.2 pounds

NAME	SOURCE AND TYPE	QUANTITY
VALRHONA GASTRONOMIE 100% CACAO	alkalized	8.82-ounce box
NESTLÉ COCOA	nonalkalized	8 ounces
SCHARFFEN BERGER NATURAL COCOA POWDER	nonalkalized	6 ounces
GHIRARDELLI PREMIUM UNSWEETENED COCOA	nonalkalized	10 ounces
MERCKENS NATURAL COCOA	nonalkalized	1 pound
PERNIGOTTI COCOA	*Williams-Sonoma* nonalkalized	13.5 ounces

specialty candy

NAME (including chocolate type and brand)	QUANTITY
DOLFIN CHOCOLAT AU LAIT AU CAFÉ MOULU Milk Chocolate with Coffee	2.47-ounce bar
DOLFIN CHOCOLAT AU LAIT AUX AMANDES GRILLÉES Milk Chocolate with Grilled Almonds	2.47-ounce bar
DOLFIN CHOCOLAT NOIR 70% DE CACAO À LA NOUGATINE Dark Chocolate 70% cocoa with Nougatine	2.47-ounce bar
DOLFIN CHOCOLAT NOIR AUX ÉCORCES D'ORANGE CONFITES Dark Chocolate with Crystallized Orange Peel	2.47-ounce bar
DOLFIN CHOCOLAT AU LAIT À LA CANNELLE DE JAVA Milk Chocolate with Cinnamon	2.47-ounce bar
DOLFIN CHOCOLAT NOIR AU GINGEMBRE FRAIS Dark Chocolate with Fresh Ginger	2.47-ounce bar
VOSGES HAUT-CHOCOLAT BLACK PEARL BAR Japanese ginger, wasabi, black sesame seeds and dark chocolate 55% cacao	3.3-ounce bar
VOSGES HAUT-CHOCOLAT RED FIRE BAR Mexican ancho y chipotle chile peppers, Ceylon cinnamon and dark chocolate 55% cacao	3.3-ounce bar

NAME (including chocolate type and brand)	QUANTITY
DOLFIN CHOCOLAT AUX FEUILLES DE THÉ Earl Grey Chocolate with Tea	2.47-ounce bar
DOLFIN CHOCOLAT AUX FEUILLES DE MENTHE Dark Chocolate with Mint Leaves	2.47-ounce bar
LAKE CHAMPLAIN MILK CHOCOLATE WITH HAZELNUTS	3-ounce bar
LAKE CHAMPLAIN MILK CHOCOLATE WITH ALMONDS	3-ounce bar
LAKE CHAMPLAIN DARK CHOCOLATE WITH ALMONDS	3-ounce bar
BERNARD CASTELAIN ARTISAN CHOCOLATIER CHOCOLAT NOIR CAFÉ Dark Chocolate-Coffee	3.5-ounce bar
BERNARD CASTELAIN ARTISAN CHOCOLATIER CHOCOLAT NOIR WITH ALMOND SPLITS	3.5-ounce bar
BERNARD CASTELAIN ARTISAN CHOCOLATIER CHOCOLAT NOIR AUX ECLATS DE FEVES DE CACAO Dark chocolate with cocoa bean splits	3.5-ounce bar
RICHARD DONNELLY ORANGE FINE DARK CHOCOLATE	1.6-ounce bar
RICHARD DONNELLY HAZELNUT ALMOND TOFFEE FINE MILK CHOCOLATE	1.6-ounce bar
RICHARD DONNELLY CAPPUCCINO FINE MILK CHOCOLATE	1.6-ounce bar
MICHEL CLUIZEL CHOCOLAT AMER AU CAFÉ Dark chocolate with coffee 60% cacao	3.5-ounce bar
MICHEL CLUIZEL CHOCOLAT GRAND LAIT CACAO PUR ILE DE JAVA Milk chocolate pure java 50% cacao	3.5-ounce bar
MICHEL CLUIZEL CHOCOLAT AMER AU PRALINÉ À L'ANCIENNE Dark chocolate with praliné 60% cacao	3.5-ounce bar
VALRHONA LE NOIR NOISETTES Dark chocolate with split hazelnuts 61% cocoa	3.5-ounce bar
VALRHONA MANJARI Dark chocolate with candied orange peel 64% cocoa	2.62-ounce bar
VALRHONA CARAÏBE ECLATS DE NOISETTES Dark chocolate with split hazelnuts	2.62-ounce bar

NAME (including chocolate type and brand)	QUANTITY
SCHARFFEN BERGER DARK CHOCOLATE MOCHA BAR Freshly roasted coffee in 62% chocolate	1-ounce bar
CÔTE D'OR SENSATIONS INTENSE BELGIAN MILK AND DARK CHOCOLATE CONFECTION	3.52-ounce bar
CHRISTOPHER NORMAN CHOCOLATES, LTD. MOCHA DOT minimum 30% COCOA	2-ounce bar
CHRISTOPHER NORMAN CHOCOLATES, LTD. BITTERSWEET CRUNCH minimum 70% COCOA	2-ounce bar
CHRISTOPHER NORMAN CHOCOLATES, LTD. WHITE CHOCOLATE MACADAMIA NUT minimum 29% COCOA	2-ounce bar
CHRISTOPHER NORMAN CHOCOLATES, LTD. DARK CHOCOLATE GINGER minimum 65% COCOA	2-ounce bar
FRAN'S GOLD BAR WITH MACADAMIA NUTS	1.75-ounce bar
DEAN & DELUCA ULTIMATE MALTED MILK BALLS SEMISWEET, WHITE AND MILK CHOCOLATE ENROBED MALTED MILK BALLS (manufactured by Koppers Chocolate)	8.5 ounces
DEAN & DELUCA CHOCOLATE TOFFEE PISTACHIOS (manufactured by Koppers Chocolate)	8 ounces
DEAN & DELUCA MINT LENTILS (manufactured by Koppers Chocolate)	9 ounces
DEAN & DELUCA BUTTER TOFFEE CARAMEL (manufactured by Koppers Chocolate)	9 ounces
DR. PETER'S PEPPERMINT CRUNCH (Jo's Candies)	9 ounces
JO'S PEPPERMINT CRUNCH DARK CHOCOLATE	6 ounces
JO'S PEANUT BUTTER MELTAWAYS MILK CHOCOLATE	6 ounces
WILLIAMS-SONOMA DARK DINNER MINTS	7.94 ounces
WILLIAMS-SONOMA CHOCOLATE-COVERED ALMONDS	15 ounces
ENSTROM'S ALMOND TOFFEE	1, 2, or 5 pounds

time-honored candy

NAME AND TYPE (including brand)	QUANTITY
DOVE SILKY DARK CHOCOLATE	1.30-ounce bar
DOVE PROMISES DARK CHOCOLATE MINIATURES	11 ounces (individual miniatures)
DOVE RICH MILK CHOCOLATE	1.30-ounce bar
DOVE PROMISES MILK CHOCOLATE MINIATURES	11-ounce bag (individual miniatures)
ORIGINAL HEATH ENGLISH TOFFEE BAR	1.4-ounce bar
ORIGINAL HEATH ENGLISH TOFFEE BAR MINIATURES	5 ounces (individual miniatures)
ORIGINAL HEATH ENGLISH TOFFEE SNACK BARS	12 ounces (individual snack bars)
YORK CHOCOLATE-COVERED PEPPERMINT PATTIES	13 ounces (individually wrapped patties)
YORK CHOCOLATE-COVERED PEPPERMINT PATTY	1.5-ounce patty
NESTLÉ CHUNKY MILK CHOCOLATE WITH PEANUTS AND RAISINS	1.4 ounces
PETER PAUL MOUNDS MINIATURES DARK CHOCOLATE COVERED COCONUT	13 ounces (individual miniatures)
PETER PAUL MOUNDS SNACK SIZE BARS DARK CHOCOLATE COVERED COCONUT	12.6 ounces (individual snack sizes bars)
PETER PAUL ALMOND JOY MILK CHOCOLATE COCONUT ALMONDS	1.76-ounce bar
REESE'S MILK CHOCOLATE PEANUT BUTTER CUPS MINIATURES	13 ounces (individual miniatures)
REESE'S MILK CHOCOLATE PEANUT BUTTER CUPS SNACK SIZE	12 ounces (individual snack size)
REESE'S MILK CHOCOLATE PEANUT BUTTER CUPS	1.5 ounces (2 peanut butter cups)
REESE'S NUTRAGEOUS PEANUT BUTTER PEANUTS MILK CHOCOLATE CARAMEL	12 ounces
NESTLÉ BUTTERFINGER FUN-SIZE bars	12 ounces (individual bars)

NAME (including chocolate type and brand)	QUANTITY
NESTLÉ BUTTERFINGER	2.1-ounce bar
ZAGNUT CRUNCHY PEANUT BUTTER-TOASTED COCONUT	1.75-ounce bar
SNICKER'S	2.07-ounce bar
SNICKER'S FUN SIZE	13.30 ounces (individual fun-size)
MILKY WAY MIDNIGHT BOLD, RICH CHOCOLATE GOLDEN CARAMEL VANILLA NOUGAT	1.76-ounce bar
MILKY WAY MIDNIGHT FUN SIZE BOLD, RICH CHOCOLATE GOLDEN CARAMEL VANILLA NOUGAT	11.30 ounces (individual fun-size)
MILKY WAY RICH CHOCOLATE CREAMY CARAMEL SMOOTH NOUGAT	2.05-ounce bar
MILKY WAY MINIATURES RICH CHOCOLATE CREAMY CARAMEL SMOOTH NOUGAT	9 ounces (individual miniatures)
CADBURY ROAST ALMOND MILK CHOCOLATE WITH ROASTED ALMONDS	4.5-ounce bar
M AND M'S SEMI-SWEET CHOCOLATE MINI BAKING BITS	12 ounces

special effect chocolate

NAME AND TYPE (including brand)	QUANTITY
INDIA TREE CHOCOLATE VERMICELLI DECORATIFS chocolate sprinkles *La Cuisine—The Cook's Resource*	5.5 ounces
GUITTARD CHOCOLATE SPRINKLES	6 ounces
INDIA TREE CHOCOLATE DECADENCE CHOCOLATE RIBBONS, CHOCOLATE BITS, CHOCOLATE CURLS	Chocolate Ribbons 1.4 ounces Chocolate Bits 2.4 ounces Chocolate Curls 1.4 ounces
BURDICK CHOCOLATES RICH SHAVED CHOCOLATE	12 ounces
PAIN AU CHOCOLAT STICKS chocolate sticks for yeast-baking *The Baker's Catalogue*	1 pound

Storing chocolate

CHOCOLATE IS PRONE TO ABSORBING HUMIDITY, in addition to the aromas so welcome in savory cooking (such as onions and garlic) but not on the sweet plate. To protect any form, flavoring, or style of this ingredient, large quantities of chocolate should be stored between 57 and 64 degrees F. in an area that is not subjected to excess humidity or sudden changes of temperature. Of course, this is the ideal. I store a working supply of chocolate in my kitchen on several cool pantry shelves far away from the direct heat of the oven and in a corner area in large apothecary jars. Avoid refrigerating any form of it. Unopened, unsweetened and bittersweet chocolate can be kept as is, wrapped in bars and blocks, for 1 year to 18 months, milk and white chocolate for 7 to 9 months. Unused portions should be enclosed in food-safe plastic wrap, then placed in a self-sealing plastic bag and used within 4 to 6 weeks (for unsweetened or bittersweet) or within 1 to 2 weeks (for white or milk). It is far better to buy chocolate in a smaller quantity and use it on an as-needed basis than to improperly store large amounts and have your expensive largess deteriorate.

Composing tiers of chocolate flavor

HOW TO DEVELOP THE FLAVOR OF CHOCOLATE

The flavor package that is chocolate has always both mystified and captivated me: what does it mean when you describe a brownie, cupcake, or slice of layer cake as chocolatey? A brownie conveys the notion of "chocolatey" when it is dark, rich, and satisfying, sweetly fragrant, buttery-tasting and fudgy, moist and creamy-textured, or cakey and swarthy. A cupcake or slice of layer cake seems "chocolatey" when the cake has a delicate, downy texture, is lusciously dark, and is covered in a blanket of frosting. That brownie, cupcake, or slice of cake must also look sumptuous, because looks often convey what we imagine the taste to be. A chocolate batter or dough should include enough chocolate to carry the flavor and create a statement. That chocolate message can be delicate or bold, light or dense—it can be chocolate inside and out, or established with accents of chocolate, but it must speak of the flavor.

The single most important discovery I have made over the years in baking with chocolate is that the flavor of chocolate is not always determined by the chocolate-based ingredient alone. On its own, chocolate is a dashing, distinguished flavor, yet it does need other elements for support in order to bring the taste front and center. After all, developing the intensity of chocolate in a batter or dough is quite different from the direct experience of eating a chocolate bar, and having that bar melt in your mouth and straightaway create all those nuances and gradations of flavor. In the baking act, chocolate, in one form or another, gets all mixed up with other components, and its depth can be diminished if a recipe doesn't establish tiers of flavor.

BUILDING TIERS OF FLAVOR

On its own, chocolate—in any form—is one-dimensional, even though a specific piece of chocolate tastes complex, with its foreground and background shades, and high and low notes of flavor that can range from winey to fruity to flowery. By one-dimensional, I mean that it conveys a single flavor. That flavor can be amplified—extended, in fact—in a batter or dough. Not until chocolate merges with other ingredients to form the structure and design of a dough or batter is its full savor established. To bring out and cultivate the taste of chocolate, it is helpful to look at all the basic baking ingredients that chocolate interacts with and the various categories of chocolate that can be used within a recipe to establish its flavor.

BAKING INGREDIENTS

Planes of chocolate flavor and their accompanying textures are created in baking by using staple ingredients—flour, cornstarch, sugar, liquid extracts, salt, whole eggs and/or egg yolks, unsalted butter, and both liquid and soft dairy ingredients—with one or more chocolate-based ingredients. The flavor of chocolate is enriched by the presence of these ingredients, for they establish and set the flavor as well as provide the working framework for the sweet. Think of this as the sweet art of construction.

FLOUR

Bleached all-purpose flour determines the structure of a chocolate-based batter or dough. It is sturdy enough to allow the chocolate element to be suspended throughout and still create a sweet that is tender and moist. It is a pivotal ingredient in a baking recipe, for it provides the critical network of support. An exception to this would be the batter for a flourless chocolate cake. This type of cake receives its strength from lots of chocolate and a fair number of eggs; the dessert is more like a fallen soufflé—dense or not—than a cake, but is still fixed in the category of cake.

Bleached cake flour can be used on its own or along with bleached all-purpose flour in many cake and cookie doughs or batters. Bleached cake flour helps to develop a tender structure and refined crumb in a chocolate-based sweet.

Unbleached all-purpose flour, used alone or in conjunction with bleached all-purpose flour, builds a yeast dough by cultivating its structure and body. Unbleached flour builds a dough that has a lovely "pull," a solid but fine-grained texture, and terrific "oven-spring," that initial impressive rise the dough makes at the onset of baking.

SUGAR

In baked goods made with unsweetened cocoa powder and/or unsweetened chocolate, the presence of sugar in the batter or dough virtually guarantees that the chocolate flavor will develop. Sugar is important as a sweetener, but it also builds texture and develops the internal grain or crumb. Both in terms of the polished flavor and the result-ing texture it creates, superfine sugar (also called "bar" sugar) is my first choice to use in batters and doughs leavened with baking powder or baking soda. The very small grains of superfine sugar, when creamed with butter, produce light and fine-textured baked goods.

Light brown and dark brown sugar, with overtones of caramel in varying degrees, have their place in a chocolate chip cookie dough, a few pancake and waffle batters, and some muffin and cake batters. When either light or dark brown sugar is used in chocolate-based recipes, I tend to combine it with granulated or superfine sugar because I prefer the caramel flavor to come through in a soft, sophisticated way; otherwise, the full chocolate impact is obstructed.

Confectioners' sugar, which has a small percentage of cornstarch (3 percent) included in its production, can be a chocolate-friendly sweetening agent when used in frostings and icings, in some cookie and scone doughs, and in a few cake batters. Confectioners' sugar doesn't mute the flavor of chocolate so much as it alters the baked texture of some sweets (like creating a rubbery texture). As a quick topping for sprinkling on a slice of coffee cake, sweet roll, or cookie, it's peerless.

BUTTER

Unsalted butter, a pearly, voluptuous fat that also includes a small percentage of water and dairy (milk) solids, adds a fullness of flavor to chocolate batters and doughs. There simply isn't any replacement for it. Butter contributes a meltingly luxurious texture to chocolate-flavored sweets, a characteristic that creates the duality of tenderness and moistness—two qualities that, in turn, drive up the chocolate taste quotient.

EGGS

Whole eggs develop the overall composition of doughs and batters; eggs are responsible for defining the all-important structure in baked goods. Egg yolks are especially welcome in chocolate-based recipes because they keep the batter or dough creamy enough to sustain and bolster the taste of the specific chocolate used. A creamy-textured batter, in turn, makes the chocolate flavor richer and more intense.

SALT

The many virtues of adding salt to a chocolate-based batter or dough should not be underestimated. Salt has a remarkable capacity to bring out the chocolate flavor in a batter or dough. Leaving out the salt would cause the cookie, muffin, or slice of cake to taste bland, for salt is an ingredient that deepens—or expands—the flavor of chocolate. As a vital component in a sweet yeast bread, salt balances out the sugar, helps to develop the flavor, and modulates the rise of the dough during the fermentation process. I use very extra-fine sea salt in doughs and batters that contain chocolate, for its clean, pure taste is flawless.

LIQUID AND SOFT DAIRY PRODUCTS

In addition to contributing liquid to a chocolate-based recipe, whole milk adds fat. In a creamed cake batter that contains chocolate in one form or another, milk develops and enriches it, and contributes to its overall volume. In most batters and thick, sturdy doughs, milk is the liquid of choice, but some benefit from the use of water to embolden the chocolate flavor (especially those that contain cocoa powder or unsweetened chocolate in the ingredient list).

Half-and-half, light (table) cream, and heavy cream smooth and round out the chocolate flavor in a batter or dough, filling, frosting, or icing. To understand just how wonderful heavy cream is when paired with chocolate, all you have to do is make the bittersweet chocolate ganache for the Cocoa-Coated Truffles on page 364 and admire the chocolate flavor. It's mellow and what I like to describe as "centered"—concentrated without being overwhelming. The heavy cream, along with some butter, creates a thick, supple, and exceptionally lustrous chocolate mixture that, in its warm and fluid state, can be treated as a glaze, or chilled and turned into a filling or into creamy spheres of candy.

A buttery, creamed cake batter that contains chips, chunks, or nuggets of chocolate is also appealing when it includes half-and-half, light cream, or heavy cream; the batter, upgraded with a little more fat, is the perfect foil for bits and fragments of chocolate.

Buttermilk and sour cream, both cultured products, create tender and moist baked goods. Sour cream generates the moistest crumb and buttermilk the tenderest crumb.

EXTRACTS

Vanilla extract makes the flavor of chocolate expand within a batter or dough. It also works with butter to build and intensify flavor. Pure almond extract is sometimes present to intensify the flavor of the nut if any form of it (almond flour, slivered skinned almonds, skinned chopped almonds, sliced skinned almonds, or almond paste) is part of a recipe. Chocolate extract may be used along with vanilla extract as an adjunct flavoring agent, but not as a substitute for vanilla extract.

CORNSTARCH

The thickening power of cornstarch binds together dairy, flavoring, and sweetening ingredients to form a pastry cream, filling, pudding, and, on occasion, cooked frosting or icing. In specific amounts, and in an ancillary way, it can also provide structure in a cake batter or cookie dough. Used in a filling or sauce, cornstarch is a gentle thickener that allows the chocolate flavor to come forward. On the whole, I prefer cornstarch to flour for thickening because the result is light on the tongue, smooth, and polished.

Chocolate compatibility

This chart profiles the compatibility of chocolate with other primary flavors.

PRIMARY FLAVOR	INGREDIENTS AND/OR RECIPE COMPONENTS THAT DELIVER THE PRIMARY FLAVOR
ALMOND	whole skinless, slivered, ground, or chopped almonds almond flour almond paste almond extract almond liqueur
APRICOT	dried apricots glazed apricots apricot jam or preserves apricot butter apricot puree
BANANA	firm but ripe bananas (sliced, mashed, crushed, or chopped)
BUTTER	unsalted butter butter-based frostings and glazes
BUTTERCRUNCH (TOFFEE)	milk-chocolate covered toffee, chopped or in chunks
CARAMEL	creamy caramel sauce clear caramel sauce light or dark brown sugar (as a caramel undertone) melted caramel candies chocolate-covered caramel and nougat candy bars chocolate-covered caramel and nut candy bars
CHERRY	dried sweet or tart cherries
COCONUT	sweetened flaked coconut coconut milk cream of coconut chocolate-covered coconut candy bars or patties
COFFEE	instant espresso powder (slaked with a liquid or flavoring extract) coffee syrup coffee glaze coffee and granulated sugar wash

PRIMARY FLAVOR	INGREDIENTS AND/OR RECIPE COMPONENTS THAT DELIVER THE PRIMARY FLAVOR
CREAM	heavy cream light (table) cream cultured sour cream crème fraîche
GINGER	ground ginger knobs of ginger preserved in syrup crystallized ginger peeled and grated fresh ginger root chocolate-covered ginger candy ginger preserves
HAZELNUT	skinned hazelnuts hazelnut flour or ground hazelnuts hazelnut liqueur hazelnut paste
PEANUT	roasted peanuts peanut butter dark or semisweet chocolate-covered peanut butter candy bars milk chocolate-covered peanut butter cups chocolate-covered peanuts
PECAN	chopped pecans; pecan halves and pieces
SWEET CHEESE	cream cheese
VANILLA	pure vanilla extract vanilla-flavored sugar (granulated, superfine, or confectioners') vanilla bean paste whole or split vanilla beans seed scrapings from the inside of split vanilla beans
WALNUT	chopped walnuts; walnut halves and pieces

Harmony of chocolate to basic baking staples

This chart reveals how chocolate synthesizes with basic baking staples.

CHOCOLATE TYPE	CHOCOLATE STATE	STAPLE INGREDIENT	HOW THE STAPLE INGREDIENT FUNCTIONS WITH CHOCOLATE
UNSWEETENED CHOCOLATE	melted	butter (softened or melted)	• establishes depth of chocolate flavor • establishes "creaminess" quotient
UNSWEETENED CHOCOLATE	melted	eggs	• deepen and enrich chocolate flavor • add volume and structure to a dough or batter
UNSWEETENED CHOCOLATE	melted	granulated sugar	• sweetens a batter or dough and develops chocolate flavor • adds moisture
UNSWEETENED CHOCOLATE	melted	vanilla extract	• points up any floral notes in dough • scents a dough or batter
UNSWEETENED CHOCOLATE	melted	salt	• intensifies chocolate flavor
SEMISWEET OR BITTERSWEET CHOCOLATE	melted or in the form of chips, chunks, or nuggets	butter (softened)	• provides lush background notes • intensifies flavor • intensifies "creamy" quality present in chocolate
SEMISWEET OR BITTERSWEET CHOCOLATE	melted or in the form of chips, chunks, or nuggets	whole eggs/egg yolks	• build texture and consistency in a batter or dough • contribute to a silky quality
SEMISWEET OR BITTERSWEET CHOCOLATE	melted or in the form of chips, chunks, or nuggets	vanilla extract	• deepens flavor of a batter or dough • rounds out chocolate flavor
MILK CHOCOLATE	chips, chunks, or nuggets	butter (softened)	• ties into smooth, dairy taste of chocolate • builds flavor in a batter or dough
MILK CHOCOLATE	chips, chunks, or nuggets	whole eggs/egg yolks	• develop richness in flavor and texture • build volume in a batter or dough
MILK CHOCOLATE	chips, chunks, or nuggets	vanilla extract	• rounds out and reinforces chocolate flavor
WHITE CHOCOLATE	chips, chunks, or nuggets	butter (softened or melted)	• builds and reinforces creamy quality • enhances flavor of cocoa butter

CHOCOLATE TYPE	CHOCOLATE STATE	STAPLE INGREDIENT	HOW THE STAPLE INGREDIENT FUNCTIONS WITH CHOCOLATE
WHITE CHOCOLATE	chips, chunks, or nuggets	whole eggs/egg yolks	• build and enrich presence of cocoa butter • develop richness and structure in a batter or dough
WHITE CHOCOLATE	chips, chunks, or nuggets	vanilla extract	• uplifts and deepens flavor of cocoa butter present in chocolate
UNSWEETENED COCOA	powder (alkalized and nonalkalized)	butter (softened or melted)	• adds textural richnes • develops moistness
UNSWEETENED COCOA	powder (alkalized and nonalkalized)	granulated sugar	• acts as a necessary sweetening agent • promotes moistness
UNSWEETENED COCOA	powder (alkalized and nonalkalized)	whole eggs/egg yolks	• establish and develop texture • promote moistness
UNSWEETENED COCOA	powder (alkalized and nonalkalized)	vanilla extract	• expands chocolate flavor • contributes contrasting floral notes

ESTABLISHING CHOCOLATE FLAVOR

The establishment of chocolate flavor in a batter or dough can be simple or complex, depending upon the recipe. A dough or batter can be flavored with chocolate in several ways: entirely with melted chocolate; with chips or chunks; with fragments of chocolate candy; with an icing, frosting, glaze, or, filling; or by a combination of chocolate ingredients.

1. MELTED UNSWEETENED CHOCOLATE, melted bittersweet chocolate, cocoa powder, or a combination can color a dough or batter. In a recipe, melted chocolate is usually added to a whisked egg-and-sugar mixture or to a creamed butter-sugar-egg mixture. Cocoa powder is introduced into the batter either by sifting it with other dry ingredients or by combining it with a liquid and adding it to the creamed mixture at the appropriate time in the procedure of the recipe.

2. CHIPS OR CHUNKS OF SEMISWEET, BITTERSWEET, MILK, OR WHITE CHOCOLATE, or chunks of chocolate candy, can define a batter or dough in a most delicious way. For chips and chunks to be assimilated into a cake batter, the batter must be creamy but sturdy, and of moderate density. A dough can contain chips and chunks and/or nuggets of candy inside and outside its unbaked network.

3. AN ICING, FROSTING, GLAZE, OR FILLING can both define and reinforce the chocolate flavor in a slice of cake, pie, or tart, or in a muffin, scone, bar, or drop cookie. Usually, an icing or glaze is thinner in consistency than a frosting; I like to use a shiny, pourable or spoonable icing or glaze over a pound cake, coffee cake, or Bundt cake, and for coating some single-layer cakes. A buttery frosting always enriches and frequently defines a chocolate layer or sheet cake. A filling should enhance but not overwhelm layers of cake, but a pie or tart filling should have a prominent and forward chocolate flavor.

4. A CHOCOLATE BATTER, graced with chips or chunks and assembled with a frosting and/or filling, is one of the most intense ways to expand—or enlarge—the flavor of chocolate in what you bake. Topping a square of fudge cake with a handmade chocolate truffle also produces a flavor-heightened sweet, and is a good example of multiplying boldly chocolate components in one dessert.

	This chart shows you how to create three separate levels of chocolate intensity in one dessert.
SINGLE INTENSITY	melted unsweetened chocolate plus vanilla extract, salt, and unsalted butter (creamed or melted) melted bittersweet chocolate plus vanilla extract, salt, and unsalted butter (creamed or melted) unsweetened cocoa powder (sifted with dry ingredients, slaked with boiling water, or combined with water and simmered) plus vanilla extract, salt, and unsalted butter (creamed or melted) semisweet or bittersweet chips, chunks, or nuggets, plus vanilla extract, salt, and unsalted butter (creamed or melted)
DOUBLE INTENSITY	melted unsweetened chocolate and semisweet or bittersweet chips, chunks, or nuggets, plus vanilla extract, salt, and unsalted butter (creamed or melted) melted unsweetened chocolate and unsweetened cocoa powder, plus vanilla extract, salt, and unsalted butter (creamed or melted) melted bittersweet chocolate and unsweetened cocoa powder, plus vanilla extract, salt, and unsalted butter (creamed or melted) melted bittersweet chocolate and semisweet or bittersweet chips, chunks, or nuggets, plus vanilla extract, salt, and unsalted butter (creamed or melted) creamed unsalted butter dough with semisweet or bittersweet chips, chunks, or nuggets, plus vanilla extract and salt, finished with chocolate glaze or chocolate frosting, or served with a chocolate sauce
TRIPLE INTENSITY	melted unsweetened chocolate with unsweetened cocoa powder and semisweet or bittersweet chips, chunks, or nuggets, plus vanilla extract, salt, and unsalted butter (creamed or melted) melted unsweetened chocolate with melted bittersweet chocolate and unsweetened cocoa powder, plus vanilla extract, salt, and unsalted butter (creamed or melted) melted unsweetened chocolate with unsweetened cocoa powder, plus vanilla extract, salt, and unsalted butter (creamed or melted) with chocolate frosting or glaze melted bittersweet chocolate with unsweetened cocoa powder and semisweet or bittersweet chips, chunks, or nuggets, plus vanilla extract, salt, and unsalted butter

BAKING IS A STEP-BY-STEP PROCESS. Each phase needs to be addressed and completed in the correct sequence and with a specific set of ingredients. Since a good part of baking centers around combining components, it is especially important to have every ingredient specified in a recipe organized and ready. This assemblage of measured or prepared ingredients is called *mise en place* and is translated as "put in place." Those who work in professional kitchens routinely employ this method of advance preparation, and so should you.

Working with chocolate— the process of using chocolate in batters and doughs

As a flavoring agent, chocolate is both exquisitely sensitive and, in certain forms, remarkably sturdy. It is a vigorous and dynamic substance and, at the same time, a delicate and vulnerable one. This juxtaposition of opposite traits is what makes working with chocolate so complex and so intriguing.

Chocolate chips and chunks are easy enough to integrate into doughs and batters, but melting chocolate correctly and introducing it into doughs and batters is pivotal to producing many chocolate-based recipes. Chocolate, in all its forms, depending on the type and quantity, can moisturize, dry out, enrich, or relax a batter or dough. If melted with an appropriate amount of butter or a liquid, chocolate will respond as a smooth, satiny, and lilting mixture.

CHOPPING AND MELTING
unsweetened, bittersweet, sweet, or semisweet, milk, and white chocolate

Before it is melted, bar or block chocolate of any type (bittersweet, semisweet, sweet, unsweetened, milk, or white) should first be chopped. This initial step is important to the melting process. The reason for chopping the chocolate at the outset is to reduce the time it takes for it to melt down, and allow the low heat applied to it to work through it in the most effective way possible. This is best done gently. Remember the phrase "low and slow" when it comes to melting chocolate—it should melt down slowly over the lowest heat possible. Rushing the melting process by increasing the heat produces pasty, gritty chocolate rather than glossy, moderately fluid chocolate.

CHOPPING CHOCOLATE

If using very large hunks of block chocolate, put them in a heavy-duty, food-safe plastic bag, seal, and tap the contents with a hammer or meat pounder to break it into manageable pieces; after the chocolate has been weighed, place it on a sturdy cutting surface. If you are using chocolate bars, line them up on the cutting surface. Carefully chop the chocolate into small chunks with a chef's knife. Use a slow up-and-down motion. Avoid rapid chopping (as you would for chopping nuts), because that would fling the chocolate around the cutting surface.

A food processor, fitted with the steel blade, does a great job of producing very finely chopped chocolate. I use this method when preparing the chocolate for the bittersweet chocolate ganache in the recipe for Cocoa-Coated Truffles on page 364. Chocolate reduced to the finely chopped state should, without exception, always be chopped into pieces not larger than ½ inch (or slightly smaller) prior to processing in order to protect the equipment and assure an even result. Fill the work bowl of the food processor no more than one-quarter full of chopped chocolate. Chop the chocolate in batches, as necessary, emptying out the work bowl before each new lot is added.

Over many baking years, I have developed guidelines for chopping chocolate destined to be melted. I should also say that these specifications were presented to me on occasion when I worked with hunks of chocolate that were too big, or used an inappropriate pan or an inaccurate ratio of chocolate to butter.

Dark chocolate is a little less sensitive to heat than milk or white chocolate, so it can be chopped into larger pieces; both milk and white chocolate are more delicate, so chopping either one into smaller pieces reduces the overall melting time.

For melting, chop unsweetened, bittersweet, sweet, or semisweet chocolate into chunks no larger than ¾ inch.

For melting, chop milk chocolate or white chocolate into pieces no larger than ⅓ inch.

PARAMETERS FOR MELTING CHOCOLATE

When melting chocolate—and this refers to all types—the pan you choose should be heavy, clean, and impeccably dry. For suggestions on equipment for melting chocolate, refer to page 66. Droplets of moisture will cause chocolate to "seize" (that is, tighten and turn clumpy, gritty, and/or grainy) during the heating process. Moisture or the smallest amount of liquid can grab onto the sugar crystals present in chocolate and cause it to coalesce into a fairly compact, thickened mass. Although many experts suggest that the chocolate can be corrected at this point, I have found that it ruins the texture of the batter or dough if any repair work takes place (such as trying to remelt it with a little solid shortening). If the chocolate-seizes, it's always best to start over with a new batch of chocolate.

Sometimes a recipe will call for several kinds of melted chocolate, usually bittersweet and unsweetened. Both can be melted together. Butter and chocolate can be melted together if their amounts follow the parameters below. Otherwise, it is important to melt them separately, and add them in the order that the method presents.

MELTING UNSWEETENED, BITTERSWEET, SWEET, OR SEMISWEET CHOCOLATE

Place the chocolate in the saucepan in an even layer and set over the lowest possible heat. When the chocolate is two-thirds to three-quarters melted, turn off the heat, remove the saucepan from the burner, and let the residual heat finish melting the chocolate. Removing the chocolate from the heat before it has melted all the way through is critical to the one-pan procedure of melting chocolate, as the remnants of heat will finish the process without scorching the contents. You should stir the chocolate very gently *once* after it has melted down at the three-quarters point, then again when finally melted. Avoid actively beating or whipping the chocolate before it has melted completely.

Always stir the chocolate with a clean, dry, heatproof spoon, flat paddle, or spatula. Use the chocolate warm, tepid, or cooled, or as directed in each recipe. When melted, you can safely whisk it with melted (or softened) butter.

The temperature of unsweetened, bittersweet, sweet, or semisweet chocolate should not exceed 117 to 118 degrees F. during the melting process.

MELTING MILK CHOCOLATE OR WHITE CHOCOLATE

Place the chocolate in the saucepan in an even layer and set over the lowest possible heat. When the chocolate is melted to the three-quarter point, turn off the heat and let the heat of the pan finish melting the chocolate, removing the pan from the burner to a heatproof surface. Stir the chocolate slowly and gently from time to time. For milk or white chocolate it is best to use the heaviest small or medium-size saucepan you own, rather than a large saucepan with an expansively wide bottom surface area. Always stir the chocolate with a clean, dry, heatproof spoon, flat paddle, or spatula. For the best assimilation into most recipes, use the chocolate in the tepid state.

The temperature of milk or white chocolate should not exceed 107 to 108 degrees F. during the melting process.

MELTING CHOCOLATE WITH A LIQUID
melting chocolate and butter in small-to-moderate ratio of chocolate-to-butter

As discussed above, a small amount of liquid in the form of moisture, condensation, a scattering of droplets, or a single teaspoon, can spoil a batch of chocolate as it melts, causing it to seize. To guard against this, I have developed the following guidelines, based on working with chocolate/liquid and chocolate/butter. To melt chocolate and liquid together, it is important to use 4 teaspoons of liquid to every 1 ounce of chocolate. If the recipe can handle it, I prefer to use 5 teaspoons of liquid to every 1 ounce of chocolate. (Using 3 teaspoons of liquid to every 1 ounce of chocolate is the bare minimum and, depending on the relative viscosity/density/ingredient or character makeup of the chocolate, can be tricky and is generally not recommended.)

To melt chocolate and butter together, a safe quantity of each is 2 ounces chocolate to 4 ounces butter (8 tablespoons or 1 stick). A large quantity of chocolate does not readily meld with a very small amount of butter unless you work very quickly to combine it, so it is far better to melt the butter and chocolate separately. The ideal ratio of chocolate to butter is 4 ounces of chocolate (bittersweet, unsweetened, or semisweet) to 8 ounces of butter. This proportion is classic in a certain number of the brownie recipes in this book. Half of that measure, 2 ounces of chocolate to 4 ounces of butter, is sometimes used to make soft and creamy, fudge-like frostings. This is also a good balance. Do not cover the saucepan.

MELTING LARGER QUANTITIES OF UNSWEETENED, BITTERSWEET, SWEET, OR SEMISWEET CHOCOLATE AND BUTTER (4 ounces or more of chocolate and 8 ounces or more of butter)

More than seventeen years ago, I came up with this method out of necessity (and by accident): I was baking loads of brownies and other chocolate-intense bar cookies and had to melt lots of butter and chocolate. Instead of melting each batch separately, which only increased my working time in the kitchen, I developed a technique of melting the two together with ease and no fuss, by pressing or mashing softened butter on the bottom of a wide, straight-sided pan (such as a *sauteuse* [see page 66]) and placing the chopped chocolate on top. For this method the chocolate must be chopped into ½- to ¾-inch pieces, and you must have at least ½ pound (16 tablespoons or 2 sticks) butter and 4 ounces of chocolate to melt; many of the brownies and bars in this book use this formula or proportions close to it. When you set the pan over very low heat, the butter begins to melt first and acts as a kind of cushion for the chocolate. The mixture melts smoothly, with a nice gloss and satiny quality. Use very low heat and a heavy pan, and stir the mixture now and again during the melting process. Do not cover the saucepan. The melted chocolate and butter mixture will be smooth and luminous. Give the mixture a good stir or whisk slowly to combine before using.

COMBINING MELTED CHOCOLATE WITH LIQUID DAIRY INGREDIENTS IN A FROSTING, GLAZE, OR ICING

Even if a correct ratio of melted chocolate is incorporated with a liquid, if the liquid isn't used warm or tepid, the chocolate may react in an unfavorable way. Have you ever made a chocolate frosting, glaze, or icing with a quantity of milk, light cream, or heavy cream and found little chocolate flecks or bits scattered throughout the mixture? This is a direct result of adding liquid that is cool or cold, rather than lukewarm, tepid, or warm. It's the cocoa butter in the chocolate that congeals to form tiny flecks as it reacts to being combined with a cold liquid; remember that melted chocolate is temperature-sensitive. To avoid this, warm the liquid dairy ingredient lightly, then proceed with the recipe. Occasionally, a frosting will be made with lukewarm or warm milk; then, once the base frosting has been blended, a small amount of cream (heavy or light, and at room temperature) will be added. I call this a "finishing cream." It does not need to be warmed, as the chocolate is already amalgamated into the base ingredients.

PREPARING CHOCOLATE CHIPS AND CHUNKS TO HIGHLIGHT BATTERS AND DOUGHS

When chips and chunks are added to a batter or dough, it's a good idea to toss them first in a small amount of the flour mixture; the amount of the flour mixture is indicated in the procedure of the recipe. Both chips and chunks benefit from this treatment when they are an ingredient in cake batters and some bar cookie batters, as they would sink if not floured. The flour particles that adhere to the surface of the chips and chunks allow them to cling to the batter and remain suspended in it during baking. Many brownie and thick blondie mixtures are compact enough to accept a stir-in of chips and chunks (or pieces of candy) without flouring them first.

As a general guide, 12 ounces (2 cups) of chips, chunks, or nuggets (either bittersweet, semisweet, milk, or white chocolate, standard-sized, or miniature) should be thoroughly tossed with 1 tablespoon of the flour mixture; for 6 ounces (1 cup) of chips, chunks, or nuggets, use about 1½ teaspoons of the flour mixture. (Note that depending on the consistency of the batter and the type of chocolate, the amount of flour used for tossing may differ slightly from the parameters above, so follow the directions in each recipe.)

A reference guide to techniques and methods

AMONG THE TECHNIQUES for assembling batters, doughs, frostings, pastry creams, and custard sauces in *ChocolateChocolate*, there are several that are used often—a "creamed" cake batter or cookie dough, a "melt and stir" batter for brownie and bar cookie batters, a "cut-in" dough for making scones and sweet biscuits, a "combined and kneaded" sweet yeast dough, a "creamed" confectioners' sugar frosting, and an egg yolk–enriched custard sauce and pastry cream.

FOR A "CREAMED" CAKE BATTER OR COOKIE DOUGH, flour and leavening (baking powder and/or baking soda) are sifted with salt and any additional ingredients, such as cocoa powder. A softened fat, usually butter, is creamed until smooth. The creamed butter is then ready to receive the sugar in several additions. A thorough beating of the butter and sugar together is important because it establishes volume and texture. The leavening present in the recipe acts only to work with the volume created by beating the sugar and fat together, for it does not expand the crumb of the baked cake beyond what is already established by the creaming process: this is an important point to remember when mixing a "creamed" cake batter. Whole eggs, a combination of whole eggs and egg yolks, or egg yolks alone are incorporated next, followed, as appropriate, by a flavoring extract and melted chocolate, if used in the recipe. The flour mixture is added alternately with the liquid, beginning and ending with the sifted ingredients. At each stage after the sifted mixture is added, the mixing should stop when the particles of flour are absorbed; additional beating may take place, depending upon the recipe. Any additions to the batter, such as chocolate chips, chocolate chunks, dried fruit, or nuts, are added at this point, usually stirred in by hand.

A full and light creamed batter with the best overall unbaked and baked texture is attained by using a freestanding electric mixer. It is my first choice for making a creamed cake batter. The strength of the mixer beats the requisite amount of air into the butter and sugar mixture, ultimately building volume. In some cases, an electric hand mixer is an adequate substitute, and some of the creamed batters in this book can be produced with one. Small-quantity cookie doughs will fare well, while larger amounts or those with heavy ingredients, such as lots of chips, nuts, and/or rolled oats, will not; and some cake batters may bake denser, with a tighter, more compact crumb, because a hand mixer beats a lesser quantity of air into a butter and sugar mixture. The lightest cakes and tenderest cookies are made in a freestanding electric mixer, and it is a worthy investment. Cake or muffin batters that call for about 3 cups of flour, more or less, should be made in a freestanding mixer; and yeast doughs, if not made by hand, must be made in a heavy-duty freestanding mixer.

FOR A "MELT AND STIR" BATTER, flour and leavening (baking powder and/or baking soda) are sifted, whisked, or stirred with salt and any additional ingredients, such as cocoa powder. Chocolate and butter are melted and combined (frequently with a whisk) until smooth. The eggs are whisked until just combined and blended with the sugar, then the vanilla extract and melted butter-chocolate mixture. For most brownie batters, the flour mixture is sifted over the whisked ingredients and the mixture is formed into a batter by combining all of the elements, using a whisk or flat wooden paddle. At this point, it is important to mix just until the particles of flour are absorbed. For blondie batters, the flour mixture is usually stirred in, using a wooden spoon or flat wooden paddle, but a whisk can be used if it is sturdy and you mix slowly. Added enrichments such as chocolate chips, chocolate chunks, candy bar nuggets, or chopped nuts are worked into the batter at the end.

FOR A "CUT-IN" DOUGH, as for sweet biscuits and scones, the flour, sugar, and leavening are whisked or sifted with salt and any additional ingredients, such as cocoa powder. Butter is strewn over the flour mixture in chunks and "cut in" using a pastry blender or two round-bladed table knives. Frequently the butter is reduced further, from small pellets or pearl-sized bits, to smaller flakes, using your fingertips. A whisked mixture—usually cream, eggs, and a flavoring extract—is poured over the flour mixture. Additions such as chocolate chips, chocolate chunks, candy bar nuggets, or chopped nuts are then scattered over, and all of the components are mixed into a dough. The dough is then kneaded lightly in the bowl for 30 seconds to 1 minute to establish its texture (the kneading can also be done on a very lightly floured work surface). The dough is shaped into disks, refrigerated, cut into wedges, and baked; occasionally, the dough is formed into wedges and baked without chilling it first.

FOR A "COMBINED AND KNEADED" SWEET YEAST DOUGH, active dry yeast, sugar, and warm water are combined and set to proof until swollen. A dough is created by combining the expanded yeast mixture with, in addition to flour (and occasionally cocoa powder), ingredients such as sugar, a liquid (frequently milk), a flavoring extract, butter, eggs, and salt. The dough is kneaded (by hand or in the mixing bowl of a heavy-duty freestanding mixer) and set to rise, either at cool room temperature or by a combination of room-temperature-and-refrigerator rise. At one point in the mixing and kneading process, if a sweet yeast dough is prepared in a heavy-duty freestanding electric mixer, the partially kneaded dough is covered and put aside for 20 minutes to rest, then the machine-kneading resumes. The purpose of this rest is to allow the flour to absorb the liquid and fat, to prevent overworking the dough, to retain its flavor, and to keep it supple. Some kneaded doughs, set to rise in a bowl, are slashed with a pair of kitchen scissors; the deep cuts in the dough encourage a good and supportive rise. The resulting dough, lightened and puffy, is compressed slightly and set to rest for a short while, covered loosely with a linen tea towel or sheet of food-safe plastic wrap; some refrigerated doughs are not treated to a short rest prior to shaping. The dough is then formed into sweet rolls, little babas, individual breads or buns, and set aside to rise again before baking. Occasionally, before the last rise, and depending on the kind of sweet bread you are making, the dough will be rolled out and spread with a filling before it is formed into small coffee cakes, individual sweet rolls, or buns. The dough itself is occasionally enriched with chocolate in the form of chips or chunks. Formed rolls or buns may be covered

with a streusel topping. Some breads containing chocolate are finished with indulgent strokes of icing or glaze.

While mixing and beating a yeast dough in a heavy-duty freestanding mixer, always stand by the mixer to make sure that it is stable on the work surface, and never leave it unattended.

FOR A "CREAMED" CONFECTIONERS' SUGAR FROSTING, confectioners' sugar, butter (melted or softened), melted chocolate, salt, vanilla extract, and a liquid and/or soft dairy ingredient are combined in stages, usually in a freestanding electric mixer fitted with the flat paddle attachment. With the mixer fully stopped, the sides of the bowl are scraped down as necessary to keep the frosting even-textured. Do this with a flexible rubber spatula. Depending on the recipe, the frosting is sometimes finished by a final, accelerated beating to achieve a creamier, fluffier texture, with or without additional light cream or heavy cream. Finally, the texture of the frosting is adjusted to spreading consistency with extra tablespoons of milk or cream or a little more confectioners' sugar. The need for extra liquid or sugar will vary according to the weather and temperature of your kitchen, or how you intend to use the frosting: as a soft and gossamer covering for a layer cake, or for piping decoratively over the surface of a smoothly frosted cake or directly onto the tops of cupcakes. The main amount of the liquid dairy ingredient (milk or cream) is frequently heated to tepid—slightly warm—before adding to the other ingredients so that it blends with the chocolate mixture; if the recipe does not call for it to be warmed first, then use it at room temperature.

For frosting that is to be put through a pastry bag and piped decoratively, beat the frosting on low to moderately low speed until all ingredients are combined at each stage, using the flat paddle attachment (refrain from beating until fluffy at any stage). If necessary, press the frosting against the sides of a mixing bowl with a spatula to expel any air bubbles. If the frosting is fluffy, you can usually restore the texture by blending in several additional tablespoons of confectioners' sugar and a tablespoon or two extra of softened butter on low speed.

To use the frosting for spreading on sheet cakes, place spaced dollops of the frosting on top of the cake, then smooth it over the surface. For cupcakes, mound the frosting in the center of each cupcake, smooth down the sides just to the ruffle of the paper cupcake liner (the frosting should conceal the surface of the cake and just touch the paper liner but not sag too far over it), then finally swirl on a top coat of frosting. For layer cakes, after the layers are spread with frosting and assembled, spread the frosting on the top of the cake, then on the sides, and, finally, touch up the entire rounded edge where the sides meet the uppermost surface layer of frosting.

Once the frosting is spread on a layer cake or sheet cake, or on an armload of cupcakes, you can swirl it decoratively into small peaks and curls—an icing spatula is particularly useful for this—but do so as soon as possible, before the frosting firms up.

To make high, thickly frosted cupcakes, use a fairly firm confectioners' sugar frosting and load it on the surface of the cupcake in the shape of an inverted cone or a teepee with the top squared off—that is, thickly at the base and narrower toward the top—then smooth the sides and top. When the frosting is still moist, decorate the surface with sprinkles, if you wish.

FOR AN EGG YOLK–ENRICHED CUSTARD SAUCE OR PASTRY CREAM, the goal is to create a satiny smooth, thoroughly cooked and thickened mixture that is free of lumps. Both a custard sauce and a pastry cream are considered a stirred custard, though the former is thicker than the latter. There are several important technical notes to remember: pastry creams, thickened with cornstarch, bound with egg yolks for richness and texture, and cooked at a reasonably low boil should reach between 199 degrees F. and 201 degrees F., averaging out at 200 degrees F. A properly cooked pastry cream will coat a wooden spoon thickly and continue to firm up as it cools. An egg yolk–enriched custard sauce must be cooked until thickened so that it reaches and maintains a temperature of 160 degrees F. To test the temperature of the custard sauce, remove the saucepan from the heat for a moment and, protecting your hands with oven mitts, tip the pan slightly so that the sauce pools to one side, then test with an instant-read thermometer. For safety, technical precision, and accuracy, always use a thermometer to verify the temperature of the completed sauce or pastry cream.

A CUSTARD SAUCE is the result of combining warmed liquid dairy ingredients with a pinch of salt into a sugar, arrowroot (if used), and egg yolk mixture, then cooking it slowly in a heavy saucepan until it reaches the correct temperature and lightly coats the back of a wooden spoon. The custard is strained through a fine-mesh sieve before flavoring with an extract or liqueur. Some custard sauces are thickened gently with arrowroot, while others rely on the thickening power of egg yolks alone to arrive at a sauce that is slightly dense, but with a good flow. For a chocolate-flavored custard sauce, egg yolks are mixed into a sifted sugar and arrowroot mixture; salt and melted chocolate are added, followed by the warmed liquid. The mixture is cooked slowly until thickened, then strained and flavored.

A PASTRY CREAM is made by combining liquid dairy ingredients and a pinch of salt with sugar and cornstarch in a heavy saucepan. The mixture is brought to a boil over moderately high heat and cooked until thickened. Lightly beaten egg yolks are introduced into the mixture off the heat after the yolks have been "tempered" with a small amount of the hot mixture. The tempering process moderates the temperature at which the yolks are introduced into the hot cream. By mixing some of the yolks with a little of the hot mixture, and so acclimating them to the heat, they can be added to the thickened cream without risking a change in texture. The saucepan is returned to the heat and the mixture is cooked to complete the thickening (and enriching) process. Depending on the recipe, the filling may be strained into a heatproof bowl or simply turned into the bowl. A flavoring extract is added at this point, and a little softened butter may be incorporated as a final enhancement.

TO CREATE A FANCIFUL TOPPING FOR DROP COOKIES, SHORTBREAD, BAR COOKIES, AND SCONES, sprinkle extra or reserved chips, chunks, nuts, or chopped candy (matched to the ingredient in the recipe) onto the surface of cookie dough mounds, sweet rolls, or blocks of bar cookies either just before baking or 5 to 10 minutes before the baking time is up. For bar cookies, scatter the chips, chunks, nuts, or chopped candy here and there on the surface (avoiding the edges). If the particular bar cookie batter is only moderately thick, add the topping before the final 5 to 10 minutes of baking because topping the sweet any sooner will lose the definition of the ingredient (as it sinks into the surface). Cookies made from a thick dough can be topped prior to baking; cookies made from a softer dough that spreads during baking should be topped about 4 minutes before the baking time is up. For scones, add a topping of extra chips or chunks of candy during the last 4 to 5 minutes of baking.

Baking expressions

APPROACHING THE BAKING PROCESS IS EASY if you understand its basic terminology. This glossary of terms reflects both the methods and techniques used in the recipes and my own baking style.

TO BEAT is to blend ingredients together using slow, moderate, or high speed. Butter is beaten to make it smooth and creamy. Butter and sugar are beaten together to establish texture and, later, volume in the baked batter or dough. A sifted (or whisked) mixture is added alternately with dry ingredients and beaten into the creamed mixture to form a batter. Different phases of the mixing process require distinct speeds. Beating is a steady process, and should be balanced and seamless no matter the speed.

TO BLEND is to combine two or more ingredients in a careful, consistent way. Blending is a way to mix ingredients without creating or losing volume. It can be accomplished simply with a wooden spoon, rubber spatula, or flat wooden spatula, or in the bowl of a freestanding electric mixer on low speed.

TO CREAM is to beat butter, alone or with sugar, to arrive at a specific texture. Creaming butter by itself until smooth and the consistency of pearly mayonnaise readies it for the addition of sugar. When sugar is added in several portions, it is beaten to create a mixture that is light and pale; this builds texture. Creaming butter is equally important when making many cookie doughs, especially shortbread, when a fragile, melting baked texture is the coveted thing.

THE CRUMB of a cake, bar or drop cookie, scone, muffin, tea bread, or sweet roll refers to its internal texture.

TO DUST is to shower the top of a cake with confectioners' sugar (or a mixture of confectioners' sugar and cocoa powder) or to lightly coat a work surface with flour in preparation for kneading a yeast dough. To *dust* also refers to the act of lightly coating the entire interior surface of a greased baking pan with flour before filling it with a batter or dough; the pan should be dusted with a haze of flour and the excess tapped out over the kitchen sink. As a general rule, use all-purpose flour for dusting the inside of the baking pans.

TO FILM is to lightly coat the interior of a baking pan with nonstick cooking spray, such as Pam.

TO FOLD is to combine two elements together in the lightest but most thorough way possible. Folding egg whites into a base batter mixture is a good example of this procedure: I incorporate—by actively stirring—about one-quarter of the beaten whites into the base batter to lighten it, then top the mixture with the remaining beaten whites. With a spatula, I dip and sweep the whites into, around, and through the batter to make the mixture as buoyant as possible. This should be done quickly, with a minimum of strokes, so as not to deflate the puffy mixture. Once the two mixtures meet each other, they should be mixed with an up-and-around motion of the spatula (going vertically down, then up while sweeping the sides), rather than circulating the bowl as if you were mixing a batter with a spoon.

TO FORM is to create shaped sections of dough, as for individual sweet breads such as scones. For scones, the dough is formed into one or more disks and cut into thick wedges. Cut the dough into equal pieces so that the quick breads bake evenly.

To FROST is to cover one or more layers of cake with frosting. Using the "crumb coat" method is especially helpful when frosting tender, freshly baked butter cake layers. For this method, brush any crumbs from the top of a sheet cake, or the top and sides of multiple layers. For a sheet cake, spread a thin layer of frosting on top and let it firm up at room temperature for 20 to 30 minutes or refrigerate it for 15 minutes, then apply the remaining frosting in sweeps and swirls. For a layer cake, cover the layers with frosting or filling, spread the entire surface with a thin coating of frosting, and let stand for 20 to 30 minutes or refrigerate for 15 minutes, then frost the cake with whirls of frosting. This method works with creamy, billowy, buttercream-style frosting. For cakes that are frosted while oven hot, such as Coca-Cola Cake (page 285), or finished with a poured or spooned-on glaze or icing or a warm, cooked frosting, it is not necessary to perform the initial "crumb coat." When frosting a cake, use an icing spatula.

To GREASE AND FLOUR a baking pan, lightly coat the inside of the pan, including the tube (if it is a Bundt or any kind of plain or decorative tube pan), with softened, unsalted butter or shortening, as specified in each recipe. In some instances the pan(s) will be lined with waxed paper; if so, grease the paper, too. Then sprinkle all-purpose flour over the entire interior greased surface and tap the pan from side to side to coat evenly in a haze of flour. Turn the pan(s) upside-down over the kitchen sink and tap out any excess flour. See also to *film,* page 36.

To LAYER elements is to uniformly assemble different levels of ingredients, such as constructing a bar cookie. Ingredients should be sprinkled over or spooned on evenly, from side to side and corner to corner, in order to arrange the elements in a balanced way that ensures even baking.

To MELT is to apply heat to an ingredient, such as chocolate, so that the texture changes from a solid to a fluid, or thickly fluid, state.

To MIX is to combine two or more ingredients carefully by whisking, stirring, or beating without overworking the mixture.

To SCATTER is to sprinkle or strew a mixture, such as a streusel, over an unbaked batter or dough. It is important to scatter an ingredient in a balanced way. Nubs of hand-made streusel should be applied in an even layer; otherwise, some sections of the sweet will bake unevenly and have a pasty texture.

To SCRAPE DOWN is to clean the sides of a bowl with a rubber spatula, sweeping down the batter that clings to the sides. In the course of mixing a batter, be sure to scrape down the sides of the bowl frequently to keep it even-textured. I do this at all of the stages—creaming butter and sugar, incorporating the eggs, adding chocolate, mixing in dry and liquid ingredients, and adding any additional flavoring components (such as nuts, chips, or chunks of candy).

To SHAPE is to compose mounds of cookie dough of a specific size on the prepared baking sheets. The actual size and contour of each unbaked cookie should be the same in order to promote even baking. When assembling the cookies on the pan, take care to leave enough space between them as recommended in each recipe. Spacing cookies too close together usually causes them to merge as they bake into sweet, interconnected chaos.

To SIFT is to pass one or a combination of dry ingredients through a sifter or sieve to aerate and eliminate lumps. This act ventilates a leavened or unleavened flour mixture, but does not mix the ingredients. To mix dry ingredients thoroughly, before or in lieu of sifting (as specified in the recipe), whisk them together in a bowl.

To SPOON is to parcel out an ingredient or mixture using a spoon. I use a large stainless-steel mixing spoon for filling a baking pan with batter. Using a spoon to fill fancy baking molds avoids the inevitable sloshes against the sides and through the tubular opening of a baking pan. To measure flour, aerate it first with a fork, then spoon into dry measuring cups and level off with a flexible palette knife or other straight-edged knife.

To STIR OR STIR IN is to blend ingredients together in a reasonably slow, careful way. For stirring, use a wooden spoon, flat wooden paddle, flexible rubber spatula, whisk, or large stainless-steel spoon, depending on the mixture involved. Many of my brownie batters suggest using a whisk or flat wooden paddle for stirring the sifted mixture into the blend of melted chocolate, butter, sugar, and eggs; if you use the whisk slowly, it does a fine job of blending in the dry ingredients.

TO SWIRL is to form curves in a mixture, such as a frosting. A filling and batter or two different batters (chocolate and vanilla, for example) may also be swirled together. To integrate a filling, a portion of cake batter is turned into a prepared cake pan, and a trench is formed with the back of a spoon or spatula. Once the filling is added and covered with the remaining batter, a round-edged table knife is swept through the mixture to move the filling around in graceful twirls or curls. When swirling, keep the knife away from the bottom and sides of the baking pan. Resist the urge to over-swirl the mixture, as this could blur the batter. The point is to keep both mixtures distinguishable while composing them for baking.

TO TOSS is to combine two or more ingredients, usually chips or chunks of chocolate with a little of the sifted flour mixture, in a bowl so that the ingredients are combined and coated, using a spoon or spatula.

TO WHIP is to actively beat an ingredient, such as egg whites or heavy cream, in order to achieve volume. No matter the stage of firmness, beaten egg whites should remain shiny and creamy-looking, not dry or grainy, and heavy cream should be smooth, cloud-like, and pillowy. Whipping builds volume by incorporating air; a hand-held whisk or electric mixer outfitted with the whisk attachment can be used. For heavy cream, I am a great fan of whipping the cream in a chilled bowl with a balloon whisk, for this generates the lightest and creamiest accompaniment of all.

TO WHISK is to combine two or more ingredients in an active way. Most whisking is a vigorous process, but it can also be less energetic. I often use a whisk to combine ingredients slowly and methodically (such as a sifted flour mixture into a butter-chocolate-sugar-egg brownie base), without robustly working them in the bowl.

TO WORK IN is to mix chocolate chips, chocolate chunks, chopped nuts, flaked coconut, bits of dried fruit, and the like into a batter or dough at the end of the procedure. To work an ingredient into a small-quantity of batter or dough: use a flexible rubber spatula or wooden spoon and mix by hand or on low speed of an electric mixer for creamy batters; use a wooden spoon or a flat paddle and mix by hand or on moderately low speed of an electric mixer for moderately thick batters. Big batches of dense or heavy and creamy-thick dough, rich in add-ins of oats, chips or chunks of chocolate, or dried fruit, are best combined in an electric mixer.

To add chocolate chips or chunks to a yeast dough, pat out the dough on a lightly floured work surface. Scatter the ingredient over the dough and push the dough into a loose jelly roll, then knead it until the addition is integrated At first, the dough will splinter and fragment, and the addition will make it look as if it is corrupting the dough and spoiling its texture, but it isn't. After a few minutes of kneading, the dough will accommodate the flavoring addition.

Elements of texture

WHEN CHOCOLATE IS INTRODUCED into a batter or dough, it determines not only its flavor, but its texture as well. Texture, along with flavor, is defined before baking by the type and amount of the ingredients, but the baking process establishes and unifies it. The type and form of chocolate used in batters and doughs are chosen for the way that they behave, bake, and taste in them.

Characteristics of chocolate-based batters and doughs

This chart lists the characteristics of chocolate-based batters and doughs.	
TYPE OF CHOCOLATE-BASED BATTER OR DOUGH	CHARACTERISTICS OF BATTER OR DOUGH
CHOCOLATE CHIP, CHUNK, OR NUGGET-ENHANCED DROP COOKIE BATTER	• creamy-textured • softly to moderately dense • silky-textured
CHOCOLATE CHIP, CHUNK, OR NUGGET-ENHANCED CAKE BATTER	• moderately to thickly dense • creamy-textured • silky-textured
CHOCOLATE CHIP, CHUNK, OR NUGGET-ENHANCED BAR COOKIE DOUGH	• dense • creamy-textured • chunky
CHOCOLATE CHIP, CHUNK, OR NUGGET-ENHANCED MUFFIN BATTER	• moderately dense • creamy-textured • buttery
CHOPPED CANDY-ENHANCED DROP COOKIE DOUGH	• moderately dense • creamy-textured • chunky • buttery and dense
CHOPPED CANDY-ENHANCED BAR COOKIE DOUGH	• dense but silky • creamy-textured • chunky • buttery and dense
MELTED CHOCOLATE-HEIGHTENED BAR COOKIE BATTER	• softly or moderately dense • silky-textured • creamy-textured • moist and buttery

TYPE OF CHOCOLATE-BASED BATTER OR DOUGH	CHARACTERISTICS OF BATTER OR DOUGH
MELTED CHOCOLATE-HEIGHTENED CAKE BATTER (USING UNSWEETENED OR BITTERSWEET CHOCOLATE)	• softly or moderately dense • creamy-textured • smooth • satiny-textured • moist and buttery
MELTED CHOCOLATE-HEIGHTENED SCONE/SWEET BISCUIT DOUGH (USING UNSWEETENED, SEMISWEET, OR BITTERSWEET CHOCOLATE)	• dense but creamy-textured • capable of suspending miniature semisweet chips, chopped or shredded chocolate, and chopped candy • buttery
UNSWEETENED COCOA POWDER–HEIGHTENED AND FLAVORED CAKE BATTER	• softly to moderately dense • firm-textured
UNSWEETENED COCOA POWDER–HEIGHTENED AND FLAVORED SCONE/SWEET BISCUIT DOUGH	• capable of suspending miniature semisweet chips, chopped or shredded chocolate, and chopped candy • compact and dense
CHOCOLATE-ENHANCED BISCOTTI BATTER OR DOUGH	• firm-textured but moist • capable of suspending miniature semisweet chips or chopped or shredded chocolate • stable and compact
CHOCOLATE-ENHANCED WAFFLE BATTER	• creamy-textured and moist • moderately thick • capable of suspending miniature semisweet chips, chopped or grated chocolate
CHOCOLATE-ENHANCED PANCAKE BATTER	• silky-textured • creamy-textured • lightly to moderately dense • capable of suspending miniature semisweet chips or grated chocolate

BASIC INGREDIENTS, ALONG WITH THE METHOD, form the structure of the recipes in *ChocolateChocolate* and draw on these baking staples. The core ingredients used in baking are important components that build texture, furnish volume, establish the level of sweetness, and determine the basic structure of a dough or batter.

KING ARTHUR FLOUR

Naturally Pure and Wholesome ®

QUEEN GUINEVERE
CAKE
FLOUR

For high-rising, tender cakes

Never Bro

A glossary of baking ingredients

PAN PREPARATION INGREDIENTS

When a recipe calls for using a combination of fat and flour (shortening/flour or butter/flour), you can also use Baker's Joy or Cake Release. Baker's Joy is a spray that combines soybean oil and flour. Cake Release is a slightly thick mixture that contains soybean oil and shortening. Cake Release, once squeezed onto the inside surface of the baking pan, must be stroked on with a pastry brush. Cake Release works beautifully in layer cake pans and Bundt pans. Pam, a reliable nonstick cooking spray, contains canola oil, and can be used for preparing pans for bar cookies and some Bundt cakes. The interior of baking pans should be covered in a film of Baker's Joy, Pam, or Cake Release, not a thick coating.

FLOUR

The recipes in *ChocolateChocolate* call for bleached all-purpose flour (12 grams of protein in 1 cup), bleached cake flour (8 grams of protein in 1 cup), and unbleached all-purpose flour (16 grams of protein in 1 cup). The level of protein in each type of flour is an indication of its "strength." Unbleached flour is designated as a "strong" flour, for its higher protein content creates a somewhat sturdier dough; in this cookbook, it is used primarily in sweet yeast breads along with bleached all-purpose flour. Cake flour, at the other end of the spectrum, is termed a "weak" (or "soft") flour because it's lower in protein; cake flour is present in some cake batter formulas, and occasionally is combined with all-purpose flour in cookie doughs and brownie batters. All-purpose flour, in terms of strength, is in between cake and unbleached flour with regard to protein content, allowing it to be used in a wide range of doughs and batters.

MEASURING FLOUR

When baking the recipes in *ChocolateChocolate,* always measure flour in dry measuring cups. First, stir the flour with a fork to aerate it, then spoon the flour into the cup(s) and level the top(s) by sweeping off the excess with the straight edge of a spatula or palette knife. If the recipe calls for a measurement of sifted flour, sift the flour first onto a sheet of waxed paper, then spoon it into the measuring cup(s) and level off the top.

LEAVENING AGENTS

Both baking soda (composed of 100 percent sodium bicarbonate, U.S.P.) and double-acting baking powder (containing calcium acid phosphate, bicarbonate of soda, and cornstarch) are known as *chemical leaveners.* Baking soda generally appears as a leavener when an acidic liquid or soft dairy product is present in the ingredient list, such as buttermilk or sour cream. Baking soda neutralizes the acidity present in the batter or dough as well as furnishing the lift. Baking soda is frequently used with nonalkalized cocoa powder. Baking powder is used with alkalized cocoa powder in some batters and doughs, as baking soda is not needed for its neutralizing effect. Baking soda will keep in an airtight container on a cool pantry shelf for up to 9 months. Once opened, a can of baking powder should be used or replaced within 6 months, as its potency and leavening ability diminishes over time; always respect the "use by" date on the can of baking powder, as well. Both baking powder and baking soda should be measured by dipping the measuring spoon into the leavening and sweeping off the excess with the straight edge of a knife or spatula. Baking soda is sometimes lumpy; lumps should be sieved out before measuring.

Yeast is considered a *nonchemical leavener* and is available as active and dry, in packets and jars, or in fresh, moist cakes, known as compressed cakes. The recipes in "Chocolate Bread" call for active dry yeast, and it is measured out in teaspoons. In the recipes, active dry yeast is combined with a little warm water and a bit of sugar, and set aside for several minutes to foam and swell, an indication that it is a viable, thriving substance.

Egg whites, whipped to billowy peaks, also provide leavening when folded into a batter. In order to get maximum volume from the beaten whites, whip them slowly at first, then increase the speed to develop mass and bulk. A bowlful of whipped egg whites—whether soft, firm, or stiff—should look satiny, sleek, and velvety, and not at all grainy. Softly whipped whites have peaks that bend and droop slightly, whereas when firmly beaten, they stand up without bowing or slouching. Whipped egg whites, no matter the degree of firmness, should appear moist.

SALT

Salt brings out the flavor of chocolate in doughs and batters. It also counterbalances the sugar present in the recipe, defines the taste of the chocolate ingredient, and brings depth to a batter or dough. I use extra-fine sea salt in my recipes. Its pure, clean taste is a revelation.

BUTTER

Mostly fat (and also containing a small amount of milk-based settlings [solids] and water), butter is a defining element in a chocolate-based batter or dough. Butter should be kept in its wrappings, in the coldest part of the refrigerator, not in a section of the door. Use fresh, not previously frozen, unsalted butter, for the consistency of butter changes as the butter defrosts, and that alteration results in a heavy, and possibly streaky, baked batter or dough. Unsalted butter has the purest, cleanest flavor and is preferable over the salted variety for baking, as salt can mask any off-flavors.

Premium butter

This chart offers an overview of premium butters that are excellent for baking.	
BUTTER (brand and package size)	RECIPES THAT MAKE THE BEST USE OF PREMIUM BUTTER
ORGANIC VALLEY UNSALTED EUROPEAN STYLE CULTURED BUTTER (8 OUNCES)	• flourless chocolate cakes • dense bar cookie batters • chocolate-based frostings • cookie doughs with a high butter content • all drop cookie doughs • sweet yeast doughs
CELLES SUR BELLE (8.82 OUNCES)	• flourless chocolate cakes • dense bar cookie batters • chocolate-based frostings • cookie doughs with a high butter content • sweet yeast doughs
HORIZON ORGANIC EXTRA CREAMY EUROPEAN-STYLE BUTTER (8 OUNCES)	• flourless chocolate cakes • dense bar cookie batters • cookie doughs with a high butter content • all drop cookie doughs
ISIGNY S^{TE} MÈRE BEURRE CRU DE NORMANDIE (250 G)	• flourless chocolate cakes • dense bar cookie batters • sweet yeast doughs
365 ORGANIC ORGANIC SWEET CREAM UNSALTED BUTTER (1 POUND)	• flourless chocolate cakes • dense bar cookie batters • chocolate-based frostings • cookie doughs with a high butter content • all drop cookie doughs • sweet yeast doughs

BUTTER (brand and package size)	RECIPES THAT MAKE THE BEST USE OF PREMIUM BUTTER
HORIZON ORGANIC EXTRA CREAMY EUROPEAN-STYLE BUTTER (8 OUNCES)	• flourless chocolate cakes • dense bar cookie batters • cookie doughs with a high butter content • sweet yeast doughs
KATE'S HOMEMADE BUTTER (8 OUNCES)	• flourless chocolate cakes • dense bar cookie batters • chocolate-based frostings • cookie doughs with a high butter content • all drop cookie doughs
BEURRE PRÉSIDENT UNSALTED FRENCH BUTTER (200 G)	• flourless chocolate cakes • dense bar cookie batters • sweet yeast doughs
PLUGRÁ EUROPEAN STYLE UNSALTED BUTTER (8 OUNCES)	• flourless chocolate cakes • dense bar cookie batters • cookie doughs with a high butter content • all drop cookie doughs • sweet yeast doughs

SUGAR

White sugar is used in two kinds of granulations in the recipes that make up *ChocolateChocolate:* granulated and superfine. Pound for pound, a 1-pound box of superfine sugar (Domino brand) is considerably more expensive than a 5-pound bag of granulated sugar, and, ideally, all bakers should use the superfine variety when making creamed butter cake batters and most cookie doughs, as superfine sugar creates a more delicate texture and an increased level of moistness in these baked goods. Another brand of superfine sugar, called Caster Sugar, is produced by India Tree (available in a 1-pound box); it, too, dissolves quickly and produces cakes with a gossamer texture.

In general, I prefer to use cane sugar rather than beet sugar because it has the best flavor and behaves properly and evenly in all baking recipes, and especially in chocolate-based recipes.

Light or dark brown sugar is used in some chocolate-centered batters and doughs, adding a rounded undertone of caramel. Both light and dark brown sugar should be moist enough to pack easily into a dry measuring cup. Before adding either kind of brown sugar to a batter or dough, it should be pressed through a sieve to remove any lumps; otherwise, the texture will be impaired because the bumps of sugar won't dissolve during baking. Both light and dark brown sugar should be measured by firmly packing it into a dry measuring cup, then leveling the top.

Confectioners' sugar, also called powdered sugar, is used in some chocolate-based frostings, icings, and glazes, and to dust over finished baked goods. This very finely pulverized sugar is combined with a small percentage of cornstarch (3 percent) to prevent excessive clumping. The sugar is available in 1-pound boxes (Domino brand sugar). Another variety of powdered cane sugar, called fondant and icing sugar, is produced by India Tree (available in a 1-pound box); this type of sugar is especially useful for making a glaze for cakes and sweet rolls, as it dries to a polished, firm finish.

Non-melting sugar, such as *Snow White Non-Melting Sugar* or *Arctic Snow Powdered Sugar* is ideal for sprinkling over baked goods if the weather is humid or hot, or if the sweet is warm, moist, or sticky. This type of sugar won't melt, disintegrate, or otherwise deteriorate.

EGGS

The combination of fat and protein in whole eggs provides structure, richness, and moisture to batters and doughs in general, and chocolate-specific doughs in particular. I use certified organic eggs in baking. Organic eggs bring out the best in chocolate-based batters and doughs, contributing a full, rounded flavor and a luxurious texture. Organic egg yolks produce wonderfully rich pastry creams and custards.

CORNSTARCH

Cornstarch is used to thicken cooked custards, custard-based fillings, puddings, and creams. Once set, the mixture is smooth and lilting, and not at all pasty or heavy. I prefer cornstarch to flour for the finished texture it conveys. Use a wooden spoon or flat wooden paddle to stir the cornstarch mixture as it cooks, and avoid stirring it vigorously when adding any flavoring additions or enrichments once it has finished cooking or when cooled. Rapidly stirred cornstarch-thickened mixtures can thin out.

One favorite brand, Rumford cornstarch, is manufactured by Hulman & Company. It is made, as the label states, from "nongenetically modified corn" and produces delicate pastry creams and custards. The cornstarch comes in a 12-ounce can that's easy to reseal with the plastic lid that accompanies it.

EXTRACTS, FLAVORING PASTE, AND VANILLA POWDER

VANILLA EXTRACT

Lochhead's Madagascar Bourbon Pure Vanilla Extract for Cookies (4-fluid-ounce bottle) is wonderful to add to cookie doughs in general and chocolate-flavored cookie doughs in particular. Its vanilla flavor resonates through a cookie dough.

Neilsen-Massey Tahitian Pure Vanilla Extract (4-fluid-ounce bottle) is an especially deep, bold, and floral vanilla flavor well-suited to flourless chocolate cakes, quick bread doughs and batters, and dark chocolate cookie doughs.

Neilsen-Massey Madagascar Bourbon Pure Vanilla Extract (4-fluid-ounce bottle) is a superior extract to use for all chocolate-specific doughs and batters. Neilsen-Massey Organic Madagascar Bourbon Pure Vanilla Extract (4-fluid-ounce bottle) is also exceptional. I love to use it in chocolate-based fillings, sauces, frostings, glazes, and toppings.

Zeron Double Intensity pure Veracruz vanilla extract (100-ml bottle) is potent. Use it in pastry creams, chocolate frostings, flourless chocolate cake batters, and any of the pound cake batters in this book.

Neilsen-Massey Madagascar Pure Bourbon Pure Vanilla Bean Paste (4-ounce jar) is a highly aromatic, spoonable mixture that includes the seeds of vanilla beans. Other ingredients are sugar, water, vanilla extract, and gum tragacanth. It is a fabulous product that should be on every baker's shelf. You can use it in almost any chocolate-based cake batter, cookie, or scone dough, pancake or waffle batter, icing, filling, glaze, or frosting for a direct impact of vanilla flavor. In cake batters that use 3 cups flour, you can safely add up to 1 teaspoon; use up to ½ teaspoon in any waffle or pancake batter; up to ¾ teaspoon in any cookie dough that contains 2 to 2½ cups of flour; or up to ½ teaspoon in an icing, filling, glaze, or frosting. Vanilla bean paste can be used along with vanilla extract.

McCormick vanilla extract is a top-quality supermarket staple. Use it straight from the bottle or intensify it further with a split vanilla bean (as in the recipe for Fortified Vanilla Extract on page 55).

Pure Bourbon Vanilla Powder from Madagascar (30-g/1-ounce bottle), a product of France, is the powder made from pure bourbon vanilla (imported by Crossings). Each bottle has a specified lot number. Incorporate it into all chocolate-based batters and doughs. Use ⅛ teaspoon in recipes that use 2 cups of flour, ¼ teaspoon in recipes that use 3 cups of flour, and ¾ teaspoon in any of the yeast doughs in this book. Use the powder along with vanilla extract or vanilla bean paste.

CHOCOLATE EXTRACT

Star Kay White's Chocolate Extract (8-fluid-ounce bottle) adds a depth of chocolate flavor and complexity to doughs and batters. The contents of the ingredient list on the bottle read as follows: "Water, alcohol and chocolate extractives." It has an alcohol content of 46.5 percent.

ALMOND EXTRACT

Star Kay White's Almond Extract (4-fluid-ounce bottle) is a superlative extract that adds a definitive, nutty edge of flavor to baked goods.

LIQUID AND SOFT DAIRY INGREDIENTS

In addition to acting as the liquid component in a recipe, whole milk, buttermilk, light cream, half-and-half, and/or heavy cream contribute flavor and build texture in chocolate-based baked goods. Most importantly, liquid dairy products add moisture and richness. Heavy cream, ideally with a butterfat content of about 40 percent, produces the best sweet biscuit and scone dough—full of flavor and creamy-textured. Buttermilk creates chocolate-based batters and doughs that are wonderfully moist, with a tender crumb. Sour cream (cultured by lactic acid) is a richly thickened dairy product that generates some of the moistest chocolate cakes imaginable.

NUTS AND NUT PASTE

Nuts are used for both flavor and crunch in a chocolate-based batter or dough. Walnuts, pecans, peanuts, and macadamia nuts in particular are appealing in many kinds of coffee cakes, Bundt cakes, scones, bar cookies, and drop cookies, for they add textural relief and a topnote of taste. Lightly toasting whole, slivered, or halved nuts before adding them to a batter or dough brings out their flavor beautifully; it is, however, unnecessary to toast them first if they are used in a topping, such as a streusel. To toast nuts, spread them in an even layer on a rimmed baking sheet and place in a preheated 350 degree F. oven for 6 to 7 minutes, or until fragrant and lightly browned. Cool the nuts completely before chopping.

BIA Organic Marzipan from Sicily (8.8 ounces; packaged in a heavy foil pouch), made from two types of

almonds, contains organic raw cane sugar and organic vanilla. It has an exceptional almond flavor and a rich, fully developed texture. It is imported by Purely Organic, Ltd. Marzipan is wonderful used in concentrated amounts as a filling, and a few tablespoons can be worked into the melted chocolate base of a flourless chocolate cake or chocolate soufflé cake, a scone or drop cookie dough, or a dense brownie batter. To integrate the marzipan into a dough or batter, crumble it into the work bowl of a food processor fitted with the steel blade along with a small amount of the sugar called for in the recipe, cover, and process for 1 minute or until reduced to small particles. Beat one of the eggs called for in the recipe in a small bowl, add it to the processed sugar/marzipan mixture, then process again until smooth and pastelike. Add this marzipan mixture to a "creamed" cake or cookie batter after adding the sugar; to a scone/sweet biscuit dough along with the beaten eggs/cream; to a "melt and stir batter" after the eggs and sugar are whisked together and before a mixture of melted butter and chocolate is added. Marzipan is best used in dense batters and craggy drop cookie doughs, not in tender shortbread doughs or light and silky cake batters.

PASTE AND SOFT GEL FOOD COLORS

Paste and soft gel food colors come in a range of hues and blend nicely into buttercream frosting and royal icing made with meringue powder. Both the paste and soft gel colors add exquisite color to icings and frostings—soft and delicate, or bold and forward.

I have had outstanding results with Cake Craft Food Paste Colors and AmeriColor Soft Gel Paste Food Color. Wilton makes concentrated paste icing colors as well. I have listed my favorite colors for tinting frostings and icings in each brand:

PASTE FOOD COLORS, available in Cake Craft Food Paste Colors brand

My favorite Standard Colors are Lemon Yellow, Golden Yellow, Yellow, Egg Yellow, Antique White, Salmon Pink, Coral, Pink, Fuchsia Pink, Lavender, Royal Blue, Sky Blue, Aqua Blue, Teal, Forest Green, Turquoise, Kelly Green, Mint Green, Leaf Green, and Moss Green.

My favorite pastels are Buttercup, Apricot, Pumpkin Orange, Peach, Mello Melon, Wild Rose, Miami Mauve, and Meadow Green.

PASTE ICING COLORS, PACKED IN SETS FROM WILTON

My favorite sets are Garden Tone Icing Colors containing, in a boxed set of four, Delphinium Blue, Aster Mauve, Juniper Green, and Buttercup Yellow; and Pastel Icing Colors containing, in a boxed set of four, Willow Green, Cornflower Blue, Creamy Peach, and Rose Petal Pink.

GEL COLORS, available in AmeriColor Soft Gel Paste Food Color brand

My favorite gel colors are Fuchsia, Deep Pink, Dusty Rose, Mauve, Peach, Soft Pink, Regal Purple, Violet, Lemon Yellow, Egg Yellow, Teal, Sky Blue, Leaf Green, and Mint Green.

FLAVORED COOKIES AND COOKIE WAFERS FOR MAKING CRUMB CRUSTS AND BAR COOKIE LAYERS

Flavored cookies and wafers, crushed into crumbs, form an excellent base for intensifying chocolate-based bar cookies, and are great for sprinkling over layered cake-and-pudding desserts, or for combining with nuts to use as a swirl-in filling for a chocolate-based butter cake. To make the crumbs, place the broken-up cookies in the work bowl of a food processor fitted with the steel blade, cover, and process to form fine crumbs. Cookie crumbs are best made in batches, filling the work bowl one-third full of crushed cookies. Any of these cookies will crumble deliciously:

Nabisco Famous Chocolate Wafers

Oreo Chocolate Sandwich Cookies

Oreo Chocolate Creme Sandwich Cookies

Nabisco Honey Maid Chocolate Grahams

Nabisco Honey Maid Grahams Chocolate Sticks

Nabisco Nilla Wafers

Keebler Fudge Shoppe Deluxe Grahams Fudge Covered Graham Crackers

Keebler Droxies Creme-Filled Chocolate Cookies

Pepperidge Farm Milano

Pepperidge Farm Double Chocolate Milano

Mint Coco Jo's chocolate mint cookies enrobed in rich dark chocolate (made by Jo's Candies)

Chocolate Grahams milk and dark chocolate graham crackers (made by Jo's Candies)

INGREDIENTS FOR ACCENTING, HIGHLIGHTING, AND DECORATING CHOCOLATE BAKED GOODS

Williams-Sonoma Australian Crystallized Ginger Puree (10-ounce jar) is a fine condiment for spicing up a chocolate-based sweet. I have combined a few tablespoons of the paste into a portion of chocolate frosting before spreading between layers of cake; mixed a few teaspoons into a chocolate glaze for an intense flavor boost (the resulting glaze looks rustic, as the puree gives it a mottled effect); and, added 2 to 3 tablespoons to a biscotti or scone dough. Zeron Early Harvest Crystallized Ginger Baker's Bits, a gorgeous product to heighten the flavor of chocolate-based batters and doughs, is available in 250-gram cans.

Williams-Sonoma Chocolate Mocha Beans (14-ounce can) and Dean & Deluca Chocolate Mocha Beans (8 ounces) are intense candies, and good for decorating frosted, iced, or glazed cakes.

Dean & Deluca Chocolate Dutch Mints (8 ounces) can be used for decorating the top of any frosted or glazed chocolate cake, tart, or torte.

Whole Candied Violets, available in a 2-ounce jar, make an elegant, sweet, and frilly trim for a tart and any glazed (or lightly iced) cake, pudding, or torte.

Mazet Amandas Nougatine au Chocolat Noir—Black Chocolate covered nougat (3 ounces) is a nougatine of roasted almonds and caramel rolled in chocolate from Equador and covered with cocoa. This intense almond confection is best used as a decorative accent for flourless chocolate cakes or chocolate tortes.

Michel Cluizel Grains d'Arôme—Grains de Café Enrobes de Chocolat Noir—coffee beans coated with dark chocolate (5.3 ounces) are an instant garnish for a chocolate tart, chocolate torte, flourless chocolate cake, or chocolate soufflé cake.

Fleur de Sel Caramels, butter caramels with salt (8.75 ounces), are a confection best used for melting and drizzling over a slice of chocolate cake, preferably a simple torte or flourless chocolate cake, served with a toffee sauce. These are small, elegant squares of caramel that are sweet with a light, appealing edge of saltiness. They are made with Charentes-Poitou butter.

Basic ingredients

This chart describes the characteristics of essential ingredients used in baking.

CORE INGREDIENT	ROLE OF THE CORE INGREDIENT
BUTTER	develops and enriches texture; develops and maintains moistness; flavors dough or batter
SHORTENING (SOLID VEGETABLE SHORTENING)	builds volume in a dough or batter; creams smoothly with softened, unsalted butter; integrates well into a "cut-in" dough for biscuits and scones
EGGS	add moisture to batters and doughs; help to develop volume; enrich and define texture
GRANULATED OR SUPERFINE SUGAR	sweetens a batter or dough; maintains moisture in baked crumb; develops the crumb; develops color of baked crust
LIGHT OR DARK BROWN SUGAR	sweetens a batter or dough; maintains moisture in a batter or dough; creates a level of density in a batter or dough
BLEACHED ALL-PURPOSE FLOUR OR BLEACHED CAKE FLOUR	defines internal crumb and overall structure of a batter or dough (all-purpose and cake); contributes to overall structure and size of a batter or dough (all-purpose and cake); softens and tenderizes baked crumb of a batter (cake flour)
DAIRY PRODUCTS (WHOLE MILK, BUTTERMILK, LIGHT [TABLE] CREAM, HEAVY CREAM, HALF-AND-HALF, SOUR CREAM, CRÈME FRAÎCHE, OR HEAVY CREAM)	work to establish baked crumb of batters and doughs; develop internal structure, whether light or dense; add moisture; add richness (especially light cream, heavy cream, sour cream, crème fraîche, or heavy cream); refine the crumb of a baked batter or dough
LEAVENING AGENTS (BAKING POWDER AND/OR BAKING SODA)	establish volume in a baked batter or dough; develop the overall structure and height of a baked batter or dough
LIQUID EXTRACTS	build flavor in a batter or dough
SALT (PREFERABLY EXTRA-FINE SEA SALT FOR THE BEST FLAVOR)	builds flavor in any batter or dough that contains chocolate; regulates process of fermentation in a sweet yeast dough
WATER	develops the chocolate intensity/flavor in a cocoa-based batter or dough

The luxury of homemade ingredients

SIMPLE TO MAKE, these are the small pleasures of baking—ingredients that are great to have on hand when composing chocolate doughs and batters. Some are plain but significant, others playful.

FORTIFIED VANILLA EXTRACT
4 ounces

Fortified is the right word for this flavoring extract, as it is reinforced with a split vanilla bean. While not pivotal to chocolate-based desserts, the strengthened extract adds a wonderful dimension of taste. And it's so easy to make.

1 small, supple vanilla bean
One 4-ounce bottle vanilla extract

With the tip of a small, sharp knife, split the vanilla bean to expose the tiny seeds, leaving the bean intact. Dip the bean several times in the bottled extract, then bend it into thirds and place in the bottle. Cap the bottle tightly and shake 2 or 3 times. Place the bottle on the pantry shelf and let it stand for about 5 days before using. The extract, with the infusing bean, will keep for 6 months.

ESSENCE-OF-VANILLA GRANULATED SUGAR
3 pounds

Vanilla-sugar adds a polished taste to chocolate-based batters and doughs. It is simple to make and returns flavorful results.

2 moist, aromatic vanilla beans
3 pounds granulated sugar

With a small, sharp knife, split each vanilla bean down the center to expose the tiny seeds, but keep the vanilla bean intact.

Pour half of the granulated sugar into a large storage container. Add one of the split vanilla beans. Fill with the remaining sugar and push in the remaining vanilla bean. Cover the container. Let the sugar stand in a cool, dark place for at least 3 days before using. The sugar will gain in intensity within the first few weeks. Over time, moist vanilla beans will cause the sugar to clump. When this happens, press the sugar through a sieve to eliminate any of the small lumps.

The vanilla-sugar will keep for 3 months.

ESSENCE-OF-VANILLA CONFECTIONERS' SUGAR

1 pound

Nestling a vanilla bean into a pound of confectioners' sugar is a simple act that will reward you with a sweetly floral ingredient to sift over baked goods or add to a dough or batter.

1 supple, aromatic vanilla bean
1 pound confectioners' sugar

With a small, sharp knife, split the vanilla bean down the center to expose the tiny seeds, but keep the vanilla bean intact.

Spoon half of the confectioners' sugar into a medium-size storage container. Add the vanilla bean and fill with the remaining sugar. Cover the container. Let the sugar stand in a cool, dark place for at least 3 days before using. The sugar will gain in intensity within the first few weeks. Over time, a moist vanilla bean will encourage the sugar to clump. When this happens, press the sugar through a strainer or sieve to break up any of the lumps. The vanilla-scented confectioners' sugar will keep for 6 months.

ESSENCE-OF-VANILLA SUPERFINE SUGAR

2 pounds

Superfine sugar takes wonderfully to the subtlety of vanilla bean flavoring.

1 moist, aromatic vanilla bean
2 pounds superfine sugar

With a small, sharp knife, split the vanilla bean down the center to expose the tiny seeds, but keep the length of the vanilla bean intact.

Pour half of the superfine sugar into a medium-size storage container. Add the vanilla bean and fill with the remaining sugar. Cover the container. Let the sugar stand in a cool, dark place (in the pantry) for at least 3 days before using. The sugar will gain in intensity within the first few weeks. As the sugar mellows, it will absorb some of the moisture present in the vanilla bean and prompt it to lump up here and there; break up the sugar nuggets into manageable pieces and press through a sieve before measuring. The scented sugar will keep for 3 to 4 months.

CHOCOLATE LIQUEUR SOAKING GLAZE

About ½ cup glaze

Lightly sweetened and syrupy, this is a good glaze to coat the top and sides of chocolate-based butter cakes, especially pound or Bundt cakes.

¼ cup granulated sugar
¼ cup water
½ cup plus 2 tablespoons chocolate liqueur
½ teaspoon vanilla extract

Place the sugar, water, and chocolate liqueur in a small, heavy, nonreactive saucepan. Cover and set over low heat. When every granule of sugar has dissolved, raise the heat to high, and bring the contents of the saucepan to the boil. Cook the liquid at a moderate boil for 7 minutes, until reduced and concentrated-looking. It should measure about ½ cup. Remove from the heat and stir in the vanilla extract. Pour the syrup into a heatproof storage container and cool completely. Cover tightly and refrigerate. The syrup will keep, stored in the refrigerator, for 1 week.

CHOCOLATE LIQUEUR AND SUGAR WASH

About ½ cup topping

This wash can be used as you would the Chocolate Liqueur Soaking Glaze (at left), but it is a bit bolder, a little more intense, and faster to make. The fact that the liqueur is not simmered but simply combined with granulated sugar and vanilla extract makes it assertive. It imparts sheen and an appealing sandy texture to the surface of a baked pound cake or Bundt cake, as the sugar, for the most part, stays suspended in the liqueur.

⅓ cup chocolate liqueur
⅓ cup granulated sugar
¼ teaspoon vanilla extract

In a small, nonreactive bowl, stir together the chocolate liqueur, sugar, and vanilla extract. Let the wash stand for at least 10 minutes, then use as directed in the recipe, for brushing over the top of chocolate-based butter cakes. The sugar will settle to the bottom of the bowl; when applying the mixture, make sure to dip, dunk, and sweep the pastry brush into the sugary bottom. The wash can be made up to 1 hour in advance.

CHOCOLATE COOKIE CRUMB WAVE
About 1¼ cups filling

You can make a crumb filling out of almost any kind of cookie, but I am partial to using dark chocolate wafers, for they are plain and dry enough to make light, sandy crumbs in the work bowl of a food processor; some cookie wafers compact when ground, contributing too moist a texture to weave through a batter or dough, but this crumb mixture maintains its integrity when marbled through almost any kind of batter. It makes for a strikingly delicious, swirly center in almost any kind of butter cake.

1 cup dark chocolate wafer cookie crumbs (such as crumbs made from Nabisco Famous Chocolate Wafers)
1 tablespoon superfine sugar
3 tablespoons ground or very finely chopped bittersweet chocolate

In a medium-size mixing bowl, combine the cookie crumbs, sugar, and ground chocolate. Use the mixture as a swirly filling for a cake. The filling can be made up to 2 days in advance and stored in a covered container.

CHOCOLATE CHIP WAVE
About 1⅓ cups filling

When chocolate cookie crumbs meet miniature chocolate chips, a happy merger of ingredients forms to compose a dandy filling. Use the filling in a plain vanilla pound cake batter to add a spark of chocolate, or in a buttery chocolate chip or sour cream coffee cake batter to double the chocolate flavor.

1 cup dark chocolate wafer cookie crumbs (such as crumbs made from Nabisco Famous Chocolate Wafers)
1 tablespoon superfine sugar
⅓ cup miniature semisweet chocolate chips

In a medium-size mixing bowl, thoroughly combine the cookie crumbs, sugar, and chocolate chips, using a wooden spoon. The filling can be made up to 1 week in advance and stored in a covered container.

COCOA-SUGAR "SOOT"
2 cups topping

Shade confectioners' sugar with cocoa powder, and you have created a simple and flattering finish for sprinkling over chocolate-based baked goods. Or, use the "soot" as a sweet finishing touch for rolling crescent cookies and butter balls after baking.

2 cups confectioners' sugar
2 tablespoons unsweetened alkalized cocoa powder

Whisk the sugar and cocoa powder well, then sift onto a sheet of waxed paper. Transfer to a container and cover tightly. Store the "soot" on a pantry shelf. It will keep for 1 month.

CHOCOLATE CHIP AND NUT "GRAVEL"
About 1 cup topping or filling

Such sweet rubble. A mixture of chocolate chips and nuts can serve as a topping or filling. As a topping, the "gravel" can be sprinkled on the surface of an unbaked cake, such as a plain coffee cake. The sugar is present to give some bulk to the cocoa powder so that it twinkles on the nuts and chips.

½ cup miniature semisweet chocolate chips
½ cup chopped nuts (walnuts, pecans, macadamia nuts, or peanuts)
1 teaspoon unsweetened alkalized cocoa powder combined with1 tablespoon granulated sugar

In a medium-size mixing bowl, combine the chocolate chips, chopped nuts, and cocoa powder/granulated sugar blend. Stir to blend well. The mixture will keep for 1 week, stored in a covered container.

CHOCOLATE "DIRT"

About 1⅓ cups filling

This is the most delicious grime you may ever encounter. "Dirt" is an affectionate name for a chocolate cookie crumb mixture mixed with cocoa powder and walnuts, and sweetened with a little granulated sugar. You could add ½ cup sweetened flaked coconut to the mix for texture and additional flavor. Use the "dirt" as a curly filling for a chocolate or vanilla pound cake, coffee cake, or Bundt cake batter, especially one made with sour cream.

1 cup dark chocolate wafer cookie crumbs (such as crumbs made from Nabisco Famous Chocolate Wafers)
3 tablespoons granulated sugar
1 tablespoon unsweetened alkalized cocoa powder
½ cup finely chopped walnuts

In a small bowl, combine the cookie crumbs, sugar, cocoa powder, and walnuts. Use the "dirt" now or spoon into a container, cover, and store at room temperature for up to 3 days.

CLARIFIED BUTTER

1 cup clarified butter

Clarified butter is an excellent fat for coating a crêpe pan or pancake griddle because it is able to tolerate moderate-to-high heat without burning. Melted clarified butter is also superb for brushing inside intricate baking molds, such as madeleine pans, before flouring them. The act of clarifying butter is simple and its taste is pure and clean. Use the best and freshest unsalted butter available for this process, preferably premium butter (refer to the chart on pages 46–47 for suggestions).

¾ pound (3 sticks) top-quality unsalted butter, cut into chunks

MELT THE BUTTER Place the butter in a heavy, medium-size saucepan (preferably enameled cast iron). Set over moderately low heat. When the butter has melted down, raise the heat slightly; after 2 minutes, remove the saucepan from the heat to a heatproof work surface.

SKIM THE MELTED BUTTER Using a teaspoon, spoon off the white surface foam, skimming the top so that you see the golden butter beneath. Make sure that the entire surface is clean. Use a damp paper towel, folded several times, to lightly graze the surface and pick up any clinging dabs.

SPOON OUT THE CLEAR BUTTER, COOL, AND STORE Tip the saucepan slightly. Spoon the clear, liquified butter into a clean, dry storage container, leaving behind the milky residue at the bottom of the pan. Cool the butter completely, cover, and refrigerate. Clarified butter keeps for about 1 month.

3

IT IS EQUIPMENT, in addition to the hands of the cook, that allows a powdery mound of flour, softened nuggets of butter, eggs that are good and fresh, a flowing amount of sugar, and luxurious chunks or silky spoonfuls of melted chocolate to be transformed into a homemade sweet assembled with all the care and attention it deserves.

By its very nature, the design of a recipe places ingredients in touch with a range of bakeware. In various stages, ingredients meet cups and spoons that parcel out specific amounts, are turned into a sifter for aeration or into a saucepan for melting, and receive a creaming and beating in an electric mixer or by hand in a sturdy bowl. Finally, the resulting dough or batter is turned into or onto a baking pan to establish its finished shape.

Classic baking equipment endures, and using an assortment of it will present you with sweets that are beautiful, shapely, and deliciously alluring. The measuring tools, implements, decorating supplies, and bakeware that follow have long been a part of my working kitchen. The equipment outlined below is catalogued by the phases a baking recipe can travel through.

Preparation materials

COOKING PARCHMENT PAPER

Parchment paper is excellent for lining cookie sheets and layer cake pans. Use food-safe parchment: Paper Maid Kitchen Parchment is a particularly good brand (20 sq. ft. roll), as is Reynolds Parchment Paper (30 sq. ft. roll). Two other reliable brands are Unbleached Parchment Paper by Beyond Gourmet, available in a 71 sq. ft. jumbo roll (the paper is free of chlorine), and Parchment Paper *Papier Sulfurisé,* a cellulose-fiber parchment that is also chlorine-free, available in a 71 sq. ft. roll.

WAXED PAPER

Waxed paper, available in 75 sq. ft. rolls, is good to have in the kitchen for lining round layer cake pans (do not use it for lining cookie sheets or sheet pans when baking cookies, scones, or yeast rolls and breads; choose parchment paper instead), and for portioning out and sifting ingredients.

NONSTICK BAKING SHEET LINER

A nonstick baking sheet liner, such as a Silpat, is useful for lining pans when baking soft, fragile cookies and tender scones. According to the description supplied on the label, it is made of "food grade silicone reinforced glass weave" and can be used in the oven up "to 480 degrees F." Baking sheet liners are best used in recipes that create soft buttery cookies, and when baking scones; cookie doughs should be firm and moldable, or of the creamy drop variety, and scone doughs solid and thick. Treat the baking sheet liner with consideration: store it flat, be careful when lifting off cookies with a spatula, and do not use cutting utensils of any kind on it. Never cut or trim the sheet.

CAKE CIRCLES

A layer cake can be assembled on cardboard cake circles, which are widely available at cake decorating supply stores and some cookware stores. Cake circles, also known as cake rounds, come in handy sizes in the following diameters: 6, 8, 10, 12, 14, and 16 inches. The circles are corrugated, with a shiny side (assemble the layers on this side) and a matte side.

Temperature gauges

OVEN THERMOMETER

A great batch of cookies, cake layers, or a pan loaded with scones all require the same two elements to attain that splendid star-quality: the proper balance of ingredients and the correct oven temperature for baking. To achieve the latter, you will need both a properly calibrated oven and a reliable oven thermometer. The Taylor Classic Oven Dial Thermometer (made of stainless steel), No. 5931, is a good model to own.

Measuring and weighing equipment

MEASURING SPOONS

Measuring spoons are lightweight and set into a ring that holds gradations of sizes, in ¼ teaspoon, ½ teaspoon, 1 teaspoon, and 1 tablespoon amounts. Bakers routinely dip into a can of baking powder, a box of baking soda or cornstarch, a container of cocoa powder, or dispenser of salt to measure a quantity of it. Baking staples, such as sugar or flour, are sometimes measured with spoons, too, as are milk, flavoring extracts, and flavoring pastes. A set of nonstick measuring spoons is especially handy to have for parceling out corn syrup, which is sticky, or peanut butter, which is dense and cohesive.

DRY MEASURING CUPS

Quantities of flour, sugar, rolled oats, and cocoa powder are routinely measured in cup gradations—⅛ cup, ¼ cup, ⅓ cup, ½ cup, 1 cup, and 2 cup amounts. The cups nest for easy storage. Dry measures are defined as such because they are used to measure ingredients like flour or sugar that can be spooned or packed in. The top of each cup is then leveled cleanly with a spatula or palette knife.

Flour is measured first by lightly aerating with a fork, then spooning it into the cup and sweeping off the excess with a firm, flat tool, such as a palette knife. Granulated sugar, superfine sugar, and cocoa powder are also measured by spooning the ingredient into the cup and leveling the top. Brown sugar is measured by packing the sugar into the cup and pressing down firmly to level the top.

LIQUID MEASURING CUPS

Liquid measuring cups may be made of clear glass or semi-transparent, heavyweight plastic. Either type should have neat, legible line indicators that mark ounces and cups. One, 2, and 4 cup measures are indispensable.

SCALE

The Edlund digital scale (Model E-80) is used routinely in my kitchen for weighing chocolate and basic baking staples. It measures ingredients consecutively with the tare function. Ingredients can be measured in ounces and grams, ranging from 0.1 ounce to 80 ounces or 1 gram to 2000 grams. The scale works by using either a 9-volt battery or the power adaptor furnished with the scale for plugging into an electrical outlet. Another model, the DS-10, also operates by a 9-volt battery or by the power supply; the weight readout in ounces or grams is revealed by holding down the ON/OFF switch, rather than pushing the switch (a feature of the E-80 scale).

Aerating device

SIFTER

The purpose of a sifter is to aerate flour and other dry ingredients, such as baking powder, baking soda, cream of tartar, salt, ground spices, and cocoa powder. Sifting dry ingredients lightens them considerably and removes any lumps before incorporating them into a dough or batter. Sometimes a mixture will be sifted twice for a batter-in-progress: once to aerate, then sifted again directly over a batter or dough. I keep a separate sifter for using with cocoa-based dry ingredients.

Melting equipment for chocolate

Of the equipment available, an enameled cast iron saucepan or a heavy (hotel weight) copper *fait-tout* or *sauteuse* gives the best overall results. I get excellent results using a stainless steel-lined or tin-lined copper *fait-tout* and a heavy (medium-size) or a small- to medium-size *sauteuse* when melting 6 ounces (or more) of chocolate. With the *sauteuse*, the surface area exposed to the heat is wider, and it melts chocolate efficiently. A *sauteuse* is a straight-sided skillet. A *fait-tout*, translated as "does everything," is a saucepan with a rounded base or an angular bottom, depending on the model that you select. It is wonderful for both melting chopped chocolate or chopped chocolate and butter together.

HEAVY ENAMELED CAST IRON SAUCEPAN

I own a nest of enameled cast iron saucepans (made by Le Creuset) and choose the size of the saucepan depending on the quantity of chopped chocolate that needs to be melted. The sizes I reach for the most are medium (7¼ inches in diameter) and medium-large (7¾ inches in diameter).

COPPER *FAIT-TOUT* AND *SAUTEUSE*

My tin-lined *fait-tout* (hotel weight), 8 inches in diameter, can melt a fair amount of chopped chocolate and butter handsomely—certainly enough for any of the brownie recipes or flourless chocolate cakes in this book.

A stainless steel-lined copper *fait-tout* (hotel weight), with its curved sides, allows you to wield a spoon or flat paddle easily around the sides. The two sizes that I own, measured across the top, are 6¾ inches and 8¼ inches.

The *sauteuse* I use most frequently for melting chocolate and butter together, or chocolate alone, measures 8 inches across the top. I also use a larger size for bulk chocolate melting and it measures nearly 9 inches across the top.

According to La Cuisine—The Cook's Resource, a preeminent source of top-quality French copper cookware, the weight of the copper can be divided into two categories, presentation weight and hotel weight. The weight is based on the overall thickness of the copper. Presentation weight, the lighter of the two, is between 1.2 and 1.5 mm, averaging about 1.3 mm. Hotel weight averages about 3 mm, with stockpots at 3.5 mm.

INSTANT READ TEMPERATURE PROBE

The Thermapen Digital Thermometer is an elegant tool to use when you need to get an instant temperature reading. The model I own is the Thermapen 5. It operates on a 12-volt battery. Its range is −50 degrees F. to 572 degrees F. You open and extend (literally, unfold) the needle-like probe from the base and insert it into what you need to read, such as a custard sauce. The thermometer quickly and clearly displays the temperature digitally on its flat side surface.

Mixing, beating, and whisking equipment

MIXING BOWLS

I keep a nested set of stainless-steel mixing bowls on my kitchen countertop. They are light but well-balanced, and invaluable for mixing batters and doughs by hand. The four bowls are graduated: small (8 inches in diameter, with a capacity of 6 to 7 cups); small-medium (9 inches in diameter, with a capacity of 10 cups); medium (10 inches in diameter, with a capacity of 16 cups); and large (11½ inches in diameter, with a capacity of 22 cups). For tossing chocolate chips in a flour mixture to prepare them for stirring into a batter or combining a small amount of melted butter and chocolate, use a small bowl; use a roomy medium-size bowl for larger quantities of melted butter and chocolate, so that the mixture can be mixed smoothly without sloshing it around in every direction.

Rolling and cutting

ROLLING OUT AND DIVIDING DOUGHS into specific shapes and cutting through baked cakes or bars are two culinary acts to manage at different points in the baking process. The following tools make each process seamless, before and after baking, and are valuable for cooks at every level of expertise to have in their working kitchen.

ROLLING PINS

A few chocolate doughs need a rolling pin to extend the size and overall shape of a yeast dough or to flatten and smooth out a scone dough. A rolling pin, made of wood or nylon, is the tool of choice to use for rolling out a dough in the quickest, most elegant way possible. My *French wooden rolling pin,* made of oak (and in use for years and years), measures 19½ inches in length and weighs just under 1 pound. This pin requires little care once you have initially washed it lightly, left it to dry thoroughly, then massaged a coating of plain vegetable oil over the entire surface. After each use, rinse and dry thoroughly. If it feels really dry, give it another light coat of oil, and always use a nylon pastry scraper (rather than a knife or any other cutting device) to loosen any small bits of caked-on dough. My *ball-bearing rolling pin,* made by Thorpe (produced in Hamden, Connecticut), is a heavy pin constructed from maple. Its weight (4 pounds) and size (the rolling surface is 18 inches) help to extend a mass of yeast dough or firm cookie to any thickness desired. My *nylon rolling pin* (20 inches in length) provides a sleek, nearly nonstick surface for rolling out cushy yeast doughs, pastry, and sticky cookie doughs.

CUTTING TOOLS

A small PARING KNIFE (about 7 inches long) is useful for light trimming and cutting, such as dividing baked bar cookies into squares or rectangles. You will also find it handy to use for splitting vanilla beans to expose the tiny seeds.

A 14-inch CHEF'S KNIFE is a necessity for chopping a quantity of nuts, chocolate candy bars, or hunks of block chocolate, and for cutting disks of scone or biscuit dough into wedges and lengths of rolled and filled yeast dough into individual pastries. My knife, made by Sabatier, has a carbon-steel blade.

A SERRATED KNIFE, made by Victorinox, with an 8-inch stainless-steel blade, is excellent for slicing through butter cakes, cake rolls, sweet yeast breads, coffee cakes, and pound cakes.

AN EXTRA-LONG SERRATED KNIFE, with a blade measuring a whopping 14 inches, is great for slicing through cake layers to split them. It is invaluable for cutting through large tube cakes to split them horizontally into layers for filling with pastry cream. My knife is an Ateco Ultra No. 1316. If you bake and fill cakes on a regular basis, this is the knife to own.

A CAKE KNIFE/SERVER, with a 7-inch triangular blade (high carbon/no stain), is a fine implement for cutting through tarts, tortes, and layer cakes. Mine is made by Friedrick Dick (No. 1105-16). It is made in Germany. This is a serious, in-the-kitchen knife, not to be confused with a fancy sterling silver cake server (pretty, dainty, and for show rather than function).

Another excellent tart/cake knife is made by Wüsthof (No. 4821) and has a 6¾-inch triangular blade. It cuts through baked tarts and tortes beautifully. I also use it whenever I slice into any of the cakes in the "Flourless and Almost-Flourless Chocolate Cakes" section (pages 405 through 416).

The Matfer "Racle Tout" (No. 82231) nylon PASTRY SCRAPER/DOUGH CUTTER is used almost on a daily basis in my baking kitchen. It can clear the surface of a cutting board with a few swipes; lift a mound of dough, chopped nuts, or chopped chocolate from the surface; and shear through an unbaked cake of scone, biscuit, or yeast dough with ease. I also reach for it when cleaning off a pastry board or other work surface. I use the nylon scraper more often than I do my straight-bladed metal scraper.

When fat meets flour for a dough or streusel mixture and needs to be reduced to large or small lumps, pearl-sized bits, or flecks, the best piece of equipment to use for the job is a PASTRY BLENDER. It breaks down the butter in a simple and effective way. Mine has a wooden handle into which 6 stainless-steel wires converge. It is swifter to use a pastry blender, but two round-bladed table knives can be used in its place.

Spreading and brushing

SPREADING AND BRUSHING are two important but often dashed-off procedures in baking. Extending a filling over an expanse of yeast dough, smoothing a filling into a tart shell, or covering a cake in a sultry coat of frosting relies on the use of an icing spatula or palette knife. Pastry brushes are essential for the application of glazes or thin, shimmery flavoring washes.

ICING SPATULAS AND FLEXIBLE PALETTE KNIVES

An *icing spatula,* also known as a frosting spatula, can serve a variety of functions. Its flexible blade is handy for smoothing over and leveling off a cake batter, for spreading frosting over a single cake layer, for spreading and smoothing frosting over the top and sides of a layer cake, or for spreading batter in a tart shell. The blade, usually made of stainless steel, is what I would describe as firmly flexible. These spatulas are all top-quality: the Ateco Ultra spatula (No. 1304) is 8½ inches long with a 4¼-inch stainless-steel blade, and the Ateco Ultra spatula (No. 1308) is 13 inches long, with an 8-inch stainless-steel blade and polypropylene handle.

A flexible palette knife can also double as an icing spatula to level a cake batter, frost cupcakes, or spread a filling in a tart shell. Mine is made by Dexter and measures 10¼ inches long, with a narrow, 6-inch stainless-steel blade. Several small flexible palette knives (with 4¼-inch-long blades that are ¾ inch wide) that I own come in handy for small baking maneuvers such as sweeping off the top of measuring cups or measuring spoons to level them and smoothing frosting against the bottom of a layer cake where it touches the cake plate.

A large *offset icing spatula,* with the blade angled about 1½ inches from the handle, is used for smoothing the top and sides of a cake once the frosting is applied. The two offset spatulas I find invaluable are Ateco Ultra No. 1307, with a 6-inch blade, and Ateco Ultra No. 1309, with a 7¾-inch blade.

The LamsonSharp high carbon-stainless-steel *spreader* is an effective tool to use for spreading a filling or soft topping. Half of one rounded edge is serrated and so handy for cutting through a pan of brownies or blondies. It looks like a slightly larger version of a sandwich spreader.

PASTRY BRUSHES

A *pastry brush* is necessary for applying washes and some finishing glazes to the tops of cakes and muffins; for brushing off and cleaning away excess flour clinging to rolled-out yeasted sweet doughs; for brushing a flavoring solution over rolled-out doughs; and for applying preserves to the top of a baked tart. The overall length of my pastry brush, made by Sparta (No. 432-1"), measures 8½ inches long, with 2-inch-wide bristles. It is made of boar bristle. All brushes used in pastry-making and desserts should be designated as food-safe, and should be reserved for use in baking or dessert-making. I keep a separate brush for dusting flour off yeast dough, a brush for using with melted butter or oil, and another for painting jam, jelly, or preserves over the surface of a tart.

Cooling and lifting

ONCE YOU'VE MADE THAT RADIANT batch of chocolate chip cookies, that cluster of scones, or those cake layers that you'll so lovingly enclose in frosting, the sweet needs to be transferred to a wire rack to cool so that its texture and form sets. The process of baking establishes the composition and overall architecture of a sweet, but the cooling stage sets it. A pair of tongs and an offset spatula are essential for transferring or lifting certain baked goods, such as biscotti, drop cookies, and bar cookies, with an easy, agile motion.

COOLING RACKS

Sturdy *wire cooling racks* are essential—and basic—to the baking process. Most chocolate-based baked goods are served at room temperature, so it is important that the contents of the pan be cool enough to cut, lift out, or otherwise detach. I own several 9 and 10-inch round racks and 13 by 22–inch rectangular cooling racks, with secure circular wires or tight square grids. A cooling rack should be judged by its stability, strength, and balance. It should sit on feet that raise the surface at least ½ inch above your counter-top. Nonstick racks are great to have for cooling butter-and-sugar-rich cookies and delicate layers of cake. Wilton makes fine nonstick cooling racks; I own several 10 by 16–inch racks (No. 2305-K-228).

TONGS

A pair of solid, strong *tongs* is ideal to use for turning batches of biscotti during their second baking and for lifting small yeast breads. My tongs are made by Edlund, and they lock into place when not in use.

OFFSET SPATULAS

An *offset spatula* is the implement of choice to use for lifting cookies from a sheet pan, pancakes from the griddle, or squares of sheet cake and bar cookies from the baking pan. The wide blade of an offset spatula slopes down flat from the handle. The following sizes (measured in overall length) are most frequently used in my kitchen: 7½, 9½, and 14½ inches. The smallest one is handy to use for detaching bar cookies and the largest for sliding off cookies cooling on parchment paper–lined pans.

Decorating equipment

DECORATING EQUIPMENT for chocolate-based desserts can be simple or elaborate, depending on the level of your interest and your passion for detail. I love to create decorations that are natural and somewhat understated, in order to allow the dessert to shine. Many chocolate tea breads and sweet rolls, cookies, and cakes need little more than their natural form to entice. But decorations of all kinds beguile me, and when I have the time, I like to make them. For that reason, my collection of decorative equipment includes pastry bags and an expansive assortment of tips.

PASTRY BAGS AND TIPS

An assortment of *pastry bags* and *pastry tips* available for filling with buttery frostings, satiny fillings, and creamy accompaniments lets you add a distinguished finish to many desserts. Piped frostings and whipped cream are fun to do and look fancy, and pretty swirls of frosting, rosettes of whipped cream, and buttercream flowers (complete with flowing, ribbony petals and ruffled edges for a layer cake) are rewarding to make and a delightful way to expand your creative horizons. Some of these flourishes, such as a rosette, are simple to master (the pastry tip does all the work), and can turn simple dollops of frosting into sweet, decorative art.

Begin by buying *Cake Decorating! The Wilton Yearbook,* which is published each year by Wilton Industries. It will introduce you to a whole galaxy of cake and cookie decorating, and provide information on the array of pastry bags and tips available. It also offers visual, technique-oriented instructions on how to make certain flowers (rose, apple blossom, and pansy, for example), a basket-weave design, a shell and rope motif, and other specialty designs.

Should you want to get ornate on any level, I find the following decorative tips and several sizes of pastry bags (8, 10, 12, 14, and 18 inches) are worth owning. You will also need several couplers to accommodate the various size tips and bags. A coupler is a two-piece accessory that allows you to exchange tips without dismantling the entire contents of the filled pastry bag. Covers for pastry tips are handy if you travel with filled and assembled pastry bags, or find yourself frequently interrupted while decorating; the plastic tip covers the decorative metal tip. Also useful: brushes for cleaning large and standard-sized tips (Wilton Maxi Tip Brush [No. 414-K-1010] and Wilton Tip Brush [No. 418-K-1123]).

The following names and numbers are standard in the Wilton tip organizational system. It's always fun to have a choice of tips in the same category; some are larger versions of each other, while others are variations on a particular theme, such as shells, stars, ruffles, or drop flowers:

ROUND TIPS for outlining edges and figures, for string-work, for creating lace, and for piping large and small dots: No. 3, No. 6, No. 8, No. 12, and No. 230 (an elongated tip, typically used for filling éclairs, but also useful for filling the centers of cupcakes and muffins).

CLOSED-STAR TIPS for piping stars, rosettes, and articulated shells: No. 26, No. 29, No. 30, and No. 35.

OPEN-STAR TIPS for piping drop flowers, rosettes, and stars: No. 15, No. 18, No. 21, No. 199, No. 364, No. 172, and No. 2110 (1M; for creating a really big swirl, perfect for covering the entire top of standard-sized cupcakes).

LEAF TIPS for piping leaves of various widths and types: No. 66, No. 69, No. 352, No. 74, No. 326, and No. 113.

DROP FLOWER TIPS for piping drop flowers: No. 107, No. 109, No. 129, No. 225, No. 191, No. 2C, and No. 2F.

PETAL TIPS for piping flower petals, some bows, and pleated gathers (ruffles): No. 59, No. 61, No. 97, No. 102, No. 104, No. 121, and No. 124.

RUFFLE TIPS for piping wavy borders and fluted ribbons: No. 86, No. 100, and No. 340.

BASKET-WEAVE TIPS for creating a woven design and wide bands (both plain or fluted): No. 46, No. 48, No. 2B, and No. 789 (known as the "Cake Icer" because its smooth, flat side can pipe out large bands of icing over the surface of the cake, ready to be leveled with an icing spatula).

ÉCLAIR/BISMARCK TIP for filling éclairs and bismarcks (also great for piping a creamy filling directly into the center of baked cupcakes or muffins, as it has a long "nose" to make inserting easy and as unobtrusive as possible): No. 230.

Ateco is another wonderful maker of pastry tips and bags. I especially like the ten-piece set of star pastry tips, for they are strong, seamless, and won't rust. The closed-star set, "10 Piece Closed Star Pastry Tube Set" (No. 850), includes tips with the following numbers: 840, 841, 842, 843, 844, 845, 846, to the whopping 847, 848, and 849). The open-star set (No. 830), called the "10 Piece Star Pastry Tube Set", includes tips numbered 820, 821, 822, 823, 824, 825, 826, 827, 828, and 829. The fine-star set, called "10 Fine Star Pastry Tubes" (No. 870), includes tips numbered 860, 861, 862, 863, 864, 865, 866, 867, 868, and 869.

PERHAPS NO OTHER SWEET ELEVATES THE FLAVOR OF CHOCOLATE to such unpretentious loftiness as the brownie. In this batter, the taste of chocolate is broadened to create the essence of fudgy. In all its luscious creaminess, a bite of brownie should convey the sensation of richness with a moistly memorable texture, making a fabulous chocolate statement. Just remember to treat the batter with consideration, as it is sensitive to prolonged or vigorous mixing and is easily overbaked.

Brownie Style

BITTERSWEET CHOCOLATE BROWNIES

*W*hen a brownie batter supports little chunks of premium bittersweet chocolate, a delectable thing happens—the small chunks of chocolate form pools of goodness throughout, and the sweet resonates with flavor. Even though I can't, you should try to restrain yourself from cutting the brownies too soon.

BITTERSWEET BROWNIE BATTER

1 cup bleached all-purpose flour

⅓ cup bleached cake flour

¼ cup plus 1 tablespoon unsweetened alkalized cocoa powder

¼ teaspoon baking powder

⅛ teaspoon salt

3 ounces bittersweet chocolate, chopped into small chunks

½ pound (16 tablespoons or 2 sticks) unsalted butter, melted and cooled to tepid

5 ounces unsweetened chocolate, melted and cooled to tepid

3 ounces bittersweet chocolate, melted and cooled to tepid

5 large eggs

2 cups superfine sugar

2 teaspoons vanilla extract

Confectioners' sugar, for sifting on top of the baked brownies (optional)

PREHEAT THE OVEN TO 325 DEGREES F. Film the inside of a 9 by 9 by 2-inch baking pan with nonstick cooking spray.

MIX THE BATTER Sift the all-purpose flour, cake flour, cocoa powder, baking powder, and salt onto a sheet of waxed paper. In a small bowl, toss the chocolate chunks with 1 teaspoon of the sifted mixture.

In a medium-size mixing bowl, whisk the melted butter, melted unsweetened chocolate, and melted bittersweet chocolate until smooth. In a large mixing bowl, whisk the eggs until blended, about 15 seconds. Add the sugar and whisk until combined, 30 to 45 seconds. Blend in the vanilla extract and melted butter-chocolate mixture. Sift the flour mixture over and stir to form a batter, mixing thoroughly until the particles of flour are absorbed, using a whisk or flat wooden paddle. Stir in the chocolate chunks.

Scrape the batter into the prepared pan and spread evenly. Smooth the top with a rubber spatula.

BAKE, COOL, AND CUT THE BROWNIES Bake the brownies in the preheated oven for 30 to 33 minutes, or until gently set. Let the brownies stand in the pan on a cooling rack for 3 hours. With a small sharp knife, cut the sweet into quarters, then cut each quarter into 4 squares. Remove the brownies from the baking pan, using a small offset metal spatula. Store in an airtight tin.

Sift confectioners' sugar on top of the brownies just before serving, if you wish.

Bake-and-serve within 3 days

STUDY The chopped bittersweet chocolate forms creamy pools of flavor in the baked brownies. The following bittersweet chocolates are worth noting for using in the recipe (both for the chunks and melted chocolate): Valrhona Extra Amer Bittersweet 61% cacao; Valrhona Le Noir Amer 71% cacao; Valrhona Le Noir Gastronomie 61% cacao; Valrhona Caraïbe Dark Chocolate 66% cocoa; Valrhona Grand Cru Noir Manjari Gastronomie Chocolat Noir Dark Chocolate 64% cocoa; Valrhona Equatoriale Chocolat de Couverture Noir Dark Bittersweet Couverture 55% cacao; Michel Cluizel Chocolat Amer Dark Chocolate 60% cacao; Michel Cluizel Ilha Toma 65% cocoa; Lindt Chocolate Créé à Berne Swiss Bittersweet Chocolate; or, Lindt Excellence Swiss Bittersweet Chocolate.

DOUBLE-DECKER FUDGE BROWNIES

16 brownies

*E*xquisite and loaded with chocolate, these are the brownies that I swoon over, for they never fail to please: the batter is plied with cocoa powder, miniature chocolate chips, melted unsweetened chocolate, and melted bittersweet chocolate. Within moments of pulling the moist block of brownies from the oven, it is covered with a thick swath of chocolate fudge that bonds irresistibly with the dark chocolate firmament below.

DARK CHOCOLATE BATTER

¾ cup bleached cake flour

½ cup bleached all-purpose flour

3 tablespoons unsweetened alkalized cocoa powder

¼ teaspoon baking powder

⅛ teaspoon salt

¾ cup miniature semisweet chocolate chips

½ pound (16 tablespoons or 2 sticks) unsalted butter, melted and cooled to tepid

4 ounces unsweetened chocolate, melted and cooled to tepid

1 ounce bittersweet chocolate, melted and cooled to tepid

4 large eggs

2 cups granulated sugar

2 teaspoons vanilla extract

TOPPING

Chocolate Fudge Topcoat (page 79)

PREHEAT THE OVEN TO 325 DEGREES F. Film the inside of a 9 by 9 by 2-inch baking pan with nonstick cooking spray.

MIX THE BATTER Sift the cake flour, all-purpose flour, cocoa powder, baking powder, and salt onto a sheet of waxed paper. In a small bowl, toss the chocolate chips with ¾ teaspoon of the sifted mixture.

In a medium-size mixing bowl, whisk the melted butter, melted unsweetened chocolate, and melted bittersweet chocolate until smooth. In a large mixing bowl, whisk the eggs until blended, about 15 seconds. Add the sugar and whisk until combined, about 30 to 45 seconds. Blend in the vanilla extract and melted butter-chocolate mixture. Sift the flour mixture over and stir to form a batter, mixing thoroughly until the particles of flour are absorbed, using a whisk or flat wooden paddle. Stir in the chocolate chips.

Scrape the batter into the prepared pan and spread evenly. Smooth the top with a rubber spatula.

BAKE THE BROWNIES Bake the brownies in the preheated oven for 35 to 40 minutes, or until set.

APPLY THE TOPPING Let the baked brownies stand in the pan on a cooling rack for 3 minutes. Carefully place dollops of the frosting on top of the hot brownie layer. Smooth and spread the frosting with a small offset palette knife or rubber spatula, taking care not to cut into the top of the brownie cake.

COOL AND CUT THE BROWNIES Let the brownies stand in the pan on a cooling rack for 5 hours, or until completely cool. The topping should be set and softly firm. With a small sharp knife, cut the sweet into quarters, then cut each quarter into 4 squares. Remove the brownies from the baking pan, using a small offset metal spatula. Store in single layers in airtight tins.

Bake-and-serve within 3 days

ACCENT Add ¼ teaspoon chocolate extract to the brownie batter along with the vanilla extract.

STUDY Applying the fudgy topcoat to the block of brownies while hot ensures that it will meld to it. The topcoat will begin to melt slightly as it is spread onto the brownie base, but will firm up as it cools.

CHOCOLATE FUDGE TOPCOAT

About 2⅔ cups frosting

This is a first-rate frosting for brownies—chocolatey and softly dense. The topcoat melts down initially as you spread it on a hot brownie slab (or on top of a single-layer sheet cake), but firms up as the sweet cools down. The topcoat is one of my favorite ways to finish a baked bar—simply the creamiest and richest counterpoint to what it conceals.

3¾ cups plus 2 tablespoons confectioners' sugar, sifted
Large pinch of salt
8 tablespoons (1 stick) unsalted butter, melted and cooled to tepid
2 ounces unsweetened chocolate, melted and cooled to tepid
2 teaspoons vanilla extract
6 tablespoons milk, at room temperature

MIX THE CONFECTIONERS' SUGAR and salt in a large mixing bowl. In a small bowl, whisk the butter and melted chocolate until smooth. Blend in the vanilla extract. Pour the chocolate mixture over the confectioners' sugar, add the milk, and beat for 2 minutes on low speed, using an electric hand mixer, or until combined and smooth. Scrape down the sides of the mixing bowl once or twice to maintain an even texture.

Use the topcoat immediately, or press a sheet of food-safe plastic wrap directly onto the surface of chocolate frosting and use within 30 minutes.

STUDY Combine the mixture only until it is smooth and creamy. Overbeating the topcoat once the confectioners' sugar is added will increase volume and spoil its texture as it sets. Using low speed will produce a smooth, almost velvety fudge topping that's not at all fluffy, which is exactly the texture you want to top the brownies (or any kind of sheet cake). The topcoat should be relatively dense, but refined.

ELEMENT Use the topcoat for covering a pan of freshly baked blondies. The same principle applies for covering blondies as it does for brownies, and that is to frost them 3 minutes after removing the pan from the oven.

SUPREMELY FUDGY BROWNIES

*T*he flavor of chocolate comes through solidly in this pan of brownies. If you like your brownies dense, buttery, and creamy, preheat the oven now.

FUDGE BROWNIE BATTER

1 cup bleached all-purpose flour

¼ cup bleached cake flour

2 tablespoons unsweetened alkalized cocoa powder

¼ teaspoon baking powder

⅛ teaspoon salt

½ pound (16 tablespoons or 2 sticks) unsalted butter, melted and cooled to tepid

4 ounces unsweetened chocolate, melted and cooled to tepid

4 large eggs

2 cups granulated sugar

1½ teaspoons vanilla extract

Confectioners' sugar, for sifting on top of the baked brownies (optional)

PREHEAT THE OVEN TO 325 DEGREES F. Film the inside of a 9 by 9 by 2-inch baking pan with nonstick cooking spray.

MIX THE BATTER Sift the all-purpose flour, cake flour, cocoa powder, baking powder, and salt onto a sheet of waxed paper.

In a medium-size mixing bowl, whisk the melted butter and melted chocolate until smooth. In a large mixing bowl, whisk the eggs until blended, about 30 seconds. Add the sugar and whisk until combined, about 30 seconds. Blend in the vanilla extract and melted butter-chocolate mixture. Sift the flour mixture over and stir to form a batter, mixing thoroughly until the particles of flour are absorbed, using a whisk or flat wooden paddle.

Scrape the batter into the prepared pan and spread evenly. Smooth the top with a rubber spatula.

BAKE, COOL, AND CUT THE BROWNIES Bake the brownies in the preheated oven for 34 to 38 minutes, or until set. Let the brownies stand in the pan on a cooling rack for 3 hours. Refrigerate for 1 hour. With a small sharp knife, cut the sweet into quarters, then cut each quarter into 4 squares. Remove the brownies from the baking pan, using a small offset metal spatula. Store in an airtight tin.

Sift confectioners' sugar on top of the brownies just before serving, if you wish.

Bake-and-serve within 3 days

STUDY The combination of all-purpose and cake flour creates a tender but substantial brownie.

PEANUT AND COCONUT CANDY FUDGE BROWNIES

16 brownies

*C*runchy chunks of candy, made of peanut butter and toasted coconut, are a bold seasoning agent for a brownie. The peanut candy–sparked batter is heightened and rounded out by a little peanut butter. Lightly salted whole peanuts (a generous ¾ cup) or three more candy bars, cut into rough chunks, can be scattered on the top of the unbaked pan of brownies—either would make an indulgent overlay.

PEANUT AND COCONUT BROWNIE BATTER

1 cup bleached all-purpose flour

¼ cup bleached cake flour

3 tablespoons unsweetened alkalized cocoa powder

¼ teaspoon baking powder

⅛ teaspoon salt

½ pound (16 tablespoons or 2 sticks) unsalted butter, melted and cooled to tepid

4 ounces unsweetened chocolate, melted and cooled to tepid

2 tablespoons smooth (creamy) peanut butter

4 large eggs

2 cups superfine sugar

2 teaspoons vanilla extract

4 (1.75 ounces each) crunchy peanut butter and toasted coconut candy bars (such as Zagnut), cut into ½-inch chunks

Confectioners' sugar, for sifting on top of the baked brownies (optional)

PREHEAT THE OVEN TO 325 DEGREES F. Film the inside of a 9 by 9 by 2-inch baking pan with nonstick cooking spray.

MIX THE BATTER Sift the all-purpose flour, cake flour, cocoa powder, baking powder, and salt onto a sheet of waxed paper.

In a medium-size mixing bowl, whisk the melted butter and melted chocolate until thoroughly combined; whisk in the peanut butter to blend well. In a large mixing bowl, whisk the eggs until blended, about 15 seconds. Add the sugar and whisk until combined, about 30 seconds; do not whisk vigorously or the batter will become overly lightened. Blend in the vanilla extract and melted butter-chocolate mixture. Sift the flour mixture over and stir to form a batter, mixing thoroughly but lightly, using a whisk or flat wooden paddle, until the particles of flour are absorbed. Stir in the candy bar chunks.

Scrape the batter into the prepared pan and spread evenly. Smooth the top with a rubber spatula.

BAKE, COOL, AND CUT THE BROWNIES Bake the brownies in the preheated oven for 33 to 38 minutes, or until set. Let the brownies stand in the pan on a cooling rack for 3 hours. Refrigerate for 45 minutes. With a small sharp knife, cut the sweet into quarters, then cut each quarter into 4 squares. Remove the brownies from the baking pan, using a small offset metal spatula. Store in an airtight tin.

Sift confectioners' sugar on top of the brownies just before serving, if you wish.

Bake-and-serve within 3 days

ACCENT To increase the intensity of the chocolate, add ½ cup semisweet chocolate chips to the batter along with the candy bar chunks. These are rich.

Add ¼ teaspoon chocolate extract to the batter along with the vanilla extract.

LAYERED CHOCOLATE COOKIE BROWNIES

*T*hese brownies are just *packed* with chocolate: a bottom chocolate cookie layer is gilded with chocolate chips, and a darkly moist, cocoa and unsweetened chocolate–charged brownie batter seals it all together.

CHOCOLATE COOKIE LAYER

8 tablespoons (1 stick) unsalted butter, melted, cooled to tepid, and combined with ¼ teaspoon vanilla extract

1½ cups plus 3 tablespoons chocolate wafer cookie crumbs (such as crumbs made from Nabisco Famous Chocolate Wafers)

CHOCOLATE CHIP LAYER

¼ cup miniature semisweet chocolate chips

BROWNIE BATTER

1 cup bleached all-purpose flour

¼ cup bleached cake flour

¼ cup unsweetened alkalized cocoa powder

¼ teaspoon baking powder

⅛ teaspoon salt

½ pound (16 tablespoons or 2 sticks) unsalted butter, melted and cooled to tepid

6 ounces unsweetened chocolate, melted and cooled to tepid

5 large eggs

2 cups superfine sugar

2 teaspoons vanilla extract

TOPPING

½ cup miniature semisweet chocolate chips

Confectioners' sugar, for sifting on top of the baked brownies (optional)

PREHEAT THE OVEN TO 325 DEGREES F. Film the bottom of a 10 by 10 by 2-inch baking pan with nonstick cooking spray.

MIX, BAKE, AND COOL THE COOKIE LAYER Pour the melted butter-vanilla mixture into the prepared pan. Spoon the cookie crumbs evenly over the bottom of the pan and press down lightly with the underside of a small offset metal spatula so that the crumbs absorb the butter. Bake the cookie layer in the preheated oven for 4 minutes. Transfer the baking pan to a cooling rack. Immediately sprinkle the chocolate chips evenly over the cookie layer. Cool for 10 minutes.

MIX THE BATTER Sift the all-purpose flour, cake flour, cocoa powder, baking powder, and salt onto a sheet of waxed paper.

In a medium-size mixing bowl, whisk the melted butter and melted chocolate until smooth. In a large mixing bowl, whisk the eggs until blended, about 15 seconds. Add the sugar and whisk until combined, about 30 seconds. Blend in the vanilla extract and melted butter-chocolate mixture. Sift the flour mixture over and stir to form a batter, mixing thoroughly until the particles of flour are absorbed, using a whisk or flat wooden paddle.

Spoon the batter in large dollops on the cookie crumb layer. Carefully spread the batter over the cookie layer, using a flexible palette knife or spatula.

BAKE, COOL, AND CUT THE BROWNIES Bake the brownies in the preheated oven for 30 minutes. Quickly sprinkle the chocolate chips on top and continue baking for 3 to 5 minutes longer, or until set. Let the brownies stand in the pan on a cooling rack for 3 hours. Refrigerate for 30 minutes. With a small sharp knife, cut the sweet into quarters, then cut each quarter into 4 squares. Remove the brownies from the baking pan, using a small offset metal spatula. Store in an airtight tin.

Sift confectioners' sugar on top of the brownies just before serving, if you wish.

Bake-and-serve within 4 days

ACCENT Add ¼ teaspoon chocolate extract to the brownie batter along with the vanilla extract.

COCONUT AND WHITE CHOCOLATE DREAM BROWNIES

16 brownies

A generous handful of flaked coconut and white chocolate chips adds a moist chewiness and a topnote of flavor to these sweet brownie squares. The batter is straightforward, but provocative—simple, creamy, and divine.

COCONUT AND WHITE CHOCOLATE BATTER

¾ cup bleached all-purpose flour

¼ cup bleached cake flour

2 tablespoons unsweetened alkalized cocoa powder

⅛ teaspoon baking powder

⅛ teaspoon salt

½ pound (16 tablespoons or 2 sticks) unsalted butter, melted and cooled to tepid

4 ounces unsweetened chocolate, melted and cooled to tepid

4 large eggs

1¾ cups plus 1 tablespoon granulated sugar

1½ teaspoons vanilla extract

4 bars (1.9 ounces each) chocolate-covered coconut candy (such as Peter Paul Mounds), cut into ½-inch chunks

¾ cup sweetened flaked coconut

¾ cup white chocolate chips (or chunks)

PREHEAT THE OVEN TO 325 DEGREES F. Film the inside of a 9 by 9 by 2-inch baking pan with nonstick cooking spray.

MIX THE BATTER Sift the all-purpose flour, cake flour, cocoa powder, baking powder, and salt onto a sheet of waxed paper.

In a medium-size mixing bowl, whisk the melted butter and melted chocolate until well blended. In a large mixing bowl, whisk the eggs until blended, about 15 seconds. Add the sugar and whisk until combined, about 30 seconds. Blend in the vanilla extract and melted butter-chocolate mixture. Sift the flour mixture over and stir to form a batter, mixing thoroughly until the particles of flour are absorbed, using a whisk or flat wooden paddle. Stir in the chunks of candy, flaked coconut, and white chocolate chips (or chunks).

Scrape the batter into the prepared pan and spread evenly. Smooth the top with a rubber spatula.

BAKE, COOL, AND CUT THE BROWNIES Bake the brownies in the preheated oven for 35 to 40 minutes, or until set. Let the brownies stand in the pan on a cooling rack for 3 hours. Refrigerate for 45 minutes. With a small sharp knife, cut the sweet into quarters, then cut each quarter into 4 squares. Remove the brownies from the baking pan, using a small offset metal spatula. Store in an airtight tin.

Bake-and-serve within 3 days

CRUMB-CRUSTED COCOA-COCONUT BROWNIES

16 brownies

Coconut in the cookie layer on the bottom of these brownies and in the batter itself is a significant ingredient for all bakers who love it as much as I do.

COCONUT-CHOCOLATE COOKIE LAYER

8 tablespoons (1 stick) unsalted butter, melted, cooled to tepid, and combined with ¼ teaspoon vanilla extract

1⅔ cups chocolate sandwich cookie crumbs (such as crumbs made from Nabisco Oreo chocolate sandwich cookies) combined with 3 tablespoons sweetened flaked coconut

COCOA-COCONUT BATTER

1¼ cups bleached all-purpose flour

¼ cup unsweetened alkalized cocoa powder

¼ teaspoon baking powder

¼ teaspoon salt

½ pound (16 tablespoons or 2 sticks) unsalted butter, melted and cooled to tepid

6 ounces unsweetened chocolate, melted and cooled to tepid

5 large eggs

1¾ cups plus 2 tablespoons superfine sugar

2 teaspoons vanilla extract

½ cup sweetened flaked coconut

PREHEAT THE OVEN TO 325 DEGREES F. Film the inside of a 10 by 10 by 2-inch baking pan with nonstick cooking spray.

MAKE THE COOKIE LAYER Pour the melted butter-vanilla mixture into the prepared pan. Spoon the cookie crumb mixture evenly over the bottom and press down lightly with the underside of a small offset metal spatula so that the crumbs absorb the butter. Bake the cookie layer in the preheated oven for 3 minutes. Place the baking pan on a rack. Cool for 10 minutes.

MAKE THE BATTER Sift the flour, cocoa powder, baking powder, and salt onto a sheet of waxed paper.

In a medium-size mixing bowl, whisk the melted butter and melted chocolate until smooth. In a large mixing bowl, whisk the eggs for 30 seconds to blend, add the sugar, and whisk for 45 seconds, or until incorporated. Blend in the melted butter-chocolate mixture. Blend in the vanilla extract. Sift the flour mixture over and stir to form a batter, mixing thoroughly until the particles of flour are absorbed, using a whisk or flat wooden paddle. Stir in the coconut.

Spoon the batter in large dollops onto the cookie crumb layer. Carefully spread the batter over the cookie layer, using a flexible palette knife or spatula. If you are too enthusiastic, it may lift patches of the bottom layer. Use smooth, short strokes.

BAKE, COOL, AND CUT THE BROWNIES Bake the brownies in the preheated oven for 35 to 40 minutes, or until set. Cool the brownies completely in the pan on a rack. Refrigerate for 1 hour, or until solid enough to cut. With a small sharp knife, cut the sweet into quarters, then cut each quarter into 4 squares. Store in an airtight tin.

Bake-and-serve within 4 days

ACCENT Reduce the vanilla extract to 1½ teaspoons. Add ½ teaspoon chocolate extract to the batter along with the vanilla extract.

CHOCOLATE NOUGAT SQUARES

*C*ocoa powder and unsweetened chocolate, along with chunks of chocolate-covered caramel and nougat candy, form an alliance of flavor in these tender, rich squares.

CHOCOLATE NOUGAT CANDY BAR BATTER

4 (1.76 ounces each) chocolate-covered caramel and nougat bars (such as Milky Way Midnight bars), cut into ½-inch chunks

1¼ cups unsifted bleached cake flour

¼ cup unsweetened alkalized cocoa powder

¼ teaspoon baking powder

⅛ teaspoon salt

½ pound (16 tablespoons or 2 sticks) unsalted butter, melted and cooled to tepid

4 ounces unsweetened chocolate, melted and cooled to tepid

4 large eggs

2 cups granulated sugar

2½ teaspoons vanilla extract

PREHEAT THE OVEN TO 325 DEGREES F. Film the inside of a 9 by 9 by 2-inch baking pan with nonstick cooking spray.

CHILL THE CANDY Refrigerate the chunks of chocolate candy for 20 minutes. Refrigerating the candy helps to keep its shape intact as it's incorporated into the batter.

MIX THE BATTER Sift the flour, cocoa powder, baking powder, and salt onto a sheet of waxed paper.

In a medium-size mixing bowl, whisk the melted butter and melted chocolate until smooth. In a large mixing bowl, whisk the eggs until blended, about 15 seconds. Add the sugar and whisk until combined, about 30 seconds. Blend in the vanilla extract and melted butter-chocolate mixture. Sift the flour mixture over and stir to form a batter, mixing thoroughly until the particles of flour are absorbed, using a whisk or flat wooden paddle. Carefully stir in the chunks of candy.

Scrape the batter into the prepared pan and spread evenly. Smooth the top with a rubber spatula.

BAKE, COOL, AND CUT THE SWEET Bake the brownies in the preheated oven for 35 to 40 minutes, or until set. Let the brownies stand in the pan on a cooling rack for 2 hours. Refrigerate for 1 hour. With a small sharp knife, cut sweet into quarters, then cut each quarter into 4 squares. Remove the squares from the baking pan, using a small offset metal spatula. Store in an airtight tin.

Bake-and-serve within 3 days

ACCENT Use 3 tablespoons unsweetened alkalized cocoa powder and 1 tablespoon Dutch-Process Black Cocoa powder in place of the ¼ cup unsweetened alkalized cocoa powder. Add ¼ teaspoon chocolate extract to the batter along with the vanilla extract.

DOUBLE-DARK FUDGE BROWNIES

16 brownies

*C*ocoa powder, bittersweet chocolate, and unsweetened chocolate consort in this batter to build a bold and intrepid brownie batter.

FUDGE BROWNIE BATTER

¾ cup bleached all-purpose flour

½ cup bleached cake flour

3 tablespoons unsweetened alkalized cocoa powder

¼ teaspoon baking powder

⅛ teaspoon salt

6 ounces bittersweet chocolate, cut into small chunks

½ pound (16 tablespoons or 2 sticks) unsalted butter, melted and cooled to tepid

6 ounces unsweetened chocolate, melted and cooled to tepid

4 large eggs

2¼ cups superfine sugar

2½ teaspoons vanilla extract

Confectioners' sugar, for sifting on top of the baked brownies (optional)

PREHEAT THE OVEN TO 325 DEGREES F. Film the inside of a 10 by 10 by 2-inch baking pan with nonstick cooking spray.

MIX THE BATTER Sift the all-purpose flour, cake flour, cocoa powder, baking powder, and salt onto a sheet of waxed paper. In a small bowl, toss the chocolate chunks with 1¼ teaspoons of the sifted mixture.

In a medium-size mixing bowl, whisk the melted butter and melted unsweetened chocolate until smooth.

In a large mixing bowl, whisk the eggs until blended, about 15 seconds. Add the sugar and whisk until combined, about 45 seconds. Blend in the vanilla extract and melted butter-chocolate mixture. Sift the flour mixture over and stir to form a batter, mixing thoroughly until the particles of flour are absorbed, using a whisk or flat wooden paddle. Stir in the chocolate chunks.

Scrape the batter into the prepared pan and spread evenly. Smooth the top with a rubber spatula.

BAKE, COOL, AND CUT THE BROWNIES Bake the brownies in the preheated oven for 35 to 40 minutes, or until set. Let the brownies stand in the pan on a cooling rack for 3 hours. Refrigerate for 1 to 2 hours, or until firm enough to cut. With a small sharp knife, cut the entire sweet into quarters, then cut each quarter into 4 squares. Remove the brownies from the baking pan, using a small offset metal spatula. Store in an airtight tin.

Sift confectioners' sugar on top of the brownies just before serving, if you wish.

Bake-and-serve within 3 days

ACCENT Reduce the vanilla extract to 1½ teaspoons. Add 1 teaspoon chocolate extract to the batter along with the vanilla extract.

STUDY As far as brownie batters go, this is a simple and elegant one, replete with chocolate in three primary—but critical—forms. The choice of bittersweet chocolate is important because the chunks merge in a batter dominated by unsweetened chocolate, so choose a substantial, forthright type, such as Scharffen Berger Bittersweet 70% cocoa; Valrhona Le Noir Amer 71% cacao; Valrhona Carré Guanaja Grand Cru de Chocolat Noir Amer 70% cocoa; Weiss Ebene Bittersweet Chocolate 72% cocoa; or, Weiss Acarigua Bittersweet Chocolate 70% cocoa.

DARK AND DUSKY BROWNIES

16 brownies

When unsweetened chocolate, bittersweet chocolate, cocoa powder, and semisweet chocolate chips converge in a brownie batter, something wonderful takes place: a complex experience of chocolate.

DARK CHOCOLATE BATTER

1 cup bleached all-purpose flour

5 tablespoons bleached cake flour

½ cup unsweetened alkalized cocoa powder

¼ teaspoon baking powder

⅛ teaspoon salt

1 cup miniature semisweet chocolate chips

½ pound (16 tablespoons or 2 sticks) unsalted butter, melted and cooled to tepid

4 ounces unsweetened chocolate, melted and cooled to tepid

2 ounces bittersweet chocolate, melted and cooled to tepid

4 large eggs

2 large egg yolks

2 cups superfine sugar

2½ teaspoons vanilla extract

Confectioners' sugar, for sifting on top of the baked brownies (optional)

PREHEAT THE OVEN TO 325 DEGREES F. Film the inside of a 10 by 10 by 2-inch baking pan with nonstick cooking spray.

MIX THE BATTER Sift the all-purpose flour, cake flour, cocoa powder, baking powder, and salt onto a sheet of waxed paper. In a small bowl, toss the chocolate chips with 1 teaspoon of the sifted mixture.

In a medium-size mixing bowl, whisk the melted butter, melted unsweetened chocolate, and melted bittersweet chocolate until smooth. In a large mixing bowl, whisk the eggs and egg yolks slowly until blended, about 15 seconds. Add the sugar and whisk until combined, about 30 seconds. Blend in the vanilla extract and melted butter-chocolate mixture. Sift the flour mixture over and stir to form a batter, mixing thoroughly until the particles of flour are absorbed, using a whisk or flat wooden paddle. Stir in the chocolate chips.

Scrape the batter into the prepared pan and spread evenly. Smooth the top with a rubber spatula.

BAKE, COOL, AND CUT THE BROWNIES Bake the brownies in the preheated oven for 30 minutes, or until set. Let the brownies stand in the pan on a cooling rack for 2 hours. Refrigerate for 1 hour. With a small sharp knife, cut the sweet into quarters, then cut each quarter into 4 squares. Remove the brownies from the baking pan, using a small offset metal spatula. Store in an airtight tin.

Sift confectioners' sugar on top of the brownies just before serving, if you wish.

Bake-and-serve within 3 days

STYLE For Dark and Dusky Brownies with Nuts, add 1 cup coarsely chopped walnuts, pecans, or macadamia nuts to the batter along with the chocolate chips.

ACCENT Add ½ teaspoon chocolate extract to the batter along with the vanilla extract.

STUDY Using 2 egg yolks in place of a whole egg in the batter makes the brownies extra-creamy.

CHOCOLATE, PURE AND STRAIGHT, BROWNIES

16 brownies

*C*hunks of bittersweet chocolate radiate flavor by clinging to the batter in dark, drifty spots. The taste is indulgent, the baking facile.

BITTERSWEET CHOCOLATE BATTER

1 cup bleached all-purpose flour

¼ cup plus 1 tablespoon bleached cake flour

¼ cup plus 1 tablespoon unsweetened alkalized cocoa powder

¼ teaspoon baking powder

¼ teaspoon salt

½ pound (16 tablespoons or 2 sticks) unsalted butter, melted and cooled to tepid

5 ounces unsweetened chocolate, melted and cooled to tepid

3 ounces bittersweet chocolate, melted and cooled to tepid

5 large eggs

2 cups superfine sugar

2 teaspoons vanilla extract

6 ounces bittersweet chocolate, cut into small chunks, tossed with 1 teaspoon unsweetened alkalized cocoa powder and 2 teaspoons unsalted butter, melted and cooled

Confectioners' sugar, for sifting on top of the baked brownies (optional)

PREHEAT THE OVEN TO 325 DEGREES F. Film the inside of a 10 by 10 by 2-inch baking pan with nonstick cooking spray.

MIX THE BATTER Sift the all-purpose flour, cake flour, cocoa powder, baking powder, and salt onto a sheet of waxed paper.

In a medium-size mixing bowl, whisk the melted butter, melted unsweetened chocolate, and melted bittersweet chocolate until smooth. In a large mixing bowl, whisk the eggs until blended, about 15 seconds. Add the sugar and whisk until combined, about 30 to 45 seconds. Blend in the vanilla extract and melted butter–chocolate mixture. Sift the flour mixture over and stir to form a batter, mixing thoroughly until the particles of flour are absorbed, using a whisk or flat wooden paddle. The batter will be creamy and thick. Stir in the bittersweet chocolate chunks.

Scrape the batter into the prepared pan and spread evenly. Smooth the top with a rubber spatula.

BAKE, COOL, AND CUT THE BROWNIES Bake the brownies in the preheated oven for 30 to 35 minutes, or until gently set. Let the brownies stand in the pan on a cooling rack for 3 hours. Refrigerate the brownies for 1 hour, or until firm enough to cut. With a small, sharp knife, cut the sweet into quarters, then cut each quarter into 4 squares. Remove the brownies from the baking pan, using a small offset metal spatula. Store in an airtight tin.

Sift confectioners' sugar on top of the brownies just before serving, if you like.

Bake-and-serve within 3 days

STUDY Tossing the chunks of bittersweet chocolate with cocoa and melted butter creates pockets of sensational richness inside a brownie batter.

For both the melted and cut-into-chunks bittersweet chocolate, select a deeply potent and heady chocolate such as Scharffen Berger Bittersweet 70% cocoa; Valrhona Extra Amer Bittersweet 61% cacao; Valrhona Le Noir Amer 71% cacao; El Ray Bucare Bittersweet Chocolate (*Carnero Superior*) 58.5% cocoa; Lindt Chocolate Créé à Berne Swiss Bittersweet Chocolate; Michel Cluizel Ilha Toma 65% cocoa; or, Lindt Excellence 70% Cocoa Extra Fine Dark Chocolate.

GO BACK IN TIME WITH ME and remember how luscious a chocolate cake or a cooling rack full of grand cupcakes made from simple ingredients can be. The texture of my cakes–in layers, one great sheet, or plump individual affairs–is moist, tender, and beguiling in all its chocolate essence; all of them are a joy to bake, great fun to frost, and a pleasure to serve. And please don't forget the classic pairing of cake and ice cream–with a fresh sweet on a pretty cake stand or plate, now is the time to scoop up your best vanilla ice cream.

CLASSIC SOUR CREAM CHOCOLATE CHIP CAKE

One 10-inch cake, creating 16 to 20 slices

A cake classic in my kitchen, the thick and creamy batter frames lots of miniature chips so that every slice is loaded with bits of chocolate.

SOUR CREAM CHOCOLATE CHIP BUTTER CAKE BATTER

3 cups bleached all-purpose flour

½ teaspoon baking soda

¾ teaspoon salt

2 cups miniature semisweet chocolate chips

½ pound (16 tablespoons or 2 sticks) unsalted butter, softened

3 cups superfine sugar, preferably Essence-of-Vanilla Superfine Sugar (page 56)

6 large eggs

2¼ teaspoons vanilla extract

1 cup sour cream

Confectioners' sugar, for sifting on top of the baked cake

PREHEAT THE OVEN TO 325 DEGREES F. Grease the inside of a plain 10-inch tube pan with shortening, line the bottom of the pan with a circle of waxed paper cut to fit, grease the paper, and dust with flour.

MIX THE BATTER Sift the flour, baking soda, and salt onto a sheet of waxed paper. In a small bowl, toss the chocolate chips with 1 tablespoon of the sifted mixture.

Cream the butter in the large bowl of a freestanding electric mixer on moderate speed for 3 minutes. Add the sugar in 4 additions, beating for 1 minute after each portion is added. Add the eggs, one at a time, beating for 30 to 45 seconds after each addition. Scrape down the sides of the mixing bowl frequently to keep the batter even-textured. Blend in the vanilla extract. On low speed, alternately add the sifted mixture in 3 additions with the sour cream in 2 additions, beginning and ending with the sifted mixture. Stir in the chocolate chips.

Spoon the batter into the prepared pan. Lightly smooth the top with a rubber spatula.

BAKE AND COOL THE CAKE Bake the cake in the preheated oven for 1 hour and 15 minutes to 1 hour and 20 minutes, or until risen, set, and a toothpick inserted in the cake withdraws clean. The baked cake will pull away slightly from the sides of the baking pan and the top will be golden.

Cool the cake in the pan on a rack for 10 to 15 minutes. Invert onto another cooling rack, peel away the waxed paper, then invert again to stand right side up. Cool completely. Sift confectioners' sugar over the top of the cake just before slicing and serving.

Bake-and-serve within 2 days

CHOCOLATE AND COCONUT LAYER CAKE

One 3-layer, 9-inch cake, creating 12 slices

The recipe for this cake, which was so much a part of my childhood, is similar to my late mother's three-layer wonder that we baked together, side by side, in the kitchen. Of course, time and my own instinct to redefine a recipe have changed it even further. I have added a little cocoa powder to the dry ingredients, changed the type of flour and chocolate used, toyed with the liquid measurements, increased the vanilla extract, and included flaked coconut in the batter.

CHOCOLATE AND COCONUT CAKE BATTER

4 ounces bittersweet chocolate, chopped

⅓ cup boiling water

2½ cups sifted bleached cake flour

2 teaspoons unsweetened alkalized cocoa powder

1 teaspoon baking soda

½ teaspoon salt

½ pound (16 tablespoons or 2 sticks) unsalted butter, softened

2 cups superfine sugar

4 large eggs, separated

2½ teaspoons vanilla extract

1 cup buttermilk, whisked well

¾ cup sweetened flaked coconut

⅛ teaspoon cream of tartar

FROSTING

Coconut and Walnut Frosting (page 100)

PREHEAT THE OVEN TO 350 DEGREES F. Lightly grease the inside of three 9-inch layer cake pans (1½ inches deep) with shortening, line the bottom of each pan with a circle of waxed paper cut to fit, grease the paper, and dust with flour.

MIX THE BATTER Place the chopped bittersweet chocolate and water in a small, heavy saucepan and place over low heat to melt the chocolate. Stir the mixture from time to time. Set aside to cool in the saucepan.

Resift the flour with the cocoa powder, the baking soda, and the salt onto a sheet of waxed paper.

Cream the butter in the large bowl of a freestanding electric mixer on moderate speed for 3 minutes. Add the sugar in 3 additions, beating for 1 to 2 minutes after each portion is added. Blend in the egg yolks. Blend in the vanilla extract and melted chocolate mixture.

On low speed, alternately add the sifted mixture in 3 additions with the buttermilk in 2 additions, beginning and ending with the sifted mixture. Scrape down the sides of the mixing bowl frequently to keep the batter even-textured. Blend in the coconut. The batter will be thick.

In a clean, medium-size mixing bowl, whip the egg whites until beginning to mound, add the cream of tartar, and continue beating until firm (not stiff) peaks are formed. Stir 3 large spoonfuls of the whipped whites into the cake batter, then fold in the remaining whites. Fold in the whites until the batter is a uniform color, free of any streaky patches of beaten whites.

Spoon the batter into the prepared pans, dividing it evenly among them. Spread the batter evenly.

BAKE AND COOL THE LAYERS Bake the cake layers in the preheated oven for 30 minutes, or until risen, set, and a toothpick inserted in the center of each layer withdraws clean. Check the layers beginning at 30 minutes. Cool the layers in the pans on racks for 10 minutes. Invert the layers onto other cooling racks, carefully peel away the waxed paper, and cool completely.

SET UP THE SERVING PLATE Tear off four 3-inch-wide strips of waxed paper. Place the strips in the shape of a square around the outer 3 inches of a cake plate.

ASSEMBLE AND FROST THE CAKE Center one cake layer on the plate (partially covering the waxed paper square; the strips should extend by at least 1 inch). Spread one-third of the frosting over the cake layer. Carefully position the second layer on top and spread with half of the remaining frosting. Top with the remaining cake layer. Spread the rest of the frosting over the top layer. Once set, gently remove and discard the strips of paper.

Let the cake stand for 1 hour before slicing and serving.

Bake-and-serve within 2 days

STUDY When peeling away the waxed paper round from each baked and inverted cake layer, do so lightly and carefully, so as not to pull away any patches of cake. The cake layers are tender and delicate, so assemble them carefully with the frosting as well. A light, but steady and balanced touch does it best.

COCONUT AND WALNUT FROSTING

About 5 cups frosting

The recipe for this frosting has evolved to include my unabashed love for coconut, to develop its depth of flavor (by using enough butter and heavy cream), and to make a big enough batch to fill and frost a three-layer cake.

12 tablespoons (1½ sticks) unsalted butter, cut into chunks, softened

1 cup firmly packed light brown sugar

½ cup granulated sugar

⅛ teaspoon salt

1 cup heavy cream

½ cup light (table) cream

6 large egg yolks, lightly beaten

3¼ cups sweetened flaked coconut

2 teaspoons vanilla extract

1 cup chopped walnuts

Place the chunks of butter, light brown sugar, granulated sugar, salt, heavy cream, light cream, egg yolks, and coconut in a large, heavy saucepan (preferably enameled cast iron). The pan must be heavy so that the heat diffuses evenly and the frosting cooks steadily without scorching. Combine the ingredients (the butter will still be in chunks), set over low heat, and cook slowly until the sugar dissolves, stirring frequently with a wooden spoon or flat wooden paddle.

When the sugar has dissolved, raise the heat to moderately high and bring the frosting to a moderate boil. Cook the frosting at a moderately low boil for 12 minutes (during this time it should bubble randomly but constantly), stir in the vanilla extract, and continue to cook for 2 minutes longer, or until nicely thickened. Stir the frosting frequently with a wooden spoon or flat wooden paddle, taking care to swipe the sides and bottom curve of the pan. The cooked frosting will be thickened and glossy.

Scrape the frosting into a large heatproof bowl, stir in the walnuts, and let it cool to warm, stirring from time to time. Use the frosting while it's still warm.

STUDY Use the heaviest pot that you own. I use a 6 to 7 quart casserole, with a top diameter measurement of 9½ inches. This, along with frequent stirring, will prevent the frosting from scorching as it cooks.

The generous amount of coconut and walnuts gives the frosting bulk and body. The brown sugar lends a light caramel undertone, which is enriched and supported by the heavy cream and butter.

THE STORY OF THIS PRESENTLY NOTORIOUS CAKE began many calendar years ago—it was a recipe that worked perfectly until, when I moved from one home to another, the day that it did not.

A recipe for a beloved chocolate cake, the basis of which was made by melting down a precise number of candy bars, was the source of enormous exasperation and what I now believe to be unfortunate baking kismet. In that (now ill-fated) recipe, the melted candy bars were added as the chocolate component in the usual way, right after the eggs were beaten into a creamed butter and sugar mixture, and followed by sifted ingredients and buttermilk added in alternating batches to complete the batter. The resulting mixture was as fine and silky a one as you could fantasize. In my previous kitchen, it rose to splendid heights and yielded one buttery and chocolatey cake, perfect for all gatherings, a good keeper, a great cake to make.

A chocolate cake even the garbage disposal refused

Until a fateful day in a spanking new kitchen.

I made the cake—and I certify this—in the usual way, without any departure whatsoever from the recipe. It ascended the sides of the pan and stayed stable, until it sank miserably. The top, if you could call it a top, was crusty and, in the strangest way possible, entirely misshapen. The sides collapsed. The inside was gummy. My cake, once prized for its excellence, was a pitiful sight. I did what any self-respecting baker would do under the circumstance: destroy the evidence. But not in the trash. I was so upset that I stuffed the cake down the garbage disposal and turned it on. In adamant reply, the disposal spit back the cake—all over my spiffy new cabinets and newly painted (cream-colored) ceiling, splattering my gleaming copper pots and clogging the ventilation return and the refrigerator-freezer grille along the way. Not even the garbage disposal tolerated it, and I have never attempted the recipe since.

VELVETY CHOCOLATE CAKE

One 2-layer, 9-inch cake, creating 12 slices

*B*uttery, satiny, oh-so-chocolatey, and glamorous—everything a layer cake must be.

CHOCOLATE MIXTURE

4 ounces unsweetened chocolate, chopped

⅓ cup plus 2 tablespoons boiling water

⅓ cup superfine sugar

LAYER CAKE BATTER

2 cups bleached cake flour

1 teaspoon baking soda

½ teaspoon salt

½ pound (16 tablespoons or 2 sticks) unsalted butter, softened

1½ cups less 1 tablespoon superfine sugar

3 large eggs

1½ teaspoons vanilla extract

½ cup plus 2 tablespoons milk

FROSTING

Chocolate Fudge Frosting (page 103) **or**

Creamy and Rich Chocolate Cupcake Frosting (page 107) **or**

White Chocolate Frosting (page 206)

PREHEAT THE OVEN TO 350 DEGREES F. Lightly grease the inside of two 9-inch layer cake pans (1½ inches deep) with shortening, line the bottom of each pan with a circle of waxed paper cut to fit, grease the paper, and dust with flour.

MIX THE CHOCOLATE MIXTURE Place the chopped chocolate in a small heatproof bowl. Pour the boiling water over it, let stand 3 minutes, add the sugar, and stir to combine. The mixture should be creamy and lustrous. Set aside to cool until warm. The mixture should be used warm, not cool or cold.

MIX THE BATTER Sift the flour, baking soda, and salt onto a sheet of waxed paper.

Cream the butter in the large bowl of a freestanding electric mixer on moderate speed for 3 minutes, or until very creamy. Add the sugar in 3 additions, beating for 1 minute after each portion is added. Add the eggs, one at a time, beating for 45 seconds after each addition. Blend in the vanilla extract and melted chocolate mixture. On low speed, add half of the sifted mixture, then the milk, then the balance of the sifted mixture. Scrape down the sides of the mixing bowl frequently to keep the batter even-textured.

Spoon the batter into the prepared pans, dividing it evenly between them. Spread the batter evenly.

BAKE AND COOL THE LAYERS Bake the cake layers in the preheated oven for 30 to 33 minutes, or until risen, set, and a toothpick inserted in the center of each layer withdraws clean. Cool the layers in the pans on racks for 10 minutes. Invert the layers onto other cooling racks, peel away the waxed paper, and cool completely.

SET UP THE SERVING PLATE Tear off four 3-inch-wide strips of waxed paper. Place the strips in the shape of a square around the outer 3 inches of a cake plate.

ASSEMBLE AND FROST THE CAKE Center one cake layer on the plate (partially covering the waxed paper square; the strips should extend by at least 1 inch). Spread a thick layer of frosting over the cake layer. Carefully position the second layer on top. Frost the top and sides of the cake, swirling the frosting as you go. Once set, gently remove and discard the strips of paper. Let the cake stand for 2 hours before slicing and serving.

Bake-and-serve within 1 day

STUDY The substantial amount of butter in the batter brings the chocolate flavor to the forefront and makes this cake ultra-moist. The superfine sugar that sweetens the batter produces a fine-grained cake.

CHOCOLATE FUDGE FROSTING

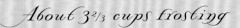

A glimmer of vanilla scents this frosting. To expand the vanilla essence further, add the seeds scraped from half of a split vanilla bean to the mixture along with the melted chocolate and butter.

4 ounces unsweetened chocolate, melted and cooled to tepid

6 tablespoons (¾ stick) unsalted butter, melted and cooled to tepid

5¼ cups confectioners' sugar, sifted

Large pinch of salt

1½ teaspoons vanilla extract

¾ cup light (table) cream, heated to tepid

Whisk the melted unsweetened chocolate and melted butter in a small bowl until smooth. The mixture will be glossy.

Place the confectioners' sugar and salt in the bowl of a heavy-duty freestanding electric mixer fitted with the flat paddle attachment. Mix on low speed to combine. Add the melted chocolate-butter mixture, vanilla extract, and cream. Beat the ingredients on moderately low speed for 2 minutes. When the frosting begins to come together, increase the speed to moderately high and beat 2 minutes longer, or until quite smooth. Scrape down the sides of the mixing bowl frequently to keep the frosting even-textured.

Increase the speed to high and beat for 2 minutes.

Adjust the texture of the frosting to spreading consistency by adding additional cream or confectioners' sugar, a tablespoon at a time, as needed.

STUDY A quarter pound of unsweetened chocolate and enough butter to convey creaminess, both in texture and taste, round out this frosting. The cream builds volume for a spreadable frosting.

If you are using the frosting for creating piped decorations (with a pastry bag and tip), mix the frosting on low to moderately low speed until just combined in order to avoid creating air bubbles, as the bubbles would break the flow of the frosting as it is squeezed from the filled pastry bag.

A LOFTY CUPCAKE, sheathed in creamy frosting and lavishly covered with sprinkles, is likely antithetical to what you'd find plated as dessert in a seriously high style restaurant. But cupcakes make grownups melt.

And I have solid evidence of this, because cupcakes, blessed with the all-important ingredient of sprinkles crowning their tops, prompt childlike reactions from adults every single time.

Throughout my baking life, it seems, guests well over the age of 21 (who, possessing an uncanny kind of radar, sight bottles of sprinkles in my kitchen) have asked for a "garnish" of these colorful bits and flakes on top of the hillock of whipped cream that sits comfortably to one side of a slice of my sultry almond soufflé cake. Or on that same swell of whipped cream covering a cup of chocolate pudding. I used to be distressed, until I realized that the reason for this came directly from the past. Sprinkles are nurturing, for they are frivolous, genuinely light-hearted, and intentionally playful.

A jar of chocolate sprinkles (although they could just as well be multicolored nonpareils or beautiful pastel sprinkles of one color, such as lavender, peach, or mint green) is the apotheosis of childhood. In a sweet way, sprinkles have long offered a sweet form of comfort and solace, stuck all over as they are to swaths of thick buttercream or a gauzy icing. The little dots and dashes promise such happy times: you can flick them on in excessive amounts. Can you ever have too many sprinkles? Certainly not.

On my kitchen counter, I have a number of antique and contemporary apothecary jars that are loaded with boutique chocolate bars, an assortment of regal French sugar cubes, and all kinds of cocoa powder, along with other baking provisions. And I have two jars that hold about a dozen varieties of sprinkles, plus a few bottles and bags of

A shower of sprinkles

chocolate sprinkles of exceptional flavor and intensity. Full disclosure here: I have more sprinkles in the pantry. And in my upstairs storage room that holds emergency "necessities" you are likely to find another supply of sprinkles in a full range of pastel colors, and jars of colored sanding sugar in an expansive range of hues (the last item is, admittedly, a sugary extension of sprinkles).

My collection began modestly one day, and really mushroomed when I began baking cupcakes in all flavors, complete with towering fluffs of frosting. As I stood in my nightgown and fleecy socks in the kitchen after dinner one night, I opened a container of multicolored sprinkles and immediately, instinctually perhaps, dipped the top of a freshly baked and lavishly frosted chocolate cupcake in it. It was a reflex reaction. Who could resist this culinary act? As I peeled away the gorgeous metallic gold baking cup and dove into moist cake that was both frosted and sprinkled, I thought: this is my madeleine.

At once, I was deep into nostalgia, immersed in a wellspring of baking memories—a simple homemade layer cake with an edging of sprinkles my mother brought to a neighborhood recreation center to celebrate my ninth birthday . . . spritz cookies topped with nonpareils from the local bakery of my childhood . . . sprinkles stuck randomly to the surface of soft, fudge-topped chocolate cookies my mother stacked in the back of our car for safekeeping as we drove the boatload of them home from New York City (a postscript here—the trip was extended in length due to inaccurate directions and, a few seriously wrong turns later, we ate all of the cookies on the way home). The flavor and texture underneath these bits are the lures. Sprinkles only happen to cloak the surface and, for the moment, transport me back in time to sweet, memory-laden places.

MY MOTHER'S BUTTERMILK CHOCOLATE CAKE

One 13 by 9-inch cake, creating 20 squares

My late mother, Irene, loved to bake with buttermilk. When I was growing up, we would drive for hours (or so it seemed) to buy fresh, thick buttermilk at the dairy of a local university. As a fidgety child, the trip made me miserable, but I was compliant (sort of) nonetheless. The result of the journey ended in this cake, the reward for my quasi-patience. As a passionate baker and cook, I now drive all over to buy ingredients, leading me to admit that my mom, of course, had just the right idea about quality. Mothers, it seems, are usually right.

This cake is a delight, simple and basic. The batter focuses gently on chocolate, the frosting more so.

BUTTERMILK CHOCOLATE CAKE BATTER
2 cups bleached cake flour
1½ teaspoons baking soda
½ teaspoon salt
1 tablespoon unsweetened alkalized cocoa powder
8 tablespoons (1 stick) unsalted butter, softened
1⅓ cups plus 3 tablespoons superfine sugar
2 large eggs
3 ounces unsweetened chocolate, melted and cooled
2 teaspoons vanilla extract
1½ cups buttermilk, whisked well

FROSTING
Rich Chocolate Frosting (page 111)

PREHEAT THE OVEN TO 350 DEGREES F. Lightly grease the inside of a 13 by 9 by 2-inch baking pan with shortening and dust with flour.

MIX THE BATTER Sift the flour, baking soda, salt, and cocoa powder onto a sheet of waxed paper.

Cream the butter in the large bowl of a freestanding electric mixer on moderate speed for 3 minutes. Add the sugar in 3 additions, beating for 1 minute after each portion is added. Add the eggs, one at a time, beating for 45 seconds after each addition. On low speed, blend in the melted chocolate and vanilla extract.

On low speed, alternately add the sifted mixture in 3 additions with the buttermilk in 2 additions, beginning and ending with the sifted mixture. Scrape down the sides of the mixing bowl frequently to keep the batter even-textured.

Scrape the batter into the prepared pan and spread evenly. Smooth the top with a rubber spatula.

BAKE AND COOL THE CAKE Bake the cake in the preheated oven for 40 minutes, or until risen, set, and a toothpick inserted in the center withdraws clean. Cool the cake in the pan on a rack.

FROST THE CAKE Spread the frosting on the cake, swirling it as you go. Let the cake stand for 1 hour before cutting into squares for serving.

Bake-and-serve within 1 day

STUDY The buttermilk in the batter renders the baked cake moist and downy.

RICH CHOCOLATE FROSTING

*I*t's the heavy cream that makes this frosting thick, rich, and deliciously smooth.

4 ounces unsweetened chocolate, melted and
cooled to tepid

6 tablespoons (¾ stick) unsalted butter, cut into
small chunks, softened

5 cups confectioners' sugar, sifted

Large pinch of salt

2 teaspoons vanilla extract

¾ cup heavy cream, heated to tepid

Whisk the melted chocolate and butter in a small bowl
until smooth.

Place the confectioners' sugar and salt in the bowl of a
heavy-duty freestanding electric mixer fitted with the flat
paddle attachment. Mix on low speed to combine. Add the
chocolate-butter mixture, vanilla extract, and heavy
cream. Beat the ingredients on moderately low speed for 2
minutes, then increase the speed to moderately high and
beat for 3 minutes longer, or until smooth. Scrape down
the sides of the mixing bowl frequently to keep the frosting even-textured. Increase the speed to high and beat for
2 minutes. Adjust the texture of the frosting to spreading
consistency by adding additional teaspoons of heavy
cream or tablespoons of confectioners' sugar as needed.

STUDY The texture of the frosting turns slightly spongy as it stands; simply beat for a minute to
restore its consistency.

CHOCOLATE CREAM CAKE

One large bowl, creating 8 servings, or 8 individual glasses or goblets

Chocolate pastry cream layered in between chunks of freshly baked buttermilk chocolate cake and topped with whipped cream combines three of my favorite things—soft, custardy pastry cream, cake, and whipped cream. This sweet combination has been a specialty of mine for more than 20 years. It all began, innocently enough, with my love of custard and cake, and blossomed into a beguiling dessert. It can be assembled in one large bowl or in individual goblets. Underneath a cape of flouncy whipped cream, you will find uninterrupted chocolate lusciousness.

CHOCOLATE PASTRY CREAM

1 tablespoon plus 2 teaspoons unsweetened alkalized cocoa powder

2 tablespoons cornstarch

¾ cup granulated sugar

Large pinch of salt

2½ cups milk

½ cup heavy cream

5 ounces bittersweet chocolate, melted

1 ounce unsweetened chocolate, melted

4 large egg yolks

2 teaspoons vanilla extract

CAKE

My Mother's Buttermilk Chocolate Cake, baked and cooled (page 110) or

A Welcoming and Old-fashioned Chocolate Sheet Cake (page 290)

TOPPING

Chocolate Cream Pie Topping (page 289)

MAKE THE PASTRY CREAM Sift the cocoa powder, cornstarch, sugar, and salt into a heavy, medium-size saucepan (preferably enameled cast iron). The pan must be heavy or the pastry cream may scorch. Whisk well to blend; the mixture must be whisked completely if the cornstarch is to combine with the sugar and cocoa. Gradually stir in the milk and heavy cream, mixing well. Blend in the melted bittersweet chocolate and melted unsweetened chocolate. The mixture will be streaky at this point, but will come together as it cooks.

Place the saucepan over moderately high heat and bring the contents to a boil, stirring slowly with a wooden spoon or flat paddle. Do not use a whisk. Adjust the heat so that the mixture boils slowly for 1 minute.

Mix the egg yolks in a small heatproof bowl to combine. Stir in ½ cup of the hot cream mixture; gradually stir this mixture back into the contents of the pan, mixing well. Return the saucepan to the heat and bring to a low boil. Cook, stirring, for 1 minute, or until the filling has thickened. The filling should reach a temperature of 200 degrees F. to achieve the correct stability and thickness. Remove from the heat. Stir in the vanilla extract.

Set a large sieve over a heatproof bowl. Scrape the pastry cream filling into the sieve and smooth it through with the back of a spoon or heatproof spatula. Pour and scrape the filling into a heatproof storage container. Press a sheet of food-safe plastic wrap directly onto the surface. Cool the filling for 15 minutes, then cover and refrigerate until well chilled, about 6 hours. The pastry cream can be made up to 1 day in advance.

ASSEMBLE THE CAKE AND PASTRY CREAM With a serrated knife, trim all firm, crusty edges from the cake. Cut the cake into rough chunks (cut 2-inch chunks if using the large bowl; 1-inch chunks if using goblets or glasses). Divide the cake chunks into thirds.

BUTTERMILK CHOCOLATE LAYER CAKE

One 2-layer, 9-inch cake, creating 12 slices

This cake has an old-fashioned flavor and fine chocolate aroma. You can extend the chocolate essence by using a chocolate butter frosting, or spread vanilla frosting over and about the layers for contrast. If you use the latter, make an extravagant double batch: spread it thickly between the two layers and flamboyantly over the top and sides of the assembled cake.

BUTTERMILK CHOCOLATE BATTER

2¼ cups bleached cake flour

1 teaspoon baking soda

½ teaspoon salt

9 tablespoons (1 stick plus 1 tablespoon) unsalted butter, softened

2 tablespoons shortening

1½ cups superfine sugar

3 large eggs

2 teaspoons vanilla extract

3 ounces unsweetened chocolate, melted and cooled

1¼ cups buttermilk, whisked well

FROSTING

Chocolate Butter Frosting (page 119) or
A double recipe of Rich Vanilla Butter Frosting (page 200)

PREHEAT THE OVEN TO 350 DEGREES F. Lightly grease the inside of two 9-inch layer cake pans (1½ inches deep) with shortening, line the bottom of each pan with a circle of waxed paper cut to fit, grease the paper, and dust with flour.

MIX THE BATTER Sift the flour, baking soda, and salt onto a sheet of waxed paper.

Cream the butter and shortening in the large bowl of a freestanding electric mixer on moderate speed for 3 minutes. Add the sugar in 2 additions, beating for 1 to 2 minutes after each portion is added. Add the eggs, one at a time, beating for 45 seconds after each is added. Blend in the vanilla extract and melted chocolate. On low speed, alternately add the sifted mixture in 3 additions with the buttermilk in 2 additions, beginning and ending with the sifted mixture. Scrape down the sides of the mixing bowl frequently to keep the batter even-textured.

Spoon the batter into the prepared pans, dividing it evenly between them. Spread the batter evenly.

BAKE AND COOL THE LAYERS Bake the cake layers in the preheated oven for 25 to 30 minutes, or until risen, set, and a toothpick inserted in the center of each layer withdraws clean (or with a few crumbs attached). Cool the layers in the pans on racks for 10 minutes. Invert the layers onto other cooling racks, peel away the waxed paper, and cool completely.

SET UP THE SERVING PLATE Tear off four 3-inch-wide strips of waxed paper. Place the strips in the shape of a square around the outer 3 inches of a cake plate.

ASSEMBLE AND FROST THE CAKE Center one cake layer on the plate (partially covering the waxed paper square; the strips should extend by at least 1 inch). Spread over a layer of frosting. Carefully position the second layer on top. Frost the top and sides of the cake, swirling the frosting as you go. Once set, gently remove and discard the strips of paper. Let the cake stand for 1 hour before slicing and serving.

Bake-and-serve within 1 day

STUDY The superfine sugar ensures that the texture of the cake layers will be fine-grained and satiny.

The buttermilk acts as a tenderizing agent in the batter.

CHOCOLATE BUTTER FROSTING

A frosting that is full of chocolate, bolstered with enough butter, and lightly fragrant with vanilla extract makes a sweet camouflage for layers of cake. The amount of salt, while small, is vital to building its flavor.

4½ cups confectioners' sugar, sifted

⅛ teaspoon salt

5 ounces unsweetened chocolate, melted and cooled to tepid

2 teaspoons vanilla extract

7 tablespoons milk, heated to tepid

8 tablespoons (1 stick) unsalted butter, cut into chunks, softened

Place the confectioners' sugar, salt, melted chocolate, vanilla extract, and milk in the bowl of a heavy-duty free-standing electric mixer fitted with the flat paddle. Scatter over the chunks of butter and beat on moderately low speed for 2 minutes to begin the mixing process. When the frosting begins to come together, raise the speed to moderate, and beat for 3 minutes, or until very smooth. Scrape down the sides of the mixing bowl to keep the frosting even-textured. Increase the speed to high and beat for 2 minutes, or until very creamy. Adjust the texture of the frosting to spreading consistency, as needed, by adding additional teaspoons of milk or tablespoons of confectioners' sugar.

STUDY The texture of the frosting will turn slightly spongy as it stands; beat on low speed for a minute to restore its consistency.

MIDNIGHT CHOCOLATE CAKE

One 13 by 9-inch cake, creating 20 squares

A generous amount of chocolate plus tenderizing buttermilk equals dark and moist cake. This is a simple dessert, oftentimes overlooked in favor of one that's more elaborate. But when presented with generous squares of this freshly baked wonder, friends press me for the recipe: such is the potency of chocolate cake, soft and gentle, and substantial strokes of chocolate frosting, brimming with butter and accented with vanilla extract.

CHOCOLATE CAKE BATTER

4 ounces unsweetened chocolate, finely chopped

⅓ cup plus 3 tablespoons boiling water

2 cups bleached cake flour

1 teaspoon baking soda

¼ teaspoon salt

14 tablespoons (1¾ sticks) unsalted butter, softened

2 tablespoons shortening

1⅔ cups plus 2 tablespoons superfine sugar

4 large eggs

2½ teaspoons vanilla extract

¾ cup buttermilk, whisked well

FROSTING

Midnight Chocolate Cake Frosting (page 121)

PREHEAT THE OVEN AND PREPARE THE CAKE PAN Preheat the oven to 350 degrees F. Film the inside of a 13 by 9 by 3-inch baking pan with nonstick cooking spray.

MIX THE BATTER Place the chopped chocolate in medium-size mixing bowl. Pour the boiling water over it and let stand until the chocolate melts completely, stirring once or twice. Mix lightly but thoroughly until smooth. The mixture should be tepid by the time it is used, not cool.

Sift the flour, baking soda, and salt onto a sheet of waxed paper.

Cream the butter and shortening in the large bowl of a freestanding electric mixer on moderate speed for 3 minutes. Add the sugar in 3 additions, beating for 1 minute after each portion is added. Add the eggs, one at a time, beating for 45 seconds after each addition. Slowly blend in the melted chocolate and vanilla extract. On low speed, alternately add the sifted mixture in 3 additions with the buttermilk in 2 additions, beginning and ending with the sifted mixture. Scrape down the sides of the mixing bowl frequently to keep the batter even-textured.

Scrape the batter into the prepared pan and spread evenly. Smooth the top with a rubber spatula.

BAKE AND COOL THE CAKE Bake the cake in the preheated oven for 35 to 40 minutes, or until risen, set, and a tooth-pick inserted in the center withdraws clean. Cool the cake in the pan on a rack.

FROST THE CAKE Place the frosting on the cake in dollops, then spread it over, using a flexible palette knife or spatula. Use a light touch. Let the cake stand for 1 hour before cutting into squares for serving.

Bake-and-serve within 2 days

MIDNIGHT CHOCOLATE CAKE FROSTING

About 4 cups frosting

*R*ich and absolutely blooming with chocolate, a frosting such as this one is a perfect covering for all kinds of sheet cakes, especially chocolate (and vanilla, too). It sets into soft fudge. Pile it on!

7 cups confectioners' sugar, sifted

⅛ teaspoon salt

6 ounces unsweetened chocolate, melted and cooled to tepid

12 tablespoons (1½ sticks) unsalted butter, melted and cooled to tepid

½ cup plus 1 tablespoon milk, heated to tepid

2½ teaspoons vanilla extract

2 tablespoons heavy cream

Place half of the confectioners' sugar and the salt in the bowl of a heavy-duty freestanding electric mixer fitted with the flat paddle attachment. Beat on low speed to combine.

Whisk the melted chocolate and melted butter in a small bowl. Pour and scrape the chocolate–butter mixture into the bowl containing the confectioners' sugar. Beat for 1 minute on low speed. Add the milk and vanilla extract. Beat on low speed for 2 minutes, or until smooth. Add the remaining confectioners' sugar and beat for 2 minutes on moderate speed. Scrape down the sides of the mixing bowl to keep the frosting even-textured. Blend in the heavy cream. Beat for 2 to 3 minutes on moderately high speed. The frosting should be creamy. Add enough additional heavy cream (up to 3 tablespoons), as needed, until the frosting reaches that point.

Use the frosting immediately.

WITH A CHOCOLATE BATTER ON THE BOTTOM and a cream cheese mixture over the top, this sweet can take the form of cupcakes, miniature tea cakes, a tart, a torte, or rich and substantial squares and bars. The best part about a black bottom dessert is the contrast between the flavor of the chocolate and the creaminess of the topping. Two strategies to remember: When swirling together the cream cheese and chocolate batter, you can either use the tip of a knife for a dramatic swirl, or a toothpick for a delicate, feathery look. Either way, the confection will look and taste delicious.

BLACK BOTTOM BROWNIE TART

One 8-inch tart, creating 8 slices

This recipe is a combination of three of my favorite things: shortbread, brownies, and cheesecake—a collusion of my black bottom bars with shortbread slipped underneath them. The layers are composed in a fluted tart pan that makes a pretty tart of contrasting textures.

VANILLA SHORTBREAD LAYER

1 cup bleached all-purpose flour

1 teaspoon cornstarch

⅛ teaspoon baking powder

Pinch of salt

8 tablespoons (1 stick) unsalted butter, softened

¼ cup superfine sugar

½ teaspoon vanilla extract

CREAM CHEESE AND CHOCOLATE CHIP TOPPING

2 packages (3 ounces each) cream cheese, softened

¼ cup granulated sugar

Large pinch salt

2 large egg yolks

½ teaspoon vanilla extract

⅓ cup plus 3 tablespoons miniature semisweet chocolate chips

BROWNIE BATTER

¾ cup bleached all-purpose flour

¼ teaspoon baking powder

Large pinch of salt

1 tablespoon unsweetened alkalized cocoa powder

8 tablespoons (1 stick) unsalted butter, melted and cooled to tepid

3 ounces unsweetened chocolate, melted and cooled to tepid

2 large eggs

2 large egg yolks

1 cup granulated sugar

1½ teaspoons vanilla extract

½ cup sweetened flaked coconut

PREHEAT THE OVEN TO 350 DEGREES F. Film the inside of a fluted 8¾-inch round tart pan (2 inches deep, with a removable bottom) with nonstick cooking spray.

MIX, BAKE, AND COOL THE SHORTBREAD LAYER Sift the flour, cornstarch, baking powder, and salt onto a sheet of waxed paper.

In the large bowl of a freestanding electric mixer, cream the butter on moderately low speed for 2 minutes. Add the sugar and beat for 1 minute longer. Blend in the vanilla extract. On low speed, add the sifted mixture in 2 additions, blending until the flour particles are absorbed. Scrape down the sides of the mixing bowl frequently to keep the dough even-textured.

Press and pat the dough on the bottom of the prepared pan in an even layer.

Bake the shortbread layer in the preheated oven for 25 minutes, or until set and golden. Transfer the pan to a cooling rack and let stand while you prepare the topping and brownie batter.

MIX THE TOPPING Using an electric hand mixer, beat the cream cheese and sugar in a medium-size mixing bowl on moderately low speed until smooth. Blend in the salt, egg yolks, and vanilla extract. Stir in the chocolate chips.

MIX THE BATTER Sift the flour, baking powder, salt, and cocoa powder onto a sheet of waxed paper.

In a small bowl, whisk the melted butter and melted chocolate until smooth. In a medium-size mixing bowl, whisk the eggs and egg yolks slowly until blended, about 15 seconds. Add the sugar and whisk until combined, about 30 seconds. Blend in the vanilla extract and melted butter-chocolate mixture. Sift the flour mixture over and stir to form a batter, mixing thoroughly until the particles of flour are absorbed, using a spoon or flat wooden paddle. Stir in the coconut.

Spoon the batter in large dollops on the shortbread layer. Carefully spread the batter over the cookie layer, using a flexible palette knife or spatula. Smooth the top with a rubber spatula.

TOP AND SWIRL THE TART Spoon the cream cheese and chocolate chip topping on top of the brownie batter. Carefully swirl together the cream cheese mixture and brownie batter, using a round-edged table knife. When swirling the two mixtures, move the knife carefully so that it doesn't touch (or dislodge) the shortbread layer.

BAKE, COOL, AND CUT THE TART Bake the tart for 45 minutes, or until set. The center of the tart should be set, without a pronounced wiggle. As with some brownie-based fillings, there will be a few hairline cracks on the top. Cool the sweet in the pan on a cooling rack. Carefully unmold the tart, leaving it on its round base. Serve the tart, cut into thick slices, using a serrated knife.

Refrigerate any leftover tart in an airtight container.

Bake-and-serve within 2 days

BITTERSWEET CHOCOLATE BLACK BOTTOM BARS

*T*he bittersweet chocolate bar cookie batter serves as a thick and intense foundation for a swirly cream cheese batter. These bars are a potent and impressive way to savor the flavor of chocolate.

VANILLA COOKIE LAYER

8 tablespoons (1 stick) unsalted butter, melted, cooled to tepid, and combined with ½ teaspoon vanilla extract

1½ cups vanilla wafer cookie crumbs (such as crumbs made from Nabisco Nilla wafers)

CREAM CHEESE TOPPING

2 packages (3 ounces each) cream cheese, softened

5 tablespoons superfine sugar

1 large egg

1 teaspoon vanilla extract

½ teaspoon bleached cake flour

Pinch of salt

BITTERSWEET CHOCOLATE BAR COOKIE BATTER

⅔ cup plus 3 tablespoons bleached cake flour

1 tablespoon unsweetened alkalized cocoa powder

¼ teaspoon baking powder

⅛ teaspoon salt

4 ounces bittersweet chocolate, chopped into small chunks

7 tablespoons (1 stick less 1 tablespoon) unsalted butter, melted and cooled to tepid

2½ ounces unsweetened chocolate, melted and cooled to tepid

2 large eggs

1 large egg yolk

¾ cup superfine sugar

1 teaspoon vanilla extract

PREHEAT THE OVEN TO 350 DEGREES F. Film the inside of a 9 by 9 by 2-inch baking pan with nonstick cooking spray.

MAKE THE COOKIE LAYER Pour the melted butter–vanilla mixture into the prepared pan. Spoon the cookie crumbs evenly over the bottom of the pan and press down lightly with the underside of a small offset metal spatula so that the crumbs absorb the butter. Bake the cookie layer in the preheated oven for 4 minutes. Place the baking pan on a rack. Cool for 10 minutes.

MIX THE TOPPING Using an electric hand mixer, beat the cream cheese and sugar in a medium-size mixing bowl on moderately low speed until smooth. Beat in the egg and vanilla extract. Blend in the flour and salt.

MIX THE BATTER Sift the flour, cocoa powder, baking powder, and salt onto a sheet of waxed paper. In a small bowl, thoroughly toss the chocolate chunks with ½ teaspoon of the sifted mixture.

In a medium-size mixing bowl, whisk the melted butter and melted chocolate until smooth. In a medium-size mixing bowl, whisk the eggs and egg yolk until blended, about 15 seconds. Add the sugar and whisk until combined, about 30 seconds. Blend in the vanilla extract and melted butter-chocolate mixture. Sift the flour mixture over and stir to form a batter, mixing thoroughly until the particles of flour are absorbed, using a whisk or flat wooden paddle. Stir in the chocolate chunks.

Spoon the batter in large dollops on the cookie crumb layer. Carefully spread the batter over the cookie layer, using a flexible palette knife or spatula. Smooth the top with a rubber spatula.

ASSEMBLE AND SWIRL THE SWEET Spoon the cream cheese mixture on top of the bittersweet batter. Carefully swirl together the cream cheese mixture and chocolate batter, using the tip of a round-edged table knife. When swirling the two mixtures, do so gently in wide sweeping movements. Do not overswirl, or the batter will look muddy.

BAKE, COOL, AND CUT THE SWEET INTO BARS Bake the sweet in the preheated oven for 27 to 30 minutes, or until set. Let the sweet stand in the pan on a cooling rack for 3 hours. Refrigerate for 1 hour. With a small sharp knife, cut the sweet into quarters, then cut each quarter into 6 bars. Or, for big bold bars, cut the entire block in half widthwise, then cut each half into long rectangular bars.

Remove the bars from the baking pan, using a small offset metal spatula.

Refrigerate all bars not served on baking day in an airtight container.

Bake-and-serve within 3 days

STYLE For Bittersweet Chocolate Black Bottom Bars with Nuts, stir ¼ cup chopped walnuts, pecans, or macadamia nuts into the bittersweet chocolate batter along with the bittersweet chocolate chunks.

For Bittersweet Chocolate–Coconut Black Bottom Bars, stir ⅓ cup sweetened flaked coconut into the bittersweet chocolate batter along with the bittersweet chocolate chunks.

ACCENT Reduce the vanilla extract in the bittersweet chocolate batter to ¾ teaspoon. Add ¼ teaspoon chocolate extract to the chocolate bar cookie batter along with the vanilla extract.

COCONUT BLACK BOTTOM BARS

2 dozen bars

*S*weetened flaked coconut adds a definable and altogether tantalizing accent to these bars. I adore the way coconut adds a subtle chewiness to a rich and fudgy batter.

COCONUT CREAM CHEESE TOPPING

2 packages (3 ounces each) cream cheese, softened

⅓ cup granulated sugar

Pinch of salt

2 large egg yolks

½ teaspoon vanilla extract

½ cup sweetened flaked coconut

⅓ cup semisweet chocolate chips

FUDGE BAR COOKIE BATTER

¾ cup plus 2 tablespoons bleached cake flour

1 tablespoon unsweetened alkalized cocoa powder

¼ teaspoon baking powder

⅛ teaspoon salt

½ cup semisweet chocolate chips

14 tablespoons (1¾ sticks) unsalted butter, melted and cooled to tepid

4 ounces unsweetened chocolate, melted and cooled to tepid

4 large eggs

1¾ cup plus 2 tablespoons superfine sugar

1 teaspoon vanilla extract

PREHEAT THE OVEN TO 350 DEGREES F. Film the inside of a 9 by 9 by 2-inch baking pan with nonstick cooking spray.

MIX THE TOPPING Using an electric hand mixer, beat the cream cheese, sugar, and salt in a medium-size mixing bowl on moderately low speed until smooth. Beat in the egg yolks and vanilla extract. Blend in the coconut and chocolate chips.

MIX THE BATTER Sift the flour, cocoa powder, baking powder, and salt onto a sheet of waxed paper. In a small bowl,

toss the chocolate chips with ½ teaspoon of the sifted mixture.

In a medium-size mixing bowl, whisk the melted butter and melted chocolate until smooth. In a medium-size mixing bowl, whisk the eggs until blended, about 15 to 20 seconds. Add the sugar and whisk until combined, about 30 seconds. Blend in the vanilla extract and melted butter-chocolate mixture. Sift the flour mixture over and stir to form a batter, mixing thoroughly until the particles of flour are absorbed, using a whisk or flat wooden paddle. Stir in the chocolate chips.

Scrape the batter into the prepared pan and spread evenly. Smooth the top with a rubber spatula.

ASSEMBLE AND SWIRL THE SWEET Spoon the coconut cream cheese mixture on top of the fudge batter. Carefully swirl together the cream cheese mixture and chocolate batter, using the tip of a round-edged table knife. When swirling the two mixtures, do so in careful gliding movements. Overswirling the batter will create a muddy look.

BAKE, COOL, AND CUT THE SWEET INTO BARS Bake the sweet in the preheated oven for up to 30 minutes, or until set. Let the sweet stand in the pan on a cooling rack for 3 hours. Refrigerate for 30 to 45 minutes, or until firm enough to cut. With a small sharp knife, cut the sweet into quarters, then cut each quarter into 6 bars. Remove the bars from the baking pan, using a small offset metal spatula.

Refrigerate all bars not served on baking day in an airtight container.

Bake-and-serve within 3 days

BLACK BOTTOM TEA CAKES

About 3 dozen tea cakes

These are flavorful cakes—bites of chocolate cake, cream cheese, and chocolate chips. A moist chocolate batter meeting a cheesecakelike topping is a delicious intersection of texture and flavor. The little gems can be used as part of a cookie plate or offered as a sweet at brunch when a taste of something chocolate is always so inviting.

CREAM CHEESE–CHOCOLATE CHIP TOPPING

1 package (8 ounces) cream cheese, softened

¼ cup plus 1 tablespoon granulated sugar

1 large egg

1 teaspoon vanilla extract

Large pinch of salt

½ teaspoon bleached all-purpose flour

¾ cup miniature semisweet chocolate chips

CHOCOLATE TEA CAKE BATTER

1½ cups bleached all-purpose flour

1 teaspoon baking soda

1 tablespoon unsweetened alkalized cocoa powder

1 cup granulated sugar

¼ teaspoon salt

1 cup water

⅓ cup plain vegetable oil (such as canola or soybean)

2¾ teaspoons distilled white vinegar

1¼ teaspoons vanilla extract

PREHEAT THE OVEN TO 350 DEGREES F. Line the inside of about 3 dozen tea cake cups (24 cups to a pan, each cup measuring 2 inches in diameter and 1³⁄₁₆ inches deep, with a capacity of 3 tablespoons) with ovenproof baking paper liners.

MIX THE TOPPING Using an electric hand mixer, beat the cream cheese and sugar in a medium-size mixing bowl on moderately low speed until smooth. Blend in the egg, vanilla extract, salt, and flour. Stir in the chocolate chips.

MIX THE BATTER Sift the flour, baking soda, cocoa powder, sugar, and salt into a large mixing bowl. Add the water, oil, vinegar, and vanilla extract. Using an electric hand mixer, mix all of the ingredients together on moderately low speed until the batter is smooth and uniform. Scrape down the sides of the bowl frequently to keep the batter even-textured. Transfer the batter to a pitcher or large measuring cup.

ASSEMBLE THE TEA CAKES Fill each cup about half full with batter. Spoon a teaspoon of the cream cheese–chocolate chip batter into the center of each tea cake.

BAKE AND COOL THE TEA CAKES Bake the tea cakes in the preheated oven for 25 minutes, or until set. Cool the tea cakes in the pan for 15 minutes, then carefully transfer them to cooling racks. Cool completely.

Refrigerate any tea cakes that remain past baking day in airtight containers.

Bake-and-serve within 3 days

STUDY Use a plain vinegar with 5 percent acidity (such as Heinz Distilled White Vinegar).

INVITING FOR THE DEPTH OF FLAVOR that chips and chunks of chocolate bring to batters and doughs, these sweet additions are a significant part of my own baking tradition. I love to use morsels, as well as chunks of bar chocolate, in recipes that feature enough butter, vanilla extract, and sugar to compose their taste and texture. Most of these doughs are a playful diversion from the more intense and solid-chocolate sweets that present a darkly powerful impact of flavor. The recipes highlight the creaminess of butter, caramel undertone of brown sugar, and flowery softness of vanilla extract.

FAVORITE CHOCOLATE CHIP COOKIES

About 3 dozen cookies

What keeps a warm, freshly baked chocolate cookie etched in my memory is the sweet presence of brown sugar and an excessive amount of chocolate chips ambushed in a buttery dough. The dough is not made with all-purpose flour alone. It contains some cake flour, and this helps to tenderize the cookies into lightly caramelized flats and lets all those chips poke through in lots of places. The baked cookies will be flat, with crispy edges and chewy centers. Is anything better than that? As the cookies bake, the ingredients mingle, and their scent draws everyone at home into the kitchen.

BUTTERY CHOCOLATE CHIP DOUGH

1¾ cups bleached all-purpose flour

¼ cup plus 2 teaspoons bleached cake flour

1 teaspoon baking soda

½ teaspoon salt

½ pound (16 tablespoons or 2 sticks) unsalted butter, softened

⅔ cup plus 3 tablespoons firmly packed light brown sugar

⅔ cup granulated sugar

2 large eggs

2 teaspoons vanilla extract

1¼ teaspoons hot water

2½ cups semisweet chocolate chips

CHOCOLATE CHIP TOPPING (OPTIONAL)

About ¾ cup semisweet chocolate chips

PREHEAT THE OVEN TO 350 DEGREES F. Line several cookie sheets or rimmed sheet pans with cooking parchment paper.

MIX THE DOUGH Sift the all-purpose flour, cake flour, baking soda, and salt onto a sheet of waxed paper.

Cream the butter in the large bowl of a freestanding electric mixer on moderately low speed for 3 minutes. Add the light brown sugar and continue creaming on moderately low speed for 2 minutes longer. Add the granulated sugar and beat for 2 minutes. Blend in the eggs, one at a time, beating until incorporated. Blend in the vanilla extract and hot water. On low speed, blend in the sifted ingredients in 2 additions, beating until the flour particles are absorbed. Scrape down the sides of the mixing bowl frequently to keep the dough even-textured. Blend in the chocolate chips.

SHAPE THE COOKIES Place rounded 2-tablespoon-size mounds of dough on the prepared pans, spacing the mounds about 3 inches apart. Sprinkle a few chocolate chips on the top of each mound of dough, if you wish.

BAKE AND COOL THE COOKIES Bake the cookies in the preheated oven for 13 to 14 minutes, or until set and golden. Let the cookies stand on the pans for 1 minute, then transfer them to cooling racks, using a wide offset metal spatula. Store in an airtight tin.

Bake-and-serve within 2 days

STYLE For Favorite Chocolate Chip Cookies with Nuts, blend 1 cup coarsely chopped walnuts, pecans, or macadamia nuts into the dough along with the chocolate chips.

For Favorite Bittersweet Chocolate Chunk Cookies, substitute 15 ounces bittersweet chocolate, cut into small chunks, for the chocolate chips.

SOFT CHOCOLATE CHUNK COOKIES

*T*hese soft and chewy cookies are buttery and mellow, with just a hint of caramel and chunks of bittersweet chocolate interspersed within the creamy, vanilla-centered dough.

CHOCOLATE CHUNK DOUGH

3 cups bleached all-purpose flour

¼ teaspoon baking soda

⅛ teaspoon cream of tartar

¾ teaspoon salt

½ pound plus 5 tablespoons (2 sticks plus 5 tablespoons) unsalted butter, softened

1 cup granulated sugar

1 cup firmly packed light brown sugar

2 large eggs

2 tablespoons vanilla extract

13 ounces bittersweet chocolate, chopped into chunks

MIX THE DOUGH Sift the flour, baking soda, cream of tartar, and salt onto a sheet of waxed paper.

Cream the butter in the large bowl of a freestanding electric mixer on moderately low speed for 3 minutes. Add the granulated sugar and beat for 2 minutes. Add the light brown sugar and beat for 2 minutes longer. Blend in the eggs, one at a time, beating until incorporated. Blend in the vanilla extract. On low speed, blend in the sifted ingredients in 3 additions, beating until the flour particles are absorbed. Scrape down the sides of the mixing bowl frequently to keep the dough even-textured. Blend in the chocolate chunks.

CHILL THE DOUGH Cover the bowl of dough and refrigerate for 1 hour.

PREHEAT THE OVEN TO 325 DEGREES F. Line several cookie sheets or rimmed sheet pans with cooking parchment paper.

SHAPE THE COOKIES Place heaping 2-tablespoon-size mounds of dough on the prepared pans, spacing the mounds about 3 inches apart. Keep the mounds high and plump.

BAKE AND COOL THE COOKIES Bake the cookies in the preheated oven for about 16 minutes, or until set and light golden on top. Let the cookies stand on the pans for 2 minutes, then transfer them to cooling racks, using a wide offset metal spatula. Store in an airtight tin.

Bake-and-serve within 2 days

STYLE For Soft Chocolate Chip Cookies, substitute 2¼ cups semisweet chocolate chips for the bittersweet chocolate.

STUDY For a more pronounced caramel flavor, use ¾ cup firmly packed dark brown sugar and ¼ cup firmly packed light brown sugar.

The cookies should be baked until they no longer look wet or shiny on top and are completely set, but avoid baking them longer than that or they will be dry instead of moist.

DARK CHOCOLATE–CHOCOLATE CHUNK COOKIES

About 20 cookies

*E*very recipe file should include a genuinely easy small-batch recipe for a good cookie dough that can be kept in the refrigerator for a few days before baking. This one is great to have on hand when you need something fresh and chocolatey.

DARK CHOCOLATE CHUNK DOUGH

1½ cups bleached all-purpose flour

1 tablespoon unsweetened alkalized cocoa powder

⅛ teaspoon salt

11 tablespoons (1 stick plus 3 tablespoons) unsalted butter, softened

¾ cup granulated sugar

¼ cup firmly packed dark brown sugar

1 large egg

2 teaspoons vanilla extract

2 ounces unsweetened chocolate, melted and cooled

8 ounces bittersweet chocolate, chopped into small chunks

PREHEAT THE OVEN TO 325 DEGREES F. Line several cookie sheets or rimmed sheet pans with cooking parchment paper.

MIX THE DOUGH Sift the flour, cocoa powder, and salt onto a sheet of waxed paper.

 Cream the butter in the large bowl of a freestanding electric mixer on moderately low speed for 3 minutes. Add the granulated sugar in 2 additions, beating on mod-erate speed for 1 minute after each portion is added; add the dark brown sugar and beat for 1 minute longer. Blend in the egg. Mix in the vanilla extract and melted choco-late. On low speed, blend in the sifted ingredients in 2 additions, beating until the flour particles are absorbed. Scrape down the sides of the mixing bowl frequently to keep the dough even-textured. Blend in the chocolate chunks. In hot weather or in a warm kitchen, refrigerate the dough for 1 hour, then proceed with the recipe, pre-heating the oven in advance of baking the cookies.

SHAPE THE COOKIES Place heaping 2-tablespoon-size mounds of dough on the prepared pans, spacing the mounds 2½ to 3 inches apart.

BAKE AND COOL THE COOKIES Bake the cookies in the pre-heated oven for 17 minutes, or until set. Let the cookies stand on the pans for 1 minute to firm up, then transfer them to cooling racks, using a wide offset metal spatula. Store in an airtight tin.

Bake-and-serve within 2 days

STYLE For Dark Chocolate–White Chocolate Chunk Cookies, substitute white chocolate, cut into chunks, for the bittersweet chocolate and blend into the dough after the flour has been added.

STUDY The cookie dough can be refrigerated up to 2 days before baking.

WHITE CHOCOLATE CHIP AND CHUNK BLONDIES

*S*ometimes I'm just not content to stir one shape of chocolate into a blondie batter—so I add both chips and chunks. This is an interesting upgrade, and the combination of chocolate and coconut makes a captivating bar cookie. A bittersweet chocolate version follows.

CHOCOLATE CHIP AND CHUNK BATTER

½ cup plus 2 tablespoons bleached cake flour

½ cup bleached all-purpose flour

¼ teaspoon baking powder

⅛ teaspoon salt

8 tablespoons (1 stick) unsalted butter, melted and cooled to tepid

½ cup plus 3 tablespoons firmly packed light brown sugar

1 large egg

1 large egg yolk

1½ teaspoons vanilla extract

6 ounces white chocolate, cut into small chunks

⅔ cup white chocolate chips

¾ cup sweetened flaked coconut

⅓ cup white chocolate chips, for sprinkling over the top (optional)

PREHEAT THE OVEN TO 350 DEGREES F. Film the inside of an 8 by 8 by 2-inch baking pan with nonstick cooking spray.

MAKE THE BATTER Sift the cake flour, all-purpose flour, baking powder, and salt onto a sheet of waxed paper.

Whisk the melted butter and sugar together in a medium-size mixing bowl, using a wooden spoon or a whisk. Blend in the egg, egg yolk, and vanilla extract. Stir in the sifted mixture with a wooden spoon, mixing until the particles of flour are absorbed. Work in the white chocolate chunks, ⅔ cup white chocolate chips, and the flaked coconut. The batter will be dense and crowded with chips and chunks.

Scrape the batter into the prepared pan and spread evenly. Smooth the top with a rubber spatula. Sprinkle the extra ⅓ cup white chocolate chips over the top, if you are using them.

BAKE, COOL, AND CUT THE BLONDIES Bake the blondies in the preheated oven for 30 minutes, or until set and a light golden color around the edges. Transfer the pan to a rack and cool completely. Cut the entire sweet into quarters with a small sharp knife, then cut each quarter into 4 squares. Carefully remove the blondies from the pan, using a small offset metal spatula. Store in an airtight tin.

Bake-and-serve within 2 days

STYLE For Bittersweet Chocolate Chip and Chunk Blondies, substitute an equal amount of bittersweet chocolate chunks and semisweet chocolate chips for the white chocolate. Use extra semisweet chips for sprinkling over the top.

PEANUT BUTTER–CHOCOLATE CHUNK BARS

2 dozen bars

The flavors of peanut butter and chocolate define this bar cookie; the batter can gracefully accept an ample stir-in (1 cup) of whole roasted peanuts. These are splendidly simple to make.

PEANUT BUTTER CHOCOLATE CHUNK BATTER

1 cup plus 1 tablespoon bleached all-purpose flour

½ teaspoon baking soda

¼ teaspoon salt

8 tablespoons (1 stick) unsalted butter, softened

1 cup firmly packed light brown sugar

2 large eggs

1½ teaspoons vanilla extract

½ cup plus 2 tablespoons smooth peanut butter

1 tablespoon plain vegetable oil (such as canola)

6 ounces bittersweet chocolate, cut into small chunks

4 packages (1.5 ounces each) milk chocolate–covered peanut butter cups (such as Reese's Milk Chocolate Peanut Butter Cups Miniatures), each cup cut into chunks

TOPPING

2 packages (1.5 ounces each) milk chocolate–covered peanut butter cups (such as Reese's Milk Chocolate Peanut Butter Cups Miniatures), each cup cut into chunks

PREHEAT THE OVEN TO 350 DEGREES F. Film the inside of a 9 by 9 by 2-inch baking pan with nonstick cooking spray.

MIX THE BATTER Sift the flour, baking soda, and salt onto a sheet of waxed paper.

Cream the butter in the large bowl of a freestanding electric mixer on moderately low speed for 3 minutes. Add the sugar and continue creaming for 3 minutes longer. Beat in the eggs, one at a time, mixing for 30 to 45 seconds after each addition. Beat in the vanilla extract, peanut butter, and oil. Scrape down the sides of the mixing bowl frequently to keep the batter even-textured. On low speed, mix in the sifted mixture. Blend in the chocolate chunks and 4 packages cut-up peanut butter candy chunks. The batter will be dense and thick.

Scrape the batter into the prepared pan and spread evenly. Smooth the top with a rubber spatula. Sprinkle the 2 packages cut-up peanut butter candy chunks on top.

BAKE AND COOL THE SWEET Bake the sweet in the preheated oven for 25 to 30 minutes, or until set. Transfer the pan to a rack and cool completely. Cut the sweet into quarters with a small sharp knife, then cut each quarter into 6 bars. Carefully remove the bars from the pan, using a small offset metal spatula. Store in an airtight tin.

Bake-and-serve within 2 days

STUDY For the moistest bar cookie, use a creamy peanut butter, such as Jif or Skippy, rather than the all-natural kind.

PEANUT BUTTER–CHOCOLATE CHUNK COOKIES

About 3½ dozen cookies

A freshly baked batch of these peanut butter–seasoned chocolate chunk cookies will fill up the cookie jar in a grand way. I especially like the mellow tone that the brown sugar and ample amount of vanilla extract add to the dense but compliant dough.

PEANUT BUTTER CHOCOLATE CHUNK DOUGH

3 cups bleached all-purpose flour

1½ teaspoons baking soda

½ teaspoon baking powder

½ teaspoon salt

12 tablespoons (1½ sticks) unsalted butter, softened

4 tablespoons shortening

1½ cups firmly packed light brown sugar

½ cup granulated sugar

2 large eggs

2½ teaspoons vanilla extract

1 cup creamy peanut butter (do not use all-natural peanut butter)

12 ounces bittersweet chocolate, chopped into small chunks

PREHEAT THE OVEN TO 350 DEGREES F. Line several cookie sheets or rimmed sheet pans with cooking parchment paper.

MIX THE DOUGH Sift the flour, baking soda, baking powder, and salt onto a sheet of waxed paper.

Cream the butter and shortening in the large bowl of a freestanding electric mixer on moderately low speed for 3 minutes. Add the light brown sugar and beat for 2 minutes. Add the granulated sugar and beat for 1 minute. Add the eggs, one at a time, beating for 45 seconds after each addition. Blend in the vanilla extract and peanut butter. On low speed, blend in the sifted ingredients in 3 additions, beating just until the flour particles are absorbed. Scrape down the sides of the mixing bowl with a rubber spatula to keep the dough even-textured. Mix in the bittersweet chocolate chunks. In hot weather or in a warm kitchen, refrigerate the dough for 45 minutes to 1 hour.

SHAPE THE COOKIES Place rounded 2-tablespoon-size mounds of dough on the prepared pans, spacing the mounds about 3 inches apart. Using the tines of a fork, press down gently on the mounds of dough in a crisscross pattern, flattening them as you do so.

BAKE AND COOL THE COOKIES Bake the cookies in the preheated oven for 12 to 14 minutes, or until set. Let the cookies stand on the pans for 1 minute, then transfer them to cooling racks, using a wide offset metal spatula. Store in an airtight tin.

Bake-and-serve within 2 days

MINI CHIP COFFEE CAKE

A cake that embraces all of the flavors present in a chocolate chip cookie is a joyful thing.

CHOCOLATE CHIP CAKE BATTER

2 cups bleached all-purpose flour

1 cup bleached cake flour

1¾ teaspoons baking soda

1¼ teaspoons baking powder

1 teaspoon salt

2 cups miniature semisweet chocolate chips

½ pound (16 tablespoons or 2 sticks) unsalted butter, softened

1 cup firmly packed light brown sugar

1 cup granulated sugar

4 large eggs

2¼ teaspoons vanilla extract

1 cup milk combined with 1 tablespoon distilled white vinegar and set aside for 15 minutes

Confectioners' sugar, for sifting on top of the baked cake (optional)

PREHEAT THE OVEN TO 350 DEGREES F. Film the inside of a 10-inch Bundt pan with nonstick cooking spray.

MIX THE BATTER Sift the all-purpose flour, cake flour, baking soda, baking powder, and salt onto a sheet of waxed paper. In a small bowl, toss the chocolate chips with 1 tablespoon of the sifted mixture.

Cream the butter in the large bowl of a freestanding electric mixer on moderate speed for 3 to 4 minutes. Add the light brown sugar in 2 additions, beating for 1 minute after each portion is added. Add the granulated sugar in 2 additions, beating for 1 minute after each portion is added. Blend in the eggs, one at a time, beating for 45 seconds after each addition. Scrape down the sides of the mixing bowl frequently to keep the batter even-textured. Blend in the vanilla extract. On low speed, alternately add the sifted mixture in 3 additions with the milk mixture in 2 additions, beginning and ending with the sifted mixture. Stir in the chocolate chips.

Spoon the batter into the prepared pan. Lightly smooth the top with a rubber spatula.

BAKE AND COOL THE CAKE Bake the cake in the preheated oven for 55 minutes, or until risen, set, and a toothpick inserted in the cake withdraws clean. The baked cake will pull away slightly from the sides of the baking pan.

Cool the cake in the pan on a rack for 10 minutes. Invert onto another cooling rack to cool completely. Store in an airtight cake keeper. Just before slicing and serving, sift confectioners' sugar over the top of the cake, if you wish.

Bake-and-serve within 2 days

STUDY Use distilled white vinegar with an acidity level of 5 percent (such as Heinz).

CHOCOLATE CHIP–BANANA TEA CAKE

One 9-inch loaf, creating about 10 slices

Mashing the bananas with an old-fashioned potato masher (or a fork) and a light hand will produce the best-textured cake—soft and moist. A full cup of miniature semisweet chocolate chips adds a terrific dimension of taste to a plain banana loaf.

CHOCOLATE CHIP-BANANA BATTER

2 cups bleached all-purpose flour

2 teaspoons unsweetened alkalized cocoa powder

½ teaspoon baking powder

½ teaspoon baking soda

¼ teaspoon salt

1 cup miniature semisweet chocolate chips

8 tablespoons (1 stick) unsalted butter, softened

1 cup granulated sugar

2 large eggs

2 teaspoons vanilla extract

1 cup mashed ripe bananas (about 3 small bananas)

PREHEAT THE OVEN TO 350 DEGREES F. Film the inside of a 9 by 5 by 3-inch loaf pan with nonstick cooking spray.

MIX THE BATTER Sift the flour, cocoa powder, baking powder, baking soda, and salt onto a sheet of waxed paper. In a small bowl, toss the chocolate chips with 1 teaspoon of the sifted mixture.

Cream the butter in the large bowl of a freestanding electric mixer on moderate speed for 3 minutes. Add the granulated sugar in two additions, beating for 2 minutes on moderate speed after each portion is added. Beat in the eggs, one at a time, blending for 30 to 45 seconds after each addition. Blend in the vanilla extract and mashed bananas. Scrape down the sides of the mixing bowl frequently to keep the batter even-textured. On low speed, add the sifted mixture in 2 additions, mixing until the particles of flour are absorbed. Stir in the chocolate chips.

Spoon the batter into the prepared pan, mounding it slightly in the center.

BAKE AND COOL THE CAKE Bake the tea cake for 1 hour, or until risen, set, and a toothpick inserted in the center withdraws clean. Cool the loaf in the pan on a rack for 10 minutes, then remove it from the pan to another rack. Cool completely. Let the tea cake mellow for 2 to 3 hours before cutting into slices for serving. Store in an airtight cake keeper.

Bake-and-serve within 2 days

CHUNKY CHOCOLATE-COVERED COCONUT CANDY COOKIES

About 2 dozen cookies

*A*lthough this recipe makes a small batch of cookies, the flavors are big and ritzy: the dough is bulky with chocolate-covered coconut candy, flaked coconut, and chocolate chips. The brown sugar adds sweetness and depth, and heightens the taste of the candy and chips.

COCONUT CANDY DOUGH

6 packages (1.9 ounces each) chocolate-covered coconut candy (such as Peter Paul Mounds), cut into small chunks

1½ cups unsifted all-purpose flour

⅛ teaspoon salt

8 tablespoons (1 stick) unsalted butter, softened

3 tablespoons shortening

½ cup granulated sugar

½ cup firmly packed light brown sugar

1 large egg

1 tablespoon vanilla extract

⅔ cup sweetened flaked coconut

¾ cup semisweet chocolate chips

CHILL THE CANDY Place the cut-up candy in a baking pan and refrigerate for 30 minutes. (Refrigerating the chunks of candy will prevent them from breaking up too much when mixed into the dough.)

MIX THE DOUGH Whisk the flour and salt in a small bowl.

Cream the butter and shortening in the large bowl of a freestanding electric mixer on moderately low speed for 3 minutes. Add the granulated sugar and beat for 1 minute on moderate speed. Add the light brown sugar and beat for 1 minute longer. Beat in the egg. Blend in the vanilla ex-tract. Scrape down the sides of the mixing bowl frequently to keep the dough even-textured. On low speed, add the sifted mixture in 2 additions, beating until the particles of flour are absorbed. Mix in the candy chunks, coconut, and chocolate chips. The dough will be chunky.

CHILL THE DOUGH Cover the bowl with a sheet of food-safe plastic wrap and refrigerate for 30 minutes.

PREHEAT THE OVEN TO 325 DEGREES F. in advance of baking. Line several cookie sheets or rimmed sheet pans with lengths of cooking parchment paper.

SHAPE THE COOKIES Place heaping and domed 2-tablespoon-size mounds of dough 3 inches apart on the prepared pans, placing about 9 mounds to a pan.

BAKE AND COOL THE COOKIES Bake the cookies in the pre-heated oven for 16 to 17 minutes, or until set, with pale golden edges. (The tops should not look like glistening, unbaked cookie dough.) Let the cookies stand on the pans for 1 minute, then remove them to cooling racks, using a wide offset metal spatula. Cool completely. Store in an airtight tin.

Bake-and-serve within 3 days

GIANT CHOCOLATE CHIP MUFFINS

*A*mple, and burdened—in the most scrumptious way possible—with chocolate chips, these muffins freeze well, so you can have a stash of them ready to warm up when the urge for something chocolatey strikes. At the coffee hour, for a late-night treat, on a lazy weekend afternoon—cakey, buttery muffins, with enough chocolate chips to crowd every bite, always please.

CHOCOLATE CHIP BATTER

3 cups bleached all-purpose flour

2¾ teaspoons baking powder

¼ teaspoon baking soda

½ teaspoon salt

2 cups semisweet chocolate chips

12 tablespoons (1½ sticks) unsalted butter, softened

½ cup granulated sugar

½ cup firmly packed light brown sugar

2½ teaspoons vanilla extract

3 large eggs

1 cup milk

PREHEAT THE OVEN TO 375 DEGREES F. Film the inside of 9 jumbo muffin/cupcake cups (6 cups to a pan, each cup measuring 4 inches in diameter and 1¾ inches deep, with a capacity of 1⅛ cups) with nonstick cooking spray. Or, line the cups with ovenproof baking paper liners.

MIX THE BATTER Sift the flour, baking powder, baking soda, and salt onto a sheet of waxed paper. In a small bowl, toss the chocolate chips with 1 tablespoon of the sifted mixture.

Cream the butter in the large bowl of a freestanding electric mixer on moderate speed for 3 minutes. Add the granulated sugar and beat for 2 minutes; add the light brown sugar and beat for 2 minutes longer. Blend in the vanilla extract. Beat in the eggs, one at a time, mixing for 30 seconds after each addition. On low speed, alternately add the sifted ingredients in 3 additions with the milk in 2 additions, beginning and ending with the sifted mixture. Scrape down the sides of the mixing bowl frequently to keep the batter even-textured. Stir in the chocolate chips.

Spoon the batter into the prepared cups, dividing it evenly among them.

BAKE AND COOL THE MUFFINS Bake the muffins in the preheated oven for 30 minutes, or until risen, set, and a toothpick inserted into the center of each muffin withdraws clean. (If you bump into a chip or two, the pick will be chocolate-stained—OK.)

Place the muffin pans on cooling racks and let them stand for 20 minutes. Carefully remove the muffins and place on cooling racks. Serve the muffins freshly baked.

Bake-and-serve within 1 day

STUDY The muffins retain their shape if kept in the baking pans for a little while to set, instead of unmolding them within the first 10 minutes of cooling. For this reason, it is preferable to use ovenproof baking paper liners.

THE BAKING PARTNERSHIP OF CHOCOLATE AND NUTS, or nut-based topping such as streusel, is a fine one, for each works to bring out the best in the other. The essential oil present in nuts complements the vitality of chocolate. Nuts add texture and flavor; when used ground or in the form of nut flour (essentially a powdery version of the nut), a dough or batter becomes softly thickened in a wonderfully refined way. Chopped nuts provide a welcome crackle against the backdrop of chocolate in any form—whether melted, in chips or chunks, or in the presence of cocoa powder.

DENSE CHOCOLATE-WALNUT CAKE

One 8-inch cake, creating 8 to 10 slices

This cake is straight chocolate delirium. The ground walnuts, a subtle addition to the solid chocolate batter, are a *discreet* way to introduce nuts into the cake. The nut-crowded candy bar chunks—used in an *indiscreet* way as a topping—simply increases the joy of it all. Crafty.

CHOCOLATE CAKE BATTER

10 ounces bittersweet chocolate, melted and cooled to tepid

12 tablespoons (1½ sticks) unsalted butter, melted and cooled to warm

¼ cup plus 1 tablespoon superfine sugar sifted with 1 tablespoon unsweetened alkalized cocoa powder

⅛ teaspoon salt

4 large eggs, separated

1 large egg yolk

3 tablespoons ground walnuts

2 teaspoons vanilla extract

⅛ teaspoon cream of tartar

TOPPING

3 packages (3.70 ounces each) chocolate and nut candy bars (such as Snickers), cut into chunks

PREHEAT THE OVEN TO 400 DEGREES F. Lightly butter the inside of an 8½-inch springform pan (2½ inches deep).

MIX THE BATTER In a large mixing bowl, whisk the melted chocolate, melted butter, and sugar–cocoa powder mixture until thoroughly blended. Blend in the salt, egg yolks, ground walnuts, and vanilla extract.

Whip the egg whites in a clean, dry bowl until just beginning to mound, add the cream of tartar, and continue whipping until firm (not stiff) peaks are formed. Stir one-quarter of the whipped whites into the chocolate batter, then fold in the remaining whites, combining the two mixtures completely so that no streaks of the beaten whites remain.

Spoon the batter into the prepared pan. Gently smooth the top with a rubber spatula.

BAKE AND COOL THE CAKE Bake the cake in the preheated oven for 19 minutes. Immediately—and carefully—remove the cake from the oven and sprinkle the chunks of candy on the surface. Return the cake to the oven and bake 4 to 5 minutes longer, or until just set.

Cool the cake completely in the pan on a rack. Refrigerate the cake for 2 hours, or until firm enough to cut neatly. Open the hinge on the side of the springform pan and remove the outer ring, allowing the cake to stand on the circular metal base. Serve the cake, cut into thick slices. Store in an airtight cake keeper.

Bake-and-serve within 2 days

WHITE CHOCOLATE, COCONUT, AND MACADAMIA NUT BARS

2 dozen bars

This plush confection, a sweet pick-up treat cut into bars, is a simple finish to a casual dinner and a great cookie to pack up for a picnic.

CHOCOLATE AND COCONUT COOKIE LAYER

8 tablespoons (1 stick) unsalted butter, melted and cooled to tepid

1½ cups plus 3 tablespoons chocolate wafer cookie crumbs (such as crumbs made from Nabisco Famous Chocolate Wafers) combined with 2 tablespoons sweetened flaked coconut

WHITE CHOCOLATE CHIP, COCONUT, AND MACADAMIA NUT LAYER

1⅓ cups white chocolate chips

1½ cups sweetened flaked coconut

1½ cups macadamia nuts (halves and pieces or wholes and halves)

1 can (14 ounces) sweetened condensed milk, combined with 1 teaspoon vanilla extract

PREHEAT THE OVEN TO 350 DEGREES F. Film the inside of a 9 by 9 by 2-inch baking pan with nonstick cooking spray.

MAKE THE COOKIE LAYER Pour the melted butter into the prepared pan. Spoon the cookie crumb mixture evenly over the bottom of the pan and press down lightly with the underside of a small offset metal spatula so that the crumbs absorb the butter. Bake the cookie layer in the preheated oven for 4 minutes. Place the baking pan on a rack. Cool for 5 minutes.

TOP THE COOKIE LAYER Sprinkle the white chocolate chips in an even layer over the cookie base, then top with the coconut and lastly with the nuts. Pour the sweetened condensed milk–vanilla mixture evenly over, making sure to drizzle it along the long edges and corners of the pan. It's important that the sweetened condensed milk be evenly distributed over the top layer if the bars are to be moistly baked throughout.

BAKE, COOL, AND CUT THE COOKIES Bake the bar cookies in the preheated oven for 25 to 30 minutes, or until set. The fully baked bars will be light golden on top.

Let the sweet stand in the baking pan on a rack until completely cool. With a small sharp knife, cut the sweet into quarters, then each quarter into 6 bars. Remove the bars with a small offset metal spatula. Store in an airtight tin.

Bake-and-serve within 2 days

STUDY The vanilla extract added to the sweetened condensed milk cultivates the overall taste of the cookie.

Overbaking the bars will make them dry instead of moist and chewy. Bake them until only just set.

SWEET CHOCOLATE STREUSEL TEA BISCUITS

1 dozen biscuits

*S*ometimes you need to fuss over a biscuit. To make it ornate with a substantial amount of butter and heavy cream. To crowd it with chocolate chips. To top it lavishly. Enter Sweet Chocolate Streusel Tea Biscuits: tender, chocolate chip–endowed, and decorated with streusel.

CHOCOLATE CHIP STREUSEL TOPPING

1¼ cups bleached all-purpose flour

¾ cup firmly packed dark brown sugar

¼ cup granulated sugar

⅛ teaspoon salt

10 tablespoons (1 stick plus 2 tablespoons) cold unsalted butter, cut into chunks

2 teaspoons vanilla extract

¾ cup semisweet chocolate chips

SWEET COCOA-CHOCOLATE CHIP DOUGH

3¾ cups plus 2 tablespoons bleached all-purpose flour

⅔ cup unsweetened alkalized cocoa powder

5 teaspoons baking powder

¾ teaspoon salt

¾ cup plus 2 tablespoons granulated sugar

12 tablespoons (1½ sticks) cold unsalted butter, cut into tablespoon-size chunks

4 large eggs

2 teaspoons vanilla extract

1 cup heavy cream

2 cups semisweet chocolate chips

MAKE THE TOPPING In a medium-size mixing bowl, thoroughly combine the flour, dark brown sugar, granulated sugar, and salt. Add the chunks of butter and, using a pastry blender or two round-bladed table knives, reduce the butter to small bits. Mix in the vanilla extract and chocolate chips. Knead the mixture vigorously between your fingertips to form large and small lumps of streusel.

MIX THE DOUGH In a large mixing bowl, sift the flour, cocoa powder, baking powder, salt, and granulated sugar. Whisk the ingredients to blend. Drop in the chunks of butter and, using a pastry blender or two round-bladed table knives, cut the fat into the flour mixture until reduced to pearl-sized pieces. Reduce the fat further to smaller flakes, using your fingertips.

In a medium-size mixing bowl, whisk the eggs, vanilla extract, and heavy cream. Pour the egg and cream mixture over the flour mixture, scatter the chocolate chips over, and stir to form a dough. Knead the dough lightly in the bowl for 30 seconds to 1 minute.

REFRIGERATE THE DOUGH Divide the dough in half. On a lightly floured work surface, pat-and-press or roll each piece into a disk about 8½ inches in diameter. Refrigerate the disks, wrapped in waxed paper, for 20 minutes.

PREHEAT THE OVEN TO 400 DEGREES F. Line 2 heavy cookie sheets or rimmed sheet pans with lengths of cooking parchment paper.

FORM THE BISCUITS With a chef's knife, cut each disk into 6 wedges. As the biscuits are cut, press in any chips that may stick out of the sides. Press some of the streusel mixture on top of each biscuit. Press down lightly on the streusel so that it adheres and plump up the sides.

Transfer the biscuits to the prepared pans, placing them 3 inches apart. Assemble 6 biscuits on each pan.

BAKE AND COOL THE BISCUITS Bake the biscuits in the preheated oven for 18 to 20 minutes, or until set. Transfer the pans to cooling racks. Let the biscuits stand on the pans for 1 minute, then carefully remove them to cooling racks, using a wide offset metal spatula. Cool completely.

Bake-and-serve within 2 days.

STUDY Don't worry if you squash the biscuits in the process of patting down the streusel topping. To restore the shape of the biscuits, place them on the pans, then lightly press together the sides with your fingertips or with a palette knife.

MAKING STREUSEL—combing flour, butter, and sugar into moist lumps—is not a gentle act. You have to get in there with your hands and squeeze and crumble the mixture to create those buttery globs that bake into a pebbly but tender topping for muffins, scones, and coffee cakes. In the delicate world of cake and pastry-making, a streusel mixture disrupts the polished and civilized pace—in the nicest way possible.

Wimpy streusel is like flaky sand. It never comes together in rich lumps, large and small. It's almost as if someone abandoned the mixture in the middle of it all. Many good cooks I know stop midway in the process, thinking that the mixture might be over-handled. They think that they are making pastry dough! Really, this is a topping that can be handled vigorously, and only reaches a certain transcendent texture during baking when it is manipulated into such clumpy submission.

A case against wimpy streusel

A streusel mixture, which becomes a grand and imposing topping, is assembled in a technically rough-and-tumble way. So get in there, and take control of that bowl of basic ingredients: it will yield one fabulous topping that's bumpy and gently crunchy. The landscape of a proper streusel is bold, craggy, buttery beyond belief, and the very best blanket for a coffee cake batter or an ample batch of scones.

SOUR CREAM–CHOCOLATE CHIP STREUSEL CAKE

One 10-inch cake, creating 12 squares

*L*ots of streusel tops this coffee cake, and to ensure that the cake and its bumpy, buttery cover bake evenly, use the proper size pan and sprinkle the streusel evenly over the surface of the batter. By evenly, I mean that you should sprinkle the streusel to the very edges of the pan in a layer that is uniformly thick. The buttery, chocolate chip–laden sour cream batter is a beauty.

CHOCOLATE CHIP STREUSEL TOPPING

1 cup bleached all-purpose flour

⅔ cup granulated sugar

Large pinch of salt

8 tablespoons (1 stick) cold unsalted butter, cut into chunks

¾ teaspoon vanilla extract

½ cup miniature semisweet chocolate chips

SOUR CREAM CHOCOLATE CHIP BATTER

2 cups bleached all-purpose flour

1 teaspoon baking powder

¼ teaspoon baking soda

½ teaspoon salt

½ cup miniature semisweet chocolate chips

8 tablespoons (1 stick) unsalted butter, softened

1 cup granulated sugar

2 large eggs

2 teaspoons vanilla extract

1 cup sour cream

Confectioners' sugar, for sprinkling on top of the baked cake (optional)

PREHEAT THE OVEN TO 350 DEGREES F. Film the inside of a 10 by 10 by 2-inch baking pan with nonstick cooking spray.

MAKE THE TOPPING Thoroughly combine the flour, sugar, and salt in a large mixing bowl. Drop in the chunks of butter and, using a pastry blender or two round-bladed table knives, cut the fat into the flour until reduced to small pieces about the size of large pearls. Sprinkle the vanilla extract and chocolate chips over it. Toss lightly. With your fingertips, knead the mixture together until moist lumps are formed, integrating the chips as you do so.

MIX BATTER Sift the flour, baking powder, baking soda, and salt onto a sheet of waxed paper. In a small bowl, toss the chocolate chips with ¾ teaspoon of the sifted mixture.

Cream the butter in the large bowl of a freestanding electric mixer on moderate speed for 3 minutes. Add half of the granulated sugar and beat for 1 minute on moderate speed. Add the remaining granulated sugar and beat for 1 minute longer. Mix in the eggs, one at a time, beating for 45 seconds after each addition. Blend in the vanilla extract. On low speed, alternately add the sifted mixture in 3 additions with the sour cream in 2 additions, beginning and ending with the sifted mixture. Scrape down the sides of the mixing bowl frequently to keep the batter even-textured. Stir in the chocolate chips.

Spoon the batter into the prepared pan. Lightly smooth the top with a rubber spatula.

Sprinkle the streusel topping evenly over the cake batter.

BAKE AND COOL THE CAKE Bake the cake in the preheated oven for 45 to 50 minutes, or until risen, set, golden, and a toothpick inserted in the cake withdraws clean, or with a few crumbs attached to it. The baked cake will pull away slightly from the sides of the baking pan.

Cool the cake in the pan on a rack. Cut the cake into squares directly from the baking pan. Sift confectioners' sugar over the squares of cake just before serving, if you wish.

Bake-and-serve within 3 days

BUTTERY AND NUT-SPECKLED, toffee—with its polished caramel taste—is the perfect addition to a creamy coffee cake batter, a cookie or sweet biscuit dough, or a thick brownie batter. It adds pools of flavor in a crunchy-chewy, mellow way. Toffee is one of those sweet seasoning agents that I find completely irresistible, so I always keep it on hand for that must-have-a-toffee-sweet kind of indulgence. Find your favorite brand of toffee to use, from bars traditionally found at the supermarket all the way to handmade artisan slabs and chunks, and start baking.

TOFFEE-MILK CHOCOLATE CHIP CAKE

One 10-inch cake, creating 16 slices

A full complement of chopped toffee, almonds, and milk chocolate chips accents this coffee cake batter. Light brown sugar not only sweetens the cake but serves to flatter the flavor of the toffee and chips. It is a happy jumble of baking ingredients.

SOUR CREAM TOFFEE-MILK CHOCOLATE CHIP BATTER

2¼ cups bleached all-purpose flour

¾ cup bleached cake flour

1¾ teaspoons baking powder

1 teaspoon baking soda

¾ teaspoon salt

7 packages (1.4 ounces each) milk chocolate-covered toffee (such as Heath Milk Chocolate English Toffee Bar), chopped

1 cup milk chocolate chips

½ cup slivered almonds

½ pound (16 tablespoons or 2 sticks) unsalted butter, softened

1¼ cups granulated sugar

¾ cup firmly packed light brown sugar

3 large eggs

2½ teaspoons vanilla extract

1⅓ cups plus 2 tablespoons sour cream

Confectioners' sugar, for sprinkling on top of the baked cake

PREHEAT THE OVEN TO 350 DEGREES F. Film the inside of a 10-inch Bundt pan with nonstick cooking spray.

MIX THE BATTER Sift the all-purpose flour, cake flour, baking powder, baking soda, and salt onto a sheet of waxed paper. In a medium-size bowl, toss the toffee, milk chocolate chips, and almonds with 4 teaspoons of the sifted mixture.

Cream the butter in the large bowl of a freestanding electric mixer on moderate speed for 3 minutes. Add half of the granulated sugar and beat for 2 minutes. Add the remaining granulated sugar and beat for 1 minute. Add the light brown sugar and beat for 2 minutes longer. Blend in the eggs, one at a time, beating for 45 seconds after each addition. Blend in the vanilla extract.

On low speed, alternately add the sifted mixture in 3 additions with the sour cream in 2 additions, beginning and ending with the sifted mixture. Scrape down the sides of the mixing bowl frequently to keep the batter even-textured. Stir in the toffee, milk chocolate chips, and almonds.

Spoon the batter into the prepared pan. Lightly smooth the top with a rubber spatula.

BAKE AND COOL THE CAKE Bake the cake in the preheated oven for 55 minutes to 1 hour, or until risen, set, and a toothpick inserted in the cake withdraws clean. The baked cake will pull away slightly from the sides of the baking pan.

Cool the cake in the pan on a rack for 10 minutes. Invert onto another cooling rack to cool completely. Store in an airtight cake keeper. Just before slicing and serving, sift confectioners' sugar over the top of the cake. (Note: All baked goods containing toffee should be served at room temperature.)

Bake-and-serve within 3 days

TOFFEE BUTTER BRITTLE CRISPS

*C*runchy and dashing, with the dominant flavors of butter and toffee, these cookies will captivate you. Bake them until they take on a golden color overall, for that is when the taste of the butter, brown sugar, and toffee will merge in a most delectable way and the texture will resemble the best nut brittle candy.

TOFFEE BUTTER DOUGH

2¼ cups sifted bleached all-purpose flour

1 teaspoon baking soda

¾ teaspoon salt

½ pound (16 tablespoons or 2 sticks) unsalted butter, softened

1 cup firmly packed light brown sugar

½ cup granulated sugar

2 large eggs

2¼ teaspoons vanilla extract

12 packages (1.4 ounces each) milk chocolate-covered toffee (such as Heath Milk Chocolate English Toffee Bar), chopped

PREHEAT THE OVEN TO 350 DEGREES F. Line several cookie sheets or rimmed sheet pans with cooking parchment paper.

MIX THE DOUGH Sift the flour, baking soda, and salt onto a sheet of waxed paper.

Cream the butter in the large bowl of a freestanding electric mixer on moderately low speed for 3 minutes. Add the light brown sugar and continue creaming on moderately low speed for 2 minutes longer. Add the granulated sugar and cream for 1 minute longer. Blend in the eggs and vanilla extract. On low speed, blend in the sifted ingredients in 3 additions, beating until the flour particles are absorbed. Scrape down the sides of the mixing bowl frequently to keep the dough even-textured. Blend in the chopped toffee.

SHAPE THE COOKIES Drop level 2-tablespoon-size mounds of dough on the prepared pans, spacing the mounds about 3½ inches apart. These cookies will spread as they bake. Crowding the mounds of dough will make one giant cookie!

BAKE AND COOL THE COOKIES Bake the cookies in the preheated oven for 15 minutes, or until set and evenly golden. The cookies will be somewhat thin, buttery, crisp, and chewy with toffee. Let the cookies stand on the pans for 1 minute, then transfer them to cooling racks, using a wide offset metal spatula. Cool completely. Store in an airtight tin. (Note: All baked goods containing toffee should be served at room temperature.)

Bake-and-serve within 2 days

STYLE For Almond-Toffee Butter Brittle Crisps, blend ½ cup slivered or coarsely chopped almonds into the dough along with the chopped toffee.

STUDY In hot weather or in a hot kitchen, the dough can soften quickly, which will cause the cookies to spread too much as they bake. If necessary, refrigerate the dough for 20 minutes before shaping the individual mounds.

The light brown sugar creates a rich and flavorful, beautifully golden cookie.

LAYERED TOFFEE BARS

*S*weet and chewy, this bar cookie is a good keeper. For the best flavor and texture, be sure to chop up whole toffee bars rather than using packaged toffee bits. These are rich.

CHOCOLATE COOKIE LAYER

8 tablespoons (1 stick) unsalted butter, melted and cooled to tepid

1⅔ cups plus 2 tablespoons chocolate wafer cookie crumbs (such as crumbs made from Nabisco Famous Chocolate Wafers)

COCONUT, TOFFEE, AND ALMOND LAYER

1¼ cups sweetened flaked coconut

1 cup slivered almonds

¾ cup semisweet chocolate chips

10 packages (1.4 ounces each) milk chocolate-covered toffee (such as Heath Milk Chocolate English Toffee Bar), coarsely chopped

1 can (14 ounces) sweetened condensed milk, combined with ½ teaspoon vanilla extract

PREHEAT THE OVEN TO 350 DEGREES F. Film the bottom of a 9 by 9 by 2-inch baking pan with nonstick cooking spray.

MIX THE COOKIE LAYER Pour the melted butter into the prepared pan. Spoon the cookie crumbs evenly over the bottom of the pan and press down lightly with the underside of a small offset metal spatula so that the crumbs absorb the butter.

TOP THE COOKIE LAYER Sprinkle the flaked coconut evenly over the cookie crumb layer. Cover with an even layer of the almonds, then the chocolate chips. Sprinkle the chopped toffee over it. Pour the sweetened condensed milk and vanilla mixture evenly over all, taking care to moisten the corners and sides of the baking pan.

BAKE, COOL, AND CUT THE BARS Bake the sweet in the preheated oven for 30 to 35 minutes, or until set and light golden on top. Transfer the pan to a cooling rack. Cool for 25 minutes. With a small sharp knife, cut the entire sweet into quarters, then cut each quarter into 6 bars. (Cutting the sweet into bars after 25 minutes lets you cut through the toffee candy neatly.) Cool completely. Recut the bars and remove them from the baking pan, using a small offset metal spatula. Store in an airtight tin. (Note: All baked goods containing toffee should be served at room temperature.)

Bake-and-serve within 2 days

STUDY Rich, richer, richest: these bars are filled with candy, nuts, chips, and coconut to confectionlike excess. Cut them into tiny, bite-size squares rather than bars, if you like, and serve as a sweetmeat with coffee.

VERY ROCKY TOFFEE BROWNIES

16 brownies

*W*hat makes this dough so sweetly and texturally rocky? A cluster of chopped toffee and miniature marshmallows and a bundle of slivered almonds. A vanilla cookie layer, sneaked under the brownie batter, is a bewitching contrast.

VANILLA COOKIE LAYER

8 tablespoons (1 stick) unsalted butter, melted and cooled to tepid

1⅔ cups vanilla wafer cookie crumbs (such as crumbs made from Nabisco Nilla wafers)

ROCKY TOFFEE BATTER

1½ cups bleached cake flour

3 tablespoons unsweetened alkalized cocoa powder

¼ teaspoon baking powder

¼ teaspoon salt

7 packages (1.4 ounces each) milk chocolate–covered toffee (such as Heath Milk Chocolate English Toffee Bar), chopped

15 tablespoons (2 sticks less 1 tablespoon) unsalted butter, melted and cooled to tepid

5 ounces unsweetened chocolate, melted and cooled to tepid

3 ounces bittersweet chocolate, melted and cooled to tepid

4 large eggs

2 cups superfine sugar

2½ teaspoons vanilla extract

1 cup slivered almonds

½ cup miniature marshmallows

½ cup semisweet chocolate chips

PREHEAT THE OVEN TO 325 DEGREES F. Film the inside of a 10 by 10 by 2-inch baking pan with nonstick cooking spray.

MAKE THE COOKIE LAYER Pour the melted butter into bottom of the prepared pan. Spoon the cookie crumbs in an even layer on the bottom and lightly press down on the crumbs with the underside of a small offset metal spatula so that the crumbs absorb the butter. Bake the cookie layer in the preheated oven for 4 minutes, then transfer to a cooling rack. Cool for 10 minutes.

MIX THE BATTER Sift the flour, cocoa powder, baking powder, and salt onto a sheet of waxed paper. In a small bowl, toss the toffee chunks with 2 teaspoons of the sifted mixture.

Whisk the melted butter, melted unsweetened chocolate, and melted bittersweet chocolate in a medium-size mixing bowl until smooth. Whisk the eggs in a large mixing bowl to blend, about 45 seconds. Add the superfine sugar and whisk for 1 minute, or until combined. Blend in the melted chocolate-butter mixture. Blend in the vanilla extract. Sift the flour mixture over and stir to form a batter, mixing thoroughly until the particles of flour are absorbed, using a whisk or flat wooden paddle. Stir in the chopped toffee, almonds, marshmallows, and chocolate chips. (You can also reserve a few tablespoons of the toffee, almonds, marshmallows, and chocolate chips to scatter on the top after you smooth the batter in the next step.)

Spoon the batter in large dollops on the cookie crumb layer. Using a flexible palette knife or spatula, spread the batter over the cookie layer.

BAKE, COOL, AND CUT THE SWEET Bake the brownies in the preheated oven for 35 to 38 minutes, or until set. Let the brownies stand in the pan on a cooling rack for 2 hours.

With a small sharp knife, cut the sweet into quarters, then cut each quarter into 4 squares. Refrigerate for 1 hour. Recut the squares and remove them from the baking pan, using a small offset metal spatula. Store in an airtight tin.

(Note: All baked goods containing toffee should be served at room temperature.)

Bake-and-serve within 4 days

STUDY The miniature marshmallows will form chewy little pools in the baked brownies. For a dramatic effect, you can scatter an extra ⅓ cup miniature marshmallows on top of the brownies 5 to 7 minutes before the baking time is up.

SWEET TOFFEE CHIP TEA BISCUITS

1 dozen biscuits

*W*ouldn't it be fantastic if all biscuits were this generously flavored? Together, heavy cream and eggs build the moist texture of the dough, and a blend of toffee and chocolate chips defines its flavor.

SWEET TOFFEE CHIP DOUGH

4 cups bleached all-purpose flour

4 ¾ teaspoons baking powder

1 teaspoon salt

¾ cup granulated sugar

¼ cup firmly packed light brown sugar

10 tablespoons (1 stick plus 2 tablespoons) cold unsalted butter, cut into chunks

3 large eggs

2 large egg yolks

1 tablespoon plus 2 teaspoons vanilla extract

1 cup heavy cream

10 packages (1.4 ounces each) milk chocolate–covered toffee (such as Heath Milk Chocolate English Toffee Bar), chopped

1½ cups semisweet chocolate chips

About ⅓ cup semisweet chocolate chips, for finishing the unbaked biscuits

MIX THE DOUGH In a large mixing bowl, whisk the flour, baking powder, salt, and granulated sugar to blend. Sieve the light brown sugar over and stir it in. Drop in the chunks of butter and, using a pastry blender or two round-bladed table knives, cut the fat into the flour mixture until reduced to pearl-sized pieces. Using your fingertips, further reduce the fat to smaller bits and flakes. In a medium-size mixing bowl, whisk the eggs, egg yolks, vanilla extract, and heavy cream. Pour the egg and cream mixture over the flour mixture. Add the chopped toffee

and chocolate chips, and stir to form a dough. Knead the dough lightly in the bowl for 30 seconds to 1 minute.

KNEAD AND REFRIGERATE THE DOUGH Turn the dough out onto a floured work surface and knead lightly for 1 minute, dusting the dough with flour as necessary to keep it from sticking.

Divide the dough in half, form each piece into an 8 to 8½-inch disk, wrap in waxed paper, and refrigerate for 20 minutes.

PREHEAT THE OVEN TO 400 DEGREES F. Line 2 heavy cookie sheets or rimmed sheet pans with lengths of cooking parchment paper.

FORM AND TOP THE BISCUITS Place each disk of dough on a lightly floured work surface, and using a chef's knife, cut into 6 wedges. As the biscuits are cut, press in any chips or bits of toffee that may stick out of the sides. Press a sprinkling of chocolate chips on the top of each biscuit.

Transfer the biscuits to the prepared pans, placing them 3 inches apart. Assemble 6 biscuits on each pan.

BAKE AND COOL THE BISCUITS Bake the biscuits in the preheated oven for 17 to 18 minutes, or until set and baked through. Transfer the biscuits to cooling racks, using a wide offset metal spatula. Cool. Serve the biscuits freshly baked. (Note: All baked goods containing toffee should be served at room temperature.)

Bake-and-serve within 1 day

STUDY As you are pressing the chocolate chips on the top of the biscuits, they may sag slightly. If this happens, plump up the sides with your fingertips or palette knife to restore their shape.

CHOCOLATE TOFFEE SLABS

*T*hick, sumptuous squares of this chocolate-and-toffee conspiracy will make you enormously popular with anyone in their vicinity, for they test the boundaries of richness in a bar cookie batter. But, when you think about it, is there really any limit to lavishness when it comes to a chocolate dessert?

DARK CHOCOLATE AND TOFFEE BAR COOKIE BATTER

1¼ cups bleached cake flour

2 tablespoons unsweetened alkalized cocoa powder

¼ teaspoon baking powder

¼ teaspoon salt

8 packages (1.4 ounces each) milk chocolate–covered toffee (such as Heath Milk Chocolate English Toffee Bar), coarsely chopped

½ pound (16 tablespoons or 2 sticks) unsalted butter, melted and cooled to tepid

6 ounces unsweetened chocolate, melted and cooled to tepid

4 large eggs

2 cups superfine sugar combined with 2 tablespoons ground almonds

1½ teaspoons vanilla extract

¾ teaspoon almond extract

PREHEAT THE OVEN TO 325 DEGREES F. Film the inside of a 10 by 10 by 2-inch baking pan with nonstick cooking spray.

MIX THE BATTER Sift the flour, cocoa powder, baking powder, and salt onto a sheet of waxed paper. In a small bowl, toss the chopped toffee with 2 teaspoons of the sifted mixture.

In a medium-size mixing bowl, whisk the melted butter and melted chocolate until smooth. In a large mixing bowl, whisk the eggs until blended, about 15 seconds. Add the sugar-almond mixture and whisk until combined, about 30 seconds. Blend in the vanilla extract, the almond extract, and the melted butter-chocolate mixture. Sift the flour mixture over and stir to form a batter, mixing thoroughly until the particles of flour are absorbed, using a whisk or flat wooden paddle. Stir in the chopped toffee.

Scrape the batter into the prepared pan and spread evenly. Smooth the top with a rubber spatula.

BAKE, COOL, AND CUT THE SWEET Bake the sweet in the preheated oven for 35 to 40 minutes, or until set. Cool for 30 minutes. With a small sharp knife, cut the sweet into quarters, then cut each quarter into 4 squares. Cutting the sweet into squares after 30 minutes lets you cut through the toffee neatly. Refrigerate for 1 hour. Recut the squares and remove them from the pan, using a small offset metal spatula. Store in an airtight tin. (Note: All baked goods containing toffee should be served at room temperature.)

Bake-and-serve within 4 days

CLASSIC TOFFEE BARS

2 dozen bars

*E*asy to put together by hand, these bar cookies are moist, with a light caramelly flavor. Shortly before the sweet has completely baked, consider topping it with extra chopped toffee for a ravishing, dramatic touch.

TOFFEE BAR COOKIE BATTER

1 cup bleached all-purpose flour

¼ teaspoon baking powder

¼ teaspoon baking soda

¼ teaspoon salt

8 tablespoons (1 stick) unsalted butter, melted and cooled to tepid

½ cup firmly packed light brown sugar

⅓ cup granulated sugar

2 large eggs

2 teaspoons vanilla extract

7 packages (1.4 ounces each) milk chocolate–covered toffee (such as Heath Milk Chocolate English Toffee Bar), chopped

1 cup sweetened flaked coconut

¾ cup semisweet chocolate chips

TOPPING (OPTIONAL)

4 packages (1.4 ounces each) milk chocolate–covered toffee (such as Heath Milk Chocolate English Toffee Bar), coarsely chopped

PREHEAT THE OVEN TO 350 DEGREES F. Film the inside of an 8 by 8 by 2-inch baking pan with nonstick cooking spray.

MAKE THE BATTER Sift the flour, baking powder, baking soda, and salt onto a sheet of waxed paper.

In a large mixing bowl, whisk the melted butter, light brown sugar, granulated sugar, eggs, and vanilla extract. Add the sifted mixture and chopped toffee, and stir to form a batter, using a wooden spoon or flat wooden paddle. Mix until the particles of flour are absorbed. Blend in the coconut and chocolate chips.

Scrape the batter into the prepared pan and spread evenly. Smooth the top with a rubber spatula.

BAKE, COOL, AND CUT THE SWEET Bake the sweet for 30 to 35 minutes or until softly set and golden on top. (If you wish, after 20 minutes, sprinkle the additional chunks of toffee over the top and continue baking for an another 10 to 15 minutes.) Cool for 30 minutes. With a small sharp knife, cut the sweet into quarters, then cut each quarter into 6 bars. Dividing the sweet into bars after 30 minutes lets you cut through the toffee neatly. Cool completely. Recut the bars and remove them from the baking pan, using a small offset metal spatula. Store in an airtight tin. (Note: All baked goods containing toffee should be served at room temperature.)

Bake-and-serve within 2 days

STYLE For Classic Toffee Bars with Almonds, blend ½ cup chopped or slivered almonds into the batter along with the coconut and chocolate chips.

TOFFEE TRIANGLES

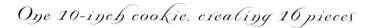

One 10-inch cookie, creating 16 pieces

The dough for these tender triangles is modeled after shortbread, but oh, what a glamorous kind of shortbread it is—the addition of chopped toffee and chocolate chips makes a sweet and fancy impression in the dough.

TOFFEE BUTTER DOUGH

1½ cups bleached all-purpose flour

¼ teaspoon baking powder

⅛ teaspoon salt

12 tablespoons (1½ sticks) unsalted butter, softened

⅓ cup plus 2 tablespoons superfine sugar

2 teaspoons vanilla extract

5 packages (1.4 ounces each) milk chocolate–covered toffee (such as Heath Milk Chocolate English Toffee Bar), chopped

½ cup semisweet chocolate chips or 4 ounces bittersweet chocolate, chopped

PREHEAT THE OVEN TO 350 DEGREES F. Have a fluted 10-inch round tart pan (1 inch deep, with a removable bottom) at hand.

MAKE THE DOUGH Sift the flour, baking powder, and salt onto a sheet of waxed paper.

Cream the butter in the large bowl of a freestanding electric mixer on low speed for 2 minutes. Add the sugar and beat on moderately low speed for 1 minute. Blend in the vanilla extract. On moderately low speed, blend in half of the sifted dry ingredients and the chopped toffee and chocolate chips (or chopped bittersweet chocolate). Blend in the remaining sifted ingredients and mix to form a dough, beating slowly until the particles of flour are absorbed. Scrape down the sides of the mixing bowl frequently to keep the dough even-textured.

Turn the dough into the pan and press it into an even layer.

BAKE, COOL, AND CUT THE COOKIE Bake the shortbread in the preheated oven for 35 to 40 minutes, or until set and golden. Cool the shortbread in the pan on a rack for 15 minutes. Carefully unmold the cookie, leaving it on its round base. Cut the cookie into 16 triangular wedges, using a chef's knife or serrated knife. Cool completely. Store in an airtight tin. (Note: All baked goods containing toffee should be served at room temperature.)

Bake-and-serve within 1 week

STUDY Press the dough into the tart pan with a light hand to avoid compacting it.

IN MY HOME, CHOCOLATE IS A CELEBRATION FLAVOR EVERY DAY, and even more so at a festive milestone event. On my birthday, I must have a slice of chocolate cake covered in a rich and buttery coconut frosting. It's a ritual. A birthday should be celebrated with a slice of *homemade* cake, baked to perfection and presented on a pretty plate or footed cake stand.

Spread the chilled, thick chocolate cream filling on the bottom layer to about ½ inch of the sides. Carefully position the second layer on top. Frost the top and sides of the cake, swirling the frosting as you go. Once set, gently remove and discard the strips of paper. Let the cake stand for 1 hour to 1 hour and 30 minutes before slicing and serving. (Any cake not eaten after 2 hours should be refrigerated in an airtight cake container.)

Bake-and-serve within 1 day

STUDY The cake batter can also be baked in a 13 by 9 by 2-inch pan for 40 to 43 minutes, or until set, and a toothpick inserted into the center withdraws clean (or with a few crumbs attached). Omit the filling. Frost the cooled cake in the pan. For serving, cut squares of cake directly from the pan.

CHOCOLATE CREAM FILLING

About 2½ cups pastry cream

*T*his gossamer filling connects two layers of cake in a sweet and nimble way.

¾ cup plus 2 tablespoons granulated sugar

¼ cup cornstarch

2 teaspoons unsweetened alkalized cocoa powder

Large pinch of salt

2 cups light (table) cream, scalded and cooled to warm

3½ ounces bittersweet chocolate, melted

5 large egg yolks

1¼ teaspoons vanilla extract

2 tablespoons unsalted butter, cut into cubes

Sift the sugar, cornstarch, cocoa powder, and salt into a heavy, medium-size saucepan (preferably enameled cast iron). The pan must be heavy (or the pastry cream may scorch) and large enough to contain the ingredients. Whisk the ingredients to combine. Slowly blend about ¼ cup of the cream into the cornstarch mixture. Gradually stir in the remaining cream and the melted chocolate, mixing slowly to combine.

Place the saucepan over moderately high heat and bring to the boil, stirring slowly with a wooden spoon or flat paddle. Do not use a whisk. When bubbles begin to appear (you'll hear the pudding make "plop-plop-plop" sounds) and the cream is thickened, reduce the heat and cook at a low boil for 1 minute. Remove the saucepan from the heat.

Mix the egg yolks in a small bowl to combine. Stir in ½ cup of the hot cream mixture. Gradually stir the mixture back into the contents of the pan, mixing well. Return the saucepan to the heat and bring to a low boil. Cook, stirring, for 1 minute or until the filling has thickened. The filling should reach a temperature of 200 degrees F. to achieve the correct stability and thickness. Remove from the heat. Stir in the vanilla extract.

Place the butter in the bottom of a medium-size heat-proof mixing bowl.

Set a large sieve on top of the bowl and scrape the pastry cream into it. Smooth the pastry cream through the sieve, using a heatproof rubber spatula. Mix slowly to incorporate the softened butter; it will melt into and combine with the pastry cream.

Immediately press a sheet of food-safe plastic wrap on the surface of the cream. Cool for 20 minutes. Remove and discard the plastic wrap. Scrape the filling into a storage container, press a clean sheet of plastic wrap on the surface, cover, and refrigerate for at least 6 hours before using.

The cream filling can be made up to 1 day in advance and stored in the refrigerator, tightly covered.

STUDY Avoid stirring or whisking the cream filling after it is made, or it may turn soupy. Work with it gently.

ELEMENT Put the chilled filling in a pastry bag fitted with the éclair tip (Wilton No. 230) and squirt it into the middle of vanilla or chocolate cupcakes, such as Grand Chocolate Chip Cakes (page 114), Big and Bountiful Chocolate Cupcakes (page 105), or The Cupcakes of My Childhood (page 291).

OLD-FASHIONED CHOCOLATE FROSTING

About 5 cups frosting

A supple chocolate frosting is always so beguiling, and especially welcome on a layered birthday cake.

9 tablespoons (1 stick plus 1 tablespoon) unsalted butter, softened

8 ounces unsweetened chocolate, melted and cooled to tepid

Large pinch of salt

1 tablespoon vanilla extract

6¾ cups confectioners' sugar, sifted

¾ cup milk, heated to tepid

Place the butter in the bowl of a heavy-duty freestanding electric mixer fitted with the flat paddle attachment. Beat on moderate speed for 1 minute. Blend in the melted chocolate, salt, vanilla extract, and 1 cup of the confectioners' sugar. Beat for 1 minute. Add the remaining confectioners' sugar in 3 additions, with the milk in 2 additions, beginning and ending with the sugar. Beat on moderately high speed for 3 to 4 minutes, or until quite smooth, lightened in texture somewhat, and nicely creamy. Scrape down the sides of the mixing bowl frequently to keep the frosting even-textured. Adjust the texture of the frosting to spreading consistency, as needed, by adding additional teaspoons of milk or tablespoons of confectioners' sugar. Use the frosting immediately.

STUDY A generous amount of butter and chocolate makes this frosting one you're not likely to forget. It's simple to make, and delightful to use for spreading over almost any kind of chocolate (or vanilla) layer or sheet cake.

DARK CHOCOLATE BIRTHDAY CAKE

One 13 by 9-inch cake, creating 20 squares

The chocolate flavor in this cake batter is substantial and expansive. Squares of the cake, covered with any of the rich frostings in this book, and nestled in ruffled individual paper cups, also make a fine bake-sale item or picnic dessert.

CHOCOLATE CAKE BATTER

1 cup milk

2 teaspoons distilled white vinegar

3 cups bleached cake flour

1 tablespoon unsweetened alkalized cocoa powder

1 teaspoon baking soda

¾ teaspoon salt

12 tablespoons (1½ sticks) unsalted butter, softened

1¾ cups plus 3 tablespoons superfine sugar

5 large eggs

4 ounces unsweetened chocolate, melted and cooled

2 teaspoons vanilla extract

FROSTING

Old-Fashioned Chocolate Frosting (page 195) or
Chocolate Butter Frosting (page 119)

PREHEAT THE OVEN TO 350 DEGREES F. Lightly grease the inside of a 13 by 9 by 2-inch baking pan with shortening and dust with flour.

MIX THE BATTER Combine the milk and vinegar in a small bowl. Set aside.

Sift the flour, cocoa powder, baking soda, and salt onto a sheet of waxed paper.

Cream the butter in the large bowl of a freestanding electric mixer on moderate speed for 3 minutes. Add the sugar in 3 additions, beating for 1 minute after each portion is added. Add the eggs, one at a time, beating for 45 seconds after each addition. On low speed, beat in the melted chocolate and vanilla extract. On low speed, alternately add the sifted mixture in 3 additions with the milk-vinegar mixture in 2 additions, beginning and ending with the sifted mixture. Scrape down the sides of the mixing bowl frequently to keep the batter even-textured.

Spoon the batter into the prepared pan and spread evenly. Smooth the top with a rubber spatula.

BAKE, COOL, AND FROST THE CAKE Bake the cake in the preheated oven for 40 minutes, or until risen, set, and a toothpick inserted in the center withdraws clean (or with a few crumbs attached). Cool the cake in the pan on a rack. Spread the frosting on the cake, swirling it as you go. Let the cake stand for 1 hour before cutting into squares for serving.

Bake-and-serve within 1 day

STUDY Use a plain (unseasoned) vinegar with 5 percent acidity.

The small amount of cocoa powder underpins the chocolate flavor in the batter.

The superfine sugar keeps the finished texture fine and light.

MY FIRST CHOCOLATE BIRTHDAY CAKE

One 2-layer, 9-inch cake, creating 12 slices

*P*lain and simple, this layer cake most likely began the tradition of chocolate-flavored birthday cakes in my small family. The Retro February 27th Birthday Cake on page 192 chronologically followed this cake years later, and both are well-preserved in my baking consciousness.

CHOCOLATE CAKE BATTER

2½ cups bleached cake flour

1½ teaspoons baking soda

¼ teaspoon salt

10⅔ tablespoons (1 stick plus 2⅔ tablespoons) unsalted butter, softened

1½ cups plus 2 tablespoons superfine sugar

2 large eggs

2 teaspoons vanilla extract

4 ounces unsweetened chocolate, melted and cooled

1 cup milk

FROSTING

Old-Fashioned Chocolate Frosting (page 195)

PREHEAT THE OVEN TO 350 DEGREES F. Lightly grease the inside of two 9-inch layer cake pans (1½ inches deep) with shortening, line the bottom of each pan with a circle of waxed paper cut to fit, grease the paper, and dust with flour.

MIX THE BATTER Sift the flour, baking soda, and salt onto a sheet of waxed paper.

Cream the butter in the large bowl of a freestanding electric mixer on moderate speed for 3 minutes. Add the sugar in 3 additions, beating for 1 minute after each portion is added. Add the eggs, one at a time, beating for 45 seconds after each addition. Blend in the vanilla extract and melted chocolate. On low speed, alternately add the sifted mixture in 3 additions with the milk in 2 additions, beginning and ending with the sifted mixture. Scrape down the sides of the mixing bowl frequently to keep the batter even-textured.

Spoon the batter into the prepared pans, dividing it evenly between them. Spread the batter evenly.

BAKE AND COOL THE LAYERS Bake the cake layers in the preheated oven for 30 minutes, or until risen, set, and a toothpick inserted in the center of each layer withdraws clean (or with a few crumbs attached). Cool the layers in the pans on racks for 10 minutes. Invert the layers onto other cooling racks, peel away the waxed paper, and cool completely.

SET UP THE SERVING PLATE Tear off four 3-inch-wide strips of waxed paper. Place the strips in the shape of a square around the outer 3 inches of a cake plate.

ASSEMBLE AND FROST THE CAKE Center one cake layer on the plate (partially covering the waxed paper square; the strips should extend by at least 1 inch). Spread over a layer of frosting. Carefully position the second layer on top. Frost the top and sides of the cake, swirling the frosting as you go. Once set, gently remove and discard the strips of paper. Let the cake stand for 1 hour before slicing and serving.

Bake-and-serve within 1 day

ACCENT Reduce the vanilla extract to 1½ teaspoons. Add ½ teaspoon chocolate extract along with the vanilla extract.

MOUNTAIN-OF-COCONUT CHOCOLATE CAKE

One 3-layer, 8-inch cake, creating 12 slices

This three-layer chocolate cake is tall, lyrical, and imposing. The frosted layers are covered in coconut, and this is my sweet, cakey tribute to a beloved ice cream dessert—the chocolate snowball—I've adored since my childhood days when I was taken to a fancy Polynesian restaurant as a treat at the end of each school year. The White Chocolate Frosting that follows is an arresting color and flavor contrast to the layers of cake, although I am charmed by the Deep Chocolate Frosting, as it peeks though the coconut on the tall sides of the cake.

CHOCOLATE CAKE BATTER

2½ cups bleached cake flour

1 teaspoon baking soda

¼ teaspoon salt

½ pound (16 tablespoons or 2 sticks) unsalted butter, softened

1½ cups superfine sugar

½ cup firmly packed light brown sugar

4 large eggs

2½ teaspoons vanilla extract

4 ounces unsweetened chocolate, melted and cooled

1½ cups buttermilk, whisked well

FROSTING

White Chocolate Frosting (page 206) or

Chocolate Satin Frosting (page 306) or

Chocolate Butter Frosting (page 119) or

Deep Chocolate Frosting (page 297)

About 6 cups sweetened flaked coconut, to finish the cake

PREHEAT THE OVEN TO 350 DEGREES F. Lightly grease the inside of three 8-inch layer cake pans (1½ inches deep) with shortening, line the bottom of each pan with a circle of waxed paper cut to fit, grease the paper, and dust with flour.

MIX THE BATTER Sift the flour, baking soda, and salt onto a sheet of waxed paper.

Cream the butter in the large bowl of a freestanding electric mixer on moderate speed for 3 minutes. Add the superfine sugar in 3 additions, beating for 1 minute after each portion is added. Add the light brown sugar and beat for 1 minute longer. Add the eggs, one at a time, beating for 45 seconds after each addition. Blend in the vanilla extract and melted chocolate.

On low speed, alternately add the sifted mixture in 3 additions with the buttermilk in 2 additions, beginning and ending with the sifted mixture. Scrape down the sides of the mixing bowl frequently to keep the batter even-textured.

Spoon the batter into the prepared pans, dividing it evenly among them. Spread the batter evenly.

BAKE AND COOL THE LAYERS Bake the cake layers in the preheated oven for 30 minutes, or until risen, set, and a toothpick inserted in the center of each layer withdraws clean (or with a few crumbs attached). Cool the layers in the pans on racks for 10 minutes. Invert the layers onto other cooling racks, peel away the waxed paper, and cool completely.

SET UP THE SERVING PLATE Tear off four 3-inch-wide strips of waxed paper. Place the strips in the shape of a square around the outer 3 inches of a cake plate.

ASSEMBLE AND FROST THE CAKE Center one cake layer on the plate (partially covering the waxed paper square; the strips should extend by at least 1 inch). Spread over a layer of frosting. Carefully position the second layer on top. Cover with a layer of frosting. Top with the remaining cake layer.

Frost the top and sides of the cake, spreading it smoothly, using a sturdy palette knife or frosting spatula.

GARNISH WITH COCONUT Lightly press the coconut on the sides of the cake. Pile more coconut on top, creating a dome. Once set, gently remove and discard the strips of paper. Sprinkle a little of the coconut on the rim of the cake plate to form a ruffled, petticoat effect, if you wish. Let the cake stand for 1 hour before slicing and serving.

Bake-and-serve within 1 day

WHITE CHOCOLATE FROSTING

About 4 cups frosting

Sweet and rich, without a doubt this is the frosting to spread in unrestrained amounts over layers of cake and cupcakes, or—for the sweetest splurge of all—over a large pan of dark chocolate brownies, like the ChocolateChocolate Squares on page 385.

12 tablespoons (1½ sticks) unsalted butter, softened

4 cups confectioners' sugar, sifted

Large pinch of salt

3 ounces white chocolate, melted and cooled to tepid

⅓ cup milk, heated to tepid

1 tablespoon vanilla extract

Place the butter in the bowl of a heavy-duty freestanding electric mixer fitted with the flat paddle attachment. Beat on moderate speed for 1 to 2 minutes. Beat in one-third of the confectioners' sugar and salt. Blend in the melted chocolate, then another third of the confectioners' sugar and milk. Beat for 2 minutes on moderately high speed. Beat in the remaining confectioners' sugar and vanilla. Beat on moderately high speed for 2 to 3 minutes, or until the frosting is very smooth. Scrape down the sides of the mixing bowl frequently to keep the frosting even-textured. Adjust the texture of the frosting to spreading consistency, as needed, by adding additional teaspoons of milk or tablespoons of confectioners' sugar. Use the frosting immediately.

STUDY In a hot kitchen, or on a humid day, you may need to add up to ½ cup additional confectioners' sugar for the frosting to spread easily. If the frosting is too soft, thicken by adding the confectioners' sugar, 2 tablespoons at a time. On a cool day or in a cold kitchen, you may need to soften the frosting by adding additional milk, 2 teaspoons at a time (there is no need to warm the milk).

For an abundant amount of frosting to use for enclosing between layers of cake and for decorative piping, make two separate batches rather than doubling the ingredients; this protects the fluidity of the melted white chocolate when combined with the confectioners' sugar.

GENTLY YEASTY. STROKED WITH CHOCOLATE. The flavor of chocolate is transported to another level when it becomes part of a yeast-risen dough. A sweet dough, developed with enough butter and eggs, is a great canvas for drawing in chocolate chips and chunks or coloring with cocoa powder; its flavor can be underscored further by adding an accessory ingredient, such as a creamy icing or crumbly topping. Or, bake high-rising Vanilla Babas, soak those little cakes in syrup, and fill with dollops of pastry cream mixed with fragments of good bittersweet chocolate. How dreamy is that?

CHOCOLATE SWIRLS

18 "panned" sweet rolls or 20 individual muffin-size rolls

These spunky buns—a cocoa powder–imbued yeast dough wrapped around a buttery chocolate chip filling—would add a fine grace note to the brunch bread basket. Who wouldn't feel pampered by something this irresistible?

COCOA YEAST DOUGH

4½ teaspoons active dry yeast

½ teaspoon granulated sugar

⅓ cup warm (105 to 110 degrees F.) water

⅔ cup plus 2 tablespoons milk

7 tablespoons granulated sugar

8 tablespoons (1 stick) unsalted butter, cut into chunks

1 tablespoon vanilla extract

2 large eggs

4 cups bleached all-purpose flour, or more as needed

½ cup plus 2 tablespoons unsweetened alkalized cocoa powder

1 teaspoon salt

CHOCOLATE CHIP FILLING

7 tablespoons (1 stick less 1 tablespoon) unsalted butter, softened

½ cup confectioners' sugar

1 teaspoon vanilla extract

1¼ cups semisweet chocolate chips

ICING

Creamy Vanilla Sweet Roll Icing (page 211)

½ cup semisweet chocolate chips, for scattering over the freshly iced swirls (optional)

MIX THE DOUGH Combine the yeast, the ½ teaspoon sugar, and the water in a small heatproof bowl. Stir well. Let stand until the yeast softens and swells, about 8 minutes. Place the milk, 7 tablespoons sugar, and butter in a small saucepan; set over moderately low heat and let stand for 5 to 8 minutes, or until the butter melts down, stirring occasionally with a wooden spoon. Remove from the heat and pour into a heatproof bowl. Stir in the vanilla extract. Cool the mixture to 110 degrees F., then whisk in the eggs. Stir in the yeast mixture.

In a large mixing bowl, thoroughly combine 3 cups of the flour, cocoa powder, and salt. Pour over the yeast-milk-egg mixture and combine the ingredients with a wooden spatula or flat paddle. Work in the remaining 1 cup of flour, ¼ cup at a time, to create a soft dough. (Depending on the absorption quality of the flour, you may need a little more or a little less.) The dough should be soft and pudgy, but not sticky or stiff. Knead the dough on a lightly floured work surface for 8 to 10 minutes.

SET THE DOUGH TO RISE Place the dough in a well-buttered bowl, and turn to coat all sides in the butter. With a pair of kitchen scissors, cut 4 slashes in the dough. (Cutting the dough in this way gives it a good initial boost and helps to strengthen it as it rises.) Cover the bowl with a sheet of food-safe plastic wrap and let rise at room temperature until doubled in bulk, about 2 hours.

MIX THE CHOCOLATE CHIP FILLING In a small bowl, blend the softened butter, confectioners' sugar, and vanilla extract until creamy. Have the chocolate chips at hand in a small bowl.

Lightly butter the inside of two 9 by 9 by 3-inch square baking pans or 20 muffin cups (12 cups to a pan, each cup measuring 2¾ inches in diameter and 1⅜ inches deep, with a capacity of ½ cup).

ROLL, FILL, AND CUT THE SWEET ROLLS Remove and discard the plastic wrap. Compress the dough with the palm of your hand to deflate lightly. Place the dough on a lightly floured work surface, cover with a sheet of food-safe plastic wrap, and let it rest for 15 minutes. Roll the dough out into a sheet measuring about 16 by 16 inches. Spread the vanilla butter over the surface of the dough. Sprinkle the chocolate chips over the butter. Press down lightly on the chips so that they stick to the butter layer.

Roll up the dough, jelly-roll style. Gently stretch the coil of dough to a length of about 25 inches. Using a chef's knife, Cut the coil into 18 slices if you are making the "panned" rolls or 20 slices if you are making individual rolls in the muffin pans. Arrange the sweet rolls, cut side up, in the prepared square pans, 9 to a pan, placing them in 3 rows of 3 each. Or, place each roll, cut side up, in the prepared muffin cup; twisting the cut pieces slightly before placing them in the muffin cups will give you a pretty, somewhat raised top (this is an optional step).

SET THE SWEET ROLLS TO RISE Cover each pan loosely with a sheet of food-safe plastic wrap. Let the rolls rise at room temperature until doubled in bulk, about 1 hour and 40 minutes.

Preheat the oven to 375 degrees F. in advance of baking. Remove and discard the plastic wrap. Bake the "panned" sweet rolls for 25 to 30 minutes, or until set. Bake the rolls in the muffin pans at 375 degrees F. for 10 minutes, reduce the oven temperature to 350 degrees F., and continue baking for 20 minutes longer, or until set. The baked rolls will pull away slightly from the sides of the pan or cups. Cool for 5 minutes.

ICE AND COOL THE SWEET ROLLS Place a sheet of waxed paper under cooling racks to catch dribbles of icing. Carefully remove the sweet rolls from the baking pans onto cooling racks. Invert the block of rolls baked in the square pan onto a cooling rack, then invert again to cool right side up.

Spoon the icing onto the surface of the warm sweet rolls, here and there. If the icing has been made in advance (or on a chilly day or in a cold kitchen), it will firm up; scoop it up with an icing spatula rather than a spoon. The icing will melt randomly over the surface of the warm rolls and cascade down the sides a bit. Ice individual rolls separately, and the whole panful as one section. Scatter the chocolate chips on top of the icing, if you are using them. Cool. Gently break apart the "panned" rolls where they've connected during the rising and baking process, using a small offset metal spatula. Serve the rolls freshly baked.

Bake-and-serve within 1 day

STYLE For Chocolate-Nut Swirls, sprinkle ¾ cup chopped walnuts or pecans on the buttery filling layer along with the chocolate chips.

STUDY The Creamy Vanilla Sweet Roll Icing is a good complement to the boldly chocolate yeast buns, but you could also use the Chocolate "Spooning" Topping on page 247 as the finishing topping— it would be thoroughly chocolate-on-chocolate, and completely wonderful.

CREAMY VANILLA SWEET ROLL ICING

About 1 cup icing

*F*reshly baked chocolate buns become even more alluring when covered, while still warm, with a soft vanilla icing.

2 cups confectioners' sugar, sifted
2 tablespoons unsalted butter, softened
2 tablespoons plus 2½ teaspoons milk
¾ teaspoon vanilla extract
Pinch of salt

Place the confectioners' sugar, butter, milk, vanilla extract, and salt in a medium-size mixing bowl. Using an electric hand mixer, beat the ingredients to blend on low speed, scraping down the sides of the mixing bowl frequently to keep the icing even-textured. Beat until smooth and creamy.

Adjust the consistency, as necessary, adding a little more milk or confectioner's sugar, to arrive at a medium-thick icing.

Press a sheet of food-safe plastic wrap directly onto the surface of the icing. The icing can be made up to 25 minutes in advance. Use the icing as directed.

CHOCOLATE CHIP CRUMB BUNS

*S*plashes of chocolate chips take over this sweet yeast bread, one that's buttery, laced with a custardy filling, and topped with streusel. As you split apart the baked buns, you will see captivating streaks of the filling—a creamy contrast to the tender crumb of the sweet bread and nubby topping.

CHOCOLATE CHIP YEAST DOUGH

4½ teaspoons active dry yeast

¾ teaspoon granulated sugar

⅓ cup warm (105 to 110 degrees F.) water

⅓ cup milk

⅓ cup granulated sugar

2½ teaspoons vanilla extract

3 large eggs

2 large egg yolks

1 cup sour cream

1½ cups unbleached all-purpose flour

3½ cups bleached all-purpose flour, or more as needed

¾ teaspoon salt

½ pound (16 tablespoons or 2 sticks) unsalted butter, cut into tablespoons, softened

½ cup miniature semisweet chocolate chips

CHOCOLATE CHIP FILLING
Chocolate Chip Cream Filling (page 215)

STREUSEL TOPPING
Chocolate Chip Streusel (page 216)

Confectioners' sugar, for dusting the top of the baked buns (optional)

MIX THE DOUGH Combine the yeast, the ¾ teaspoon granulated sugar, and the warm water in a small heatproof bowl. Stir well. Let stand until the yeast softens and swells, about 8 minutes. In the meantime, place the milk and ⅓ cup granulated sugar in a small saucepan and set over low heat to dissolve the sugar. Remove from the heat and pour into a heatproof bowl; stir in the vanilla extract. Cool the mixture to 110 degrees F., then blend in the swollen yeast mixture, eggs, egg yolks, and sour cream.

In the bowl of a heavy-duty freestanding mixer fitted with the flat paddle attachment, combine the unbleached all-purpose flour, 3 cups of the bleached all-purpose flour, and salt. Add the yeast-egg-milk-sour cream mixture. Mix the dough on low speed for 2 minutes, or until combined. The dough will be shaggy at this point. Scrape off the paddle and the sides of the mixing bowl, cover the bowl with a sheet of food-safe plastic wrap, and let stand for 20 minutes. Remove and discard the plastic wrap.

Replace the flat paddle and continue with the recipe. Add the softened butter, two tablespoons at a time, beating until incorporated before adding the next chunk. Stop the mixer and scrape down the sides of the mixing bowl and the flat paddle frequently during this time. Replace the flat paddle with the dough hook attachment. Beat the dough on moderate to moderately low speed until very smooth and glossy, about 7 to 8 minutes. During the beating process, the dough will make a slapping sound against the sides of the mixing bowl. On low speed, gradually add the remaining ½ cup of flour. When all of the flour is absorbed, beat for 3 to 4 minutes longer on moderately low speed. The dough should be smooth and satiny, and gently elastic.

SET THE DOUGH TO RISE Place the dough into a heavily buttered bowl and turn the dough in the bowl to coat all sides in a film of butter. Using a pair of kitchen scissors, cut several deep slashes in the top of the dough. Slashing the top of the dough helps a yeast dough rich in eggs and butter to rise. Cover the bowl with a sheet of food-safe plastic wrap. Let the dough rise at room temperature until doubled in bulk, about 1 hour and 45 minutes to 2 hours.

DEFLATE, WORK IN THE CHOCOLATE CHIPS, AND REFRIGERATE THE DOUGH Remove and discard the plastic wrap. Lightly deflate the dough by compressing it with the cupped palm of your hand.

Place the dough in a large bowl, scatter over the chocolate chips, and fold the dough over on itself several times. Knead the dough lightly in the bowl for 2 to 3 minutes, or until the chocolate chips are incorporated. Some chips will remain on the surface here and there—OK.

Place the dough in a large food-safe self-sealing plastic bag and refrigerate overnight, lightly deflating it with the palm of your hand 3 times during the first 6 hours. So as to preserve its texture, do not actively punch down the dough or unduly compact it.

Film the inside of two 9 by 9 by 2-inch baking pans with nonstick cooking spray.

ROLL, FILL, AND CUT THE CRUMB BUNS Using a floured rolling pin, roll out the dough on a floured work surface to a sheet measuring about 17 by 17 inches. Spread the chocolate chip cream filling evenly over the surface of the dough. Roll up the dough, jelly-roll style, as tightly as possible. As the dough is rolled, brush off any excess flour with a clean, dry pastry brush. The filling may ooze slightly as you roll—OK. Pinch the long seam end closed. Gently stretch the coil until it measures about 22 inches in length.

Cut the coil into 16 slices. The filling will ooze as the rolls are cut—OK—and any seepage will be covered up later on by the streusel topping. Gently elongate the slices to make rectangles with oval sides. Place the slices in the prepared pans, arranging them in 2 rows of 4, 8 buns to pan.

SET THE CRUMB BUNS TO RISE Cover each pan loosely with a sheet of food-safe plastic wrap. Let the buns rise until doubled in bulk at room temperature, 2 hours to 2 hours and 15 minutes. (The buns need to double in bulk during a leisurely rise in order to establish a fine, gossamer texture on baking.) The crumb buns will have merged together at this point, leaving a few patches of the baking pan peeking through.

Preheat the oven to 375 degrees F. in advance of baking. Remove and discard the plastic wrap covering the buns.

TOP THE BUNS AND BAKE Scatter and crumble the streusel evenly over the buns without pressing down on them. Use all of the streusel. Bake the buns in the preheated oven for 35 minutes, or until set and golden. The baked crumb buns will have risen close to the top of each pan.

COOL THE BUNS Let the buns stand in the pan on cooling racks for 45 minutes. On cooling, the surface of the block of buns will form natural high and low points as the streusel mixture settles, giving the sweet bread a natural, homestyle look. Using the tip of a flexible palette knife, disconnect the buns at their natural divisions and pull apart in blocks of two. Or, invert each pan of buns onto a cooling rack, invert again to stand right side up, then pull apart the buns. When they are very fresh, actually cutting into the crumb buns with a knife will compress their lovely texture. Dust the tops with confectioners' sugar, letting the streusel mixture peek through, if you wish.

Bake-and-serve within 2 days

STUDY Throughout the time that you are mixing and beating the dough, be sure to stand by the mixer to make sure that it is stable on the work surface.

The chocolate chips are added to the yeast dough after the first rise and before the overnight refrigeration takes place. The texture of the dough needs to be established in the first rise, and this is accomplished prior to adding the chips. The chips are then lightly kneaded into the dough, which is now ready to accept them.

Deflating the dough lightly during the first 6 hours of refrigeration establishes its texture and flavor. Make sure to use a large enough bag to contain the dough as it rises, or it may create an opening at the self-sealing side to break through it.

The chocolate chip cream filling adds both flavor and moisture to the crumb buns.

Finishing the buns with the streusel at the end of the second rise keeps them light and tender while maintaining their risen height.

CHOCOLATE CHIP CREAM FILLING

About 1²⁄₃ cups pastry cream

*N*ot content to leave a pastry cream alone, I've added chocolate chips to this one. The filling is lush and a perfect counterpoint to a yeast dough with a nubby topping. When I make the topping with farm-fresh organic eggs, its color is golden yellow—lovely.

2 tablespoons cornstarch

5 tablespoons granulated sugar

Large pinch of salt

¾ cup heavy cream

½ cup milk

3 large egg yolks

1 teaspoon vanilla extract

1 tablespoon unsalted butter, softened

½ cup miniature semisweet chocolate chips

Sift the cornstarch, sugar, and salt into a heavy, small-to-medium-size saucepan (preferably enameled cast iron). The saucepan must be heavy. Whisk the mixture to combine.

Gradually stir in the heavy cream and milk.

Place the saucepan over moderately high heat and bring to the boil, stirring slowly with a wooden spoon. (Do not use a whisk.) When the mixture comes to a gentle boil (bubbles will plop randomly on the surface), reduce the heat to low and cook for 1 to 2 minutes, or until thickened. Remove the saucepan from the heat.

Beat the egg yolks in a small heatproof bowl. Stir in about ¼ cup of the thickened cream. Slowly stir the tempered egg yolk mixture back into the thickened mixture in the saucepan. Return the saucepan to the heat and cook at a low boil for 1 minute, or until nicely thickened—like pudding. The filling should reach a temperature of 200 degrees F. to achieve the correct stability and thickness.

Strain the pastry cream through a fine-mesh sieve into a heatproof bowl. Slowly stir in the vanilla extract and softened butter. Place a sheet of food-safe plastic wrap directly onto the surface of the filling. Cool the filling for 20 minutes. Remove and discard the plastic wrap.

Scrape the pastry cream into a storage container, press a clean sheet of plastic wrap on the surface, cover, and refrigerate. Chill the pastry cream for 6 hours before using. The pastry cream can be prepared to this point (without the addition of the chocolate chips) up to 1 day in advance.

Just before spreading over the rolled-out yeast dough, slowly stir the chocolate chips into the cold pastry cream. The pastry cream must be cold, otherwise the chips will melt.

STUDY Sifting the cornstarch with the sugar and salt helps to disperse it evenly and frees it of any small lumps. Whisking this mixture before adding the cream and milk distributes the ingredients further.

When stirring the pastry cream as it cooks, use a wooden spoon or flat wooden paddle, not a whisk. Whisking the pastry cream as it cooks can reduce the thickening power of the cornstarch, as the wires of the whisk can break through the swollen starch network, causing it to thin out and turn soupy instead of beautifully thickened.

When mixing the chocolate chips into the chilled pastry cream, do so slowly. Stirring the thickened pastry cream too energetically may thin it out.

CHOCOLATE CHIP STREUSEL

*L*umpy and chunky, sweet and loaded with chocolate chips, this is one of my favorite toppings for yeast-raised coffee cakes and sweet rolls.

1½ cups bleached all-purpose flour

⅛ teaspoon salt

1 cup granulated sugar

12 tablespoons (1½ sticks) cold unsalted butter, cut into chunks

2 teaspoons vanilla extract

I cup miniature semisweet chocolate chips

Thoroughly combine the flour, salt, and sugar in a large mixing bowl. Scatter over the chunks of butter and, using a pastry blender or two round-bladed table knives, cut the fat into the flour until reduced to small pieces about the size of large pearls. Sprinkle the vanilla extract over. With your fingertips, begin to knead the mixture together until moist lumps are formed. Sprinkle the chocolate chips over, work them into the mixture, and continue kneading until cohesive lumps are formed. Crumble the streusel to form as even-size lumps as possible so the topping bakes evenly on the buns and doesn't weigh down any particular section of them.

Use the topping immediately, or refrigerate for up to 1 day in a covered container. If the topping is made in advance, bring it to cool room temperature before using.

STYLE For Chocolate Chip–Nut Streusel, add ⅓ cup chopped walnuts or pecans to the streusel mixture along with the chocolate chips.

A FACTUAL, EMOTIONAL, AND MENU-RELATED ADMISSION: I long for chocolate in the morning.

While others are tending to their bowl of oatmeal, buttering toast, or pouring milk over a pile of flakes, I am assembling my own plate of bread and chocolate or, rather, some kind of chocolatey bread. A tall and daring slice of chocolate chip panettone, a deeply moist crumb bun, a swirl of cocoa-colored dough that wraps chocolate chips in its pleats and creases, a big tear of flatbread buzzing with random pieces of bittersweet chocolate—just put any one of these on a dish next to my coffee and I'll promise to be good for the rest of the day. A few chocolate biscotti could stand in for something yeasty, too, if absolutely necessary, but the aroma of *raised* chocolate bread is part of the naughty stratagem of it all. To be perfectly candid, I'd be grief-stricken if presented with a plain English muffin.

In the absence of actual yeast-risen, chocolate-heightened bread, I have been known to prepare one of the following:

Sunrise sweets, or she even eats chocolate for breakfast

1. To undo one of my homemade croissants, insert a stick of bittersweet chocolate, reroll, and heat briefly (somewhat messy, but entirely viable)
2. To cut a slice from a loaf of brioche, conceal the surface with squares of bittersweet chocolate, then toast gingerly to create a wide basin of melted, just-warm chocolate (the seepage of melted chocolate onto the fingers as you pick up the bread is part of the allure)
3. To fix some chocolate butter, for spreading on a griddled waffle (or failing that, toast)

The third option is a weak substitute for selection number one or two, but a smear of chocolate butter (melted bittersweet chocolate mixed into softened butter lightly scented with vanilla extract) is a ready substitute. Which leads me to a second and final confession: I really use the butter on chocolate bread. Chocolate-lovers, I just know you understand the nature of this act.

NOTE: This is a personal statement of fact, not a cluster of breakfast suggestions. And please, don't send the nutrition patrol to my house, because I won't answer the door.

VANILLA BABAS WITH BITTERSWEET CHOCOLATE CHUNK CREAM

10 babas

*T*his is the baba dough I've been refining for almost twenty years—it's fragrant with vanilla, and the combination of butter and eggs gives these little treasures a beautifully enriched texture, with a fine, golden "crumb."

For a yeast dough, this is an easy-going one. The dough rises leisurely twice (once as a dough ball and again portioned out into small molds) and bakes to a bronzed, lightly sweetened finish. The warm baked babas are doused with an almond syrup, split open slightly, and filled with a glamorous bittersweet chocolate cream filling. Enough rhapsodizing. Let the baking begin.

VANILLA YEAST DOUGH

2¼ teaspoons active dry yeast

½ teaspoon granulated sugar

¼ cup warm (105 to 110 degrees F.) water

1 large egg

2 large egg yolks

3 tablespoons plus 1 teaspoon granulated sugar

2 teaspoons vanilla extract

Seeds scraped from ½ small split vanilla bean

5 tablespoons unsalted butter, melted and cooled to warm

⅓ cup unbleached all-purpose flour

1⅓ cups bleached all-purpose flour

Large pinch of salt

SYRUP

Almond Soaking Syrup (page 227)

FILLING

Chocolate Chunk Cream Filling (page 228)

Softly Whipped and Scented Cream (page 229), to accompany (optional)

MIX THE DOUGH Combine the yeast, the ½ teaspoon granulated sugar, and the warm water in a small heatproof bowl. Stir well. Let stand until the yeast softens and swells, about 8 minutes. Whisk the egg, egg yolks, 3 tablespoons plus 1 teaspoon sugar, the vanilla extract, vanilla bean seeds, and melted butter in a small bowl. Combine the unbleached flour, 1 cup of the bleached flour, and the salt in the bowl of a heavy-duty freestanding electric mixer fitted with the flat paddle attachment. Blend the yeast mixture into the egg mixture, add to the flour, and mix on low speed until a dough is formed. Beat on moderately low speed for 3 minutes. Turn off the mixer, remove the flat paddle, and scrape down any dough clinging to it and the sides of the work bowl. Cover the bowl with a sheet of food-safe plastic wrap and let it rest for 20 minutes. Outfit the mixer with the dough hook attachment. Beat for 4 minutes longer on moderate speed, adding the remaining ⅓ cup bleached flour by degrees to make a soft and elastic, but not sticky, dough; you may not need to add all of the final ⅓ cup (on a damp day, the dough may take most or all of the ⅓ cup, on a cool day, about 2 to 3 tablespoons of the final amount). While beating, stand by the mixer to make sure that it is stable on the work surface.

SET THE DOUGH TO RISE Place the dough into a heavily buttered bowl and turn to coat all sides with the butter. With a pair of kitchen scissors, make 4 deep cuts in the dough. Cover the bowl tightly with a sheet of food-safe plastic wrap. Let the dough rise at room temperature until doubled in bulk, about 1 hour and 45 minutes to 2 hours.

COMPRESS THE DOUGH Remove and discard the plastic wrap. With the cupped palm of your hand, lightly press down on the dough to deflate it. Actively punching down the dough would spoil the delicate network established by the fermentation process. Cover the bowl of dough with a tea towel or sheet of food-safe plastic wrap and let rest for 15 minutes, then remove the plastic wrap.

Butter the inside of 10 baba or timbale molds (each mold measuring 2¼ inches high and 2½ inches in diameter across the top, with a capacity of ½ cup plus 1 tablespoon). For extra unmolding insurance, line the inside of each mold with a 10 by 3¾-inch length of cooking parchment paper rolled loosely around itself, then tucked into the mold, letting the paper extend past the top.

FORM THE BABAS Divide the dough into 10 equal pieces. Form each piece into a ball. (The dough balls will be casual because they are so soft—OK.) Place a ball of dough in the bottom of each mold. Set the molds on a cookie sheet or sheet pan. Loosely cover the group of molds with food-safe plastic wrap. (It is unnecessary to cover the molds individually.) Let rise at room temperature for 1 hour and 30 minutes. The dough will be puffy. Carefully remove and discard the plastic wrap. Let rise for

20 to 30 minutes longer uncovered, or until the babas are puffy and have fully rounded crowns.

Preheat the oven to 375 degrees F. in advance of baking.

BAKE AND COOL THE BABAS Bake the babas in the preheated oven for 15 minutes, or until golden brown and set. Let the babas stand in the molds on a cooling rack for 45 minutes. Removing them while they are too hot can cause sagging. (The babas can be baked ahead to this point: remove them from the molds, and store airtight for up to 2 days. Carefully bundle the babas loosely in aluminum foil and warm in a 325 degree F. oven for 10 to 12 minutes before proceeding.)

MAKE THE SYRUP While the babas are baking, make the syrup.

MOISTEN THE BABAS Place the warm babas on a large nonreactive, heatproof platter (such as ovenproof porcelain) on their sides. Spoon the warm syrup over the babas to moisten them.

FILL THE BABAS Place a baba (or two) on a dessert plate and, using a serrated knife, slice open (along the center or on the diagonal) without cutting the cake completely in half. Spread open lightly and fill with a spoonful of the chocolate chunk cream. Serve with a spoonful of whipped cream dolloped over each filled baba, if you wish.

ALMOND SOAKING SYRUP

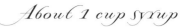

This is a light syrup, gently flavored with almond liqueur. The hint of almond in the syrup that bathes the babas is a good flavor contrast to the creamy, chocolate-mottled vanilla cream.

1 cup water
¾ cup granulated sugar
¼ cup almond liqueur (such as Amaretto)
¼ teaspoon vanilla extract

Place the water and sugar in a small, heavy saucepan (preferably enameled cast iron). Set over low heat to dissolve the sugar. When every last granule of sugar has dissolved, uncover the saucepan, bring to a boil, and cook at a moderate boil for 3 minutes. Add the almond liqueur and boil slowly for 2 to 3 minutes, or until lightly condensed. There should be about 1 cup of syrup (if there is a little more syrup, return it to the saucepan and simmer gently for a minute or two). Remove from the heat and stir in the vanilla extract. Use the syrup warm.

To store, cool the syrup, pour into a storage container, cover, and refrigerate for up to 4 days. Gently reheat the syrup in a saucepan (uncovered) to warm it before using.

CHOCOLATE CHUNK CREAM FILLING

About 2¼ cups pastry cream

Creamy, tinged with vanilla, and dappled with little knobs of bittersweet chocolate.

1¼ cups milk

1 cup light (table) cream

Large pinch of salt

⅔ cup granulated sugar

2 tablespoons cornstarch

6 large egg yolks

1 tablespoon unsalted butter, softened

1 tablespoon pure vanilla extract

3 ounces bittersweet chocolate, chopped

Combine the milk, cream, and salt in a medium-size saucepan and set over moderate heat. When the liquid is warm, remove it from the heat. Sift the sugar and cornstarch into a large, heavy saucepan (preferably enameled cast iron). Whisk thoroughly to disperse the cornstarch. Slowly stir in the warmed milk-cream mixture.

Place the saucepan over moderately high heat and cook, stirring slowly with a wooden spoon or flat paddle, until bubbles begin to break at the surface. Cook at a low boil for 1 to 2 minutes, stirring slowly but completely, until moderately thick. The mixture will become thicker after the next step.

In a small bowl, beat the egg yolks lightly until combined. Quickly stir about ½ cup of the thickened cream into the yolks. Off the heat, stir the tempered egg yolk mixture into the thickened cream base. Return the saucepan to the heat and boil slowly (small-to-medium bubbles will appear on the surface) for 1 minute or until thickened, stirring constantly. The filling should reach a temperature of 200 degrees F. to achieve the correct stability and thickness.

Carefully pour the cream filling into a heatproof bowl. Stir in the softened butter and vanilla extract. Press a sheet of food-safe plastic wrap directly onto the surface of the cream. Cool for 30 minutes. Remove and discard the plastic wrap. Scrape the filling into a container, press a clean sheet of plastic wrap on the surface, cover, and refrigerate for 6 hours, or up to 1 day. Just before serving, lightly stir in the chopped chocolate.

ELEMENT Spread the cold cream filling between layers of chocolate cake, such as the Buttermilk Chocolate Layer Cake (page 118) or Heirloom Devil's Food Layer Cake (page 116).

# SOFTLY WHIPPED AND SCENTED CREAM

About 3 cups whipped cream

*R*omantic overtones of vanilla in the whipped cream accentuate any deep chocolate-flavored dessert it accompanies in an exquisite way.

1½ cups cold heavy cream

2 tablespoons superfine sugar

½ teaspoon vanilla bean paste (optional)

1½ teaspoons vanilla extract

Chill the beater(s) and medium-size mixing bowl for 1 hour. This is an optional step, but creates whipped cream with a dreamy quality. Starting with a cold bowl and beaters facilitates the whipping process and adds smooth density to the finished cream. Pour the cream into the mixing bowl and whip until beginning to thicken. Sprinkle over the sugar, add the optional vanilla bean paste, and beat lightly to combine. Blend in the vanilla extract and continue whipping until a soft mound holds its shape in a spoon when dipped up from the bowl. Use the whipped cream immediately.

STYLE For a cocoa-topped cream, place 1 tablespoon unsweetened alkalized cocoa powder in a small sieve. Mound the finished whipped cream in a serving bowl, sift the cocoa over the top, and serve.

STUDY In place of the vanilla bean paste, you can substitute the seeds scraped from ½ small split vanilla bean. If both the paste and bean are unavailable, add an extra ¾ teaspoon vanilla extract.

Using a cold bowl and cold beaters (or whisk) builds volume quickly and smoothly, and gives the whipped cream its silky smooth texture. The cream can be whipped in a bowl with a whisk or with an electric hand mixer, or in the bowl of a freestanding electric mixer. The best texture is achieved by whipping the cream by hand.

BITTERSWEET CHOCOLATE CHUNK BREAD

1 sweet, free-form flatbread, creating about 20 pieces

Tender within and filled with the surprise of bittersweet chocolate chunks, this lightly sweetened and buttery flatbread is fanciful indeed. Partner roughly torn pieces with strong coffee at any time of the day. I love it freshly baked, when the texture of the chocolate is luxuriously melty.

VANILLA CHOCOLATE CHUNK DOUGH

2¼ teaspoons active dry yeast

¾ teaspoon granulated sugar

½ cup warm (105 to 110 degrees F.) water

¼ cup unbleached all-purpose flour

1 large egg

2 large egg yolks

3 tablespoons granulated sugar

2 teaspoons vanilla extract

1¾ cups unbleached all-purpose flour

⅛ teaspoon salt

8 tablespoons (1 stick) unsalted butter, cut into chunks, softened but cool

5 ounces bittersweet chocolate, cut into small chunks

TOPPING

2 tablespoons cold unsalted butter, cubed

About 3 tablespoons sparkling sugar (or substitute granulated sugar)

MIX THE DOUGH Combine the yeast, the ¾ teaspoon granulated sugar, and the warm water in a small heatproof bowl. Stir well. Let stand until the yeast softens and swells, about 8 minutes. Combine the yeast mixture with the ¼ cup of the unbleached flour and mix well; it will be somewhat thin. Scrape the mixture into a heavy, small-to-medium size mixing bowl, cover with a sheet of food-safe plastic wrap, and let stand for 25 to 35 minutes at room temperature until medium-size bubbles appear and break on the surface.

Place the yeast mixture in the bowl of a heavy-duty freestanding electric mixer fitted with the flat paddle attachment. Add the egg, egg yolks, the 3 tablespoons granulated sugar, and the vanilla extract. Mix on low speed until combined. Add about two-thirds of the 1¾ cups unbleached flour and the salt and mix well to combine. Add the remaining flour and beat to combine. While beating, be sure to stand by the mixer to make sure that it is stable on the work surface. Scrape the dough from the flat paddle and the sides of the work bowl, cover the bowl with a sheet of plastic wrap, and let stand for 15 minutes. Remove and discard the plastic wrap.

Replace the flat paddle with the dough hook attachment. Beat in the butter, a tablespoon at a time, mixing until integrated before the next addition. Once the last tablespoon of butter is added and incorporated, the dough will look smooth and velvety. This dough won't clean the sides of the mixing bowl (there will be a film of dough). Beat for 2 minutes longer.

SET THE DOUGH TO RISE Turn the dough into a heavily buttered bowl. Cover the bowl tightly with a sheet of food-safe plastic wrap and let the dough rise at room temperature until doubled in bulk, about 1 hour and 20 minutes.

INTEGRATE THE CHOCOLATE IN STAGES Remove and discard the plastic wrap. With the dough remaining in the bowl, sprinkle half of the chocolate chunks on top. Fold the dough over the chocolate chunks, then over itself, and knead lightly. Sprinkle the remaining chocolate over, fold the dough over, and knead lightly in the bowl to assimilate the chocolate chunks into the dough. Initially, the dough will resist the chunks, but most of them will fuse with it. Cover the dough with a sheet of food-safe plastic wrap and let it rest for 15 minutes.

Thickly butter a heavy 13 by 18 by 1-inch rimmed sheet pan, leaving an unbuttered 2- to 3-inch border. The pan must be heavy in order to diffuse heat evenly, or the dough will brown on the bottom before the interior is baked through.

FORM THE FLATBREAD Remove and discard the plastic wrap. Turn the dough onto the prepared pan. Lightly press it into a freeform oval shape about 12 inches long. If a few chunks of chocolate pop out onto the surface and resist being embedded, it's fine. Cover the dough loosely with a sheet of food-safe plastic wrap. Let rise at room temperature for 50 minutes, or until puffy and about 1¼ inches high. Remove and discard the plastic wrap.

Preheat the oven to 400 degrees F. in advance of baking.

TOP THE BREAD Scatter the cubes of butter on the surface of the risen flatbread, keeping them about 1 inch from the edges. Sprinkle with the sparkling sugar.

BAKE AND COOL THE BREAD Bake the bread in the pre-heated oven for 20 minutes, or until set, and golden on the top and bottom. Watch the bread carefully during the final 4 minutes of baking time and begin checking the bread at 16 minutes. Let the bread cool in the pan for 10 minutes, then carefully transfer it to a cooling rack.

Serve the bread freshly baked, torn into pieces.

STYLE For Bittersweet Chocolate Chunk Bread with Chocolate Chips, substitute 6 ounces semisweet chocolate chips for the chunks of bittersweet chocolate. Integrate the chocolate chips into the dough in the same way as you would work in the chunks of bittersweet chocolate, following the directions in the method on page 231.

For Bittersweet Chocolate Chunk Bread with Nuts, integrate ¾ cup coarsely chopped walnuts, pecans, or macadamia nuts into the dough along with the chunks of bittersweet chocolate.

ACCENT The seed scrapings from a small vanilla bean would be an extra and gently perfumed addition to the bread. Reduce the vanilla extract to 1 teaspoon. Add the seeds along with, and in addition to, the vanilla extract.

STUDY This is a casual, free-form bread that will impress you with its tender and buttery quality and casual puffiness. To preserve its texture, the dough should be handled lightly at each juncture—while incorporating the chocolate chunks, as well as during the final phase of pressing the dough onto the surface of the buttered baking sheet

This lightly sweetened dough can embrace an expansive reach of bittersweet chocolate, such as Scharffen Berger Bittersweet 70% cocoa; Valrhona Le Noir Amer 71% cacao; Valrhona Le Noir Gastronomie 61% cacao; Valrhona Caraïbe Dark Chocolate 66% cocoa; Valrhona Grand Cru Noir Manjari Chocolat Noir Dark Chocolate 64% cocoa; Michael Cluizel Chocolat Amer Dark Chocolate 60% cacao; Michel Cluizel Ilha Toma 65% cocoa; Michel Cluizel Chocolat Amer Brut Bitter Chocolate 72% cacao; Côte d'Or Intense Noir de Noir Intense Belgian Dark Chocolate; or, Lindt Chocolate Créé à Berne Swiss Bittersweet Chocolate.

THICK SOUR CREAM, BUTTERMILK, WHOLE MILK, AND EGGS shape the contour and composition of my collection of easy-going cakes. Collectively, these big, buttery, full-flavored cakes that form a rich backdrop to the taste of chocolate are so welcome to have lounging on the kitchen counter for slicing and serving at brunch, for the tea and coffee hour, or simply as an informal dessert. When a cake batter reveals chocolate in any form, it's virtually guaranteed to be coveted throughout the day. So, really, do I need to offer you a time or reason to dish it up?

BUTTERMILK–CHOCOLATE CHIP CRUMB CAKE

One 13 by 9-inch cake, creating 27 fingers or 20 squares

The abundance of crumbs that covers this tender and light coffee cake is simply a mixture of butter-bound flour and sugar, with a little vanilla extract added as a fragrant seasoning. Miniature chocolate chips languish in a graceful batter and they add flavor and texture to the cake. Although the cake takes well to baking ahead and reheating, I urge you to savor it warm from the oven, when the combination of crumbly, soft, buttery, and chocolatey jumps forward.

BUTTER CRUMB TOPPING

1½ cups bleached all-purpose flour

¾ cup granulated sugar

¾ cup firmly packed light brown sugar

⅛ teaspoon salt

12 tablespoons (1½ sticks) cold unsalted butter, cut into chunks

2 teaspoons vanilla extract

BUTTERY BUTTERMILK–CHOCOLATE CHIP BATTER

2½ cups bleached all-purpose flour

½ cup bleached cake flour

1½ teaspoons baking powder

½ teaspoon baking soda

1 teaspoon salt

1½ cups miniature semisweet chocolate chips

½ pound (16 tablespoons or 2 sticks) unsalted butter, softened

1¾ cups superfine sugar

3 large eggs

2½ teaspoons vanilla extract

1 cup buttermilk

¾ cup miniature semisweet chocolate chips, for sprinkling on top of the baked cake

Confectioners' sugar, for sifting on top of the baked cake

PREHEAT THE OVEN TO 350 DEGREES F. Lightly grease the inside of a 13 by 9 by 3-inch baking pan with shortening and dust with flour.

MAKE THE TOPPING Thoroughly mix the flour, granulated sugar, light brown sugar, and salt in a large mixing bowl. Drop in the chunks of butter and, using a pastry blender or two round-bladed table knives, cut the fat into the flour until reduced to small pieces about the size of large pearls. Sprinkle the vanilla extract over. With your fingertips, knead the mixture together until moist, clumpy lumps are formed. You can't overwork this topping, so dig in.

MIX THE BATTER Sift the all-purpose flour, cake flour, baking powder, baking soda, and salt onto a sheet of waxed paper. In a small bowl, toss the chocolate chips with 1½ teaspoons of the sifted mixture.

Cream the butter in the large bowl of a freestanding electric mixer on moderate speed for 3 minutes. Add the superfine sugar in 3 additions, beating for 1 minute after each portion is added, then beat another minute. Blend in the eggs, one at a time, beating for 45 seconds after each addition. Mix in the vanilla extract. On low speed, alternately add the sifted mixture in 3 additions with the buttermilk in 2 additions, beginning and ending with the sifted mixture. Scrape down the sides of the mixing bowl frequently to keep the batter even-textured. Stir in the chocolate chips.

Spoon the batter into the prepared pan and spread evenly. Smooth the top with a rubber spatula.

Sprinkle the streusel topping evenly over the cake batter, taking care to cover the four corners and long edges. (If the topping is sprinkled over unevenly, a few buttery pools may form as the cake bakes but reabsorb as the cake cools—OK.) Use all of the topping—the covering will be generous.

BAKE AND COOL THE CAKE Bake the cake in the preheated oven for 1 hour, or until risen, set, golden, and a toothpick inserted in the center withdraws clean. The baked cake will pull away slightly from the sides of the baking pan.

Place the pan of cake on a rack. Immediately sprinkle the ¾ cup chocolate chips on top of the hot cake. Cool completely.

Sift confectioners' sugar lightly over the top of the cake just before cutting into fingers or squares directly from the baking pan.

Bake-and-serve within 3 days

CHOCOLATE CHIP AND WALNUT COFFEE CAKE

One 10-inch cake, creating 16 slices

I love a coffee cake that features sour cream in the batter, for it is practically guaranteed to be moist and have a fantastic texture. This one won't disappoint, and it's great topped with a simple dusting of confectioners' sugar.

SOUR CREAM CHOCOLATE CHIP AND WALNUT BATTER

2 cups bleached all-purpose flour

1 cup bleached cake flour

1¾ teaspoons baking powder

1 teaspoon baking soda

¾ teaspoon salt

2 cups semisweet chocolate chips

½ pound (16 tablespoons or 2 sticks) unsalted butter, softened

1½ cups granulated sugar

½ cup firmly packed light brown sugar

4 large eggs

2 teaspoons vanilla extract

1 cup sour cream

2 tablespoons milk

¾ cup chopped walnuts

Confectioners' sugar, for sprinkling on top of the baked cake

PREHEAT THE OVEN TO 350 DEGREES F. Film the inside of a 10-inch Bundt pan with nonstick cooking spray.

MIX THE BATTER Sift the all-purpose flour, cake flour, baking powder, baking soda, and salt onto a sheet of waxed paper. In a small bowl, toss the chocolate chips with 1 tablespoon of the sifted mixture.

Cream the butter in the large bowl of a freestanding electric mixer on moderate speed for 3 minutes. Add half of the granulated sugar and beat for 2 minutes. Add the remaining granulated sugar and beat for 1 minute longer. Add the light brown sugar and beat for 2 minutes. Add the eggs, one at a time, beating for 45 seconds after each addition. Blend in the vanilla extract. On low speed, alternately add the sifted mixture in 3 additions with the sour cream in 2 additions, beginning and ending with the sifted mixture. On low speed, blend in the milk. Scrape down the sides of the mixing bowl frequently to keep the batter even-textured. Stir in the chocolate chips and walnuts.

Spoon the batter into the prepared pan. Smooth the top with a rubber spatula.

BAKE AND COOL THE CAKE Bake the cake in the preheated oven for 55 minutes, or until risen, set, and a toothpick inserted in the cake withdraws clean. The baked cake will pull away slightly from the sides of the baking pan.

Cool the cake in the pan on a rack for 10 minutes. Invert onto another cooling rack to cool completely. Store in an airtight cake keeper. Just before slicing and serving, sift confectioners' sugar over the top of the cake.

Bake-and-serve within 2 days

ACCENT Top the finished cake with the Chocolate "Spooning" Topping on page 247, omitting the confectioners' sugar finish.

MILK CHOCOLATE CHIP COOKIE COFFEE CAKE

One 10-inch cake, creating 16 slices

*P*lenty of milk chocolate chips grace this buttery, eggy cake batter: it is a splendid cake to bake when you crave the flavors of a chocolate chip cookie, but would rather have a tender, fine-grained slice of cake instead.

BROWN SUGAR–CHOCOLATE CHIP BATTER

2 cups bleached all-purpose flour

1 cup bleached cake flour

2 teaspoons baking powder

½ teaspoon baking soda

1 teaspoon salt

2¼ cups milk chocolate chips

½ pound (16 tablespoons or 2 sticks) unsalted butter, softened

1½ cups firmly packed light brown sugar

½ cup granulated sugar

4 large eggs

1 large egg yolk

2 teaspoons vanilla extract

1 cup milk

Confectioners' sugar, for sifting on top of the baked cake (optional)

PREHEAT THE OVEN TO 350 DEGREES F. Film the inside of a 10-inch Bundt pan with nonstick cooking spray.

MIX THE BATTER Sift the all-purpose flour, cake flour, baking powder, baking soda, and salt onto a sheet of waxed paper. In a small bowl, toss the chocolate chips with 4 teaspoons of the sifted mixture.

Cream the butter in the large bowl of a freestanding electric mixer on moderate speed for 3 minutes. Add half of the light brown sugar and beat for 1 minute. Add the remaining light brown sugar and beat for 2 minutes. Add the granulated sugar and beat for 1 minute. Add the eggs, one at a time, beating for 45 seconds after each addition. Blend in the egg yolk and vanilla extract. On low speed, alternately add the sifted mixture in 3 additions with the milk in 2 additions, beginning and ending with the sifted mixture. Scrape down the sides of the mixing bowl frequently to keep the batter even-textured. Stir in the chocolate chips.

Spoon the batter into the prepared pan. Smooth the top with a rubber spatula.

BAKE AND COOL THE CAKE Bake the cake in the preheated oven for 1 hour, or until risen, set, and a toothpick inserted in the cake withdraws clean. (If you bump into a chip or two, the pick will be chocolate-stained—OK.) The baked cake will pull away slightly from the sides of the baking pan.

Cool the cake in the pan on a rack for 10 minutes. Invert onto another cooling rack to cool completely. Just before slicing and serving, sift confectioners' sugar over the top of the cake, if you wish. Store in an airtight cake keeper.

Bake-and-serve within 2 days

SOUR CREAM–MILK CHOCOLATE CHIP POUND CAKE

One 10-inch cake, creating 16 to 20 slices

*O*f all the chocolate chip pound cakes I have baked, I turn to this one again and again, because it's simple and straightforward. And the flavors are so pure. Using superfine sugar produces such a fine-textured pound cake that it's worth keeping a box or two on the pantry shelf to have on hand for this recipe.

MILK CHOCOLATE CHIP BATTER

3 cups bleached all-purpose flour

¼ teaspoon baking soda

1 teaspoon salt

2 cups milk chocolate chips

½ pound (16 tablespoons or 2 sticks) unsalted butter, softened

3 cups superfine sugar

6 large eggs

2½ teaspoons vanilla extract

1 cup sour cream

Confectioners' sugar, for sifting on top of the baked cake

PREHEAT THE OVEN TO 325 DEGREES F. Grease the inside of a plain 10-inch tube pan with shortening, line the bottom of the pan with a circle of waxed paper cut to fit, grease the paper, and dust with flour.

MIX THE CAKE BATTER Sift the flour, baking soda, and salt twice onto a sheet of waxed paper. In a small bowl, toss the chocolate chips with 1 tablespoon of the sifted mixture.

Cream the butter in the large bowl of a freestanding electric mixer on moderate speed for 4 minutes. Add the sugar in 4 additions, beating for 45 seconds to 1 minute after each portion is added. Add the eggs, one at a time, beating for 30 seconds after each addition. Blend in the vanilla extract. On low speed, add the sifted mixture in 3 additions alternately with the sour cream in 2 additions, beginning and ending with the sifted mixture. Scrape down the sides of the mixing bowl frequently to keep the batter even-textured. Stir in the chocolate chips.

Spoon the batter into the prepared pan. Smooth the top with a rubber spatula.

BAKE AND COOL THE CAKE Bake the cake in the preheated oven for 1 hour and 15 minutes to 1 hour and 20 minutes, or until risen, set, and a toothpick inserted in the cake withdraws clean. (If you bump into a chip or two, the pick will be chocolate-stained—OK.) The baked cake will pull away slightly from the sides of the baking pan.

Cool the cake in the pan on a rack for 10 to 15 minutes. Invert onto another cooling rack, peel away the waxed paper, then invert again to stand right side up. Cool completely. Store in an airtight cake keeper. Sift confectioners' sugar over the top of the cake just before slicing and serving.

Bake-and-serve within 3 days

CHOCOLATE-ALMOND POUND CAKE

One 10-inch cake, creating 16 slices

Ground almonds, almond extract, and chocolate chips flavor this sour cream–based cake batter cake—a coffee-hour or tea-time delight. The finishing glaze, made of chocolate liqueur and sugar, gives the surface a sweet, moisturizing crackle.

CHOCOLATE CHIP–ALMOND BATTER

2½ cups bleached all-purpose flour

½ cup bleached cake flour

½ teaspoon baking soda

1 teaspoon salt

¼ cup ground almonds

2¼ cups miniature semisweet chocolate chips

½ pound (16 tablespoons or 2 sticks) unsalted butter, softened

3 cups granulated sugar

5 large eggs

2 teaspoons vanilla extract

1 teaspoon almond extract

1 cup sour cream

FINISHING GLAZE

Chocolate Liqueur and Sugar Wash (page 57)

PREHEAT THE OVEN TO 325 DEGREES F. Film the inside of a 10-inch Bundt pan with nonstick cooking spray.

MIX THE BATTER Sift the all-purpose flour, cake flour, baking soda, and salt into a large bowl. Whisk in the ground almonds. In a small bowl, toss the chocolate chips with 4 teaspoons of the sifted mixture.

Cream the butter in the large bowl of a freestanding electric mixer on moderate speed for 3 minutes. Add the sugar in 3 additions, beating for 1 minute after each portion is added. Add the eggs, one at a time, beating for 30 to 45 seconds after each addition. Blend in the vanilla extract and almond extract. On low speed, alternately add the sifted mixture in 3 additions with the sour cream in 2 additions, beginning and ending with the sifted mixture. Scrape down the sides of the mixing bowl frequently to keep the batter even-textured. Stir in the chocolate chips.

Spoon the batter into the prepared pan. Smooth the top with a rubber spatula.

BAKE AND COOL THE CAKE Bake the cake in the preheated oven for 1 hour and 15 minutes to 1 hour and 20 minutes, or until risen, set, and a toothpick inserted in the cake withdraws clean. The baked cake will pull away slightly from the sides of the baking pan.

Cool the cake in the pan on a rack for 10 minutes. Invert onto another cooling rack. Brush the Chocolate Liqueur and Sugar Wash over the top and sides of the cake, using a soft pastry brush. Cool completely. Store in an airtight cake keeper.

Bake-and-serve within 2 days

One 10-inch cake, creating 16 to 20 slices

A full cup of cocoa powder makes the deepest, darkest chocolate pound cake ever. Two dairy liquids, milk and heavy cream, create a rich, well-structured batter and, along with the vanilla extract and vanilla bean seeds, round out the overall flavor.

CHOCOLATE CAKE BATTER

3 cups bleached all-purpose flour

1 cup unsweetened alkalized cocoa powder

3 teaspoons baking powder

1 teaspoon salt

½ pound (16 tablespoons or 2 sticks) unsalted butter, softened

3 cups superfine sugar

3 large eggs

2¾ teaspoons vanilla extract

Seeds scraped from a small split vanilla bean

1¼ cups milk

½ cup heavy cream

Confectioners' sugar, for sifting on top of the baked cake (optional)

PREHEAT THE OVEN TO 325 DEGREES F. Grease the inside of a plain 10-inch tube pan with shortening, line the bottom of the pan with a circle of waxed paper cut to fit, grease the paper, and dust with flour.

MIX THE BATTER Sift the flour, cocoa powder, baking powder, and salt twice onto a sheet of waxed paper.

Cream the butter in the large bowl of a freestanding electric mixer on moderate speed for 3 to 4 minutes. Add the sugar in 4 additions, beating for 1 minute after each portion is added. Add the eggs, one at a time, beating for 30 seconds after each addition. Blend in the vanilla extract and vanilla bean seeds. On low speed, alternately add the sifted mixture in 3 additions with the milk in 2 additions, beginning and ending with the sifted mixture. Scrape down the sides of the mixing bowl frequently to keep the batter even-textured. Add the heavy cream and beat for 1 minute.

Spoon the batter into the prepared pan. Smooth the top with a rubber spatula.

BAKE AND COOL THE CAKE Bake the cake in the preheated oven for 1 hour and 20 minutes, or until risen, set, and a toothpick inserted in the cake withdraws clean. The baked cake will pull away slightly from the sides of the baking pan.

Cool the cake in the pan on a rack for 15 minutes. Invert onto another cooling rack, peel away the waxed paper, then invert again to stand right side up. Cool completely. Store in an airtight tin. Sift confectioners' sugar over the top of the cake just before slicing and serving, if you wish.

Bake-and-serve within 3 days

STUDY This cake is really defined by the type of cocoa powder you use and the quality of the butter and heavy cream. For it, I use Droste, as I adore the flavor it imparts to the cake. As for the butter, I have used the following with great success: Keller's European Style Butter, The Organic Cow of Vermont, Kate's Homemade Butter, Celles sur Belle, Vermont Cultured Butter, Président, Isigny Ste Mère Beurre Cru de Normandie, or, Beurre D'Isigny Extra-Fin.

PLUMP AND DISTINGUISHED, SWEET BISCUITS, MUFFINS, AND SCONES crafted with a generous amount of chocolate are guaranteed to tempt anyone who expects—if not requires—this flavor to be present in a morning (or afternoon) quick bread. Although I love the taste of cinnamon in a.m. pastries, chocolate eclipses it as a seasoning agent: I'll take my oatmeal breakfast scone charged with chocolate chips and my coffee cake–styled muffin threaded inside and out with yet another bonanza of chips.

*T*he topping for these cakelike muffins is made by mixing chocolate chips and chopped walnuts with melted butter and brown sugar. It is a step away from the typical streusel because the flour component is absent. Instead, the melted butter and sugar glaze the chips and nuts to make a glimmering topping for a bundle of muffins.

CHOCOLATE CHIP AND WALNUT TOPPING

¾ cup semisweet chocolate chips

⅔ cup chopped walnuts

3 tablespoons firmly packed light brown sugar

3 tablespoons unsalted butter, melted and cooled

CHOCOLATE CHIP BATTER

3 cups bleached all-purpose flour

2¼ teaspoons baking powder

¼ teaspoon baking soda

¾ teaspoon salt

1⅓ cups semisweet chocolate chips

12 tablespoons (1½ sticks) unsalted butter, softened

⅔ cup plus 1 tablespoon firmly packed light brown sugar

⅓ cup granulated sugar

3 large eggs

2½ teaspoons vanilla extract

1 ounce unsweetened chocolate, melted and cooled

¾ cup milk combined with ¼ cup light (table) cream

Confectioners' sugar, for sifting on top of the baked muffins (optional)

PREHEAT THE OVEN TO 375 DEGREES F. Line the inside of 10 jumbo muffin/cupcake cups (6 cups to a pan, each cup measuring 4 inches in diameter and 1¾ inches deep, with a capacity of 1⅛ cups) with ovenproof baking paper liners. Or, film the inside of each cup with nonstick cooking spray.

MIX THE TOPPING Mix the chocolate chips, walnuts, light brown sugar, and melted butter in a small bowl.

MIX THE BATTER Sift the flour, baking powder, baking soda, and salt onto a sheet of waxed paper. In a small bowl, toss the chocolate chips with 2½ teaspoons of the sifted mixture.

Cream the butter in the large bowl of a freestanding electric mixer on moderately low speed for 3 minutes. Add the light brown sugar and beat for 2 minutes; add the granulated sugar and beat for 2 minutes longer. Beat in the eggs, one at a time, mixing for 30 seconds after each addition. Blend in the vanilla extract and the melted chocolate. On low speed, alternately add the sifted ingredients in 3 additions with the milk-cream mixture in 2 additions, beginning and ending with the sifted mixture. Scrape down the sides of the mixing bowl frequently to keep the batter even-textured. Stir in the chocolate chips.

FILL THE MUFFIN CUPS AND TOP Divide the batter among the prepared cups, mounding it slightly. Sprinkle a little of the topping over each of the muffins.

BAKE AND COOL THE MUFFINS Bake the muffins in the preheated oven for 25 minutes, or until risen, set, and a toothpick inserted into the center of each muffin withdraws clean (if you bump into a milk chocolate chip, it will be stained—OK).

Place the muffin pans on cooling racks and let them stand for 20 minutes. Carefully remove the muffins and place on cooling racks. Dust the tops lightly with confectioners' sugar, if you wish. Cool. Serve the muffins freshly baked.

Bake-and-serve within 1 day

STUDY Just 1 ounce of melted unsweetened chocolate tinges the muffin batter enough to bring out the flavor of all those chocolate chips.

Allowing the baked muffins to remain in the pans for 20 minutes before unmolding maintains their shape.

The batter for the muffins can also be baked in jumbo "crown top" muffin cups (6 cups to a pan, each cup measuring 3¼ inches in diameter and 2 inches deep, with a capacity of a scant 1 cup). To prepare the pans, film the inside of each cup with nonstick cooking spray.

MILK CHOCOLATE CHIP MUFFINS

1 dozen muffins

 big batch of muffins with milk chocolate chips tucked into the batter are sweet parcels of flavor and tender texture.

BUTTERY MILK CHOCOLATE CHIP BATTER

2½ cups bleached all-purpose flour

½ cup bleached cake flour

2 teaspoons baking powder

1 teaspoon baking soda

1 teaspoon salt

2 cups milk chocolate chips

½ pound plus 4 tablespoons (2½ sticks) unsalted butter, softened

1 cup firmly packed light brown sugar

½ cup granulated sugar

2 large eggs

1 tablespoon plus 2 teaspoons vanilla extract

2 ounces unsweetened chocolate, melted and cooled

1 cup plus 2 tablespoons half-and-half

PREHEAT THE OVEN TO 375 DEGREES F. Film the inside of 12 jumbo muffin/cupcake cups (6 cups to a pan, each cup measuring 4 inches in diameter and 1¾ inches deep, with a capacity of 1⅛ cups) with nonstick cooking spray. Or, line the cups with ovenproof baking paper liners.

MIX THE BATTER Sift the all-purpose flour, cake flour, baking powder, baking soda, and salt onto a sheet of waxed paper. In a small bowl, toss the milk chocolate chips with 1 tablespoon of the sifted mixture.

Cream the butter in the large bowl of a freestanding electric mixer on moderate speed for 3 minutes. Add the light brown sugar and beat for 2 minutes; add the granulated sugar and beat 2 minutes longer. Beat in the eggs, one at a time, mixing for 30 seconds after each addition. Blend in the vanilla extract and the melted chocolate. On low speed, alternately add the sifted ingredients in 3 additions with the half-and-half in 2 additions, beginning and ending with the sifted mixture. Scrape down the sides of the mixing bowl frequently to keep the batter even-textured. Stir in the chocolate chips.

Divide the batter among the prepared cups, mounding it slightly.

BAKE AND COOL THE MUFFINS Bake the muffins in the preheated oven for 26 to 30 minutes, or until risen, set, and a toothpick inserted into the center of each muffin withdraws clean (if you bump into a milk chocolate chip, it will be stained—OK).

Place the muffin pans on cooling racks and let them stand for 20 minutes. Carefully remove the muffins and place on cooling racks. Cool. Serve the muffins freshly baked.

Bake-and-serve within 1 day

STUDY For a properly domed, high-rising muffin top, the muffin batter should be mounded in the center of each cup, cresting in a slight curve (not a peak).

BITTERSWEET CHOCOLATE TEA BISCUITS

1 dozen biscuits

*F*ull of bittersweet chocolate chunks, these biscuits are both a confection and a quick bread, and so very tantalizing served freshly baked, when the nuggets of chocolate caught up in the framework of dough are bold and rich.

BITTERSWEET CHOCOLATE DOUGH

4 cups bleached all-purpose flour

5 teaspoons baking powder

¼ teaspoon baking soda

1 teaspoon salt

⅔ cup granulated sugar

6 tablespoons firmly packed light brown sugar

12 tablespoons (1½ sticks) cold unsalted butter, cut into tablespoon-size chunks

4 large eggs

1 tablespoon plus 2 teaspoons vanilla extract

1 cup heavy cream

12 ounces bittersweet chocolate, chopped into chunks

About ⅓ cup granulated sugar (or crystallized sugar), for sprinkling on the tops of the unbaked scones

MIX THE DOUGH In a large mixing bowl, thoroughly whisk the flour, baking powder, baking soda, salt, and granulated sugar. Sieve the light brown sugar over and whisk again to combine. Drop in the chunks of butter and, using a pastry blender or two round-bladed knives, cut the fat into the flour mixture until reduced to pearl-size pieces. Reduce the fat further to smaller flakes, using your fingertips. In a medium-size mixing bowl, whisk the eggs, vanilla extract, and heavy cream. Pour the egg and cream mixture over the flour mixture, scatter the chunks of chocolate over, and stir to form a dough.

KNEAD AND REFRIGERATE THE DOUGH Knead the dough lightly in the bowl for 30 seconds to 1 minute. Divide the dough in half and form each half into an 8 to 8½-inch disk. Refrigerate the disks, wrapped in waxed paper, for 20 minutes.

Preheat the oven to 400 degrees F. in advance of baking the biscuits. Line 2 heavy cookie sheets or rimmed sheet pans with lengths of cooking parchment paper.

FORM AND TOP THE BISCUITS Place each disk of dough on a lightly floured work surface and, using a chef's knife, cut into 6 wedges. As the biscuits are cut, press in any chunks of chocolate that may stick out of the sides. Transfer the biscuits to the prepared pans, placing them 3 inches apart. Assemble 6 biscuits on each pan.

Sprinkle a little sugar on top of each biscuit.

BAKE AND COOL THE BISCUITS Bake the biscuits in the preheated oven for 19 to 20 minutes, or until set and baked through. Begin checking the biscuits at 18 minutes. Transfer the pans to cooling racks. Let the biscuits stand on the pans for 2 minutes, then carefully remove them to cooling racks, using a wide offset metal spatula. Cool. Serve the biscuits freshly baked.

Bake-and-serve within 1 day

STYLE For Nutty Bittersweet Chocolate Tea Biscuits, scatter ¾ cup chopped walnuts, pecans, or macadamia nuts over the dough mixture along with the bittersweet chocolate chunks.

COCOA–CHOCOLATE CHIP MUFFINS

*B*ig muffins, bold muffins, wild-with-chips muffins.

DOUBLE CHOCOLATE BATTER

2¾ cups bleached all-purpose flour

6 tablespoons unsweetened alkalized cocoa powder

1¾ teaspoons baking powder

¼ teaspoon baking soda

¾ teaspoon salt

1¼ cups semisweet chocolate chips

¾ cup chopped walnuts

13 tablespoons (1 stick plus 5 tablespoons) unsalted butter, softened

¾ cup firmly packed light brown sugar

¼ cup granulated sugar

2 teaspoons vanilla extract

3 large eggs

2 ounces unsweetened chocolate, melted and cooled

1 cup milk

PREHEAT THE OVEN TO 375 DEGREES F. Line the inside of 9 jumbo muffin cups (each cup measuring 4 inches in diameter and 1¾ inches deep, with a capacity of 1⅛ cups) with ovenproof baking paper liners or film the inside of each cup with nonstick cooking spray.

MIX THE BATTER Sift the all-purpose flour, cocoa powder, baking powder, baking soda, and salt onto a sheet of waxed paper. In a medium-size bowl, toss the chocolate chips and walnuts with 2½ teaspoons of the sifted mixture.

Cream the butter in the large bowl of a freestanding electric mixer on moderate speed for 3 minutes. Add the light brown sugar and beat for 2 minutes; add the granulated sugar and beat for a minute longer. Blend in the vanilla extract. Beat in the eggs, one at a time, mixing for 30 seconds after each addition. Blend in the melted chocolate.

On low speed, alternately add the sifted ingredients in 3 additions with the milk in 2 additions, beginning and ending with the sifted mixture. Scrape down the sides of the mixing bowl frequently with a rubber spatula to keep the batter even-textured. Stir in the chocolate chips and walnuts.

Spoon the batter into the muffin cups, dividing it evenly among them.

BAKE AND COOL THE MUFFINS Bake the muffins in the preheated oven for 25 to 30 minutes, or until risen and set, and a wooden pick inserted into the center of a muffin withdraws clean. Place the muffin pans on cooling racks and let them stand for 30 minutes. Carefully remove the muffins and place on cooling racks. Cool completely. Serve the muffins very fresh.

Bake-and-serve within 1 day

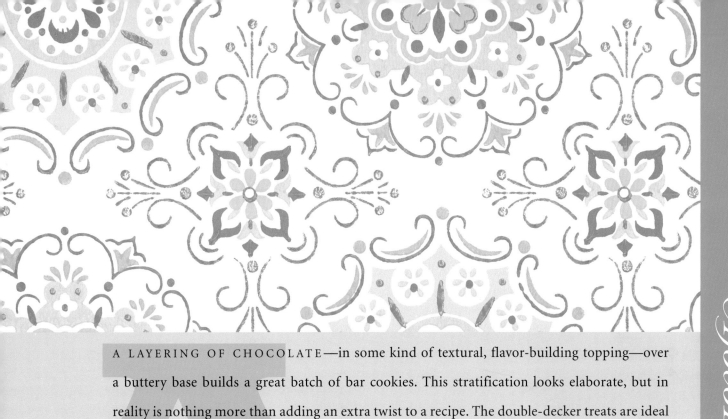

A LAYERING OF CHOCOLATE—in some kind of textural, flavor-building topping—over a buttery base builds a great batch of bar cookies. This stratification looks elaborate, but in reality is nothing more than adding an extra twist to a recipe. The double-decker treats are ideal for packing up as a bread-and-butter gift or for serving with coffee as a sweet pick-up at any-time in the afternoon or evening. And for bake sales or other collaborative events, such as potluck suppers and picnics, bar cookies can be made ahead and held until it is time to cut them into individual pieces.

LAYERED CHOCOLATE AND CARAMEL FUDGE CHIP SQUARES

16 squares

*T*his sweet is composed of two layers of chocolate richness: a dark cookie layer and a fudgy chocolate batter bolstered with chocolate chips and diced chocolate, caramel, and nougat candy bars. All of the elements converge to make a deluxe bar cookie.

CHOCOLATE COOKIE LAYER

8 tablespoons (1 stick) unsalted butter, melted and cooled to tepid

1½ cups plus 3 tablespoons chocolate cookie crumbs (such as crumbs made from Nabisco Famous Chocolate Wafers) combined with 3 tablespoons miniature semisweet chocolate chips

CHOCOLATE FUDGE CHIP BATTER

1 cup bleached cake flour

2 tablespoons unsweetened alkalized cocoa powder

¼ teaspoon baking powder

⅛ teaspoon salt

½ pound (16 tablespoons or 2 sticks) unsalted butter, melted and cooled to tepid

4 ounces unsweetened chocolate, melted and cooled to tepid

4 large eggs

1¾ cups plus 2 tablespoons superfine sugar

2 teaspoons vanilla extract

⅔ cup miniature semisweet chocolate chips

4 (1.76 ounces each) dark chocolate, caramel, and vanilla nougat candy bars (such as Milky Way Midnight bars), cut into chunks

PREHEAT THE OVEN TO 325 DEGREES F. Film the inside of a 9 by 9 by 2-inch baking pan with nonstick cooking spray.

MIX, BAKE, AND COOL THE COOKIE LAYER Pour the melted butter into the prepared pan. Spoon the cookie crumb mixture evenly over the bottom of the pan and press down lightly with the underside of small offset metal spatula so that the crumbs absorb the butter. Bake the cookie layer in the preheated oven for 4 minutes. Place the baking pan on a rack. Cool for 10 minutes.

MIX THE BATTER Sift the flour, cocoa powder, baking powder, and salt onto a sheet of waxed paper.

In a medium-size mixing bowl, whisk the melted butter and melted chocolate until smooth. In a large mixing bowl, whisk the eggs until blended, about 30 seconds. Add the sugar and whisk until combined, about 30 to 45 seconds. Blend in the vanilla extract and melted butter-chocolate mixture. Sift the flour mixture over and stir to form a batter, mixing thoroughly until the particles of flour are absorbed, using a whisk or flat wooden paddle. Stir in the chocolate chips and diced candy bars. Or, stir in half of the chocolate chips and half of the candy bar chunks, and sprinkle the remaining chocolate chips and candy bar chunks on top 5 minutes before the baking time is up.

Spoon the batter in large dollops on the cookie crumb layer. Carefully spread the batter over the cookie layer, using a flexible palette knife or spatula.

BAKE, COOL, AND CUT THE SWEET Bake the sweet in the preheated oven for 35 minutes, or until set. Let the sweet stand in the pan on a cooling rack for 3 hours. With a small sharp knife, cut the sweet into quarters, then cut each quarter into 4 squares. Remove the squares from the baking pan, using a small offset metal spatula. Store in an airtight tin.

Bake-and-serve within 4 days

STYLE For Layered Chocolate and Caramel Fudge Chip Squares with Nuts, stir ½ cup chopped walnuts or pecans into the batter along with the chocolate chips and diced candy bars.

STUDY Double-sifting, or sifting the dry ingredients once to aerate, then again over the whisked chocolate mixture, helps to make a gossamer fudge batter.

LAYERED CHOCOLATE AND PEANUT GRAHAM BARS

2 dozen bars

*I*f you use lightly salted peanuts, you will have a provocative bar cookie with the sublime contrast of salty and sweet. That sparkle of salt adds an interesting, differentiating dimension, and its presence would be a flavor foil to the sweetness of the condensed milk and flaked coconut.

VANILLA-GRAHAM CRACKER LAYER

8 tablespoons (1 stick) unsalted butter, melted, cooled to tepid, and combined with ½ teaspoon vanilla extract

1½ cups plus 3 tablespoons graham cracker crumbs

CHOCOLATE CHIP, COCONUT, AND PEANUT LAYER

1¼ cups sweetened flaked coconut

1⅓ cups semisweet chocolate chips

1⅓ cups whole roasted peanuts

1 can (14 ounces) sweetened condensed milk

PREHEAT THE OVEN TO 350 DEGREES F. Film the inside of a 10 by 10 by 2-inch baking pan with nonstick cooking spray.

MIX THE COOKIE LAYER Pour the melted butter–vanilla mixture into the prepared pan. Spoon the graham cracker crumbs evenly over the bottom of the pan and press down lightly with the underside of a small offset metal spatula so that the crumbs absorb the butter.

TOP THE COOKIE LAYER Sprinkle the coconut in an even layer over the cookie base, then top with an even layer of the chocolate chips. Top with an even layer of the peanuts. Some chocolate chips will peek through the peanut layer. Pour the sweetened condensed milk evenly over, making sure to drizzle some along the edges and at the corners of the baking pan so that the bars will be nicely moist throughout.

BAKE, COOL, AND CUT THE BARS Bake the sweet in the preheated oven for 30 minutes, or until set and light golden on top. To keep the bars moist and chewy, take care not to overbake them.

Let the sweet stand in the baking pan on a rack until completely cool. With a small sharp knife, cut the sweet into quarters, then cut each quarter into 6 bars. Remove the bars from the baking pan, using a small offset metal spatula. Store in an airtight tin.

Bake-and-serve within 2 days

LAYERED BROWNIE SQUARES

My passion for building chocolate flavor led me to hatch this chocolate-on-chocolate recipe for a wild bar cookie that uses chocolate in all its basic forms. This is the sweet to take to a bake sale, to make when your craving for chocolate needs to be indulged, and of course, when you want to impress someone—easily—with your baking know-how.

CHOCOLATE COOKIE LAYER

8 tablespoons (1 stick) unsalted butter, melted, cooled to tepid, and combined with ¼ teaspoon vanilla extract

1½ cups plus 3 tablespoons chocolate wafer cookie crumbs (such as crumbs made from Nabisco Famous Chocolate Wafers)

COCOA BROWNIE BATTER

1⅓ cups bleached cake flour

5 tablespoons unsweetened alkalized cocoa powder

¼ teaspoon baking powder

⅛ teaspoon salt

⅓ cup miniature semisweet chocolate chips

½ pound (16 tablespoons or 2 sticks) unsalted butter, melted and cooled to tepid

5 ounces unsweetened chocolate, melted and cooled to tepid

5 large eggs

2 cups granulated sugar

1¾ teaspoons vanilla extract

TOPPING

⅔ cup miniature semisweet chocolate chips

PREHEAT THE OVEN TO 325 DEGREES F. Film the inside of a 10 by 10 by 2-inch baking pan with nonstick cooking spray.

MIX, BAKE, AND COOL THE COOKIE LAYER Pour the melted butter–vanilla mixture into the prepared pan. Spoon cookie crumbs evenly over the bottom of the pan and press down lightly with the underside of a small offset metal spatula so that the crumbs absorb the butter. Bake the cookie layer in the preheated oven for 4 minutes.

Place the baking pan on a rack. Cool for 10 minutes.

MIX THE BATTER Sift the flour, cocoa powder, baking powder, and salt onto a sheet of waxed paper. In a small bowl, toss the chocolate chips with ½ teaspoon of the sifted mixture.

In a medium-size mixing bowl, whisk the melted butter and melted chocolate until smooth. In a large mixing bowl, whisk the eggs until blended, about 15 to 30 seconds. Add the sugar and whisk until combined, about 30 seconds. Blend in the vanilla extract and melted butter-chocolate mixture. Sift the flour mixture over and stir to form a batter, mixing thoroughly until the particles of flour are absorbed, using a whisk or flat wooden paddle. Stir in the chocolate chips.

Spoon the batter in large dollops on the cookie crumb layer. Carefully spread the batter over the cookie layer, using a flexible palette knife or spatula.

BAKE, COOL, AND CUT THE SWEET Bake the sweet in the preheated oven for 27 minutes. Quickly sprinkle the chocolate chips evenly on top. Bake 6 to 10 minutes longer, or until set. Let the sweet stand in the pan on a cooling rack for 3 hours. Refrigerate for 1 hour. With a small sharp knife, cut the sweet into quarters, then cut each quarter into 4 squares. Remove the squares from the baking pan, using a small offset metal spatula. Store in an airtight tin.

Bake-and-serve within 4 days

STYLE For Nutty Layered Brownie Squares, stir ½ cup chopped walnuts, pecans, or macadamia nuts into the brownie batter along with the chocolate chips.

For Layered White Chocolate Chip–Brownie Squares, substitute white chocolate chips for the miniature semisweet variety in the batter and for the topping.

STUDY Miniature semisweet chocolate chips are added to the batter and, a little while before the block of brownies is fully baked, more chips are sprinkled on top. The look is definitely one of abundance.

ACCENT Reduce the vanilla extract to 1¼ teaspoons in the brownie batter. Add ½ teaspoon chocolate extract along with the vanilla extract.

LAYERED BLONDIE SQUARES

*T*he contrast of a dark cookie crumb layer and golden, chocolate chip–dotted blondie batter is a striking—and inviting—one.

CHOCOLATE COOKIE LAYER

8 tablespoons (1 stick) unsalted butter, melted and cooled to tepid

1½ cups plus 2 tablespoons chocolate cookie crumbs (such as crumbs made from Nabisco Famous Chocolate Wafers)

CHOCOLATE CHIP BATTER

¾ cup plus 2 tablespoons bleached all-purpose flour

¼ cup bleached cake flour

¼ teaspoon baking powder

⅛ teaspoon salt

8 tablespoons (1 stick) unsalted butter, softened

½ cup firmly packed dark brown sugar

3 tablespoons granulated sugar

1 large egg

1 large egg yolk

1½ teaspoons vanilla extract

1 cup plus 2 tablespoons semisweet chocolate chips

¾ cup sweetened flaked coconut

PREHEAT THE OVEN AND PREPARE THE BAKING PAN Preheat the oven to 350 degrees F. Film the inside of an 8 by 8 by 2-inch baking pan with nonstick cooking spray.

MIX, BAKE, AND COOL THE COOKIE LAYER Pour the melted butter into the prepared pan. Spoon the cookie crumbs evenly over the bottom of the pan and press down lightly with the underside of a small offset metal spatula so that the crumbs absorb the butter. Bake the cookie layer in the preheated oven for 4 minutes. Place the baking pan on a rack. Cool for 10 minutes.

MIX THE BATTER Sift the all-purpose flour, cake flour, baking powder, and salt onto a sheet of waxed paper.

Cream the butter in the large bowl of a freestanding electric mixer on moderately low speed for 2 minutes. Add the dark brown sugar and beat for 2 minutes. Add the granulated sugar and beat for 1 minute longer. Blend in the egg, egg yolk, and vanilla extract. On low speed, add the sifted mixture in 2 additions, beating until the particles of flour are absorbed. Stir in the chocolate chips and coconut.

Spoon the batter in large dollops on the cookie crumb layer. Carefully spread the batter over the cookie layer, using a flexible palette knife or spatula and gentle, short strokes.

BAKE, COOL, AND CUT THE SWEET Bake the sweet for 25 minutes, or until the blondie topping is set (the center should be stable, not wobbly) and light golden on top. Cool the sweet in the pan on a rack. With a small sharp knife, cut the sweet into quarters, then cut each quarter into 4 squares. Remove the squares from the baking pan, using a small offset metal spatula. Store in an airtight tin.

Bake-and-serve within 2 days

LAYERED SEMISWEET, WHITE CHOCOLATE, AND VANILLA BARS

2 dozen bars

*A*ll bar cookies should be this quick, simple, and satisfying: a crumb base supports a chewy mingle of two kinds of chips, walnuts, and coconut. Sumptuous.

VANILLA COOKIE LAYER

8 tablespoons (1 stick) unsalted butter, melted, cooled to tepid, and combined with ½ teaspoon vanilla extract

1⅔ cups vanilla wafer cookie crumbs (such as crumbs made from Nabisco Nilla wafers)

CHOCOLATE CHIP, COCONUT, AND WALNUT LAYER

1 cup semisweet chocolate chips

½ cup white chocolate chips

1 cup chopped walnuts

1½ cups sweetened flaked coconut

1 can (14 ounces) sweetened condensed milk

PREHEAT THE OVEN TO 350 DEGREES F. Film the inside of a 9 by 9 by 2-inch baking pan with nonstick cooking spray.

MAKE THE COOKIE LAYER Pour the melted butter–vanilla mixture into the prepared pan. Spoon the cookie crumbs evenly over the bottom of the pan and press down lightly with the underside of a small offset metal spatula so that the crumbs absorb the butter.

TOP THE COOKIE LAYER Sprinkle the semisweet chocolate chips in an even layer over the cookie base, then top with an even layer of the white chocolate chips and walnuts. Top with an even layer of the coconut. Pour the sweetened condensed milk evenly over, making sure to drizzle some along the edges and at the corners of the baking pan so that the bars will be nicely moist throughout.

BAKE, COOL, AND CUT THE BARS Bake the sweet in the preheated oven for 30 minutes, or until set and light golden on top. Take care not to overbake the bars, or they will be tough, rather than moist and chewy.

Let the sweet stand in the baking pan on a rack until completely cool. With a small sharp knife, cut the sweet into quarters, then cut each quarter into 6 bars. Remove the bars from the baking pan, using a small offset metal spatula. Store in an airtight tin.

Bake-and-serve within 2 days

LAYERED CHUNKS-OF-CHOCOLATE SQUARES

16 squares

*T*he complex flavor of chocolate in this bar cookie is reinforced by a vanilla crumb crust layer. These squares are bold and stylish.

VANILLA COOKIE LAYER

8 tablespoons (1 stick) unsalted butter, melted and cooled to tepid

1⅔ cups vanilla wafer cookie crumbs (such as crumbs made from Nabisco Nilla wafers)

DARK CHOCOLATE BATTER

1¼ cups bleached all-purpose flour

¼ cup unsweetened alkalized cocoa powder

¼ teaspoon baking powder

¼ teaspoon salt

½ pound (16 tablespoons or 2 sticks) unsalted butter, melted and cooled to tepid

6 ounces unsweetened chocolate, melted and cooled to tepid

5 large eggs

2 cups superfine sugar

2½ teaspoons vanilla extract

6 ounces bittersweet chocolate, chopped into small chunks

TOPPING

4 ounces bittersweet chocolate, coarsely chopped, for sprinkling on the dark chocolate batter

Confectioners' sugar, for sifting over the top of the squares (optional)

PREHEAT THE OVEN TO 325 DEGREES F. Film the inside of a 10 by 10 by 2-inch baking pan with nonstick cooking spray.

MIX, BAKE, AND COOL THE COOKIE LAYER Pour the melted butter into the prepared pan. Spoon the cookie crumbs evenly over the bottom of the pan and press down lightly with the underside of a small offset metal spatula so that the crumbs absorb the butter. Bake the cookie layer in the preheated oven for 4 minutes. Place the baking pan on a rack. Cool for 10 minutes.

MIX THE BATTER Sift the flour, cocoa powder, baking powder, and salt onto a sheet of waxed paper.

Whisk the melted butter and melted chocolate in medium-size mixing bowl until smooth. In a large mixing bowl, whisk the eggs for 1 minute to blend, add the sugar, and whisk for 45 seconds to 1 minute, or until incorporated. Blend in the melted butter and chocolate mixture, mixing thoroughly. Blend in the vanilla extract. Sift the flour mixture over and slowly stir (or whisk) it in, mixing until the particles of flour are absorbed. Stir in the 6 ounces chopped chocolate.

Spoon the batter in large dollops on the cookie crumb layer. Carefully spread the batter over the cookie layer, using a flexible palette knife or spatula. Scatter the 4 ounces chopped chocolate on the top of the batter.

BAKE, COOL, AND CUT THE SWEET Bake the sweet in the preheated oven for 35 to 40 minutes, or until set. Let the sweet stand in the pan on a cooling rack for 2 hours, then refrigerate for 1 hour, or until firm enough to cut.

With a small sharp knife, cut the sweet into quarters, then cut each quarter into 4 squares. Remove the squares from the baking pan, using a small offset metal spatula. Store in an airtight tin. Sift confectioners' sugar on top of the squares just before serving, if you wish.

Bake-and-serve within 4 days

STYLE For Layered Chunks-of-White Chocolate Squares, substitute 6 ounces of white chocolate, cut into chunks, for the bittersweet variety in the dark chocolate batter.

For Nutty Layered Chunks-of-Chocolate Squares, stir ½ cup chopped walnuts, pecans, or macadamia nuts into the dark chocolate batter along with the chocolate chunks.

ACCENT Reduce the vanilla extract to 2 teaspoons in the dark chocolate batter. Add ½ teaspoon chocolate extract along with the vanilla extract.

I WAS BORN INTO A CHOCOLATE-LOVING FAMILY. Is it any wonder that I'm so pre-occupied with this flavor? Reflecting on the way chocolate has brightened my recipes over the years, I remember—with sweet sentimentality—many of the cakes, cookies, and pies that have long been a part of my own baking tradition and of two home bakers closely related to me, my mother, and paternal grandmother. My grandma's recipe for marble cake, written in her own hand on the now faint blue-lined page, continually reminds me of all the sweetness I have inherited.

GRANDMA LILLY'S MARBLE CAKE

One 10-inch cake, creating 16 slices

I cherish the memory of my paternal grandmother's kitchen, where pound cake was often found on her sleek and expansive stainless-steel countertop. Marble cake was one of Grandma Lilly's specialties, a treat that appears in her little black book of handwritten recipes which was passed down to me. (Her private "cookbook" defines the word *homemade*.) I have made some small adjustments in the recipe, but, in the main, the following formula represents it well.

This noble cake, with its genteel crumb and genuinely pure taste, is honest and understated but sophisticated—qualities that my grandma both possessed and admired, in baking and in life.

CHOCOLATE MIXTURE

3 ounces unsweetened chocolate, finely chopped

¼ cup granulated sugar

¼ cup boiling water

¼ teaspoon baking soda

VANILLA BATTER

3 cups bleached cake flour

3 teaspoons baking powder

½ teaspoon salt

12 tablespoons (1½ sticks) unsalted butter, softened

2 cups granulated sugar

4 large eggs, separated

1 teaspoon vanilla extract

¾ cup milk

¼ teaspoon cream of tartar

Confectioners' sugar, for sifting on top of the baked cake (optional)

PREHEAT THE OVEN TO 350 DEGREES F. Film the inside of a 10-inch Bundt pan with nonstick cooking spray.

PREPARE THE CHOCOLATE MIXTURE In a small, heavy saucepan, place the chopped chocolate, the ¼ cup sugar, and the boiling water. Place over low heat and cook slowly, stirring frequently, until the mixture is smooth. Remove from the heat and cool. Blend in the baking soda.

MIX THE BATTER Sift the flour, baking powder, and salt onto a sheet of waxed paper.

Cream the butter in the large bowl of a freestanding electric mixer on moderate speed for 3 minutes. Add the 2 cups granulated sugar in 3 additions, beating for 1 minute after each portion is added. Add the egg yolks and beat for 30 seconds. Blend in the vanilla extract. On low speed, alternately add the sifted mixture in 3 additions with the milk in 2 additions, beginning and ending with the sifted mixture. Scrape down the sides of the mixing bowl frequently to keep the batter even-textured.

Spoon half of the batter into another bowl. Into one amount, stir in the cooled chocolate mixture.

In a clean dry bowl, whip the egg whites until just beginning to swell, add the cream of tartar, and continue whipping until firm (not stiff) peaks are formed. Spoon half of the egg white mixture into each bowl of batter. Fold the whites into each batter until incorporated.

ASSEMBLE THE CHOCOLATE AND VANILLA BATTERS Spoon the vanilla batter into the prepared pan. Spoon the chocolate batter over it. Lightly swirl the two mixtures together, using a flexible palette knife or round-edged table knife, taking care to keep the knife from scraping against the bottom or sides of the baking pan.

BAKE AND COOL THE CAKE Bake the cake in the preheated oven for 1 hour, or until risen, set, and a toothpick inserted in the cake withdraws clean. The baked cake will pull away slightly from the sides of the baking pan.

Cool the cake in the pan on a rack for 10 to 15 minutes. Invert onto another cooling rack to cool completely. Store in an airtight cake keeper. Just before slicing and serving, sift confectioners' sugar over the top of the cake, if you wish.

Bake-and-serve within 2 days

CHOCOLATE CHIP MACAROONS

1 dozen cookies

*P*lacing these macaroons in one specific time frame is nearly impossible for me, as I have baked versions of them since forever (or so it seems). Dainty little macaroons: my miniature baking phase. Macaroons encased in both dark and white chocolate, with and without more chocolate circulating in swirls inside: my baroque baking phase. Large and slightly lofty, with surprises-of-chocolate-chips macaroons: my current baking phase. The recipe below makes a wildly rich batch of macaroons because it calls for sweetened flaked coconut and a certain amount of granulated sugar; combined, both ingredients make the moistest, chewiest cookies. Be sure to savor them freshly baked. These are like candy.

COCONUT MIXTURE

⅔ cup plus 1 tablespoon granulated sugar

2 large egg whites

Large pinch of salt

1¾ teaspoons vanilla extract

3 cups sweetened flaked coconut

⅔ cup miniature semisweet chocolate chips

PREHEAT THE OVEN TO 350 DEGREES F. Line a heavy cookie sheet or rimmed sheet pan with cooking parchment paper.

MIX THE COCONUT MIXTURE Whisk the sugar, egg whites, salt, and vanilla extract in a large mixing bowl. Add the coconut and chocolate chips. Mix the ingredients thoroughly to moisten the flakes of coconut evenly. Lightly knead the mixture together to form a damp, cohesive, and clingy mass.

SHAPE THE COOKIES Divide the coconut mixture into 12 portions. Form each portion into a pyramid-shaped mound, pressing the mixture together lightly. Place the mounds 2 inches apart on the prepared pan. With your fingertips, slightly compress the base and sides of each macaroon to give it definition and height, keeping the edges flaky. This will prevent the cookies from collapsing as they bake.

BAKE AND COOL THE COOKIES Bake the cookies in the preheated oven for 21 to 25 minutes, or until set and light golden. The macaroons will be spotty golden on the sides where the flakes gently protrude. There will be a small syrupy pool at the base of the macaroons—OK. Use a small palette knife to scrape the syrup toward the edge of each macaroon after removing the pan of cookies from the oven. Let the macaroons stand on the pan for 15 minutes, then transfer them to a clean sheet of parchment paper, using a wide offset metal spatula. Cool the macaroons completely on the parchment paper. Store in an airtight tin.

Bake-and-serve within 3 days

STUDY It is important to use parchment paper for lining the pan because the macaroon mixture is sticky.

Baker's packages the moistest, most flavorful flaked coconut to use in these macaroons.

Avoid using an insulated cookie sheet for baking macaroons, for it will only extend the baking time and cause the cookies to dry out.

Overbaking the macaroons will dry them out.

About 3½ dozen cookies

Just heaped with chocolate chips, these are the oatmeal cookies that will brighten a disconsolate mood, fill up a tin with ease, and charm all those dedicated oatmeal-cookie-lovers you know. Can you ever have too many recipes for oatmeal cookies that include chocolate?

CHUNKY OATMEAL DOUGH

2 cups bleached all-purpose flour

1 teaspoon baking soda

½ teaspoon salt

½ pound (16 tablespoons or 2 sticks) unsalted butter, softened

1¾ cups firmly packed light brown sugar

¼ cup granulated sugar

2 large eggs

1 tablespoon vanilla extract

2 cups "quick-cooking" (not instant) rolled oats

2½ cups semisweet chocolate chips

1⅔ cups sweetened flaked coconut

¾ cup chopped walnuts (optional)

PREHEAT THE OVEN TO 350 DEGREES F. Line several cookie sheets or rimmed sheet pans with cooking parchment paper.

MIX THE DOUGH Whisk the flour, baking soda, and salt in a medium-size mixing bowl.

Cream the butter in the large bowl of a freestanding electric mixer on moderately low speed for 3 minutes. Add the light brown sugar in 2 additions, beating for 1 minute after each portion is added. Add the granulated sugar and beat for 2 minutes longer. Blend in the eggs,

one at a time, beating until just incorporated. Blend in the vanilla extract. At this point, the batter will be creamy and dense. On low speed, blend in the sifted ingredients in 2 additions, beating until the flour particles are absorbed. Scrape down the sides of the mixing bowl frequently to keep the dough even-textured. Blend in the rolled oats, chocolate chips, coconut, and walnuts (if you are using them). The batter will be buttery, thick, and chunky. (On a hot day or in a warm kitchen, spread the dough out in a baking pan and refrigerate for 45 minutes before shaping and baking.)

SHAPE THE COOKIES Place heaping 3-tablespoon-size mounds of dough on the prepared pans, spacing the mounds about 3 inches apart. Keep the edges craggy.

BAKE AND COOL THE COOKIES Bake the cookies in the preheated oven for 13 to 14 minutes, or until set and lightly golden. The baked cookies will be softly set (and no longer look like moist dough). Do not overbake. Let the cookies stand on the pans for 2 to 3 minutes (or until stable enough to move), then transfer them to cooling racks, using a wide offset metal spatula. Store in an airtight tin.

Bake-and-serve within 2 days

STYLE For Home on the Range Cookies with Bittersweet Chocolate, substitute 12 ounces bittersweet chocolate, chopped into small chunks, for the semisweet chocolate chips.

STUDY Keep the edges of the cookie dough craggy as you assemble them on the baking pans. Don't bother to smooth them, for the roughhewn borders are an earthy, textural relief to the chewy crumb.

BOSTON CREAM CAKELETTES

A buttery cake, split, filled with pastry cream, and lacquered with chocolate glaze, is especially tempting. The cream filling is a gentle, willowy contrast to the vanilla-flavored cake and the chocolate glaze makes the entire sweet worth the splurge. This is my version of the beloved Boston Cream Pie.

If you like, decorate the top of each finished cake with a rosette of buttercream frosting, a candied violet, a tiny bouquet of crystallized mint leaves, a sprinkle of nuts, shards of nut brittle, or shavings of bittersweet chocolate.

BUTTER CAKE BATTER

2 cups bleached all-purpose flour

1 cup bleached cake flour

2¼ teaspoons baking powder

¾ teaspoon salt

½ pound (16 tablespoons or 2 sticks) unsalted butter, softened

2 cups granulated sugar

3 large eggs

2 large egg yolks

2 teaspoons vanilla extract

1 cup milk

FILLING

Vanilla Cream Filling (page 294)

GLAZE

Dark Chocolate Glaze (page 295)

PREHEAT THE OVEN TO 350 DEGREES F. Lightly grease the insides of 11 Mini Wonder Mold cups (each pan contains 4 cups; each cup measures 3½ inches in diameter across the top and 2¾ to 3 inches deep, with a capacity of 1⅛ cups) with shortening and dust with flour.

MIX THE BATTER Sift the all-purpose flour, cake flour, baking powder, and salt twice onto a sheet of waxed paper.

Cream the butter in the large bowl of a freestanding electric mixer on moderate speed for 3 minutes. Add the sugar in 3 additions, beating for 1 to 2 minutes after each portion is added. The butter and sugar mixture should be thoroughly beaten. Add the eggs, one at a time, beating for 30 to 45 seconds after each addition. Blend in the egg yolks and vanilla extract. On low speed, alternately add the sifted mixture in 3 additions with the milk in 2 additions, beginning and ending with the sifted mixture. Scrape down the sides of the mixing bowl frequently to keep the batter even-textured.

Spoon the batter into the prepared molds, dividing it evenly among them. Each mold should be filled a little less than half-full. If the molds are filled with too much batter, it will creep over the top onto the surface of the pan and form baked-on ledges.

BAKE AND COOL THE CAKELETTES Bake the cakelettes in the preheated oven for 27 minutes, or until risen, set, and a toothpick inserted in the center of each cake withdraws clean. Cool the cakelettes in the pans on racks for 10 minutes, then invert onto other cooling racks. Cool completely.

ASSEMBLE THE CAKELETTES WITH THE FILLING AND GLAZE Cut each cakelette in half horizontally about 1¾ inches from the bottom, using a serrated knife. Place the bottom half of a cakelette on a dessert plate, spoon some of the cream filling on the surface and set the top on, pressing lightly. Repeat with remaining cakelettes. Spoon some of the warm glaze on top of each filled cakelette, allowing it to trickle down the sides, and garnish the top, if you wish.

Serve the filled and glazed cakelettes at once.

STUDY A word about size: *cakelettes* may be a bit of false advertising here, for these aren't miniature cakes; they are, perhaps, smaller than large and much larger than miniature. And very good.

The Chocolate Fudge Sauce (page 376) can also be used to nap the top of each cakelette. Heat the sauce to warm, then spoon it over each filled cake.

 # VANILLA CREAM FILLING

About 2 cups pastry cream

Perfect for sandwiching together freshly baked cakelette halves, this filling is sleek and sensual.

⅔ cup granulated sugar

3 tablespoons cornstarch

Pinch of salt

½ cup heavy cream

½ cup light (table) cream

1 cup milk

4 large egg yolks

2 teaspoons vanilla extract

2 tablespoons cold unsalted butter, cut into small cubes

½ teaspoon vanilla bean paste (optional)

Sift the sugar, cornstarch, and salt into a heavy, medium-size saucepan (preferably enameled cast iron). Whisk the mixture to thoroughly integrate the cornstarch. Gradually stir in the heavy cream, then the light cream and milk. Place the saucepan over moderately high heat and bring to a low boil, stirring constantly with a wooden spoon or flat wooden paddle. Let the cream mixture bubble until lightly thickened (it will resemble soft pudding), about 1 to 2 minutes.

In a small heatproof mixing bowl, mix the egg yolks to blend. Remove the saucepan of thickened cream from the heat, and blend two large spoonfuls (about ½ cup) of the hot cream into the yolks, mixing well. Slowly stir the tempered egg yolk mixture into the cream base. Return the saucepan to the heat and cook at a gentle boil, stirring slowly, for 1 to 2 minutes, or until nicely thickened. The filling should reach a temperature of 200 degrees F. to achieve the correct stability and thickness.

Place the vanilla extract, cubes of butter, and vanilla bean paste (if you are using it) into a medium-size heatproof mixing bowl. Place a sieve on top, scrape the cream filling into it, and smooth it through with a heatproof spatula. Stir to combine the vanilla extract, butter, and (optional) vanilla bean paste into the hot filling. Immediately press a sheet of food-safe plastic wrap directly onto the surface of the filling.

Cool for 15 minutes. Remove and discard the plastic wrap. Scrape the filling into a container, press a clean piece of plastic wrap on the surface, cover tightly, and refrigerate for 2 hours before using. The pastry cream can be stored in the refrigerator for up to 1 day.

 # DARK CHOCOLATE GLAZE

About 2¼ cups glaze

A dazzling overlay. This compelling glaze is a glossy way to coat the surface of any cake—especially a butter cake graced with a center of vanilla, chocolate, or coconut pastry cream.

6 ounces unsweetened chocolate, chopped

8 tablespoons (1 stick) unsalted butter, cut into chunks

1 cup granulated sugar

2 tablespoons cornstarch

Pinch of salt

1 cup milk

2 teaspoons vanilla extract

Place the chopped chocolate and butter in a small, heavy saucepan (preferably enameled cast iron) and set over low heat. Stir from time to time to melt the two together completely. Whisk until smooth. Remove from the heat.

Sift the sugar, cornstarch, and salt into a heavy, medium-size saucepan (preferably enameled cast iron). Whisk the mixture to thoroughly incorporate the cornstarch and sugar. Slowly pour in the milk, blending well. Blend in the chocolate mixture with a wooden spoon or flat wooden paddle.

Place the saucepan over moderately high heat and bring to a low boil, stirring slowly and constantly with a wooden spoon or flat wooden paddle. When the mixture begins to bubble, reduce the heat to moderate, and let it bubble slowly for 1 to 2 minutes, or until lightly thickened. The glaze should coat a wooden spoon.

Place a sieve on top of a medium-size heatproof mixing bowl. Pour the hot glaze into the sieve and press it through with a heatproof spatula. Blend in the vanilla extract, stirring until smooth.

Use the glaze warm to spoon over a whole cake or individual cakelettes.

STUDY Sifting, then whisking the sugar, cornstarch, and salt distributes the thickening agent evenly.

"CHOCOLATE" LAYER CAKE

One 3-layer, 8-inch cake, creating 12 slices

*I*n a long-ago cake-baking era (and as early as the 1930s), a white or yellow butter cake layered and covered with chocolate frosting was called a "chocolate layer cake." If the frosting is dark and substantial enough, and absolutely radiating chocolate, this kind of cake fits my definition of bliss. You will love this buttery white cake—it's moist, softly textured, a gem.

VANILLA CAKE BATTER

3 cups plus 2 tablespoons bleached cake flour

3 teaspoons baking powder

¾ teaspoon salt

12 tablespoons (1½ sticks) unsalted butter, softened

2 cups superfine sugar

2½ teaspoons vanilla extract

1⅓ cups plus 2 tablespoons ice-cold water

4 large egg whites

¼ teaspoon cream of tartar

FROSTING

Deep Chocolate Frosting (page 297)

PREHEAT THE OVEN TO 350 DEGREES F. Lightly grease the inside of three 8-inch layer cake pans (1½ inches deep) with shortening, line the bottom of each pan with a circle of waxed paper cut to fit, grease the paper, and dust with flour.

MIX THE BATTER Sift the flour, baking powder, and salt twice onto a sheet of waxed paper.

Cream the butter in the large bowl of a freestanding electric mixer on moderate speed for 3 minutes. Add the superfine sugar in 3 additions, beating for 1 minute on moderately high speed after each portion is added. Blend in the vanilla extract. On low speed, alternately add the sifted mixture in 3 additions with the ice-cold water in 2 additions, beginning and ending with the sifted mixture. Scrape down the sides of the mixing bowl frequently to keep the batter even-textured. Until the batter comes together fully, it will appear curdled in some of the mix-

ing stages—OK. Beat the completed batter on moderate speed for 15 seconds.

In a clean, dry bowl, whip the egg whites until beginning to swell, add the cream of tartar, and continue whipping until firm (not stiff) peaks are formed. Stir about one-quarter of the whipped whites into the batter to lighten it, then fold in the remaining whites lightly and completely.

Spoon the batter into the prepared pans, dividing it evenly among them. Spread the batter evenly.

BAKE AND COOL THE LAYERS Bake the cake layers in the preheated oven for 25 to 30 minutes, or until risen, set, and a toothpick inserted in the center of each layer withdraws clean. Cool the layers in the pans on racks for 10 minutes. Invert the layers onto cooling racks, peel away the waxed paper, and cool completely.

SET UP THE SERVING PLATE Tear off four 3-inch-wide strips of waxed paper. Place the strips in the shape of a square around the outer 3 inches of a cake plate.

ASSEMBLE AND FROST THE CAKE Center one cake layer on the plate (partially covering the waxed paper square; the strips should extend by at least 1 inch). Spread over a layer of frosting. Carefully position the second layer on top. Cover with a layer of frosting. Top with the remaining cake layer. Frost the top and sides of the cake, spreading it with a sturdy palette knife. Once set, gently remove and discard the strips of paper. Let the cake stand for at least 1 hour before slicing and serving.

Bake-and-serve within 1 day

STUDY The butter must be completely softened and the water icy, icy cold.

To make icy cold water, fill a large measuring cup with ice cubes. Pour on enough cold water to cover the ice and let stand for 15 to 20 minutes. When very cold, remove the ice, measure out the correct amount of water, and use immediately.

For the finest textured cake, use superfine sugar and sift the dry ingredients twice.

The cake layers are very tender when freshly baked. Spread the frosting over gently and carefully to keep the layers from splitting or cracking.

DEEP CHOCOLATE FROSTING

About 4 cups frosting

*T*his frosting pulsates with chocolate intensity.

6½ cups confectioners' sugar, sifted, or more as needed

⅛ teaspoon salt

5 ounces unsweetened chocolate, melted and cooled to tepid

8 tablespoons (1 stick) unsalted butter, melted and cooled to tepid

2 teaspoons vanilla extract

½ cup milk, heated to tepid

¼ cup heavy cream, or more as needed

Place the confectioners' sugar and salt in the bowl of a heavy-duty freestanding electric mixer fitted with the flat paddle attachment. Beat on low speed to combine. Add the melted chocolate, melted butter, vanilla extract, and milk. Beat the ingredients on low speed for a minute to combine, then continue beating on moderately low speed for 2 minutes. Increase the speed to moderate and beat for 4 minutes longer, or until smooth. Scrape down the sides of the mixing bowl to keep the frosting even-textured. Beat in the heavy cream. Increase the speed to moderately high and beat for 3 minutes, or until increased in volume and creamy.

Adjust the texture of the frosting to spreading consistency as needed, adding additional tablespoons of heavy cream or confectioners' sugar, a little at a time.

STUDY The texture of the frosting turns slightly spongy as it stands; simply beat again for a minute to restore its consistency.

In cold or dry weather, you may need more heavy cream than ¼ cup. The texture of the frosting should be supple enough so that it spreads easily. If the frosting is too stiff, it will cause the cake layers to split.

VANILLA-SCENTED WHIPPED CREAM

3 cups whipped cream

*P*early mounds of whipped cream, light, graceful, and sweetened just so—this is my favorite accompaniment to anything made with chocolate, be it pudding, cake, or pie.

1½ cups cold heavy cream
1 tablespoon plus 1½ teaspoons superfine sugar
1 teaspoon vanilla extract

Chill a mixing bowl and whisk (or beaters). Pour the cream into the bowl and whip the cream until floppy, cas-cading mounds are formed. Sprinkle the sugar and vanilla extract over and beat lightly to combine. Continue whipping the cream until soft, willowy peaks are formed. Use the freshly whipped cream immediately.

STYLE For a sweeter version, increase the superfine sugar to 2 tablespoons.

A BLISSFUL LAYER CAKE

One 3-layer, 9-inch cake, creating 12 slices

This layer cake maximizes the flavor of chocolate. The combination of its rounded buttery flavor and seriously unrivaled moistness is what makes it so delicious. And when the tender, moist layers meet a satiny chocolate frosting—a wild composite of chocolate, confectioners' sugar, sour cream, butter, and heavy cream—the two combine to create a handsome cake, big and bold.

MOIST CHOCOLATE CAKE BATTER

4 ounces unsweetened chocolate, melted

½ cup plus 3 tablespoons boiling water

2⅔ cups bleached all-purpose flour

2 teaspoons baking powder

1¼ teaspoons baking soda

½ teaspoon salt

½ pound (16 tablespoons or 2 sticks) unsalted butter, softened

1¾ cups granulated sugar

½ cup firmly packed light brown sugar

4 large eggs

2 teaspoons vanilla extract

1⅓ cups plus 2 tablespoons sour cream

FROSTING

Chocolate Satin Frosting (page 306)

PREHEAT THE OVEN TO 375 DEGREES F. Lightly grease the inside of three 9-inch layer cake pans (1½ inches deep) with shortening, line the bottom of each pan with a circle of waxed paper cut to fit, grease the paper, and dust with flour.

MIX THE BATTER Combine the melted chocolate and boiling water in a small, heatproof bowl. Mix well. Cool to tepid. When tepid, the chocolate mixture will have the consistency of moderately thick pudding. Use the mixture tepid, not cold.

Sift the flour, baking powder, baking soda, and salt onto a sheet of waxed paper.

Cream the butter in the large bowl of a freestanding electric mixer on moderate speed for 3 minutes. Add the granulated sugar in 4 additions, beating for 1 minute after each portion is added. (Do not skimp on the beating time.) Add the light brown sugar and beat for 1 minute. Add the eggs, one at a time, beating for 45 seconds after each addition. Blend in the vanilla extract and chocolate mixture. On low speed, alternately add the sifted mixture in 3 additions with the sour cream in 2 additions, beginning and ending with the sifted mixture. Scrape down the sides of the mixing bowl frequently to keep the batter even-textured.

Spoon the batter into the prepared pans, dividing it evenly among them. Spread the batter evenly.

BAKE AND COOL THE LAYERS Bake the cake layers in the preheated oven for 30 minutes, or until risen, set, and a toothpick inserted in the center of each layer withdraws clean or with a few crumbs attached. Cool the layers in the pans on racks for 10 minutes. Invert the layers onto other cooling racks, peel away the waxed paper, and cool completely.

SET UP THE SERVING PLATE Tear off four 3-inch-wide strips of waxed paper. Place the strips in the shape of a square around the outer 3 inches of a cake plate.

ASSEMBLE AND FROST THE CAKE Center one cake layer on the plate (partially covering the waxed paper square; the strips should extend by at least 1 inch). Spread over a layer of frosting. Carefully position the second layer on top. Cover with a layer of frosting. Top with the remaining cake layer. Frost the top and sides of the cake. Once the frosting is set, gently remove and discard the strips of paper.

Let the cake stand for 1 hour before slicing and serving.

Bake-and-serve within 1 day

CHOCOLATE SATIN FROSTING

About 6 cups frosting

*V*elvety and creamy as can be, and chocolatey to boot.

9 ounces unsweetened chocolate, melted and cooled

13 tablespoons (1 stick plus 5 tablespoons) unsalted butter, melted and cooled

4¾ cups confectioners' sugar, sifted

Large pinch of salt

1½ cups plus 2 tablespoons sour cream

2 tablespoons heavy cream

2½ teaspoons vanilla extract

Place the melted chocolate and melted butter in the bowl of a heavy-duty freestanding electric mixer fitted with the whisk attachment. Beat on low speed to mix until smooth. Blend in half of the confectioners' sugar and the salt. Beat on low speed for 1 minute. Add the remaining confectioners' sugar and beat to combine. Add the sour cream and vanilla extract. Beat on low speed for 1 minute. Increase the speed to moderately low and beat for 2 minutes. Add the heavy cream. Increase the speed to moderately high (#7 on a heavy-duty KitchenAid free-standing mixer) and beat until shiny and very creamy, about 8 minutes longer.

Cover the frosting and refrigerate for 1 hour, or until firm enough to spread. Rebeat the frosting for 1 to 2 minutes on moderately high speed just before using. If the frosting seems slack, or in a hot kitchen, beat in up to ⅔ cup confectioners' sugar, 2 tablespoons at a time.

STUDY For years I have been making a sour cream–chocolate ganache for covering various firm-textured cakes and tortes. Adding both confectioners' sugar and heavy cream to the ganache makes a frosting that's perfect for assembling between and about downy layers of cake.

Refrigerating the frosting for 1 hour before spreading sets its texture.

In hot weather or in a warm kitchen, always refrigerate a finished cake (and any leftovers) put together with this frosting.

THE VITALITY OF CHOCOLATE COMES FORWARD IN SOME OF THE MOST UNEXPECTED PLACES, like in pancake and waffle batters. The batters are fashioned with cocoa powder, unsweetened chocolate, miniature semisweet chocolate chips, white chocolate chips, and milk chocolate chips, all the better to add uninterrupted chocolate flavor to what you griddle on the stovetop or enclose between the grids of a waffle iron.

HEAVENLY BITTERSWEET CHOCOLATE CHUNK WAFFLES

7 Belgian-style 2-sided waffles

*T*he best way to describe these waffles is "fully loaded"—with cream, butter, and chocolate. A portion of cake flour conveys a tender quality to the batter, acting as a delicate backdrop to the chopped bittersweet chocolate that laces the waffles. A full tablespoon of vanilla extract heightens their buttery, sweet cream flavor.

2¼ cups bleached all-purpose flour

¾ cup bleached cake flour

3 teaspoons baking powder

⅛ teaspoon salt

½ cup granulated sugar

1½ cups heavy cream

6 large eggs

1 tablespoon vanilla extract

10 tablespoons (1 stick plus 2 tablespoons) unsalted butter, melted and cooled to tepid

6 ounces bittersweet chocolate, chopped

Confectioners' sugar, for sprinkling on the finished waffles

MIX THE BATTER Sift the all-purpose flour, cake flour, baking powder, salt, and granulated sugar into a large mixing bowl.

In a medium-size mixing bowl, whisk the heavy cream, eggs, and vanilla extract. Add the melted butter and blend well. Pour the liquid ingredients over the sifted mixture, scatter the chopped chocolate over, and stir to form a batter, taking care to scrape the sides and bottom of the bowl as you are mixing. The batter will be slightly lumpy—OK.

MAKE THE WAFFLES Preheat a deep-dish waffle iron composed of two 4½-inch squares (the entire grid section measures about 4½ by 9 inches). Spoon ⅓ to ½ cup batter onto each square of the preheated iron. Cook the waffles for about 1½ to 2 minutes, or until set, cooked through, and golden. Lift the waffles onto warm serving plates. Wait a moment before serving the waffles to allow the chunks of chocolate to cool. Serve the waffles sprinkled with confectioners' sugar.

SOUR CREAM–MINI CHIP PANCAKES

About 18 pancakes

This batter is just a sneaky way of working miniature chocolate chips into flapjacks. Who would disapprove of having a plateful of these gracefully tender pancakes for brunch? Or as a late-night treat? Certainly not me. When the day needs to be brightened with chocolate, heat up the griddle and spoon on the batter.

SOUR CREAM MINI CHIP BATTER

1⅓ cups plus 2 tablespoons bleached all-purpose flour

¾ teaspoon baking powder

½ teaspoon baking soda

Large pinch of salt

¼ cup granulated sugar

2 large eggs

1 large egg yolk

6 tablespoons unsalted butter, melted and cooled to tepid

1¼ cups sour cream

⅔ cup light (table) cream, or more as needed

1¼ teaspoons vanilla extract

¾ cup miniature semisweet chocolate chips

Unsalted butter, for the griddle or skillet

Confectioners' sugar, for sprinkling on the griddled pancakes

MIX THE BATTER Sift the all-purpose flour, baking powder, baking soda, salt, and sugar into a medium-size bowl.

In another medium-size mixing bowl, whisk the eggs, egg yolk, melted butter, sour cream, light cream, and vanilla extract until blended. Pour the whisked mixture over the sifted dry ingredients, add the chocolate chips, and stir to form a batter, using a wooden spoon or spatula. The batter should be moderately thick. Adjust the consistency as needed by adding more table cream, 1 to 2 tablespoons at a time.

GRIDDLE THE PANCAKES Heat a griddle and swipe the surface with butter. The coating of butter should be filmy. The griddle should be just moderately hot so that the batter sizzles lightly, as intense heat will scorch the chocolate chips in the batter.

Spoon 3-tablespoon portions of batter on the griddle, placing them about 3 inches apart. Cook the pancakes for about 45 seconds, or until set and a few bubbles appear on the tops. Flip the pancakes, using a wide offset metal spatula, and griddle for 45 seconds to 1 minute longer, or until cooked through. Continue to griddle pancakes with the remaining batter, cooking them in batches, and filming the griddle with more butter as needed. If the batter becomes very thick as it stands, thin it with a little extra cream.

Lift the griddled pancakes onto warm serving plates. Sprinkle the tops of the pancakes with confectioners' sugar. For an excessive but divine fillip, dollop the spray of pancakes with Softly Whipped and Scented Cream (page 229).

STUDY The duo of light cream and sour cream fortifies a pancake batter beautifully. The two dairy ingredients develop a creamy-textured, ultra-moist crumb.

DARK CHOCOLATE WAFFLES

5 Belgian-style 2-sided waffles or about 10 heart-shaped waffles

Cocoa powder cultivates a waffle batter in a deep, dark, and enchanted way, making such a fine dessert waffle—simply delicious served warm with a pour of hot fudge sauce, a cold and creamy scoop of vanilla ice cream, or breeze of whipped cream. Once you've lingered over these on a casual late-night weekend, you may forget about making plain waffles ever again.

DARK CHOCOLATE BATTER

1½ cups bleached all-purpose flour

⅔ cup plus 2 tablespoons unsweetened alkalized cocoa powder

1¾ teaspoons baking powder

¼ teaspoon baking soda

⅛ teaspoon salt

1 cup superfine sugar

9 tablespoons (1 stick plus 1 tablespoon) unsalted butter, melted and cooled to tepid

3 large eggs

⅓ cup plus 2 tablespoons sour cream

2 teaspoons vanilla extract

1⅓ cups milk

¾ cup miniature semisweet chocolate chips

Confectioners' sugar, for sprinkling over the waffles

MIX THE BATTER Sift the flour, cocoa powder, baking powder, baking soda, salt, and sugar into a medium-size mixing bowl.

In another medium-size mixing bowl, whisk the melted butter, eggs, sour cream, vanilla extract, and milk. Pour the whisked mixture over the sifted mixture, add the chocolate chips, and stir to form a batter, using a wooden spoon or flat paddle, mixing until the particles of flour are absorbed. Be sure to sweep the bottom and sides of the mixing bowl to thoroughly incorporate the dry ingredients.

MAKE THE WAFFLES Preheat a deep-dish waffle iron composed of two 4½-inch squares (the entire grid section measures about 4½ by 9 inches). Or, preheat a 5-interconnected-heart waffler.

Spoon ⅓ to ½ cup batter onto each square of the preheated deep-dish iron; spoon about ⅔ batter into the center of the single 5-heart waffler. Cook the waffles for about 1½ to 2 minutes, or until completely cooked through and set. Lift waffles onto warm serving plates. The heart-shaped waffle can be served whole, or divided into individual hearts. Wait a moment before serving them to allow the chips to cool down. Sprinkle the waffles with confectioners' sugar and serve.

DARK CHOCOLATE–WHITE CHOCOLATE CHIP PANCAKES

About 22 pancakes

A scattering of red, ripe strawberries, small and intense, and wafts of freshly whipped cream would make a plate of these tender white chocolate and cocoa powder–suffused pancakes shine.

DARK CHOCOLATE BATTER

1⅔ cups bleached all-purpose flour

¼ cup unsweetened alkalized cocoa powder

⅛ teaspoon salt

1¾ teaspoons baking powder

6 tablespoons (¾ stick) unsalted butter, melted and cooled to tepid

1 ounce unsweetened chocolate, melted and cooled to tepid

2 large eggs

⅓ cup granulated sugar

1¾ teaspoons vanilla extract

1⅓ cups milk

¾ cup white chocolate chips

Unsalted butter, for the griddle or skillet

Vanilla-Scented Whipped Cream (page 303)

Confectioners' sugar, for sprinkling on the griddled pancakes (optional)

MIX THE BATTER Sift the flour, cocoa powder, salt, and baking powder into a medium-size mixing bowl.

In another medium-size mixing bowl, whisk the melted butter, melted chocolate, eggs, sugar, and vanilla extract to combine; whisk in the milk. Pour the egg mixture over the sifted ingredients, add the white chocolate chips, and stir to form a batter, using a wooden spoon or flat wooden paddle. Take care to incorporate any lingering pockets of the sifted mixture at the bottom and sides of the bowl.

GRIDDLE THE PANCAKES Heat a griddle and swipe the surface with butter. The coating of butter should be filmy. The griddle should be just moderately hot so that the batter sizzles lightly, as intense heat will scorch the cocoa powder and unsweetened chocolate–enriched batter.

Spoon 3-tablespoon amounts of batter on the griddle, placing them about 3 inches apart. Cook the pancakes for about 45 seconds, or until set and a few bubbles appear on the tops. Flip the pancakes, using a wide offset metal spatula, and griddle for about 45 seconds longer, or until cooked through. Continue to griddle pancakes with the remaining batter, cooking them in batches, and filming the griddle with more butter as needed. If the batter becomes very thick as it stands, thin it with a little more milk.

Lift the griddled pancakes onto serving plates, layering them between dollops of whipped cream. Sprinkle the pancakes with confectioners' sugar, if you wish, and serve.

STYLE For Dark Chocolate–Bittersweet Chocolate Chunk Pancakes, omit the white chocolate chips and stir 3 ounces bittersweet chocolate, chopped into small chunks, into the pancake batter.

CHOCOLATE–MILK CHOCOLATE CHIP PANCAKES

About 36 pancakes

This pancake batter is seasoned—delightfully—with cocoa powder and milk chocolate chips.

COCOA–MILK CHOCOLATE CHIP BATTER

1¾ cups bleached all-purpose flour

¼ cup unsweetened alkalized cocoa powder

Large pinch of salt

2½ teaspoons baking powder

⅓ cup granulated sugar

2 large eggs

5 tablespoons unsalted butter, melted and cooled to tepid

1½ teaspoons vanilla extract

1½ cups milk

¾ cup milk chocolate chips

Unsalted butter, softened, for the griddle or skillet

MIX THE BATTER Sift the flour, cocoa powder, salt, baking powder, and sugar into a large mixing bowl.

Whisk the eggs, melted butter, vanilla extract, and milk in a medium-size mixing bowl. Pour the egg mixture over the sifted ingredients, add the milk chocolate chips, and stir to form a batter, using a wooden spoon or flat wooden paddle. The batter will be moderately thick.

GRIDDLE THE PANCAKES Heat a griddle and swipe the surface with softened butter. The griddle should be hot enough so that the batter sizzles and cooks, but not so hot that it scorches the bottom of the pancakes as they're griddling.

Spoon generous 2-tablespoon amounts of batter on the griddle, placing them about 3 inches apart. Cook the pancakes for about 45 seconds, or until set and a few bubbles appear on the tops. Flip the pancakes, using a wide, offset metal spatula, and griddle for about 1 minute longer, or until cooked through. Continue to griddle pancakes with the remaining batter, cooking them in batches and filming the griddle with more butter as needed. If the batter becomes too thick, thin it with a little more milk.

Lift the griddled pancakes onto warm serving plates. Wait a moment before serving the pancakes to allow the chips to cool down.

CHOCOLATE, AS I HAVE LEARNED OVER THE YEARS IN WORKING WITH SO MANY INTENSITIES AND STYLES, is a highly expressive substance, capable of generating all kinds of appealing textures. In addition to the silkiness of a buttery batter that makes a cake downy and moist, a chocolate dough can be tender-textured in a dense and buttery way, gently soft and firmly cakey at the same time, or outright crunchy. These characteristics occur beautifully in a press-in-the-pan shortbread, shortbread-like butter cookies, delicate madeleines, and snappy, crumbly biscotti.

OATMEAL–CHOCOLATE CHIP SHORTBREAD

One 11-inch cookie, creating 16 pieces

Rolled oats make an otherwise smooth dough craggy, and add a definable earthiness to this cookie. I adore the way that both the chocolate chips and sweet coconut interrupt the composition of the dough.

OATMEAL AND CHOCOLATE CHIP DOUGH

1 cup bleached all-purpose flour

¼ teaspoon baking powder

⅛ teaspoon salt

12 tablespoons (1½ sticks) unsalted butter, softened

⅓ cup firmly packed light brown sugar

2 tablespoons granulated sugar

1½ teaspoons vanilla extract

⅔ cup "quick-cooking" (not "instant") rolled oats

⅔ cup lightly packed sweetened flaked coconut

1 cup semisweet chocolate chips

1½ to 2 tablespoons granulated sugar, for sprinkling on top of the baked shortbread

PREHEAT THE OVEN TO 350 DEGREES F. Have a fluted 11-inch round tart pan (1 inch deep, with a removable bottom) at hand.

MIX THE DOUGH Sift the flour, baking powder, and salt onto a sheet of waxed paper.

Cream the butter in the large bowl of a freestanding electric mixer on moderately low speed for 2 minutes. Add the light brown sugar and granulated sugar; beat for 2 min-utes on low speed. Blend in the vanilla extract. On moderately low speed, blend in half of the sifted ingredients, then the rolled oats, coconut, and chocolate chips. Blend in the remaining sifted mixture, mixing until the particles of flour are absorbed. Scrape down the sides of the mixing bowl frequently to keep the dough even-textured.

Place the dough in the tart pan and press it into an even layer.

BAKE, COOL, AND CUT THE SHORTBREAD Bake the shortbread in the preheated oven for 35 to 40 minutes, or until firm, set, and golden. The baked shortbread will have risen and filled the entire tart pan. Remove the shortbread from the oven and immediately sprinkle the granulated sugar on the surface. Cool the shortbread in the pan on a rack for 15 minutes. Carefully unmold the shortbread, keeping it on the base. Cut into 16 triangular-shaped pieces while still warm, using a serrated knife or chef's knife; cool. Or, cool completely and break the shortbread into casually jagged pieces. Store in an airtight tin.

Bake-and-serve within 1 week

STUDY For a crumblier shortbread, and a good contrast to the rolled oats, replace ¼ cup of the all-purpose flour with rice flour.

BITTERSWEET CHOCOLATE CHUNK SHORTBREAD

One 9-inch cookie, creating 12 pieces

This dough contains enough chunks of bittersweet chocolate to please even me. And I require a lot of chocolate. The rice flour in the dough keeps it lightly splintery, with a fine shear to it, and provides the right textural backdrop to the chunks of chocolate.

BITTERSWEET CHOCOLATE CHUNK DOUGH

1¼ cups bleached all-purpose flour

¼ cup rice flour

¼ teaspoon baking powder

⅛ teaspoon salt

12 tablespoons (1½ sticks) unsalted butter, softened

½ cup superfine sugar

2 teaspoons vanilla extract

4 ounces bittersweet chocolate, chopped into small chunks

About 1 tablespoon granulated sugar, for sprinkling on top of the baked shortbread

PREHEAT THE OVEN TO 325 DEGREES F. Have a fluted 9½-inch round tart pan (1 inch deep, with a removable bottom) at hand.

MAKE THE DOUGH Sift the all-purpose flour, rice flour, baking powder, and salt onto a sheet of waxed paper.

Cream the butter in the large bowl of a freestanding electric mixer on moderately low speed for 2 minutes. Add the sugar and beat on moderately low speed for 2 minutes. Blend in the vanilla extract. On moderately low speed, blend in half of the sifted dry ingredients, then the bittersweet chocolate. Blend in the remaining sifted mixture, mixing until the particles of flour are absorbed. Scrape down the sides of the mixing bowl frequently to keep the dough even-textured.

Place the dough in the tart pan and press it into an even layer.

BAKE, COOL, AND CUT THE SHORTBREAD Bake the shortbread in the preheated oven for 40 to 45 minutes, or until firm, set, and golden. Remove the shortbread from the oven and immediately sprinkle the granulated sugar on the surface. Cool the shortbread in the pan on a rack for 15 minutes. Carefully unmold the shortbread, keeping it on the base. Cut into 12 triangular-shaped pieces while still warm, using a serrated knife or chef's knife; cool. Or, cool completely and break the shortbread into rough pieces. Store in an airtight tin.

Bake-and-serve within 1 week

STUDY If rice flour is unavailable, use 1½ cups bleached all-purpose flour. The shortbread will still be delicious, but a shade denser.

INTENSELY CHOCOLATE SHORTBREAD

Two 8-inch cookies, creating 10 pieces each

*I*t's the cocoa powder in the dough, supported by the butter, that frames the chocolate flavor, but it's those tiny chocolate chips that make the shortbread so endearing.

COCOA CHOCOLATE CHIP DOUGH

2¾ cups bleached all-purpose flour

¼ cup rice flour

¾ teaspoon baking powder

¼ teaspoon salt

¾ cup unsweetened alkalized cocoa powder

¾ pound (3 sticks) unsalted butter, softened

1⅓ cups plus 3 tablespoons confectioners' sugar

2½ teaspoons vanilla extract

¾ cup miniature semisweet chocolate chips

2 tablespoons granulated sugar, for sprinkling on the baked shortbread

PREHEAT THE OVEN TO 325 DEGREES F. Have two fluted 8½-inch round tart pans (each 1 inch deep, with a removable bottom) at hand.

MIX THE DOUGH Sift the all-purpose flour, rice flour, baking powder, salt, and cocoa powder onto a sheet of waxed paper.

Cream the butter in the large bowl of a freestanding electric mixer on moderately low speed for 2 minutes. Add the sugar and beat on moderately low speed for 2 minutes. Blend in the vanilla extract. On low speed, blend in half of the sifted dry ingredients, a little at a time, then the chocolate chips. Blend in the remaining sifted mixture, mixing until the particles of flour are absorbed. Scrape down the sides of the mixing bowl frequently to keep the dough even-textured.

Divide the dough in half. Place half of the dough in the tart pan and press it into an even layer with your fingertips; repeat with the remaining dough. Prick each shortbread dough round with the tines of a fork in 12 to 15 random places.

BAKE, SUGAR, COOL, AND CUT EACH SHORTBREAD Bake the shortbreads in the preheated oven for 45 to 50 minutes, or until firm and set. Remove the shortbreads from the oven to cooling racks and immediately sprinkle the surface of each with granulated sugar. Cool for 15 minutes.

Carefully unmold each shortbread, keeping it on the base. Cut into 10 triangular-shaped pieces while still warm, using a serrated knife or chef's knife; cool. Or, cool completely and break the shortbread into rough pieces. Store in an airtight tin.

Bake-and-serve within 1 week

STUDY My favorite cocoa powder to use in this shortbread is Droste.

TRIPLE-CHOCOLATE BISCOTTI

About 3 dozen cookies

As far as I'm concerned, chocolate nudges out all other flavors in the world of biscotti-baking. This dough, which contains a triple measure of chocolate, is easy to manage; the amount of butter and sugar in the recipe makes for tender cookies. The recipe for Mocha Rusks that appeared in my last book, *Baking by Flavor,* was crafted from this set of ingredients, a formula I've been perfecting for years.

TRIPLE CHOCOLATE DOUGH

3 cups bleached all-purpose flour

⅔ cup plus 2 tablespoons unsweetened alkalized cocoa powder

1¼ teaspoons baking powder

¼ teaspoon baking soda

½ teaspoon salt

13 tablespoons (1 stick plus 5 tablespoons) unsalted butter, softened

1⅓ cups plus 3 tablespoons superfine sugar

3 large eggs

2 ounces unsweetened chocolate, melted and cooled

1 tablespoon plus 1 teaspoon vanilla extract

1⅔ cups miniature semisweet chocolate chips or 10 ounces bittersweet chocolate, chopped into small pieces

PREHEAT THE OVEN TO 350 DEGREES F. Line 3 cookie sheets or rimmed sheet pans with cooking parchment paper.

MIX THE DOUGH Sift the flour, cocoa powder, baking powder, baking soda, and salt onto a sheet of waxed paper.

Cream the butter in the large bowl of a freestanding electric mixer on moderately low speed for 2 minutes. Add the sugar in 2 additions, beating for 1 to 2 minutes on moderate speed after each portion is added. Blend in the eggs, one at a time, beating for 45 seconds after each addition. Blend in the melted chocolate and vanilla extract. On low speed, add the sifted ingredients in 3 additions, beating until the particles of flour are absorbed. Scrape down the sides of the mixing bowl fre-

quently to keep the dough even-textured. Blend in the chocolate chips or bittersweet chocolate pieces. The dough will be dense.

ASSEMBLE THE DOUGH ON THE PANS Using a sturdy spatula, place one-third of the dough in an elongated oval on one of the prepared pans. Shape and smooth the dough into a slightly elongated oval, measuring about 5 inches wide and 7 inches long. Moisten your fingers with cold water and pat the sides of the dough to neaten the edges. Place half of the remaining dough on the second baking pan and the rest of the dough on the third pan; shape, smooth, and pat each portion of dough.

BAKE THE DOUGH OVALS AND COOL Bake the ovals of dough in the preheated oven for 35 to 38 minutes, or until risen and set. A toothpick inserted in the center of each baked oval will withdraw clean. Reduce the oven temperature to 275 degrees F.

Let the ovals stand on the baking sheets for 5 minutes. Carefully transfer them (still on their parchment paper bases) to cooling racks. Cool for 20 minutes. Cool the pans, as you'll be using them again.

SLICE THE OVALS OF DOUGH Have the cooled baking pans at hand. Working with one oval at a time, slip a long and narrow offset metal spatula under the oval to release it from the parchment paper, and slide it onto a cutting board. Using a serrated knife, cut each cooled oval into ¾-inch-thick slices. Arrange the biscotti on the cooled pans, cut side down.

SLOW-BAKE AND COOL THE BISCOTTI Bake the biscotti for about 18 minutes, or until they are firm and dry. Turn them twice during this time. (Baking the cookies a second time at a low temperature makes them crunchy and firm.) Let the biscotti stand on the baking pans for 10 minutes, then care-fully transfer them to cooling racks, using a pair of tongs. Cool completely. Store in an airtight tin.

Bake-and-serve within 1 month

STYLE For Triple-Chocolate-Nut Biscotti, blend ¾ cup chopped walnuts, pecans, or macadamia nuts into the dough along with the chocolate chunks.

CHOCOLATE CHIP SABLÉS

About 4 dozen cookies

This is my version of a French cookie called *sablés*—delicate and reasonably light butter cookies—which I have been baking for so many years. The dough is rolled into sheets and chilled thoroughly, then frozen for an hour before cutting and baking. The overnight chilling sets the shape. The freezing time refines and maintains the edges on baking; this is especially important if you are using a fancy scalloped or fluted cookie cutter.

I serve *sablés* with ice cream, mousse, a fruit compote, or simply alone, with good strong coffee. They are beguiling.

BUTTER COOKIE DOUGH

4 cups bleached cake flour

½ teaspoon baking powder

⅛ teaspoon cream of tartar

½ teaspoon salt

1 pound (4 sticks) unsalted butter, softened

1 cup superfine sugar

1 tablespoon vanilla extract

1 cup miniature semisweet chocolate chips

Sanding or sparkling sugar, for sprinkling on the unbaked cookies (or substitute granulated sugar)

MIX THE DOUGH Sift the flour, baking powder, cream of tartar, and salt onto a sheet of waxed paper.

Cream the butter in the large bowl of a freestanding electric mixer on moderately low speed for 5 minutes, or until very creamy. The 5-minute creaming time develops the texture of the dough. Add the sugar in 3 additions, beating for 1 minute after each portion is added. Blend in the vanilla extract.

On low speed, blend in the sifted ingredients in 4 additions, beating just until the flour particles are absorbed. Scrape down the sides of the mixing bowl frequently to keep the dough even-textured. Blend in the chocolate chips.

ROLL THE DOUGH Divide the dough into 4 portions. Roll each portion of dough between two sheets of waxed paper to a thickness of a ¼ inch. Layer the waxed paper–covered sheets of dough on a cookie sheet. Refrigerate the dough overnight.

FREEZE THE COOKIE DOUGH Place the sheets of dough in the freezer for 1 hour before cutting out the cookies. The dough must be firm; freeze the dough longer than 1 hour, if necessary.

PREHEAT THE OVEN TO 350 DEGREES F. in advance of baking. Line several cookie sheets with parchment paper.

CUT, TOP, BAKE, AND COOL THE COOKIES Working with one sheet of dough at a time, peel off both sheets of wax paper and place on a lightly floured work surface. Stamp out cookies with a 3-inch cutter.

Place the cookies 2 inches apart on the lined cookie sheets. Top each with a sprinkling of sugar.

Bake the cookies for 17 to 20 minutes, or until set. Cool the cookies on the sheets for 3 minutes, then remove them to cooling racks with a wide, offset metal spatula. Cool completely. Store in airtight tins.

Bake-and-serve within 5 days

DARK CHOCOLATE MADELEINES

2 dozen madeleines

*I*like my chocolate madeleines dark and intense, blotchy with miniature semisweet chocolate chips. And buttery, too. Using the creamed method for preparing the batter lets you pack a lot of chocolate into the little cakes, as this batter can easily support enough sugar, butter, and eggs to highlight the chocolate flavor and develop its fetching texture.

DARK CHOCOLATE BATTER

⅔ cup bleached cake flour

6 tablespoons plus 1 teaspoon unsweetened alkalized cocoa powder

¼ teaspoon baking powder

Large pinch of salt

½ cup miniature semisweet chocolate chips

7 tablespoons (1 stick less 1 tablespoon) unsalted butter, softened

½ cup superfine sugar

3 large eggs

1½ teaspoons vanilla extract

2 ounces unsweetened chocolate, melted and cooled

Confectioners' sugar, for sprinkling on top of the baked madeleines

PREHEAT THE OVEN TO 350 DEGREES F. Film the inside of 24 shell-shaped madeleine molds, *plaques à madeleines* (each shell measuring 3 inches in length), with melted clarified butter (using a soft pastry brush), let stand for 5 minutes, then dust with flour. Or, film the insides of the madeleine molds with nonstick cooking spray.

MIX THE BATTER Sift the flour, cocoa powder, baking powder, and salt onto a sheet of waxed paper. In a small bowl, toss the chocolate chips with ½ teaspoon of the sifted mixture.

Using an electric hand mixer, cream the butter in a medium-size mixing bowl on moderate speed for 2 minutes. Add the superfine sugar and beat for 2 minutes longer. Beat in the eggs, one at a time, mixing for 20 sec-

onds after each addition. Scrape down the sides of the mixing bowl frequently to keep the batter even-textured. Blend in the vanilla extract and melted chocolate. On low speed, add the sifted ingredients in 2 additions, mixing just until the particles of flour and cocoa powder are absorbed. The batter will be thick but creamy. Stir in the chocolate chips.

Let the batter stand for 5 minutes.

FILL THE MOLDS Fill the prepared molds with the batter, dividing it evenly among them and mounding it lightly. Mounding the batter helps to maintain the shape of each little baked cake. Dividing the batter among the 24 shell-shaped molds will produce rounded, well-developed madeleines that, when baked, fill the molds to capacity without overflowing the rims. Some shell-shaped molds are slightly under 3 inches in length, and if you own these, you will need to fill an extra mold or two. (To achieve the classic bump on the surface of the baked madeleines, you can refrigerate the batter for several hours—about 4—then continue with the recipe, increasing the baking time by about 2 minutes.)

BAKE AND COOL THE MADELEINES Bake the madeleines in the preheated oven for 10 to 12 minutes, or until set. A toothpick inserted in the center of a madeleine will withdraw clean (but will be tinted if you bump into a chocolate chip—OK).

Cool the madeleines in the pans on racks for 3 to 5 minutes, then lightly prod them out of the pan, using the rounded tip of a flexible palette knife. Place the madeleines, rounded (ridged) side up, on cooling racks. Dust the madeleines with confectioners' sugar and serve very fresh.

Bake-and-serve within 2 to 3 hours

STUDY To prepare clarified butter, see page 62.

Allowing the batter to stand for several minutes firms it up slightly and creates moist, dreamy cakes.

# CHOCOLATE CHIP MADELEINES

20 madeleines

*C*hocolate chips mingled in a buttery batter and baked in beautiful shell-shaped forms yield one exquisite batch of moist, lightly sweetened cakes. A tray of madeleines, arranged in an artistic curve, *is* dessert, and a classic teatime treat. The batter for the cakes is baked in the madeleine molds called *plaques à coques.* Lovely.

CHOCOLATE CHIP BATTER

¾ cup plus 2 tablespoons bleached all-purpose flour

¼ teaspoon baking powder

Large pinch of salt

½ cup miniature semisweet chocolate chips

7 tablespoons (1 stick less 1 tablespoon) unsalted butter, softened

½ cup superfine sugar

1 large egg

2 large egg yolks

1½ teaspoons vanilla extract

Confectioners' sugar, for sprinkling on top of the baked madeleines

PREHEAT THE OVEN TO 375 DEGREES F. Film the inside of 20 shell-shaped madeleine shells, *plaques à coques* (each shell measuring about 2½ inches at its widest point), with melted clarified butter (using a soft pastry brush), let stand for 5 minutes, then dust with flour. Or, film the inside of each mold with nonstick cooking spray.

MIX THE BATTER Sift the flour, baking powder, and salt onto a sheet of waxed paper twice. In a small bowl, toss the chocolate chips with ½ teaspoon of the sifted mixture.

Using an electric hand mixer, cream the butter in a medium-size mixing bowl on moderate speed for 2 minutes. Add the sugar in 2 additions, beating for 1 minute after each portion is added. Add the egg and beat for 30 seconds. Add the egg yolks and vanilla extract, and beat for 45 seconds longer. Add the sifted ingredients and mix on low speed until the particles of flour are absorbed. Scrape the sides of the mixing bowl frequently to keep the batter even-textured. The batter will be somewhat thick but satiny-textured. Stir in the chocolate chips.

Let the batter stand for 5 minutes.

FILL THE MOLDS Fill the prepared molds with the batter, dividing it evenly among them. Lightly mound the batter in the center of each shell to create the plumpest cakes. (To achieve the classic bump on the surface of the baked madeleines, you can refrigerate the batter for several hours—about 4—then continue with the recipe, increasing the baking time by about 2 minutes.)

BAKE AND COOL THE MADELEINES Bake the cakes in the pre-heated oven for 10 minutes, or until set. A toothpick inserted in the center of a madeleine will withdraw clean (but will be tinted if you bump into a chocolate chip—OK). The edges of the fully baked cakes will be light golden.

Cool the madeleines in the pans on racks for 3 minutes, then lift them out of the pan, using the tip of a flexible palette knife. Place the madeleines, rounded (ridged) side up, on cooling racks. Dust the madeleines with confectioners' sugar and serve very fresh.

Bake-and-serve within 2 to 3 hours

STUDY To prepare clarified butter, see page 62.

For delightful little bites, bake the batter in the petite madeleine molds called *plaques à madeleinettes.* They are a joy to use and bake adorable sweets—each plaque contains twenty 1¾-inch-long shells (1⅛ inches wide, with a capacity of 1¼ teaspoons each). These bake in about 7 to 8 minutes.

CHOCOLATE CRESCENTS

These tender chocolate cookies nearly vaporize as you devour them.

CHOCOLATE BUTTER DOUGH

2 cups plus 2 tablespoons bleached all-purpose flour

5 tablespoons unsweetened alkalized cocoa powder

¾ teaspoon baking powder

⅛ teaspoon salt

½ pound (16 tablespoons or 2 sticks) unsalted butter, melted and cooled

½ cup confectioners' sugar

2½ teaspoons vanilla extract

¼ cup finely chopped walnuts or pecans

¾ cup miniature semisweet chocolate chips

About 2 cups confectioners' sugar, for dredging the cookies

PREHEAT THE OVEN TO 350 DEGREES F. Line several heavy cookie sheets or rimmed sheet pans with cooking parchment paper.

MIX THE DOUGH Sift the flour, cocoa powder, baking powder, and salt onto a sheet of waxed paper.

Place the melted butter in a large mixing bowl. Add the sugar and mix it in with a wooden spoon or flat wooden paddle. At this point, the melted butter–sugar mixture will appear somewhat lumpy—OK. Blend in the vanilla extract and chopped nuts. Stir in half of the sifted mixture and all of the chocolate chips. Add the remaining sifted mixture and blend it in to form a dough. Let the dough rest for 10 minutes.

SHAPE THE COOKIES Spoon up level 1-tablespoon-size quantities of dough and roll into thick logs. Arrange the logs of dough 1½ to 2 inches apart on the prepared pans, placing 12 on each pan. Bend and shape each log into a crescent shape, tapering the ends slightly as you go.

BAKE, DREDGE, AND COOL THE CRESCENTS Bake the cookies in the preheated oven for 14 to 15 minutes, or until set. The top of the baked cookies will have occasional hairline cracks—OK. Let the cookies stand on the pans for 1 minute, then carefully remove them to cooling racks, using a wide offset metal spatula. Cool for 10 minutes. Carefully (the cookies are fragile at this point) dredge the warm cookies in the confectioners' sugar. Transfer them to a large sheet of parchment paper to cool completely. Once the cookies have cooled, dredge them lightly again. Store in an airtight tin.

Bake-and-serve within 3 days

STUDY For a crescent cookie that is a shade more delicate, increase the baking powder to 1 teaspoon. With this amount, the dough will be a little more expansive.

Use Essence-of-Vanilla Confectioners' Sugar (page 56) to dredge the baked cookies for an elegant finish. The vanilla-scented sugar plays up the chocolate intensity and aroma of the baked crescents.

I use Droste alkalized cocoa powder in the cookie dough.

CHOCOLATE-PECAN BUTTER CRESCENTS

About 2½ dozen cookies

*T*he baking powder in the dough opens up the crumb and establishes a fine and fragile texture. The blend of chopped pecans, cocoa powder, and miniature chocolate chips accents the buttery dough, which is easy to shape.

CHOCOLATE PECAN BUTTER DOUGH

2 cups plus 2 tablespoons bleached all-purpose flour

5 tablespoons unsweetened alkalized cocoa powder

¾ teaspoon baking powder

⅛ teaspoon salt

½ pound (16 tablespoons or 2 sticks) unsalted butter, melted and cooled

½ cup plus 3 tablespoons confectioners' sugar

2 teaspoons vanilla extract

3 tablespoons finely chopped pecans

¾ cup miniature semisweet chocolate chips

CONFECTIONERS' SUGAR AND COCOA DREDGING MIXTURE

2 cups confectioners' sugar

1 tablespoon unsweetened alkalized cocoa powder

PREHEAT THE OVEN TO 350 DEGREES F. Line several heavy cookie sheets or rimmed sheet pans with cooking parchment paper.

MIX THE DOUGH Sift the flour, cocoa powder, baking powder, and salt onto a sheet of waxed paper.

Place the melted butter in a large mixing bowl. Add the sugar and mix it in with a wooden spoon or flat wooden paddle. At this point, the melted butter–sugar mixture will appear somewhat lumpy—OK. Blend in the vanilla extract and pecans. Stir in half of the sifted mix-

ture and all of the chocolate chips. Add the remaining sifted mixture and blend it in to form a dough. Let the dough rest for 10 minutes.

SHAPE THE COOKIES Spoon up rounded 2-teaspoon-size quantities of dough and roll into thick logs. Arrange the logs of dough 1½ to 2 inches apart on the prepared pans, placing 12 on each pan. Bend and shape each log into a crescent shape, tapering the ends slightly as you go.

BAKE THE CRESCENTS Bake the cookies in the preheated oven for 14 to 15 minutes, or until firm and set. The tops of the baked cookies will have random hairline cracks— OK. Let the cookies stand on the pans for 1 minute, then carefully remove them to cooling racks, using a wide offset metal spatula. Cool for 10 minutes.

MAKE THE DREDGING MIXTURE Sift the confectioners' sugar and cocoa into a small mixing bowl. Whisk well to blend the cocoa powder thoroughly.

DREDGE AND COOL THE CRESCENTS Carefully dredge the warm cookies in the confectioners' sugar–cocoa mixture to coat. Transfer them to a large sheet of parchment paper to cool completely. Once the cookies have cooled, dredge them lightly again. Store in an airtight tin.

Bake-and-serve within 3 days

THE FLAVOR AND TEXTURE OF TURTLE CANDY—that terrific alliance of chocolate, caramel, and nuts—can be highlighted in baked batters, doughs, sauces, and toppings. All you have to do is pair a chocolate or chocolate chip–based sweet with some form of caramel and nuts—in a topping, sauce, or confectionlike ingredient—and a simple dessert becomes an easily and extravagantly flavored one.

Chocolate, caramel, and nuts–a turtle twist

TOFFEE-ALMOND TURTLE BARS

*T*he almonds in the batter echo the type of nut in the toffee candy, and so create another dimension of taste.

TOFFEE CHOCOLATE BAR COOKIE BATTER

1 cup bleached all-purpose flour

2 tablespoons unsweetened alkalized cocoa powder

¼ teaspoon baking powder

⅛ teaspoon salt

5 packages (1.4 ounces each) milk chocolate–covered toffee (such as Heath Milk Chocolate English Toffee Bar), chopped

½ pound (16 tablespoons or 2 sticks) unsalted butter, melted and cooled to tepid

4 ounces unsweetened chocolate, melted and cooled to tepid

4 large eggs

1¾ cups plus 2 tablespoons superfine sugar

2 teaspoons vanilla extract

½ cup chopped or slivered almonds

TOPPING

Turtle Topping (page 360) or

Nutty Turtle Topping (page 360), using almonds, or

Turtle Topping and 2 packages (1.4 ounces each) milk chocolate–covered toffee (Heath Milk Chocolate English Toffee Bar), cut into large chunks

PREHEAT THE OVEN TO 325 DEGREES F. Film the inside of a 9 by 9 by 2-inch baking pan with nonstick cooking spray.

MIX THE BATTER Sift the flour, cocoa powder, baking powder, and salt onto a sheet of waxed paper. In a small bowl, toss the chopped toffee with ½ teaspoon of the sifted mixture.

In a medium-size mixing bowl, whisk the melted butter and melted chocolate until smooth. In a large mixing bowl, whisk the eggs until blended, about 15 seconds. Add the sugar and whisk until combined, about 45 seconds to 1 minute. Blend in the vanilla extract and melted butter-chocolate mixture. Sift the flour mixture over and stir to form a batter, mixing thoroughly until the particles of flour are absorbed, using a whisk or flat wooden paddle. Stir in the chopped toffee and almonds.

Scrape the batter into the prepared pan and spread evenly. Smooth the top with a rubber spatula.

BAKE, COOL, TOP, AND CUT THE SWEET Bake the sweet in the preheated oven for 33 to 37 minutes, or until set. Let the sweet stand in the pan on a cooling rack to cool completely. Spoon and spread the topping randomly over the chocolate bar base. After 1 minute, sprinkle the almonds or toffee on the topping, if you wish. Let stand until the topping is set, about 1 hour. With a small sharp knife, cut the sweet into quarters, then cut each quarter into 6 bars. Remove the bars from the baking pan, using a small offset metal spatula. Store the bars, in single layers, in airtight tins.

Bake-and-serve within 2 days

COCONUT–CHOCOLATE CHIP TURTLE COOKIES

About 3½ dozen cookies

*E*xceptionally buttery, these caramel-topped cookies are indulgent. The flavor accent of butterscotch, which comes from the light brown sugar, ties in perfectly with the taste of the chocolate chips and coconut.

COCONUT CHOCOLATE CHIP DOUGH

3 cups bleached all-purpose flour

¼ teaspoon baking soda

¾ teaspoon salt

½ pound plus 4 tablespoons (2 sticks plus 4 tablespoons) unsalted butter, softened

1⅓ cups firmly packed light brown sugar

1 cup granulated sugar

2 large eggs

2 teaspoons vanilla extract

3 cups semisweet chocolate chips

2 cups sweetened flaked coconut

1 cup chopped pecans

TOPPING

Two recipes Turtle Topping (page 360)

About ¾ cup semisweet chocolate chips, for sprinkling on the topped cookies

PREHEAT THE OVEN TO 325 DEGREES F. Line several cookie sheets or rimmed sheet pans with cooking parchment paper.

MIX THE DOUGH Sift the flour, baking soda, and salt onto a sheet of waxed paper.

Cream the butter in the large bowl of a freestanding electric mixer on moderate speed for 3 minutes. Add the light brown sugar and continue creaming on moderately low speed for 2 minutes longer. Add the granulated sugar and beat for 2 minutes longer. Beat in the eggs, one at a time, mixing until incorporated. Blend in the vanilla extract. On low speed, blend in the sifted ingredients in 3 additions, beating until the flour particles are absorbed. Scrape down the sides of the mixing bowl frequently to keep the dough even-textured. Mix in the chocolate chips, coconut, and pecans.

SHAPE THE COOKIES Place heaping 2-tablespoon-size mounds of dough on the prepared pans, spacing the mounds about 3 inches apart.

BAKE, COOL, AND TOP THE COOKIES Bake the cookies in the preheated oven for 16 to 17 minutes, or until set and a spotty golden color on top. The centers should not look wet, but do not overbake or they will be dry instead of moist. Let the cookies stand on the pans for 1 minute, then transfer them to cooling racks, using a wide offset metal spatula. Cool completely. Spoon and spread the topping randomly over the cookies. After 1 minute, scatter a few chocolate chips on the topping of each cookie. Let the cookies stand until the topping is set, about 1 hour. Store the cookies, in single layers, in airtight tins.

Bake-and-serve within 2 days

STUDY When forming the dough mounds, keep the edges craggy and the mounds pudgy for cookies with the best appearance and texture.

PEANUT FUDGE TURTLE TORTE

One 9-inch torte, creating 10 slices

*T*he batter for this dark and fudgy torte is pampered, for it includes chunks of chocolate, peanut and caramel candy, and peanuts. The topping is an entrancing way to finish the cake, but you could also serve the slices with Turtle Sauce or Nutty Turtle Sauce, and skip the topping entirely: it's a mood thing—the dessert will taste good either way—so do what appeals to you.

TORTE BATTER

4 bars (2.07 ounces each) chocolate-covered peanut and caramel candy bars (Snickers), cut into chunks

1 cup plus 2 tablespoons bleached cake flour

1 tablespoon unsweetened alkalized cocoa powder

¼ teaspoon baking powder

⅛ teaspoon salt

14 tablespoons (1¾ sticks) unsalted butter, melted and cooled to tepid

4 ounces unsweetened chocolate, melted and cooled to tepid

4 large eggs

1¾ cups plus 1 tablespoon superfine sugar

2 teaspoons vanilla extract

¾ cup whole roasted peanuts

TOPPING

Turtle Topping (page 360) or Nutty Turtle Topping (page 360), using peanuts

SAUCE (OPTIONAL)

Turtle Sauce (page 358) or Nutty Turtle Sauce (page 358), using peanuts

PREHEAT THE OVEN TO 350 DEGREES F. Film the inside of a 9-inch springform pan (2¾ inches deep) with nonstick cooking spray.

CRUSH THE CHUNKS OF CANDY With the broad side of a knife, lightly crush the candy chunks.

MIX THE BATTER Sift the flour, cocoa powder, baking powder, and salt onto a sheet of waxed paper.

In a medium-size mixing bowl, whisk the melted butter and melted chocolate until smooth. In another a medium-size mixing bowl, whisk the eggs until blended, about 15 seconds. Add the sugar and whisk until combined, about 30 seconds. Blend in the vanilla extract and melted butter-chocolate mixture. Sift the flour mixture over and stir to form a batter, mixing thoroughly until the particles of flour are absorbed, using a whisk or flat wooden paddle. Stir in the chunks of candy and peanuts.

Scrape the batter into the prepared pan and spread evenly. Smooth the top with a rubber spatula.

BAKE, COOL, AND TOP THE TORTE Bake the torte in the preheated oven for 10 minutes. Reduce the oven heat to 325 degrees F., and continue baking for 25 to 30 minutes longer, or until set. The center of the baked torte should be slightly soft, but not wobbly-liquidy. Cool the torte in the pan on a rack. Release the sides of the springform pan.

Spoon and spread the topping randomly over the surface of the torte. After 1 minute, sprinkle the peanuts on the topping (if you are using them). Let the torte stand until the topping is set, about 1 hour, then slice and serve with spoonfuls of sauce, if you wish. Store the cake in an airtight cake keeper.

Bake-and-serve within 2 days

STYLE For a bold turtle presence, top the unbaked torte with 2 additional candy bars (cut into chunks) and ½ cup whole roasted peanuts—spectacular.

STUDY In hot weather (or in a warm kitchen), refrigerate the chunks of crushed candy for 20 minutes before adding to the batter. This keeps the candy intact and prevents it from melding into the batter before baking.

MILK CHOCOLATE CHIP TURTLE SHORTBREAD

One 9-inch cookie, creating 12 pieces

The surface of a tender round of shortbread is a perfect base for a covering in caramel and topping with nuts or chocolate chips. This cookie is fun to make and serve, and entirely tempting. At my house, it is a beloved part of the (really) big holiday cookie plate.

CHOCOLATE CHIP DOUGH

1¼ cups bleached all-purpose flour

¼ cup rice flour

¼ teaspoon baking powder

⅛ teaspoon salt

12 tablespoons (1½ sticks) unsalted butter, softened

¼ cup firmly packed light brown sugar

¼ cup granulated sugar

1 teaspoon vanilla extract

¾ cup milk chocolate chips

TOPPING

Turtle Topping (page 360) and ¾ cup milk chocolate chips, or Nutty Turtle Topping (page 360), using macadamia nuts, walnuts, or pecans

PREHEAT THE OVEN TO 350 DEGREES F. Have a fluted 9 to 9½-inch round tart pan (1 inch deep, with a removable bottom) at hand.

MIX THE DOUGH Sift the all-purpose flour, rice flour, baking powder, and salt onto a sheet of waxed paper.

Cream the butter in the large bowl of a freestanding electric mixer on low speed for 2 minutes. Add the light brown sugar and granulated sugar and beat on moderately low speed for 2 minutes. Blend in the vanilla extract. On moderately low speed, blend in half of the sifted dry ingredients, then the chocolate chips; blend in the remaining sifted mixture, mixing until the particles of flour are absorbed. Scrape down the sides of the mixing bowl frequently to keep the dough even-textured.

Place the dough on the bottom of the tart pan and press it into an even layer.

BAKE, COOL, TOP, AND CUT THE SHORTBREAD Bake the shortbread in the preheated oven for 35 to 40 minutes, or until set and golden. Cool the shortbread in the pan on a rack. Spoon and spread the topping randomly over the surface of the shortbread. After 1 minute, sprinkle the milk chocolate chips or nuts on the topping. Let the shortbread stand until the topping is set, about 1 hour. Carefully unmold the shortbread, leaving it on its round base. Cut into 12 triangular-shaped pieces, using a serrated knife. Or, cut-and-break the shortbread into irregular pieces. Store the shortbread pieces, in single layers, in airtight tins.

Bake-and-serve within 2 days

STYLE For Chocolate Chip Turtle Shortbread, substitute semisweet chocolate chips for the milk chocolate variety in the shortbread dough and the topping.

STUDY If rice flour is unavailable, use a total of 1½ cups bleached all-purpose flour.

CHUNKY TURTLE SCONES

A basket of buttery scones, stubby with chocolate chips and walnuts throughout and topped with caramel, is my idea of luscious.

CHUNKY SCONE DOUGH

4 cups bleached all-purpose flour

4¾ teaspoons baking powder

1 teaspoon salt

⅔ cup granulated sugar

12 tablespoons (1½ sticks) cold unsalted butter, cut into tablespoon-size chunks

4 large eggs

1 cup heavy cream

1 tablespoon vanilla extract

1½ cups semisweet chocolate chips

1 cup chopped walnuts

TOPPING

Turtle Topping (page 360), or

Nutty Turtle Topping (page 360), using walnuts

MIX THE DOUGH In a large mixing bowl, thoroughly whisk the flour, baking powder, salt, and granulated sugar. Drop in the chunks of butter and, using a pastry blender or two round-bladed knives, cut the fat into the flour mixture until reduced to pieces the size of large pearls. Reduce the fat further to smaller flakes, using your fingertips. In a medium-size mixing bowl, whisk the eggs, heavy cream, and vanilla extract. Pour the egg and cream mixture over the flour mixture, scatter the chocolate chips and walnuts over, and stir to form a dough.

KNEAD AND REFRIGERATE THE DOUGH Turn the dough out onto a floured work surface and knead lightly for 1 minute, sprinkling the dough with flour as necessary to keep it from sticking. Divide the dough in half and form each into 8 to 8½-inch disks. Wrap the disks in waxed paper and refrigerate for 20 minutes.

Preheat the oven to 400 degrees F. in advance of baking the scones. Line 2 heavy cookie sheets or rimmed sheet pans with lengths of cooking parchment paper.

FORM THE SCONES Place each disk of dough on a lightly floured work surface and, using a chef's knife, cut into 6 wedges. As the scones are cut, press in any chocolate chips or nuts that poke out of the sides. Transfer the scones to the prepared pans, placing them 3 inches apart. Assemble 6 scones on each pan.

BAKE, COOL, AND TOP THE SCONES Bake the scones in the preheated oven for 18 to 20 minutes, or until set and baked through. Transfer the pans to cooling racks. Let the scones stand on the pans for 1 minute, then carefully remove them to cooling racks, using a wide offset metal spatula. Cool completely.

Spoon and spread the topping randomly on top of the scones. After 1 minute, place the walnuts (if you are using them) here and there on the topping. Let the scones stand until the topping is set, about 1 hour. Serve the scones freshly baked.

Bake-and-serve within 1 day

TURTLE TOPPING

Vanilla-flavored caramels are the foundation for a fast and incredibly easy topping for bar cookies, cakes, tortes, and quick breads.

24 vanilla-flavored caramels (a generous 6 ounces), unwrapped

3 tablespoons plus 2 teaspoons milk

Pinch of salt

½ teaspoon vanilla extract

Place the caramels, milk, and salt in a small, heavy saucepan and set over moderately low heat. Cook until the caramels melt down, about 9 to 10 minutes. Stir from time to time with a wooden spoon or flat wooden paddle. Bring the mixture to a gentle simmer, stir in the vanilla extract, and simmer for 1 minute. Use the topping immediately.

STYLE For Nutty Turtle Topping, make the Turtle Topping (above). Use the topping as directed in the recipe, by spooning or spreading it over the baked sweet, then immediately sprinkle with ¾ cup whole, halved or slivered nuts, such as walnuts, pecans, almonds, roasted peanuts, or macadamia nuts.

NOTE: Any sweet accented with either topping should be served at room temperature.

THE DEEP AND COMPLEX QUALITY OF BITTERSWEET CHOCOLATE frames, cultivates, and polishes the taste of batters and doughs. Used along with bittersweet chocolate cut from big blocks or bars (in chunks or melted down), unsweetened chocolate and cocoa powder both balance and embolden the chocolate intensity to shape a dessert that is rich and refined. The depth of good bittersweet chocolate always impresses me, for its temperate but commanding strength functions superbly with unsalted butter, pure vanilla extract, whole eggs and egg yolks, the moist seed scrapings from vanilla beans, and thick cream.

BITTERSWEET CHOCOLATE TRUFFLE SQUARES

*A*creamy and moist square of fudgy cake topped with a handmade truffle is unrestrained chocolate at its best. Though most people would call this a fudge cake, it's really a brownie. Sort of. (A fudge cake. A brownie. What does it matter?) I'm always searching for yet another way to make any batter into a brownie because a brownie is a transcendental thing.

With a silky truffle sitting on top of a fudgy, dense square, this is the sweet I want to have around for supreme chocolate sustenance.

DARK CHOCOLATE BATTER

1⅓ cups bleached all-purpose cake flour

¼ cup unsweetened alkalized cocoa powder

¼ teaspoon baking powder

⅛ teaspoon salt

½ pound (16 tablespoons or 2 sticks) unsalted butter, melted and cooled to tepid

5 ounces unsweetened chocolate, melted and cooled to tepid

5 large eggs

2 cups granulated sugar

1½ teaspoons vanilla extract

HANDMADE TRUFFLES TO TOP THE BAKED SQUARES

Cocoa-Coated Truffles (page 364)

CHOCOLATE FOR ATTACHING THE TRUFFLES

About 3 ounces bittersweet chocolate, melted, for attaching the truffles to the top of the baked brownies

Confectioners' sugar, for sifting on top of the baked squares (optional)

PREHEAT THE OVEN TO 325 DEGREES F. Film the inside of a 10 by 10 by 2-inch baking pan with nonstick cooking spray.

MIX THE BATTER Sift the flour, cocoa powder, baking powder, and salt onto a sheet of waxed paper.

Whisk the melted butter and melted chocolate in a medium-size mixing bowl until smooth. In a large mixing bowl, whisk the eggs for 45 seconds to blend, add the sugar and whisk for 45 seconds to 1 minute, or until

incorporated. Blend in the melted butter-chocolate mixture and vanilla extract. Sift the flour mixture over and stir it in, using a whisk or flat wooden paddle. Mix until the particles of flour are absorbed.

Scrape the batter into the prepared pan and spread evenly. Smooth the top with a rubber spatula.

BAKE, COOL, AND CUT THE SWEET Bake the sweet for 35 minutes, or until set. Cool the sweet completely in the pan on a rack. With a small sharp knife, cut the sweet into quarters, then cut each quarter into 4 squares. Remove the squares from the pan, using a small offset metal spatula.

APPLY THE TRUFFLES TO THE SQUARES Carefully dip a truffle into the melted bittersweet chocolate. Quickly place it on a chocolate square.

Refrigerate the squares in a single layer to set the truffles, about 1 hour. Store the truffle-topped squares in the refrigerator, assembling them in rigid, airtight containers with tight-fitting lids. Just before serving, dust the surface of each square with a haze of confectioners' sugar, if you wish. Serve the squares at room temperature or cool, not cold.

Bake-and-store the squares, without the truffle topping, for up to 3 days. The refrigerated truffle-topped squares for 2 days

16 squares

oist and darkly chocolate, and flecked with enough coconut to please, these squares are chewy and very chocolatey. For a bonus layer of flavor, scrape the seeds from half a pliant vanilla bean into the batter—the extra surge of vanilla does wonders for uniting the flavors of chocolate and coconut.

CHOCOLATE COOKIE LAYER

8 tablespoons (1 stick) unsalted butter, melted and cooled to tepid

1⅔ cups chocolate sandwich cookie crumbs (such as crumbs made from Nabisco Oreo chocolate sandwich cookies)

BITTERSWEET CHOCOLATE MACAROON BATTER

1 cup bleached all-purpose flour

¼ cup bleached cake flour

2 tablespoons unsweetened alkalized cocoa powder

¼ teaspoon baking powder

⅛ teaspoon salt

½ pound (16 tablespoons or 2 sticks) unsalted butter, melted and cooled to tepid

4 ounces unsweetened chocolate, melted and cooled to tepid

4 large eggs

1¾ cups plus 3 tablespoons superfine sugar

2 teaspoons vanilla extract

5 ounces bittersweet chocolate, chopped into small chunks

¾ cup sweetened flaked coconut

2 ounces bittersweet chocolate, chopped into small chunks

PREHEAT THE OVEN TO 325 DEGREES F. Film the inside of a 9 by 9 by 2-inch baking pan with nonstick cooking spray.

MAKE THE COOKIE LAYER Pour the melted butter into the prepared pan. Spoon the cookie crumbs evenly over the bottom and press down on the crumbs with the underside of a small offset metal spatula so that the crumbs absorb the butter. Bake the cookie layer in the preheated oven for 4 minutes. Transfer the pan to a rack. Cool for 10 minutes.

MIX THE BATTER Sift the all-purpose flour, cake flour, cocoa powder, baking powder, and salt onto a sheet of waxed paper.

In a medium-size mixing bowl, whisk the melted butter and melted chocolate until smooth. In a large mixing bowl, whisk the eggs until blended, about 15 seconds. Add the sugar and whisk until combined, about 30 seconds. Blend in the vanilla extract and melted butter-chocolate mixture. Sift the flour mixture over and stir to form a batter, using a whisk or flat wooden paddle. Stir in the 5 ounces of chopped bittersweet chocolate and the coconut.

Spoon the batter in large dollops on the cookie crumb layer. Carefully spread the batter over the cookie layer, using a flexible palette knife or spatula.

BAKE, COOL, AND CUT THE SWEET Bake the sweet for in the preheated oven 30 minutes. Quickly sprinkle the remaining 2 ounces bittersweet chocolate on top and bake for 5 minutes longer, or until set. Let the sweet stand in the pan on a cooling rack for 3 hours. Refrigerate for 1 hour. With a small sharp knife, cut the sweet into quarters, then cut each quarter into 4 squares. Remove the squares from the baking pan, using a small offset metal spatula. Store in an airtight tin.

Bake-and-serve within 4 days

STUDY Any of these bittersweet chocolates would partner beautifully with the coconut: Scharffen Berger Bittersweet 70% cocoa; Valrhona Extra Amer Bittersweet 61% cacao; Valrhona Caraïbe Dark Chocolate 66% cocoa; Michel Cluizel Chocolat Amer Dark Chocolate 60% cacao; Michel Cluizel Ilha Toma 65% cocoa; or, Lindt Excellence 70% Cocoa Extra Fine Dark Chocolate.

BITTERSWEET CHOCOLATE BLONDIES

16 blondies

*C*hunks of bittersweet bar chocolate converge with the soft caramel-like mellowness of brown sugar to create a chewy and rich bar cookie.

BITTERSWEET CHOCOLATE CHUNK BATTER

1 cup plus 2 tablespoons bleached all-purpose flour

½ teaspoon baking powder

⅛ teaspoon salt

8 tablespoons (1 stick) unsalted butter, melted and cooled

¼ cup plus 2 tablespoons firmly packed light brown sugar

⅓ cup plus 1 tablespoon granulated sugar

2 large eggs

2 teaspoons vanilla extract

6 ounces bittersweet chocolate, cut into chunks

¾ cup sweetened flaked coconut

PREHEAT THE OVEN TO 350 DEGREES F. Film the inside of a 9 by 9 by 2-inch baking pan with nonstick cooking spray.

MAKE THE BATTER Sift the flour, baking powder, and salt onto a sheet of waxed paper.

Whisk the melted butter, light brown sugar, and granulated sugar in a medium-size mixing bowl. Blend in the eggs and vanilla extract. Stir in the sifted mixture, using a wooden spoon or flat wooden paddle, mixing until the particles of flour are absorbed. Blend in the bittersweet chocolate chunks and flaked coconut. The batter will be dense and chunky.

Scrape the batter into the prepared pan and spread evenly. Smooth the top with a rubber spatula.

BAKE, COOL, AND CUT THE BLONDIES Bake the blondies in the preheated oven for 25 minutes, or until set. Transfer the pan to a rack and cool completely. Cut the sweet into four quarters, then cut each quarter into 4 squares. Remove the squares from the baking pan, using a small offset metal spatula. Store in an airtight tin.

Bake-and-serve within 2 days

STYLE For Bittersweet Chocolate Blondies with Walnuts or Pecans, work ½ cup coarsely chopped walnuts or pecans into the batter along with the chocolate chunks and coconut.

A fusion of chocolate cake and tea bread, these little gems are tender and moist. The batter is a quick-bread version of the Deep Chocolate Pound Cake on page 244—more or less—recast as little tea cakes. My favorite way to serve them is with a petite cup of chocolate cream. The creamy, intense cups of custard resonate so well with the buttery tea cakes.

BITTERSWEET CHOCOLATE BATTER

1⅔ cups plus 2 tablespoons bleached all-purpose flour

5 tablespoons unsweetened alkalized cocoa powder

2½ teaspoons baking powder

¼ teaspoon salt

½ cup plus 2 tablespoons superfine sugar

¾ cup miniature semisweet chocolate chips

9 tablespoons (1 stick plus 1 tablespoon) unsalted butter, melted and cooled

4 ounces bittersweet chocolate, melted and cooled

2 large egg yolks

2 teaspoons vanilla extract

⅓ cup plus 3 tablespoons half-and-half

TOPPING

About ⅓ cup miniature semisweet chocolate chips

TO SERVE WITH THE TEA CAKES

Bittersweet Chocolate Creams (page 374)

PREHEAT THE OVEN TO 375 DEGREES F. Line 24 teacake cups (each cup measuring 2 inches in diameter by 1³⁄₁₆ inches deep, with a capacity of 3 tablespoons) with ovenproof baking paper liners. Or, film the insides with nonstick cooking spray.

MIX THE BATTER Sift the flour, cocoa powder, baking powder, salt, and sugar into a large mixing bowl. In a small bowl, toss the chocolate chips with ¾ teaspoon of the sifted mixture.

In a medium-size mixing bowl, whisk the melted butter, melted chocolate, egg yolks, and vanilla extract. Whisk in the half-and-half. Pour the liquid ingredients over the sifted ingredients, add the chocolate chips, and stir to form a batter, using a wooden spoon or flat wooden paddle. Mix the ingredients thoroughly to dispel any pockets of flour lingering at the bottom and sides of the bowl.

Divide the batter among the prepared cups, mounding it slightly, and sprinkle with chocolate chips.

BAKE AND COOL THE CAKES Bake the tea cakes for 18 to 20 minutes, or until risen, set, and a toothpick inserted in the center of each cake withdraws clean. The baked tea cakes will pull away slightly from the sides of the baking pan.

Let the tea cakes cool in the pan on a rack for 10 minutes, then carefully remove them to another cooling rack. Cool completely. Store in an airtight cake keeper. Serve the tea cakes with ramekins of Bittersweet Chocolate Cream.

Bake-and-serve within 2 days

STUDY Using paper liners keeps the pretty figure of the cakes.

BITTERSWEET CHOCOLATE–OATMEAL–DRIED CHERRY COOKIES

About 3½ dozen cookies

*T*he combination of bittersweet chocolate, rolled oats, cashews, and dried cherries is bold, toothsome, and, for a batch of cookies, quite full-bodied.

BITTERSWEET CHOCOLATE–OATMEAL–DRIED CHERRY DOUGH

1½ cups bleached all-purpose flour

¼ teaspoon baking soda

½ teaspoon salt

½ pound (16 tablespoons or 2 sticks) unsalted butter, softened

5 tablespoons shortening

1⅓ cups firmly packed light brown sugar

1 cup granulated sugar

2 large eggs

1 tablespoon plus 1 teaspoon vanilla extract

2½ cups "quick-cooking" (not "instant") rolled oats

14 ounces bittersweet chocolate, chopped

1⅔ cups sweetened flaked coconut

1 cup moist, dried sweet or tart cherries

1¼ cups cashews (wholes and halves, or halves and pieces)

PREHEAT THE OVEN TO 325 DEGREES F. Line several cookie sheets or rimmed sheet pans with cooking parchment paper.

MIX THE DOUGH Whisk the flour, baking soda, and salt in small mixing bowl.

Cream the butter and shortening in the large bowl of a freestanding electric mixer on moderate speed for 3 min-utes. Add the light brown sugar in 2 additions, beating for 1 minute on moderate speed after each portion is added; add the granulated sugar in 2 additions, beating for 1 minute af-ter each portion is added. Add the eggs, one at a time, beat-ing until just incorporated. Blend in the vanilla extract. On low speed, blend in the sifted ingredients in 2 additions, beating until the flour particles are absorbed. Scrape down the sides of the mixing bowl frequently to keep the dough even-textured. Beat in the rolled oats. On low speed, blend in the chocolate chunks, coconut, cherries, and cashews. The dough will be thick and chunky.

SHAPE THE COOKIES Place heaping 2-tablespoon-size mounds of dough on the prepared pans, spacing the mounds about 3 inches apart.

BAKE AND COOL THE COOKIES Bake the cookies in the pre-heated oven for 16 to 17 minutes, or until set. The tops of the baked cookies will no longer look wet or glossy. Let the cookies stand on the pans for 1 minute, then transfer them to cooling racks, using a wide offset metal spatula. Store in an airtight tin.

Bake-and-serve within 2 days

STYLE For Chocolate Chip–Oatmeal–Dried Cherry Cookies, substitute 2½ cups semisweet chocolate chips for the chopped bittersweet chocolate.

BITTERSWEET CHOCOLATE TART

I love the integrity of this filling, a composite of good bittersweet chocolate (and a little unsweetened chocolate), egg yolks, unsalted butter, and flavoring in the form of vanilla extract and the seed scrapings from half of a vanilla bean. The pastry dough that insulates the truffle-like chocolate filling is upgraded by the addition of vanilla extract as well. For a dividend of flavor and the ultimate in chocolate pampering, place a ring of Cocoa-Coated Truffles (page 364) on the surface of the filling once it has been baked and lightly chilled. Arrange the truffles so that they embrace the inner edge of the tart crust.

SCENT-OF-VANILLA BITTERSWEET CHOCOLATE FILLING

7 large egg yolks

⅓ cup plus 1 tablespoon superfine sugar sifted with
2 teaspoons unsweetened alkalized cocoa powder
and ⅛ teaspoon salt

8 ounces bittersweet chocolate, melted and cooled to tepid

1 ounce unsweetened chocolate, melted and cooled to tepid

9 tablespoons (1 stick plus 1 tablespoon) unsalted butter, melted and cooled to tepid

1½ teaspoons vanilla extract

Seeds scraped from ½ small split vanilla bean

Butter and Vanilla Bean Pastry Shell, baked (page 382)

ENHANCEMENT FOR THE FINISHED TART (OPTIONAL)

Cocoa-Coated Truffles (page 364)

Confectioners' sugar, for sifting over the baked tart

ACCOMPANIMENT

Vanilla-Scented Whipped Cream (page 303)

PREHEAT THE OVEN TO 325 DEGREES F.

MIX THE FILLING In a small mixing bowl, whisk the egg yolks and sugar–cocoa powder mixture to combine.

In a medium-size mixing bowl, whisk the melted bittersweet chocolate, melted unsweetened chocolate, and melted butter until smooth. Stir in the vanilla extract and vanilla bean seeds. Pour and scrape the chocolate over the egg yolk–sugar mixture; mix slowly to form a smooth batter, using a wooden spoon or flat wooden paddle. (Actively beating or whisking the mixture at this point would introduce too much air and create foam.)

Pour and scrape the filling into the prebaked tart shell, spreading it evenly. Lightly smooth the top with a rubber spatula.

BAKE AND COOL THE TART Bake the tart in the preheated oven for 20 minutes, or until set. The outer band of the filling will puff ever-so-slightly—OK. Let the tart stand in the pan on a cooling rack for at least 3 hours.

FINISH THE TART If you are ornamenting the tart with the truffles, place a ring of truffles around the interior rim. Carefully unmold the tart, leaving it on its round base.

Bake-and-serve within 1 day

STUDY Baking the tart slowly in a moderately low oven keeps the filling lissome and smooth throughout.

A centered, rich chocolate makes the best filling, and for that I prefer Scharffen Berger Bittersweet 70% cocoa; Valrhona Extra Amer Bittersweet 61% cacao; Valrhona Le Noir Amer 71% cacao; Valrhona Grand Cru Noir Manjari Gastronomie Chocolat Noir Dark Chocolate 64% cocoa; Michel Cluizel Ilha Toma 65% cocoa; Côte d'Or Intense Noir de Noir Intense Belgian Dark Chocolate; Lindt Excellence Swiss Bittersweet Chocolate; or, Lindt Excellence 70% Cocoa Extra Fine Dark Chocolate.

BUTTER AND VANILLA BEAN PASTRY SHELL

Pastry dough for one 9 to 9½-inch tart pan

*T*he vanilla bean seeds—in addition to a full teaspoon of vanilla extract—contribute a rounded flavor and fine aroma to the pastry dough.

BUTTER AND VANILLA BEAN DOUGH

1½ cups bleached all-purpose flour

⅛ teaspoon salt

8 tablespoons (1 stick) cold unsalted butter, cut into tablespoon chunks

2 tablespoons granulated sugar

1 large egg yolk, cold

1 teaspoon vanilla extract, preferably Fortified Vanilla Extract (page 55)

2 tablespoons ice water

Seeds scraped from ½ small split vanilla bean

TO MAKE THE DOUGH BY HAND Place the flour and salt in a medium-size mixing bowl and mix to combine. Drop in the chunks of butter and, using a pastry blender or two round-bladed table knives, cut the fat into the flour until reduced to small, pearl-size pieces.

Mix in the sugar. Dip into the flour-butter mixture and crumble it lightly between your fingertips, rubbing the butter into the flour until reduced to small bits and flakes. In a small bowl, whisk the egg yolk, vanilla extract, ice water, and vanilla bean seeds. Pour the egg yolk mixture over the flour and mix to form a dough, using a flat wooden paddle. It will come together in clumps. Pat the dough into a thick disk, wrap it up in a sheet of waxed paper, and refrigerate for 10 minutes.

TO MAKE THE DOUGH IN A FOOD PROCESSOR Place the flour and salt in the work bowl of a food processor fitted with the steel blade. Cover and process, using a quick on-off pulse, to combine the flour and salt. Add the chunks of butter, cover, and process to reduce the butter into small

bits, using 7 to 8 on-off pulses. Sprinkle the sugar over, cover, and pulse once or twice to combine. Whisk the egg yolk, vanilla extract, ice water, and vanilla bean seeds in a small bowl. Pour the egg yolk mixture over the flour mixture and process, using about 10 on-off pulses, until the mixture gathers together into small, moist clumps.

Turn the fragments of dough onto a work surface and gather into one mass of dough, forming it into a thick cake. Wrap the dough in a sheet of waxed paper and refrigerate for 10 minutes.

ROLL THE DOUGH AND LINE THE TART PAN Have a fluted 9 to 9½-inch round tart pan (1 inch deep, with a removable bottom) at hand. Roll the dough between 2 sheets of waxed paper to a round about 11 inches in diameter. Refrigerate the dough on a cookie sheet for 30 minutes.

Remove the top layer of waxed paper from the sheet of dough. Quickly invert the dough round, centering it, into the tart pan. Press the dough on the bottom of the tart pan, then press it up the sides. With your thumb, press back a ¼-inch ridge of dough, using the dough that extends past the rim (the overhang), all around the edges of the pan. Roll over the top of the dough with a rolling pin to cut away any excess tart dough. Press up the tucked-in ¼-inch ridge of dough to create a reinforcing edge to extend about ⅛ inch above the rim of the tart pan. Prick the bottom of the pastry dough lightly with the tines of a table fork.

REFRIGERATE THE DOUGH-LINED PAN Wrap the tart crust loosely in food-safe plastic wrap and carefully slip into a large self-sealing plastic bag. Refrigerate for at least 3 hours, or overnight, if you wish.

BAKE THE TART SHELL On baking day, preheat the oven to 425 degrees F. About 10 minutes before prebaking the tart shell, place a sheet pan or cookie sheet on the oven rack.

Line the dough-lined tart pan with a sheet of aluminum foil, very lightly pressing the foil against the bottom and sides of the dough. Fill the lined tart pan with raw rice or dried beans. (The rice or beans should be used exclusively for this purpose.) Place on the preheated pan and bake for 10 minutes. Carefully spoon out about one-third of the rice or beans, then lift away the foil with its contents and return to the container. (Cool the rice or beans before storing.)

Reduce the heat to 375 degrees F. Return the tart shell to the oven (still on the pan) and continue baking for 15 minutes longer, or until set, fully baked, and golden. Transfer the tart shell to a cooling rack and let stand for 10 minutes. The tart shell is now ready to be filled.

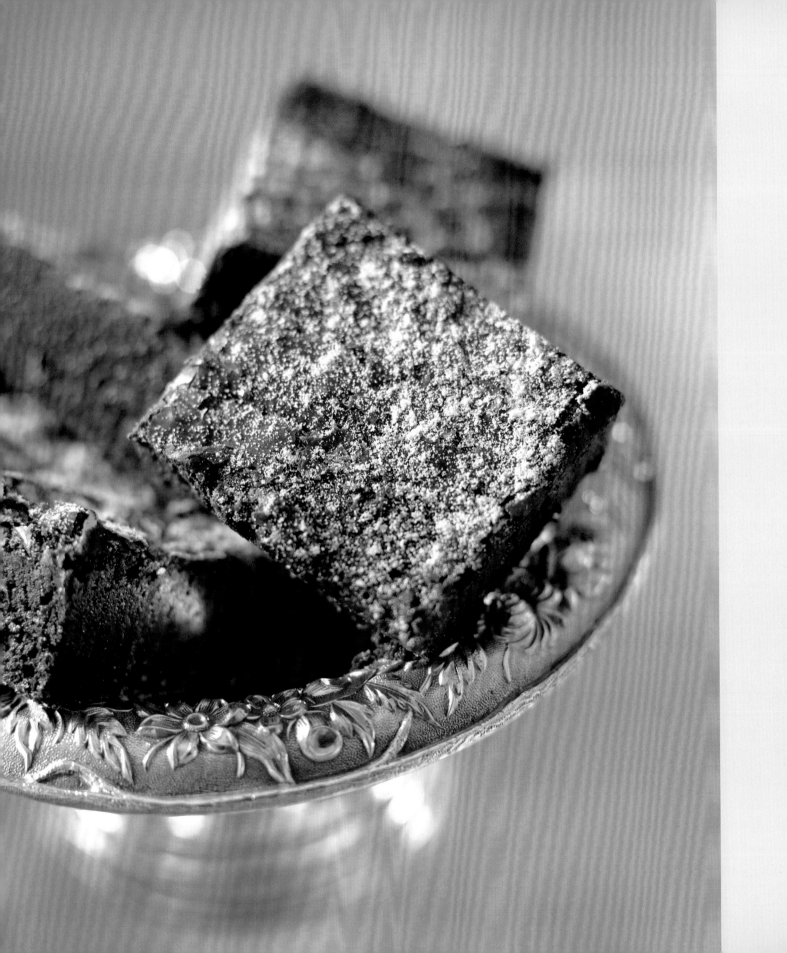

DOUBLE CHOCOLATE–COCONUT-PECAN COOKIES

About 2 dozen cookies

*D*rop cookies tinted with melted unsweetened chocolate, showered with chocolate chips, and dappled with pecans are delectable on their own or as an accompaniment to ice cream or pudding.

DOUBLE CHOCOLATE CHIP DOUGH

1 cup plus 2 tablespoons bleached all-purpose flour

½ teaspoon baking soda

¼ teaspoon salt

8 tablespoons (1 stick) unsalted butter, softened

1 cup granulated sugar

1 large egg

2 teaspoons vanilla extract

2 ounces unsweetened chocolate, melted and cooled

1 cup semisweet chocolate chips

¾ cup coarsely chopped pecans

½ cup sweetened flaked coconut

TOPPING (OPTIONAL)

¾ cup pecans (halves and pieces)

½ cup semisweet chocolate chips

PREHEAT THE OVEN TO 400 DEGREES F. Line several cookie sheets or rimmed sheet pans with cooking parchment paper.

MIX THE DOUGH Sift the flour, baking soda, and salt onto a sheet of waxed paper.

Cream the butter in the large bowl of a freestanding electric mixer on moderate speed for 2 to 3 minutes. Add the sugar in 2 additions, beating on moderate speed after each portion is added. Beat in the egg. Blend in the vanilla extract and melted unsweetened chocolate. On low speed, add the sifted ingredients in 2 additions, beating until the flour particles are absorbed. Scrape down the sides of the mixing bowl frequently to keep the dough even-textured. Mix in the chocolate chips, pecans, and coconut.

SHAPE THE COOKIES Place heaping 2-tablespoon-size mounds of dough on the prepared pans, spacing the mounds about 3 inches apart. Top each mound of dough with some pecans and chocolate chips, if you wish.

BAKE AND COOL THE COOKIES Bake the cookies in the preheated oven for 11 to 12 minutes, or until set. Let the cookies stand on the pans for 1 minute, then transfer them to cooling racks, using a wide offset metal spatula. Store in an airtight tin.

Bake-and-serve within 2 days

STUDY Topping the unbaked mounds of dough with extra pecans and chocolate chips makes a lavish batch of cookies.

DOUBLE CHOCOLATE–COCONUT HEAVENS

About 3 dozen cookies

*S*oft and chewy, and delightfully coconutty—make these cookies with good bittersweet chocolate. The cookie dough can be spooned on the pans and be baked immediately as drop cookies, or chilled, formed into balls, and rolled in more coconut for a delicious flourish.

DOUBLE CHOCOLATE–COCONUT DOUGH

2¾ cups bleached all-purpose flour

¼ cup bleached cake flour

1 tablespoon unsweetened alkalized cocoa powder

¼ teaspoon baking soda

¾ teaspoon salt

½ pound plus 5 tablespoons (2 sticks plus 5 tablespoons) unsalted butter, softened

1 cup firmly packed light brown sugar

1 cup granulated sugar

2 large eggs

3 ounces unsweetened chocolate, melted and cooled

1 ounce bittersweet chocolate, melted and cooled

2 tablespoons vanilla extract

14 ounces bittersweet chocolate, chopped into small chunks

2½ cups sweetened flaked coconut

COCONUT ROLL (OPTIONAL)

About 1½ cups sweetened flaked coconut

PREHEAT THE OVEN TO 325 DEGREES F. If you are rolling the chilled balls of dough in coconut (for the *coconut roll*, see the optional step later in the recipe), preheat the oven after the dough has chilled and prior to baking the cookies. Line several cookie sheets or rimmed sheet pans with cooking parchment paper.

MIX THE DOUGH Sift the all-purpose flour, cake flour, cocoa powder, baking soda, and salt onto a sheet of waxed paper.

Cream the butter in the large bowl of a freestanding electric mixer on moderate speed for 2 minutes. Add the light brown sugar in 2 additions, beating for 1 minute after each portion is added. Add the granulated sugar in 2 additions, beating for 1 minute after each portion is added. Beat in eggs. Blend in the melted unsweetened chocolate, melted bittersweet chocolate, and vanilla extract. On low speed, blend in the sifted ingredients in 3 additions, beating until the flour particles are absorbed before adding the next portion. Scrape down the sides of the mixing bowl frequently to keep the dough even-textured. Blend in the bittersweet chocolate chunks and coconut.

CHILL THE DOUGH, ROLL, AND SHAPE THE COOKIES (IF USING THE COCONUT ROLL) Refrigerate the dough, covered, for 5 hours, or until firm. (The dough can be stored in the refrigerator overnight.) Preheat the oven to 325 degrees F. Roll heaping 2-tablespoon-size mounds of dough between the palms of your hands, roll in the coconut to coat, and place on the prepared pans, spacing them about 3 inches apart. Bake as directed below in "Bake and cool the cookies." If you are not using the coconut roll step, proceed directly to shaping the cookies, below.

SHAPE THE COOKIES Place heaping 2-tablespoon-size mounds of dough on the prepared pans, spacing the mounds about 3 inches apart. Keep the mounds of dough plump. The dough does not need to be chilled if used for drop cookies.

BAKE AND COOL THE COOKIES Bake the cookies in the preheated oven for 16 to 17 minutes, or until set. Let the cookies stand on the pans for 1 minute, then transfer them to cooling racks, using a wide offset metal spatula. Store in an airtight tin.

Bake-and-serve within 2 days

DOUBLE CHOCOLATE–COOKIE CHIP SCONES

1 dozen scones

Go crazy and mix chocolate sandwich cookie chunks into a luxurious scone dough.

COCOA-COOKIE-CHIP DOUGH

3½ cups bleached all-purpose flour

½ cup plus 2 tablespoons unsweetened alkalized cocoa powder

4½ teaspoons baking powder

¾ teaspoon salt

⅔ cup plus 3 tablespoons granulated sugar

12 tablespoons (1½ sticks) cold unsalted butter, cut into tablespoon-size chunks

3 large eggs

2 large egg yolks

1 tablespoon plus 2 teaspoons vanilla extract

1 cup heavy cream

15 chocolate sandwich cookies (such as Nabisco Oreo Chocolate Sandwich Cookies), cut into ½-inch chunks

1 cup semisweet chocolate chips

MIX THE DOUGH Sift the flour, cocoa powder, baking powder, salt, and granulated sugar into a large mixing bowl. Whisk to blend the cocoa powder thoroughly into the flour mixture. Drop in the chunks of butter and, using a pastry blender or two round-bladed table knives, cut the fat into the flour mixture until reduced to pieces the size of large pearls. Reduce the fat further to smaller flakes, using your fingertips.

In a medium-size mixing bowl, whisk the eggs, egg yolks, vanilla extract, and heavy cream to blend well; pour over the flour mixture. Add the chocolate chips and cookie chunks, and stir to form a dough. Gather the dough into a rough mass.

KNEAD AND REFRIGERATE THE DOUGH Knead the dough lightly in the bowl for 30 seconds to 1 minute. Divide the dough in half. On a lightly floured work surface, pat or roll each portion of dough into an 8 to 8½-inch disk. Chill the disks of dough, wrapped in waxed paper, for 20 minutes.

Preheat the oven to 400 degrees F. in advance of baking the scones. Line 2 heavy cookie sheets or rimmed sheet pans with lengths of cooking parchment paper.

FORM THE SCONES With a chef's knife, cut each disk into 6 wedges. As the scones are cut, press in any chips or cookie pieces that may stick out of the sides. Transfer the scones to the prepared pans, placing them 3 inches apart.

BAKE AND COOL THE SCONES Bake the scones in the preheated oven for 18 to 20 minutes, or until set. Transfer the pans to cooling racks. Let the scones stand on the pans for 1 minute, then carefully remove them to cooling racks, using a wide offset metal spatula. Cool. Serve the scones freshly baked.

Bake-and-serve within 1 day

DARK CHOCOLATE PEANUT BUTTER CANDY SQUARES

16 squares

Oh-so-rich, oh-so-peanutty—these squares are like eating candy within candy. You can cut them into properly large blocks or dainty smaller squares. I love them in looming, substantial pieces, big and bold.

DARK CHOCOLATE AND PEANUT BUTTER BAR COOKIE BATTER

1 cup bleached all-purpose flour

3 tablespoons unsweetened alkalized cocoa powder

¼ teaspoon baking powder

¼ teaspoon salt

½ pound (16 tablespoons or 2 sticks) unsalted butter, melted and cooled to tepid

4 ounces unsweetened chocolate, melted and cooled to tepid

4 large eggs

2 cups less 2 tablespoons superfine sugar

1¾ teaspoons vanilla extract

One 9-ounce bag miniature milk chocolate–covered peanut butter cups (such as Reese's Milk Chocolate Peanut Butter Cups Miniatures), each cup cut into thirds

⅔ cup roasted peanuts

PREHEAT THE OVEN TO 325 DEGREES F. Film the inside of a 9 by 9 by 2–inch baking pan with nonstick cooking spray.

MIX THE BATTER Sift the flour, cocoa powder, baking powder, and salt onto a sheet of waxed paper.

In a medium-size mixing bowl, slowly whisk the melted butter and melted unsweetened chocolate until smooth. In a large mixing bowl, whisk the eggs slowly until just blended, about 30 to 40 seconds. Add the sugar and whisk until combined, about 45 seconds. Blend in the vanilla extract and whisked melted butter–chocolate mixture. Sift over the flour mixture and stir to form a batter, mixing thoroughly until the particles of flour are absorbed, using a whisk or flat wooden paddle. Stir in the chunks of peanut butter candy and peanuts.

Scrape the batter into the prepared pan, spreading it evenly into the corners. Smooth the top with a rubber spatula.

BAKE, COOL, AND CUT THE SWEET Bake the sweet in the preheated oven for 33 to 38 minutes, or until set. Let the sweet stand in the pan on a cooling rack for 3 hours. Refrigerate for 45 minutes, or until firm enough to cut. With a small, sharp knife, cut the sweet into quarters, then cut each quarter into 4 squares. Remove the squares from the baking pan, using a small offset metal spatula. Store in an airtight tin.

Bake-and-serve within 3 days

BUTTERY AND SOFT CHOCOLATE CAKE FOR A CROWD

One 13 by 9-inch cake, creating 20 squares

Butter and sour cream combine to develop a lush framework for a batter that bakes into an exceedingly tender, feathery, yet moist chocolate cake. Its composition is downy rather than compact and, as chocolate desserts go, texturally lighter than any of the flourless chocolate cakes in this book, but no less rich. This cake calls out for an abundant stretch of frosting, and when nothing less than that will do, the Soft and Luxurious Chocolate Frosting that follows is simply ideal.

BUTTER AND SOUR CREAM CHOCOLATE BATTER

4 ounces unsweetened chocolate, chopped

½ cup plus 2 tablespoons and 1½ teaspoons water

2 cups bleached cake flour

1 teaspoons baking powder

1 teaspoon baking soda

½ teaspoon salt

½ pound (16 tablespoons or 2 sticks) unsalted butter, softened

1¼ cups firmly packed light brown sugar

¼ cup plus 2 tablespoons granulated sugar

3 large eggs

1 large egg yolk

2 teaspoons vanilla extract

1 cup sour cream

FROSTING

Soft and Luxurious Chocolate Frosting (page 404)

PREHEAT THE OVEN TO 350 DEGREES F. Lightly grease the inside of a 13 by 9 by 2-inch baking pan with shortening and dust with flour.

MIX THE BATTER Place the chocolate and water in a small, heavy saucepan (preferably enameled cast iron) and set over low heat. As the chocolate begins to melt, stir it from time to time with a wooden spoon or flat paddle. When the chocolate has melted, stir slowly to blend until smooth. By the time you need to use it, it should be slightly warm and the texture of thick pudding.

Sift the flour, baking powder, baking soda, and salt onto a sheet of waxed paper.

Cream the butter in the large bowl of a freestanding electric mixer on moderate speed for 2 to 3 minutes. Add the light brown sugar in 2 additions, beating for 1 minute after each portion is added. Add the granulated sugar and beat for 1 minute longer. Add the eggs, one at a time, beating for 45 seconds after each addition. Beat in the egg yolk. Blend in the chocolate mixture and vanilla extract. The mixture may look slightly curdled at this point—OK—but will be restored once the sifted mixture and sour cream are added to complete the batter. On low speed, alternately add the sifted mixture in 3 additions with the sour cream in 2 additions, beginning and ending with the sifted mixture. Scrape down the sides of the mixing bowl frequently to keep the batter even-textured. The batter will be soft, light, and very creamy.

Spoon the batter into the prepared pan and spread evenly. Smooth the top with a rubber spatula.

BAKE, COOL, AND FROST THE CAKE Bake the cake in the preheated oven for 35 to 40 minutes, or until risen, set, and toothpick inserted in the center withdraws clean. The baked cake will pull away slightly from the sides of the pan. Cool the cake in the pan on a rack. Spread the frosting over the cake. Let the cake stand for 1 hour before cutting into squares for serving.

Bake-and-serve within 1 day

SOFT AND LUXURIOUS CHOCOLATE FROSTING

About 4 cups frosting

*I*ndulgent in all the best ways—buttery, chocolate-endowed, creamy.

6 tablespoons (¾ stick) unsalted butter, softened

4 ounces unsweetened chocolate, melted and cooled to tepid

Large pinch of salt

2½ teaspoons vanilla extract

5½ cups confectioners' sugar, sifted

⅔ cup milk, heated to tepid

Place the butter in the bowl of a heavy-duty freestanding electric mixer fitted with the flat paddle attachment. Beat on moderate speed for 1 minute. Blend in the melted chocolate, the salt, the vanilla extract, half of the milk, and 1½ cups of the confectioners' sugar. Add the balance of the milk and beat for 1 minute. Add half of the remaining confectioners' sugar and beat for 1 minute, or until smooth. Add the balance of the confectioners' sugar, beat on low speed to blend, then beat on moderately high speed until very creamy and somewhat lightened in texture, about 3 minutes. Scrape down the sides of the mixing bowl frequently to keep the frosting even-textured.

Adjust the texture of the frosting to soft spreading consistency, as needed, by adding additional teaspoons of milk or tablespoons of confectioners' sugar.

STUDY This frosting is especially suited for spreading on the top of a sheet cake because it is so soft and creamy. The qualities that make it so enticing for spreading over a single layer preclude it from being used for piping, when a stiffer consistency is desired.

DARKLY LUXURIOUS, any one of these cakes is likely to provide you with your minimum daily requirement of chocolate. These one-layer charmers are easy to assemble and invitingly rich. Each cake tastes complex, relying on the use of excellent bittersweet chocolate—an ample amount of this essential component is melted down in order to integrate it into a buttery batter. Richer than a candy bar, and more powerful than any type of cookie, a flourless chocolate cake is purely and inescapably chocolate, and so much fun to bake.

FLOURLESS BITTERSWEET CHOCOLATE CAKE

One 9-inch cake, creating 8 slices

A little cocoa powder strengthens the batter and, along with the bittersweet chocolate, extends the flavor. The cake's delicacy is most appreciated at room temperature, several hours after baking, when the flavors are unified and the texture settles into something lightly creamy but chocolate-rich. A puffy cascade of Vanilla-Scented Whipped Cream (page 303) would be a perfect plate-mate to a slice of this cake.

BITTERSWEET CHOCOLATE BATTER

⅔ cup plus 2 tablespoons superfine sugar

1 tablespoon plus 2 teaspoons unsweetened alkalized cocoa powder

Large pinch of salt

9 ounces bittersweet chocolate, melted and cooled to tepid

8 tablespoons (1 stick) unsalted butter, melted and cooled to tepid

5 large eggs, separated

2½ teaspoons vanilla extract

¼ teaspoon cream of tartar

1 tablespoon unsweetened alkalized cocoa powder and confectioners' sugar, for sifting on top of the baked cake (optional)

PREHEAT THE OVEN TO 350 DEGREES F. Lightly butter the inside of a 9-inch springform pan (2¾ inches deep).

MIX THE BATTER Sift the superfine sugar, cocoa powder, and salt onto a sheet of waxed paper.

Whisk the melted chocolate and melted butter in a small bowl until smooth.

In a large mixing bowl, whisk the egg yolks and sifted sugar mixture for 1 to 2 minutes, or until combined and very lightly thickened. Whisk in the vanilla extract. Blend in the melted chocolate-butter mixture.

Whip the egg whites in a clean, dry bowl until beginning to mound, add the cream of tartar, and continue whipping until firm (not stiff) peaks are formed. Stir 2 or 3 large spoonfuls of the whipped whites into the chocolate mixture, then fold in the remaining whites lightly but thoroughly.

Spoon the batter evenly into the prepared pan. Gently smooth the top with a rubber spatula.

BAKE AND COOL THE CAKE Bake the cake in the preheated oven for 35 to 40 minutes, or until gently set. The baked cake will form puffs and fissures here and there.

Cool the cake completely in the pan on a rack. It will sink, and collapse at the cracks. Open the hinge on the side of the pan and remove the outer ring, allowing the cake to stand on the circular metal base. Sift the 1 tablespoon cocoa powder over the surface of the cake and a little confectioners' sugar on the entire circular edge, if you wish. Serve the cake, cut into thick slices. Store in an airtight cake keeper.

Bake-and-serve within 2 days

STYLE For Double Vanilla Flourless Bittersweet Chocolate Cake, add 1½ teaspoons vanilla bean paste to the batter along with the vanilla extract.

STUDY The following chocolates bring out the best in this cake: Callebaut Bittersweet Chocolate; Scharffen Berger Bittersweet 70% cocoa; Valrhona Extra Amer Bittersweet 61% cacao; Valrhona Le Noir Amer 71% cacao; Valrhona Grand Cru Noir Manjari Gastronomie Chocolat Noir Dark Chocolate 64% cocoa; Michel Cluizel Chocolat Amer Dark Chocolate 60% cacao; Lindt Chocolate Crée à Berne Swiss Bittersweet Chocolate; Lindt Excellence Swiss Bittersweet Chocolate; or, Lindt Excellence 70% Cocoa Extra Fine Dark Chocolate.

CHOCOLATE WALNUT SOUFFLÉ CAKE

One 9-inch cake, creating 8 slices

Ground walnuts add an elusive richness to this cake batter, while intensifying the flavor of the bittersweet chocolate and fortifying the batter along the way. In its own transcendent way, a slice of the cake is rich enough unescorted, but even more heavenly with just a little Nutty Turtle Sauce (page 358) and a side of whipped cream.

CHOCOLATE WALNUT SOUFFLÉ BATTER

⅔ cup superfine sugar

1 tablespoon bleached cake flour

2 tablespoons unsweetened alkalized cocoa powder

Large pinch of salt

13 ounces bittersweet chocolate, melted and cooled to tepid

12 tablespoons (1½ sticks) unsalted butter, melted and cooled to tepid

5 large eggs, separated

2 teaspoons vanilla extract

¼ cup ground walnuts

¼ teaspoon cream of tartar

Walnut halves, lightly toasted and cooled completely (optional)

Preheat the oven to 350 degrees F. Lightly butter the inside of a 9-inch springform pan (2¾ inches deep).

MIX THE BATTER Sift the sugar, flour, cocoa powder, and salt onto a sheet of waxed paper.

Whisk the melted chocolate and melted butter in a medium-size mixing bowl until smooth.

In a large mixing bowl, whisk the egg yolks and sugar–cocoa powder mixture for 1 minute. Blend in the vanilla extract. Thoroughly stir in the melted chocolate-butter mixture, then the ground walnuts.

Whip the egg whites in a clean, dry bowl until beginning to mound, add the cream of tartar, and continue whipping until firm (not stiff) peaks are formed. Stir 3 large spoonfuls of the whipped whites into the batter, then fold in the remaining whites, combining the two mixtures lightly but thoroughly.

Spoon the batter evenly into the prepared pan. Gently smooth the top with a rubber spatula.

BAKE AND COOL THE CAKE Bake the cake in the preheated oven for 30 minutes, or until gently set throughout (the center should be stable).

Cool the cake completely in the pan on a rack. The cake will fall somewhat on cooling. Open the hinge on the side of the pan and remove the outer ring, allowing the cake to stand on the circular metal base. Cut the cake into thick slices, scatter over a few walnuts (if using), and serve. Store in an airtight cake keeper.

Bake-and-serve within 2 days

STUDY The gently nutty and enriching influence of the ground walnuts calls out for a relatively intense chocolate, such as Valrhona Le Noir Amer 71% cacao; Valrhona Guanaja Dark Bitter Chocolate 70% cacao; Michel Cluizel Chocolat Amer Brut Bitter Chocolate 72% cacao; or, Weiss Ebene Bittersweet Chocolate 72% cocoa.

ESSENCE-OF-VANILLA CHOCOLATE SOUFFLÉ CAKE

One 9-inch cake, creating 8 slices

This cake—simple but elegant in its simplicity—has a lovely moist texture and defined chocolate flavor. The vanilla lends a shadowy, sweetly perfumelike undertone to the batter. Lightly sweetened whipped cream or good vanilla ice cream—and a handful of bright fresh raspberries—would be an amiable contrast to the cake's rich texture and depth of flavor.

VANILLA-SCENTED CHOCOLATE SOUFFLÉ BATTER

⅔ cup plus 2 tablespoons superfine sugar, preferably Essence-of-Vanilla Superfine Sugar (page 56)

2 tablespoons unsweetened alkalized cocoa powder

Large pinch of salt

10 ounces bittersweet chocolate, melted and cooled to tepid

12 tablespoons (1½ sticks) unsalted butter, melted and cooled to tepid

Seeds scraped from a small split vanilla bean

5 large eggs, separated

2 teaspoons vanilla extract

¼ teaspoon cream of tartar

PREHEAT THE OVEN TO 350 DEGREES F. Lightly butter the inside of a 9-inch springform pan (2¾ inches deep).

MIX THE BATTER Sift the sugar, cocoa powder, and salt onto a sheet of waxed paper.

Whisk the melted chocolate, melted butter, and vanilla bean seeds in a medium-size bowl until smooth.

In a large mixing bowl, whisk the egg yolks and sugar–cocoa powder blend for 1 to 2 minutes, or until combined. Blend in the vanilla extract and the melted chocolate-butter mixture and whisk to mix well.

Whip the egg whites in a clean, dry bowl until just beginning to mound, add the cream of tartar, and continue whipping until firm (not stiff) peaks are formed. Stir 3 large spoonfuls of the whipped whites into the chocolate batter, then fold in the remaining whites, combining the two mixtures lightly but thoroughly.

Spoon the batter evenly into the prepared pan. Gently smooth the top with a rubber spatula.

BAKE AND COOL THE CAKE Bake the cake in the preheated oven for 30 minutes, or until gently set.

Cool the cake completely in the pan on a rack. The cake will settle as it cools. Open the hinge on the side of the pan and remove the outer ring, allowing the cake to stand on the circular metal base. Serve the cake, cut into thick slices (the top—especially the rounded edges—will splinter and crack when cut). Store in an airtight cake keeper.

Bake-and-serve within 2 days

STUDY This cake benefits from using chocolate with a rounded and centered cocoa presence, such as Valrhona Le Noir Gastronomie 61% cacao; Valrhona Caraïbe Dark Chocolate 66% cocoa; Valrhona Grand Cru Noir Manjari Gastronomie Chocolat Noir Dark Chocolate 64% cocoa; Valrhona Equatoriale Chocolat de Couverture Noir Dark Bittersweet Couverture 55% cacao; or, Michel Cluizel Ilha Toma 65% cocoa.

CANDYLIKE CHOCOLATE CAKE

One 8-inch cake, creating 8 to 10 slices

Fudgy, and indisputably containing more than a suggestion of chocolate, this confection of a cake presents chocolate at its potent best. I can't tell you the number of times I've made the cake for dessert hurriedly late in the morning for unexpected dinner guests that evening because it's so easy to put together. Though rich in its own right, I like to have a bowl of whipped cream primed to spoon over each slice.

BITTERSWEET CHOCOLATE BATTER

⅓ cup superfine sugar

2 tablespoons unsweetened alkalized cocoa powder

Large pinch of salt

10 ounces bittersweet chocolate, melted and cooled to tepid

12 tablespoons (1½ sticks) unsalted butter, melted and cooled to tepid

4 large eggs, separated

1 large egg yolk

2 teaspoons vanilla extract

¼ teaspoon cream of tartar

PREHEAT THE OVEN TO 400 DEGREES F. Lightly butter the inside of an 8½-inch springform pan (2½ inches deep).

MIX THE BATTER Sift the superfine sugar, cocoa powder, and salt onto a sheet of waxed paper.

Whisk the melted chocolate and melted butter in a large mixing bowl until smooth. Whisk in the sugar–cocoa powder mixture. Blend in the 5 egg yolks and the vanilla extract, mixing well.

In a clean, dry medium-size mixing bowl, whip the egg whites until just beginning to mound and swell, add the cream of tartar, and continue whipping until firm (not stiff) peaks are formed. Stir 3 large spoonfuls of the whipped whites into the chocolate batter, then fold in the remaining whites, combining the two mixtures lightly but thoroughly.

Spoon the batter evenly into the prepared pan. Gently smooth the top with a rubber spatula.

BAKE AND COOL THE CAKE Bake the cake in the preheated oven for 20 minutes. The surface of the cake will be uneven—OK. As the cake cools, it will settle and firm up.

Cool the cake completely in the pan on a rack. If necessary, speed the firming process by refrigerating the cake for 1 hour. Open the hinge on the side of the pan and remove the outer ring, allowing the cake to stand on the circular metal base. Serve the cake, cut into thick slices. Store in an airtight cake keeper.

Bake-and-serve within 2 days

STUDY The texture of this cake is wonderfully dense and creamy. The cake must be cooled completely to be cut into neat, clean slices.

It is important to use a bittersweet chocolate with enough depth in this cake batter and any one of the following would generate just the right complexity of flavor: Callebaut Bittersweet Chocolate; Scharffen Berger Bittersweet 70% cocoa; Valrhona Le Noir Amer 71% cacao; Valrhona Grand Cru Noir Manjari Gastronomie Chocolat Noir Dark Chocolate 64% cocoa; Valrhona Equatoriale Chocolat de Couverture Noir Dark Bittersweet Couverture 55% cacao; or, El Ray Bucare Bittersweet Chocolate (*Carenero Superior*) 58.5% cocoa.

CHOCOLATE TORTE

One 9-inch cake, creating 8 to 10 slices

An ample amount of butter, combined with an equally substantial quantity of bittersweet chocolate, imparts a certain density to this cake and underlines its richness. It is moist and elegant, with a complex taste. The winy intensity of black mission figs, when in season and available fresh, is an engaging accompaniment to slices of the torte; the contrast is unexpected but the pairing underscores the fruity aroma occasionally present in certain types of bittersweet chocolate.

BUTTERY CHOCOLATE BATTER

7 tablespoons superfine sugar

2 tablespoons unsweetened alkalized cocoa powder

3 tablespoons bleached cake flour

⅛ teaspoon salt

14 ounces bittersweet chocolate, melted and cooled to tepid

½ pound (16 tablespoons or 2 sticks) unsalted butter, melted and cooled to warm

8 large eggs, separated

2 large egg yolks

2½ teaspoons vanilla extract

½ teaspoon cream of tartar

Confectioners' sugar, for sifting on top of the baked cake (optional)

PREHEAT THE OVEN TO 375 DEGREES F. Lightly butter the inside of a 9-inch springform pan (2¾ inches deep).

MIX THE BATTER Sift the sugar, cocoa powder, flour, and salt onto a sheet of waxed paper.

Whisk the melted chocolate and melted butter in a medium-size mixing bowl until smooth.

In a large mixing bowl, whisk the 10 egg yolks to blend. Add the sifted sugar–cocoa powder mixture and whisk for 1 minute. Blend in the melted chocolate and butter mixture, add the vanilla extract, and mix well.

Whip the egg whites in a large mixing bowl until just beginning to mound and swell. Add the cream of tartar and continue whipping until firm (not stiff) peaks are formed. Stir 4 large spoonfuls of the whipped egg whites into the chocolate mixture to lighten it, then fold in the remaining whites lightly but thoroughly. The batter will be moderately thick.

Spoon the batter evenly into the prepared pan. Gently smooth the top with a rubber spatula.

BAKE AND COOL THE CAKE Bake the cake in the preheated oven for 25 to 30 minutes, or until gently set throughout the outer two-thirds. The center will wobble slightly. The baked cake will rise up ¼ to ⅓ inch above the rim of the baking pan. Begin checking the cake at 25 minutes.

Cool the cake completely in the pan on a rack. The cake will settle as it cools—OK. Refrigerate the cake for about 1 hour, or until firm enough to cut cleanly. Open the hinge on the side of the pan and remove the outer ring, allowing the cake to stand on the circular metal base. Serve the cake, cut into thick slices. For serving, sift confectioners' sugar onto the edges or the entire top of each slice, if you wish. Store in an airtight cake keeper.

Bake-and-serve within 2 days

STUDY For a somewhat sweeter cake, you can increase the sugar to ½ cup plus 1 tablespoon.

I have baked a beautifully flavored torte with these chocolates: Michel Cluizel ("*Hacienda Concepcion*") Chocolat Amer Dark Chocolate 66% cacao; Michel Cluizel Chocolat Amer Dark Chocolate 60% cacao; Michel Cluizel Ilha Toma 65% cocoa; Côte d'Or Intense Noir de Noir Intense Belgian Dark Chocolate; Weiss Ebene Bittersweet Chocolate 72% cocoa; Weiss Acarigua Bittersweet Chocolate 70% cocoa; Lindt Chocolate Créé à Berne Swiss Bittersweet Chocolate; Lindt Excellence Swiss Bittersweet Chocolate; Lindt Excellence 70% Cocoa Extra Fine Dark Chocolate; Domori Sur Del Lago Clasificado Cocoa Estate Couverture 75% cocoa; or, Domori Caranero Superior Cocoa Estate Couverture 75% cocoa.

EVERYONE WHO LOVES TO BAKE HAS, at one time or another, called me to find out if I have some special method to make a flourless chocolate cake, well, beautiful. Picture perfect. Do I have a recipe for one that bakes into an absolutely flat top and straight-as-a-soldier sides, worthy of a highly polished veneer of ganache or shiny chocolate icing? The answer is an underscored "no!" This is a cake that frequently sinks, the edges might (okay, usually) buckle or crease, and the top bakes into occasional humps and bumps, peaks and valleys.

And I'm the wrong one to ask, because I love this cake even though it looks funky—in a natural kind of way.

You could certainly make a flourless chocolate cake with a few ingredients—butter, bittersweet chocolate, vanilla extract, and eggs (or a combination of whole eggs and egg yolks)—and bake it carefully so that only the edges are slightly higher and the surface is smooth and varnished, almost like a polished wood table with a patina that has

Chocolate, glorious and rich—but can't win a beauty contest

been acquired over a period of years. But why limit the ingredients for looks alone? I adore the subtle shadings in taste a flourless (or nearly flourless) chocolate cake gets from the addition of ingredients (or the way you play with them) that might upend the batter, and I find its uneven look—an inherent quirkiness—appealing. In a sexy kind of way, all those rich and dark curves are provocative. So, I don't care if it looks craggy, and if I want to make a cake with a perfectly constructed figure, I'm just as happy to choose a recipe for a different kind of cake.

THESE BUTTERY, CHOCOLATE-LADEN COOKIE RECIPES have a fair amount of nostalgia mixed into the various doughs. What makes the collective assortment of them an anchor in my recipe file is their easy-going nature, inviting style, indulgent flavor, and appealing texture—rich, sometimes chewy, occasionally fudgy, crammed with rolled oats now and then, and, of course, swarming with chocolate. What makes each kind of cookie so distinctly special is its own form of chocolate presence and, quite naturally, the baking aroma that radiates so sweetly from every batch.

Heirloom chocolate cookies

DARK AND WHITE CHOCOLATE COOKIES

About 4 dozen cookies

*T*hese cookies have a chewy-crunchy texture, and they are dramatically dark and white chocolate through-and-through. The dark chocolate batter is enlarged by the addition of white chocolate chips. The concept of a color-flavor contrast is one you could easily apply to many of the chocolate-focused doughs and batters in this book.

BUTTERY CHOCOLATE DOUGH

2¼ cups bleached all-purpose flour

1 teaspoon baking soda

½ teaspoon salt

½ pound (16 tablespoons or 2 sticks) unsalted butter, softened

2 cups granulated sugar

2 large eggs

2½ teaspoons vanilla extract

4 ounces unsweetened chocolate, melted and cooled

1 cup white chocolate chips

CHOCOLATE CHIP TOPPING (OPTIONAL)

About ½ cup white chocolate chips

PREHEAT THE OVEN TO 375 DEGREES F. Line several cookie sheets or rimmed sheet pans with cooking parchment paper.

MIX THE DOUGH Sift the flour, baking soda, and salt onto a sheet of waxed paper.

Cream the butter in the large bowl of a freestanding electric mixer on moderately low speed for 3 minutes. Add the sugar in 3 additions, beating for 1 minute on moderate speed after each portion is added. Blend in the eggs, one at a time, beating until just incorporated. On low speed, blend in the vanilla extract and melted chocolate. On low speed, blend the sifted ingredients in 3 additions, beating just until the flour particles are absorbed. Scrape down the sides of the mixing bowl frequently to keep the dough even-textured. Blend in the chocolate chips. The dough will be moderately dense but buttery-textured.

SHAPE THE COOKIES Place heaping 2-tablespoon-size mounds of dough on the prepared pans, spacing the mounds 3 inches apart. The cookies will spread as they bake.

BAKE AND COOL THE COOKIES Bake the cookies in the preheated oven for 12 to 13 minutes, or until set. The cookies will puff lightly as they bake, then settle down. Begin to check the cookies after 10 minutes of baking. After 9 minutes of baking, you can quickly sprinkle the additional white chocolate chips randomly on top of the cookies, if you wish. Let the cookies stand on the pans for 1 to 2 minutes, then transfer them to cooling racks, using a wide offset metal spatula. Store in an airtight tin.

Bake-and-serve within 2 days

STYLE For Dark and White Chocolate Cookies with Nuts, blend ¾ cup chopped walnuts, pecans, or macadamia nuts into the dough along with the white chocolate chips.

CHOCOLATE HANDFULS

*R*aid the cookie jar for this handful-of-a-cookie, crawling with chunks of chopped bittersweet chocolate. Although these monsters can be baked ahead, I usually try to serve them within a few hours of baking, when they are utterly and irresistibly delicious.

ULTRA-BITTERSWEET CHOCOLATE CHUNK DOUGH

3 cups bleached all-purpose flour

¼ teaspoon baking powder

¾ teaspoon salt

¾ pound (3 sticks) unsalted butter, softened

1½ cups superfine sugar

2 tablespoons vanilla extract

1 tablespoon hot water

1 pound 6 ounces (22 ounces) bittersweet chocolate, coarsely chopped

PREHEAT THE OVEN TO 350 DEGREES F. Line several cookie sheets or rimmed sheet pans with cooking parchment paper.

MIX THE DOUGH Sift the flour, baking powder, and salt onto a sheet of waxed paper.

Cream the butter in the large bowl of a freestanding electric mixer on moderately low speed for 3 minutes. Add the sugar in 3 additions, beating for 1 minute on moderate speed after each portion is added. Blend in the vanilla extract and hot water. On low speed, blend in the sifted ingredients in 3 additions, beating just until the flour particles are absorbed. Scrape down the sides of the mixing bowl frequently to keep the dough even-textured. Work in the chocolate chunks with a wooden spoon or flat wooden paddle. The dough will be firm (like shortbread) and chunky.

SHAPE THE COOKIES Place rounded ¼-cup-size mounds of dough on the prepared pans, spacing the mounds about 3½ inches apart and arranging 6 cookies on each pan.

BAKE AND COOL THE COOKIES Bake the cookies in the preheated oven for 16 to 17 minutes, or until golden and set. Let the cookies stand on the pans for 1 to 2 minutes, then transfer them to cooling racks, using a wide offset metal spatula. Store in an airtight tin.

Bake-and-serve within 3 days

STYLE For Chocolate Handfuls with Nuts, reduce the amount of bittersweet chocolate to 1 pound 3 ounces. Work 1 cup coarsely chopped walnuts, pecans, or macadamia nuts into the dough along with the bittersweet chocolate chunks.

STUDY These cookies are a combination of buttery shortbread and candy, buttery and intense, with pockets of bittersweet chocolate throughout. The dough keeps in the refrigerator for 3 days, so it's easy to bake and serve these gems very fresh, almost on impulse.

CHOCOLATE SAVANNAHS, REMODELED

*S*avannahs, as they are known in my kitchen, are deep, dark, and fudgy-rich drop cookies. The intense flavor reaches a chocolatey plateau in the dough through the use of cocoa powder, bittersweet chocolate, unsweetened chocolate, and chocolate chips in the dough.

In my hands, untold ways have surfaced to refashion what was a favorite chocolate cookie recipe of my late mother's: to make them with or without bittersweet chocolate chunks; with or without unsweetened alkalized cocoa powder; with varying amounts of salt; with baking powder alone or a combination of baking powder and baking soda; with an amended oven temperature; with or without the seed scrapings from a vanilla bean; with cake flour, all-purpose flour, or a combination of the two; and *on and on*. But in every one of its incarnations, these cookies embody chocolate in all its dark glory.

INTENSE CHOCOLATE DOUGH

⅓ cup bleached all-purpose flour

⅓ cup bleached cake flour

3 tablespoons unsweetened alkalized cocoa powder

½ teaspoon baking powder

⅛ teaspoon salt

1⅓ cups plus 2 tablespoons superfine sugar

4 large eggs

1 large egg yolk

10 tablespoons (1 stick plus 2 tablespoons) unsalted butter, melted and cooled to tepid

12 ounces bittersweet chocolate, melted and cooled to tepid

4 ounces unsweetened chocolate, melted and cooled to tepid

2 tablespoons vanilla extract

3 cups semisweet chocolate chips

PREHEAT THE OVEN TO 325 DEGREES F. Line several cookie sheets or rimmed sheet pans with cooking parchment paper.

MIX THE DOUGH Sift the all-purpose flour, cake flour, cocoa powder, baking powder, and salt onto a sheet of waxed paper.

In a large mixing bowl, beat the sugar, eggs, and egg yolk on moderate speed for 1 minute, using an electric hand mixer. Add the melted butter, melted bittersweet chocolate, melted unsweetened chocolate, and vanilla extract, and beat for 1 to 2 minutes longer, or until thoroughly combined. Sift the flour mixture over the chocolate mixture and blend it in completely. Mix in the chocolate chips. Let the cookie dough rest for 5 minutes.

SHAPE THE COOKIES Place rounded 2-tablespoon-size mounds of dough on the prepared pans, spacing the mounds about 2 inches apart. Arrange 12 mounds of dough on each pan.

BAKE AND COOL THE COOKIES Bake the cookies for 12 minutes, or until just set. Begin checking the cookies at 10 minutes. The baked cookies will no longer look wet on top, and they will be somewhat soft—OK. Let the cookies stand on the pans for 3 to 4 minutes. Transfer the cookies, still on the parchment paper, to racks and cool completely. Remove the cookies from the parchment paper, using a wide offset metal spatula. Store in an airtight tin.

Bake-and-serve within 2 days

STYLE For Bittersweet Chocolate Savannahs, Remodeled, substitute 1 pound bittersweet chocolate, coarsely chopped, for the semisweet chocolate chips. These are very rich.

For Chocolate and White Chocolate Chip Savannahs, Remodeled, use 2 cups semisweet chocolate chips and 1 cup white chocolate chips.

For Chocolate and Macadamia Nut Savannahs, Remodeled, mix 1 cup macadamia halves and pieces to the dough along with the chocolate chips. These are chunky.

STUDY Melt the butter and chocolates separately (although both the bittersweet and unsweetened chocolate can be melted together).

Do not substitute granulated for superfine sugar, as the baked cookies will have a gritty texture.

Allowing the cookie dough to rest for 5 minutes before shaping and baking helps to establish its texture and composition. In that time, the melted chocolate has the opportunity to lightly set, which contributes to the overall density and fudginess of the baked cookie.

To make the dough by hand, whisk the sugar and eggs/egg yolk for 3 minutes. Add the melted chocolate and vanilla and blend well, mixing for 2 to 3 minutes. Blend in the sifted flour mixture, using a wooden spoon or flat wooden paddle, then mix in the chocolate chips.

I AM TRANSFIXED BY THESE CHOCOLATE SAVANNAHS.

Inspired by a recipe of my mother's, they are possibly the most intense chocolate cookies I know of, for the flavor is dark and compelling. I have made countless versions of them, not initially with a view towards improving the recipe. In my kitchen, armed with more ingredients and intensities of chocolate than ever imaginable, the flow of the recipe has changed according to my mood, my baking whim and, perhaps, a little inspiration.

In my mixing bowl, the dough has morphed into a very creamy and moist one. I've crammed plenty of chocolate into it, upgraded the vanilla flavor, and baked larger mounds of the dough at a lower oven temperature. A moderately high oven temperature, I have found, is the enemy of many a chocolate cookie dough, especially this one.

Possessed by a cookie recipe

Many recipes have influenced this one—my mom's recipe for a Southern fudge nut cookie (Savannah Chocolate Drops), a French chocolate cake, and one of my paternal grandmother's brownie recipes. My mother baked a lot with nuts, so you would likely crunch into walnuts or pecans in her batch of cookies. Although I have a mocha version in *Baking by Flavor* and offer a macadamia variation in this book, I am most partial to the all-chocolate, nut-free, best-of-the-best version on page 423.

This recipe has a long personal history, one that chronicles an exchange of ingredients, a modified technique and baking method, and pivotal elevations in flavor: the way this recipe has evolved over time, and from cook to cook, is what good baking is all about.

CHOCOLATE CHIP SAND COOKIES

About 4 dozen cookies

As soon as I was able, I took charge of the kitchen at home. As the only child in a single-parent household, this was easy to do. With my own personal baking file in hand, I began to "test" recipes on my mother's friends, who were always willing to try out a new batch of something sweet. Looking back now, I appreciate how patient they all were. It helped that my mother was so interested in baking, and that she had so many steadfast and agreeable friends; they, and our neighbors, frequently received the overrun of my kitchen capers—especially cookies like these and double or triple-layer chocolate cakes.

The vanilla version of this recipe has long been part of my baking repertoire, and my mother had variations of it in her file, too. She used it during the Christmas holidays and was too impatient to roll small balls of dough, so she made them large. But not one of the recipes included chocolate chips. To bring the evolution of this recipe full circle, I must tell you that my friend Anna Saint John (chef and owner of Catering by Anna Saint John), who is also a devoted baker, tells me that she makes the vanilla cookies from my recipe larger than originally designed, and I do, too. But when Anna and I spoke about how wonderful the larger version can be, she informed me that lately she's been baking the cookies in miniature for presentation on an assorted cookie platter.

Following is a prized recipe with a new twist—the addition of chocolate chips—and the results are splendid. No matter the size. (But make them large.)

CHOCOLATE CHIP DOUGH

4 cups bleached all-purpose flour

1 teaspoon baking soda

1 teaspoon cream of tartar

½ teaspoon salt

½ pound (16 tablespoons or 2 sticks) unsalted butter, softened

1 cup plain vegetable oil (such as canola)

1 cup superfine sugar

1 cup confectioners' sugar

4 large egg yolks

2½ teaspoons vanilla extract

1¾ cups miniature semisweet chocolate chips

SUGAR FOR ROLLING THE UNBAKED BALLS OF COOKIE DOUGH

About 2 cups granulated sugar

MIX THE DOUGH Sift the flour, baking soda, cream of tartar, and salt onto a sheet of waxed paper.

Cream the butter in the large bowl of a freestanding electric mixer on moderate speed for 3 minutes. With the mixer on moderately high speed, beat in the oil in a thin, steady stream. The mixture will be soupy. Add the superfine sugar and beat for 2 minutes on moderate speed. Add the confectioners' sugar and beat for 2 minutes longer. On moderate speed, blend in the egg yolks and vanilla extract. The mixture will look lightly creamy. On low speed, blend in half of the sifted ingredients. Mix in the chocolate chips. Blend in the balance of the sifted mixture in 2 batches, beating just until the flour particles are absorbed. Scrape down the sides of the mixing bowl frequently to keep the dough even-textured. The dough will be soft.

REFRIGERATE (OR FREEZE) THE DOUGH Scrape the dough onto a baking pan lined with food-safe plastic wrap, press into a flat cake, cover, and refrigerate for about 5 hours, or until firm enough to shape without sticking to your hands. Or, freeze the dough for about 1 hour, or until firm. The dough must be cold in order to roll into balls and coat in sugar. The dough may be stored in the refrigerator for up to 3 days in advance of baking.

Preheat the oven to 375 degrees F. in advance of rolling the cookies. Line several cookie sheets or rimmed sheet pans with cooking parchment paper.

SHAPE THE COOKIES AND ROLL IN SUGAR Take up heaping 2-tablespoon-size mounds of dough and roll them into balls. Gently roll the balls in the granulated sugar to coat lightly.

Place the dough balls 2 to 2½ inches apart on the prepared pans. Flatten each cookie lightly and evenly with the tines of a fork, dipping the fork in a little granulated sugar to keep it from sticking to the dough. You can flatten the dough balls in a crisscross pattern (like peanut butter cookies) or in parallel lines (I think that parallel lines look best).

BAKE AND COOL THE COOKIES Bake the cookies in the preheated oven for 15 to 16 minutes, or until set and golden. Do not underbake, or the centers will not be sandy-textured like the outsides, but be careful about over-browning them. The cookies are sensitive to hot spots in the oven, so it would be wise to rotate the pans halfway through baking. Let the cookies stand on the pans for 2 minutes, then transfer them to cooling racks, using a wide offset metal spatula. Store in an airtight tin.

Bake-and-serve within 4 days

BITTERSWEET CHOCOLATE–OATMEAL COOKIES WITH MACADAMIA NUTS

About 3½ dozen cookies

*M*asses of bittersweet chocolate chunks impose themselves in an oatmeal cookie dough that's rounded out with the tropical richness of coconut and macadamia nuts.

OATMEAL–BITTERSWEET CHOCOLATE–MACADAMIA NUT DOUGH

1½ cups bleached all-purpose flour

1 teaspoon baking soda

¾ teaspoon salt

½ pound (16 tablespoons or 2 sticks) unsalted butter, softened

1 cup firmly packed light brown sugar

½ cup granulated sugar

2 large eggs

2½ teaspoons vanilla extract

½ teaspoon hot water

15 ounces bittersweet chocolate, hand-cut into ½-inch-thick chunks

2 cups "quick-cooking" (not "instant") rolled oats

1⅔ cups sweetened flaked coconut

1 cup macadamia nuts (whole and halves or halves and pieces)

PREHEAT THE OVEN TO 375 DEGREES F. Line several cookie sheets or rimmed sheet pans with cooking parchment paper.

MIX THE DOUGH Sift the flour, baking soda, and salt onto a sheet of waxed paper.

Cream the butter in the large bowl of a freestanding electric mixer on moderately low speed for 3 minutes. Add the light brown sugar in 2 additions, beating for 1 minute on moderate after each portion is added. Add the granulated sugar and beat for 2 minutes longer. Blend in the eggs, one at a time, beating until incorporated. Blend in the vanilla extract and hot water. On low speed, blend in the sifted ingredients in 2 additions, beating until the flour particles are absorbed. Scrape down the sides of the mixing bowl frequently to keep the dough even-textured. Blend in the rolled oats, chocolate chunks, coconut, and macadamia nuts.

SHAPE THE COOKIES Drop generous 2-tablespoon-size mounds of dough on the prepared pans, spacing the mounds about 3 inches apart.

BAKE AND COOL THE COOKIES Place the cookies in the pre-heated oven for 12 to 13 minutes, or until set. Let the cookies stand on the pans for 2 minutes, then transfer them to cooling racks, using a wide offset metal spatula. Store in an airtight tin.

Bake-and-serve within 2 days

BUTTERSCOTCH CHOCOLATE CHIP COOKIES

About 3 dozen cookies

A chocolate chip cookie sweetened entirely with brown sugar tastes complex and confection-like, with its deep caramel flavor acting as backdrop for all those chocolate chips. Its flavor is a jot more sophisticated than my Favorite Chocolate Chip Cookies on page 138. There are a lot of chocolate chips in this dough, and skimping on the amount would be very sad indeed. When pecans are added, the cookies are reminiscent of praline candy—but with a very buttery, faintly fragile, crisp and crunchy-chewy edge.

BUTTERSCOTCH CHOCOLATE CHIP DOUGH

2 cups bleached all-purpose flour

¼ cup plus 2 teaspoons bleached cake flour

1 teaspoon baking soda

½ teaspoon salt

½ pound (16 tablespoons or 2 sticks) unsalted butter, softened

1½ cups firmly packed light brown sugar

2 large eggs

2 teaspoons vanilla extract

1½ teaspoons hot water

2¾ cups semisweet chocolate chips

CHOCOLATE CHIP TOPPING (OPTIONAL)

About ¾ cup semisweet chocolate chips

PREHEAT THE OVEN TO 350 DEGREES F. Line several cookie sheets or rimmed sheet pans with cooking parchment paper.

MIX THE DOUGH Sift the all-purpose flour, cake flour, baking soda, and salt onto a sheet of waxed paper.

Cream the butter in the large bowl of a freestanding electric mixer on moderately low speed for 3 to 4 minutes. Add the light brown sugar in 2 additions, beating for 2 minutes on moderate speed after each portion is added. Beat in the eggs, one at a time, mixing for 30 seconds after each addition. Blend in the vanilla extract and hot water. On low speed, blend in the sifted ingredients in 2 additions, beating until the flour particles are absorbed. Scrape down the sides of the mixing bowl frequently to keep the dough even-textured. The dough will be creamy-textured. Mix in the chocolate chips.

SHAPE THE COOKIES Place heaping 2-tablespoon-size mounds of dough on the prepared pans, spacing the mounds about 3 inches apart. Place 9 mounds on a pan. Top each mound with a few chocolate chips at this point, if you wish.

BAKE AND COOL THE COOKIES Bake the cookies in the preheated oven for 13 minutes, or until set and an even golden color. The cookies will spread and flatten as they bake. Let the cookies stand on the pans for 2 minutes, then transfer them to cooling racks, using a wide offset metal spatula. Store in an airtight tin.

Bake-and-serve within 2 days

STYLE For Butterscotch Chocolate Chip Cookies with Nuts, mix 1 cup coarsely chopped walnuts, pecans, or macadamia nuts into the dough along with the chocolate chips.

STUDY The blend of all-purpose flour and cake flour makes a cookie dough that is both tender-crisp and stable.

CANDYLIKE BUTTERSCOTCH BRITTLE CHIP COOKIES

About 4 dozen cookies

Crunchy, chewy, and absolutely crowded with semisweet chocolate chips, these are genuinely buttery cookies, with a resounding butterscotch edge to them. The dough mounds bake into fabulously golden rounds with a deeper color than some chocolate chip–styled cookies—brown sugar is a prominent ingredient that surely resonates—and this is what makes them so distinctive. Warm from the oven, one bite will enchant you. An unresolved question lingers: Is this a cookie or a confection?

BROWN SUGAR CHOCOLATE CHIP DOUGH

3 cups bleached all-purpose flour

1½ teaspoons baking soda

¾ teaspoon salt

¾ pound (3 sticks) unsalted butter, softened

1¼ cups firmly packed light brown sugar

1 cup granulated sugar

3 large eggs

2¾ teaspoons vanilla extract

1 teaspoon hot water

3 cups semisweet chocolate chips

PREHEAT THE OVEN TO 350 DEGREES F. Line several heavy cookie sheets or rimmed sheet pans with cooking parchment paper.

MIX THE DOUGH Sift the flour, baking soda, and salt onto a sheet of waxed paper.

Cream the butter in the large bowl of a freestanding electric mixer on moderately low speed for 3 minutes. Add the light brown sugar in 2 additions, beating for 1 minute on moderate speed after each portion is added. Add the granulated sugar in 2 additions and beat for 1 minute after each portion is added. Blend in the eggs, one at a time, beating until incorporated. Blend in the vanilla extract and hot water. On low speed, blend in the sifted ingredients in 3 additions, beating just until the flour particles are absorbed. Scrape down the sides of the mixing bowl frequently to keep the dough even-textured. Blend in the chocolate chips.

CHILL THE DOUGH Cover the bowl and refrigerate the dough for 45 minutes.

SHAPE THE COOKIES Place heaping 2-tablespoon-size mounds of dough on the prepared pans, spacing the mounds about 3 inches apart. The cookies will spread as they bake.

BAKE AND COOL THE COOKIES Bake the cookies in the preheated oven for 12 to 13 minutes, or until set and golden. Let the cookies stand on the pans for 2 minutes, then transfer them to cooling racks, using a wide offset metal spatula. Store in an airtight tin.

Bake-and-serve within 2 days

HOMESTYLE CHOCOLATE CHIP–OATMEAL COOKIES

About 3½ dozen cookies

From my family's file of favorite recipes to yours comes this wonderful—and wonderfully simple—oatmeal cookie recipe. The dough is exceptionally buttery. Both my mother and grandmother loved coconut and chocolate chips (me too!), so you know that both ingredients would figure in such a beloved recipe.

OATMEAL-COCONUT-CHOCOLATE CHIP DOUGH

1½ cups bleached all-purpose flour

1 teaspoon baking soda

¾ teaspoon salt

½ pound (16 tablespoons or 2 sticks) unsalted butter, softened

1 cup firmly packed light brown sugar

⅓ cup plus 3 tablespoons granulated sugar

2 large eggs

2½ teaspoons vanilla extract

1½ teaspoons hot water

2 cups "quick-cooking" (not "instant") rolled oats

2⅓ cups semisweet chocolate chips

2 cups sweetened flaked coconut

MIX THE DOUGH Sift the flour, baking soda, and salt onto a sheet of waxed paper.

Cream the butter in the large bowl of a freestanding electric mixer on moderately low speed for 3 minutes. Add the light brown sugar in 2 additions, beating for 1 minute on moderate speed after each portion is added. Add the granulated sugar and beat for 1 minute longer. Beat in the eggs, one at a time, blending until incorpo-

rated. Beat in the vanilla extract and hot water. On low speed, blend in the sifted ingredients in 2 additions, beating just until the flour particles are absorbed. Scrape down the sides of the mixing bowl frequently to keep the dough even-textured. Blend in the rolled oats, chocolate chips, and coconut.

CHILL THE DOUGH Refrigerate the bowl of dough, covered, for 30 minutes.

Preheat the oven to 375 degrees F. in advance of baking the cookies. Line several cookie sheets or rimmed sheet pans with cooking parchment paper.

SHAPE THE COOKIES Place rounded 2-tablespoon-size mounds of dough on the prepared pans, spacing the mounds about 3 inches apart.

BAKE AND COOL THE COOKIES Bake the cookies in the preheated oven for 12 to 13 minutes, or until set. Let the cookies stand on the pans for 1 to 2 minutes, then transfer them to cooling racks, using a wide offset metal spatula. Store in an airtight tin.

Bake-and-serve within 2 days

STYLE For Homestyle Chocolate Chip–Oatmeal Cookies with Nuts, mix ¾ cup coarsely chopped walnuts, pecans, or macadamia nuts into the dough along with the rolled oats, chocolate chips, and coconut.

BUTTERSCOTCH PEANUT CANDY-CHIP SAUCERS

About 4 dozen cookies

A mellow butterscotch flavor, along with chocolate chips and pieces of peanut butter–coconut candy, makes these cookies wonderfully rich, almost like a buttery, fully-loaded candy bar.

3 cups bleached all-purpose flour

1½ teaspoons baking soda

1 teaspoon salt

¾ pound (3 sticks) unsalted butter, softened

1¼ cups firmly packed light brown sugar

1 cup granulated sugar

3 large eggs

1 tablespoon plus 1 teaspoon vanilla extract

2⅓ cups semisweet chocolate chips

8 packages (1.75 ounces each) crunchy peanut butter toasted coconut candy bars (such as Zagnut), chopped

PREHEAT THE OVEN TO 350 DEGREES F. Line several heavy cookie sheets or rimmed sheet pans with cooking parchment paper.

MIX THE DOUGH Sift the flour, baking soda, and salt onto a sheet of waxed paper.

Cream the butter in the large bowl of a freestanding electric mixer on moderate speed for 3 minutes. Add the light brown sugar in 2 additions, beating for 1 minute after each portion is added. Add the granulated sugar in 2 additions, beating for 1 minute after each portion is added. Blend in the eggs, one at a time, beating until incorporated. Blend in the vanilla extract. On low speed, blend in the sifted ingredients in 3 additions, beating just until the flour particles are absorbed. Scrape down the sides of the mixing bowl frequently to keep the dough even-textured. Blend in the chocolate chips and chopped candy.

SHAPE THE COOKIES Place heaping 2-tablespoon-size mounds of dough on the prepared pans, spacing the mounds about 3 inches apart. Assemble 9 cookies on each pan. The cookies will spread as they bake.

BAKE AND COOL THE COOKIES Bake the cookies in the preheated oven for 13 minutes, or until set and golden. Let the cookies stand on the pans for 1 minute, then transfer them to cooling racks, using a wide offset metal spatula. Store in an airtight tin.

Bake-and-serve within 3 days

CHOCOLATE-TOPPED VANILLA COOKIES

About 4 dozen cookies

$\mathcal{A}$ dramatic collaboration of chocolate and vanilla springs from piping swirls of rich chocolate frosting onto equally lush vanilla cookies.

COOKIES
1 recipe dough for Chocolate Chip Sand Cookies, without the chocolate chips (page 425)

CHOCOLATE TOPPING
Chocolate Cookie Frosting (page 440)

PREPARE THE DOUGH Mix the dough according to the directions on page 425, omitting the final addition of chocolate chips. Refrigerate (or freeze) the dough according to the directions on page 427.

SHAPE, BAKE, AND COOL THE COOKIES Roll the dough into balls as described on page 427, but omit the final rolling in granulated sugar. Flatten the dough balls slightly with the smooth bottom of a glass (rather than with a fork). Bake and cool the cookies as directed on page 427.

ASSEMBLE A PASTRY BAG AND TIP Fit a 12-inch pastry bag with a star tip (Ateco #4F [a four-pointed star]; Wilton #1M [No. 2110, a large six-pointed star]; or Wilton No. 17, No. 18, No. 19, or No. 20) depending on the size of the frosting rosette desired (a coupler may need to be put in place depending on the size of the tip). I like having a big, bold rosette of chocolate cookie frosting on top of each cookie, but you may prefer a smaller one.

TOP THE COOKIES WITH THE FROSTING Fill the pastry bag about half full of frosting (an overfilled bag will be difficult to hold and maneuver). Place the cookies in a single layer on sheets of waxed paper. Pipe a rosette of frosting onto each cookie, letting the tip barely graze the top as you pipe the base. Let the frosting stand until firm, about 1 hour. Store the cookies (in single layers) in airtight tins.

Bake-and-serve within 3 days

CHOCOLATE COOKIE FROSTING

Buttery and chocolatey, this is an ideal frosting to use for piping decorative swirls on top of baked cookies for a boost of flavor and richness, or to sandwich in between cookies to sweetly seal them together. The frosting should be moderately firm but creamy enough to squeeze from a pastry bag. On a cold day in winter, you may have to increase the amount of milk, while on a humid day in summer, you may need to use more confectioners' sugar.

4 cups confectioners' sugar, or more as needed

⅛ teaspoon salt

6 ounces unsweetened chocolate, melted and cooled to tepid

2½ teaspoons vanilla extract

½ cup plus 1 tablespoon milk, heated to tepid

8 tablespoons (1 stick) unsalted butter, softened

Sift the confectioners' sugar and salt into the bowl of a freestanding electric mixer fitted with the flat paddle attachment. Add the melted chocolate, vanilla extract, and milk. Beat the ingredients on moderately low speed for 2 minutes to begin the mixing process. Blend in the butter, 2 tablespoons at a time, beating just until incorporated. Beat for 1 to 2 minutes on moderate speed, or until smooth. Scrape down the sides of the mixing bowl frequently to keep the frosting even-textured.

Adjust the texture of the frosting to piping consistency as needed, beating in additional milk about 2 teaspoons at a time (it is not necessary to warm the extra milk for this), or confectioners' sugar, 2 to 3 teaspoons at a time.

Fill the pastry bag with the frosting as directed on page 439.

If, when piped in the beginning, the frosting does not come away cleanly from the decorative tip and looks shaggy, you will need to add more milk. Conversely, if the frosting does not hold a defined shape or sit up in a plump swirl, spiral, or rosette, you will need to add more confectioners' sugar. To do this, unload the pastry bag, beat the contents and remaining frosting with the ingredient needed, and load into a clean, dry pastry bag.

Use the frosting immediately for loading into a pastry bag and piping on baked cookies. Press a sheet of food-safe plastic wrap on the surface of the rest of the frosting to prevent a crust from forming until you are ready to use it.

ELEMENT Swirls of the frosting can be applied to a flourless chocolate cake, chocolate torte, or tart in a ring around the outermost edge for a rich and provocative finish. Or, for a flavor and color contrast, pipe decorative rosettes on top of cupcakes or a layer cake assembled with white chocolate frosting. Use the frosting to sandwich together miniature chocolate, vanilla, or chocolate chip madeleines or to squiggle onto the tops of baked brownie or blondie squares or bars.

CHOCOLATE-TIMES-FOUR MUD SQUARES

16 squares

This batch of brownies reminds me of a soft candy bar, but one that's supple and completely saturated with chocolate. If you love your brownies fudgy and dense with chips and chunks, these are for you.

ULTRA-CHOCOLATE BATTER

1¼ cups bleached cake flour

¼ cup bleached all-purpose flour

¼ teaspoon baking powder

⅛ teaspoon salt

4 ounces white chocolate, chopped into small chunks

¾ cup miniature semisweet chocolate chips

½ pound (16 tablespoons or 2 sticks) unsalted butter, melted and cooled to tepid

5 ounces unsweetened chocolate, melted and cooled to tepid

3 ounces bittersweet chocolate, melted and cooled to tepid

4 large eggs

2 cups superfine sugar

2 teaspoons vanilla extract

TOPPING

4 ounces white chocolate, chopped into chunks

PREHEAT THE OVEN AND PREPARE THE BAKING PAN Preheat the oven to 325 degrees F. Film the inside of a 10 by 10 by 2-inch baking pan with nonstick cooking spray.

MIX THE BATTER Sift the cake flour, all-purpose flour, baking powder, and salt onto a sheet of waxed paper. In a small bowl, toss the white chocolate chunks and the chocolate chips with 1 teaspoon of the sifted mixture.

In a medium-size mixing bowl, whisk the melted butter, melted unsweetened chocolate, and melted bittersweet chocolate until smooth. In a large mixing bowl, whisk the eggs until blended, about 15 seconds. Add the sugar and whisk until combined, about 45 seconds to 1 minute. Blend in the vanilla extract and melted butter-chocolate mixture. Sift the flour mixture over and stir to form a batter, mixing thoroughly until the particles of flour are absorbed, using a whisk or flat wooden paddle. Stir in the white chocolate chunks and chocolate chips.

Scrape the batter into the prepared pan and spread evenly. Smooth the top with a rubber spatula.

BAKE, COOL, AND CUT THE SQUARES Bake the sweet in the preheated oven for 30 minutes. Quickly scatter the white chocolate chunks on top, then continue baking for 5 to 8 minutes longer, or until set. Let the sweet stand in the pan on a cooling rack for 3 hours. With a small sharp knife, cut the sweet into quarters, then cut each quarter into 4 squares. Remove the squares from the baking pan, using a small offset metal spatula. Store in an airtight tin.

Bake-and-serve within 3 days

STYLE For Nutty Chocolate-Times-Four Mud Squares, stir ¾ cup chopped walnuts, pecans, or macadamia nuts into the batter along with the white chocolate chunks and semisweet chocolate chips.

PECAN MUD BARS

*G*ood and nutty, these dense bars are filled with a generous mosaic of pecans winding their way through the dark chocolate batter. Pecan-lovers, you will fancy this easy-to-mix sweet.

CHOCOLATE COOKIE LAYER

8 tablespoons (1 stick) unsalted butter, melted and cooled to tepid

1⅔ cups chocolate sandwich cookie crumbs (such as crumbs made from Nabisco Oreo chocolate sandwich cookies) combined with 2 tablespoons ground pecans

CHOCOLATE PECAN BAR COOKIE BATTER

1 cup plus 1 tablespoon bleached all-purpose flour

¼ cup unsweetened alkalized cocoa powder

¼ teaspoon baking powder

⅛ teaspoon salt

½ pound (16 tablespoons or 2 sticks) unsalted butter, melted and cooled to tepid

4 ounces unsweetened chocolate, melted and cooled to tepid

4 large eggs

2 cups superfine sugar

2 teaspoons vanilla extract

1 cup coarsely chopped pecans

¾ cup coarsely chopped pecans, for topping the unbaked brownies (optional)

Confectioners' sugar, for sifting over the top of the brownies (optional)

PREHEAT THE OVEN TO 325 DEGREES F. Film the inside of a 9 by 9 by 2-inch baking pan with nonstick cooking spray.

MIX, BAKE, AND COOL THE COOKIE LAYER Pour the melted butter into the prepared baking pan. Spoon the cookie crumb mixture evenly over the bottom of the pan and press down lightly with the underside of a small offset metal spatula so that the crumbs absorb the butter. Bake the cookie layer in the preheated oven for 4 minutes. Place the baking pan on a rack. Cool for 10 minutes.

MIX THE BAR COOKIE BATTER Sift the flour, cocoa powder, baking powder, and salt onto a sheet of waxed paper.

Whisk the melted butter and melted chocolate in a medium-size mixing bowl until smooth. Whisk the eggs in a large mixing bowl to blend well, about 45 seconds, then add the superfine sugar and whisk for 45 seconds, or until combined. Blend in the melted chocolate-butter mixture. Blend in the vanilla extract. Sift the flour mixture over and mix until the particles of flour are absorbed into the batter, using a whisk, wooden spoon, or flat wooden paddle. Stir in the pecans.

Spoon the batter in large dollops on the cookie crumb layer. Carefully spread the batter over the cookie layer, using a flexible palette knife or spatula. Sprinkle the ¾ cup chopped pecans over the top, if you are using them.

BAKE, COOL, AND CUT THE SWEET Bake the sweet in the preheated oven for 30 to 33 minutes, or until set. Let the sweet stand in the pan on a cooling rack for 4 hours, then refrigerate for 1 hour, or until firm enough to cut. With a small sharp knife, cut the sweet into quarters, then cut each quarter into 6 bars. Remove the bars from the baking pan, using a small offset spatula. Store in an airtight tin. Just before serving, sift confectioners' sugar on top of the bars, if you wish.

Bake-and-serve within 3 days

ROCKY ROAD MUD BARS

2 dozen bars

*P*aved with these bars, a rough and rugged road is certainly sweeter: a chocolate cookie crumb layer forms a buttery base for a brownie batter packed with a madness of walnuts, chocolate chips, and miniature marshmallows. About 5 minutes before the bars have finished baking, you can toss a booster amount of chopped walnuts, chips, and marshmallows over the surface.

CHOCOLATE COOKIE LAYER

8 tablespoons (1 stick) unsalted butter, melted and cooled to tepid

1½ cups plus 3 tablespoons chocolate sandwich cookie crumbs (such as crumbs made from Nabisco Oreo chocolate sandwich cookies)

MUD BROWNIE BATTER

1¼ cups bleached cake flour

¼ cup unsweetened alkalized cocoa powder

¼ teaspoon baking powder

⅛ teaspoon salt

¾ cup semisweet chocolate chips

½ pound (16 tablespoons or 2 sticks) unsalted butter, melted and cooled to tepid

6 ounces unsweetened chocolate, melted and cooled to tepid

5 large eggs

2 cups superfine sugar

2 teaspoons vanilla extract

1 cup chopped walnuts

⅓ cup miniature marshmallows

PREHEAT THE OVEN TO 325 DEGREES F. Film the inside of a 10 by 10 by 2-inch baking pan with nonstick cooking spray.

MIX THE COOKIE LAYER Pour the melted butter into the prepared pan. Sprinkle the chocolate cookie crumbs evenly over the melted butter. Press down on the crumbs with the underside of an offset metal spatula so that the crumbs absorb the butter. Bake the cookie layer in the preheated oven for 4 minutes. Place the baking pan on a cooling rack and let stand for 10 minutes.

MIX THE BATTER Sift the flour, cocoa powder, baking powder, and salt onto a sheet of waxed paper. In a small bowl, toss the chocolate chips with ½ teaspoon of the sifted mixture.

Whisk the melted butter and melted chocolate in a medium-size mixing bowl until smooth. In a large mixing bowl, whisk the eggs for 1 minute to blend, add the sugar and whisk for 45 seconds to 1 minute, or until just incorporated. Blend in the melted butter-chocolate mixture, mixing thoroughly. Blend in the vanilla extract. Sift the flour mixture over and slowly stir it in, mixing until the particles of flour are absorbed, using a whisk, wooden spoon, or flat wooden paddle. Blend in the chocolate chips, walnuts, and marshmallows.

Spoon the batter in large dollops on the cookie crumb layer. Carefully spread the batter over the cookie layer, using a flexible palette knife or spatula.

BAKE, COOL, REFRIGERATE, AND CUT THE SWEET Bake the sweet in the preheated oven for 40 minutes, or until set. Cool the sweet completely in the pan on a rack. Refrigerate for 1 hour, or until firm enough to cut neatly. With a small sharp knife, cut the sweet into quarters, then cut each quarter into 6 bars. Store in an airtight tin.

Bake-and-serve within 3 days

MILK CHOCOLATE CHIP MUD SQUARES

*T*he sweet luxury of a dark chocolate batter intertwined with milk chocolate chips will please those who favor a little creaminess in a bar cookie. The milk chocolate chips are a sweet relief from all that dark chocolate. I love the squares inundated with pecans.

MILK CHOCOLATE CHIP MUD BATTER

1 cup plus 2 tablespoons bleached all-purpose flour

2 tablespoons unsweetened alkalized cocoa powder

¼ teaspoon baking powder

⅛ teaspoon salt

¾ cup milk chocolate chips

½ pound (16 tablespoons or 2 sticks) unsalted butter, melted and cooled to tepid

5 ounces unsweetened chocolate, melted and cooled to tepid

4 large eggs

2 cups granulated sugar

2 teaspoons vanilla extract

1¼ cups coarsely chopped nuts (walnuts, pecans, or macadamia nuts)

NUT AND CHIP TOPPING

¾ cup chopped nuts (the same type used in the batter)

½ cup milk chocolate chips

Confectioners' sugar, for sifting over the top of the squares (optional)

PREHEAT THE OVEN TO 325 DEGREES F. Film the inside of a 10 by 10 by 2-inch baking pan with nonstick cooking spray.

MIX THE BATTER Sift the flour, cocoa powder, baking powder, and salt onto a sheet of waxed paper. In a small bowl, toss the chocolate chips with ½ teaspoon of the sifted mixture.

Whisk the melted butter and melted chocolate in a medium-size mixing bowl until smooth. In a large mixing bowl, whisk the eggs for 1 minute to blend, add the sugar and whisk for 45 seconds to 1 minute, or until just incorporated. Blend in the melted butter-chocolate mixture. Blend in the vanilla extract. Sift the flour mixture over and stir it in, mixing until the particles of flour are absorbed, using a wooden spoon, whisk, or flat paddle. Stir in the chocolate chips and nuts.

Scrape the batter into the prepared pan and spread evenly. Smooth the top with a rubber spatula.

BAKE, COOL, AND CUT THE SWEET Bake the sweet in the preheated oven for 25 minutes. Carefully sprinkle with the nuts and chocolate chips, and continue baking 10 to 15 minutes longer, or until set. Let the sweet stand in the pan on a cooling rack for 4 hours, then refrigerate for 1 hour, or until firm enough to cut. With a small sharp knife, cut the sweet into quarters, then cut each quarter into 4 squares. Remove the squares from the baking pan, using a small offset spatula. Store in an airtight tin. Just before serving, sift confectioners' sugar on top of the squares, if you wish.

Bake-and-serve within 3 days

MUDSLIDES

*S*eriously chocolate, fudgelike, and entirely unforgettable. Oh my.

MUDSLIDE COOKIE DOUGH

7 tablespoons bleached cake flour

3 tablespoons unsweetened alkalized cocoa powder

½ teaspoon baking powder

Large pinch of salt

3 large eggs

1 cup plus 1 tablespoon granulated sugar

8 tablespoons (1 stick) unsalted butter, melted and cooled to tepid

10 ounces bittersweet chocolate, melted and cooled to tepid

2 ounces unsweetened chocolate, melted and cooled to tepid

2½ teaspoons vanilla extract

1¾ cups semisweet chocolate chips

PREHEAT THE OVEN TO 325 DEGREES F. Line several cookie sheets or rimmed sheet pans with cooking parchment paper.

MIX THE DOUGH Sift the flour, cocoa powder, baking powder, and salt onto a sheet of waxed paper.

In a large mixing bowl, beat the eggs and sugar on moderate speed for 1 minute, using an electric hand mixer. On low speed, beat in the melted butter, melted bittersweet chocolate, melted unsweetened chocolate, and vanilla extract. Sift the flour mixture over the chocolate mixture and blend it in completely. Stir in the chocolate chips. The dough will be soft and glossy. Place the bowl of dough in the refrigerator. Refrigerate for 15 minutes.

SHAPE THE COOKIES Place rounded 3-tablespoon-size mounds of dough on the prepared pans, spacing the mounds about 3 inches apart.

BAKE AND COOL THE COOKIES Bake the cookies for 14 to 15 minutes, or until just set. Begin checking the cookies at 13 minutes. The baked cookies will be soft but stable, and will look dry on top (not like wet batter). Let the cookies stand on the pans for 1 minute, then transfer them, still on the parchment paper, to cooling racks. Cool completely. Remove the cookies from the parchment paper, using a wide offset metal spatula. Store in an airtight tin.

Bake-and-serve within 2 days

STUDY Melt the butter and chocolates separately (although both the bittersweet and unsweetened chocolate can be melted together).

Baking the cookies at 325 degrees F. creates a soft, moist cookie through-and-through.

Cooling the baked cookies on the parchment paper helps to define their shape and set their texture.

A CHARMING, PROFOUNDLY VANILLA-FRAGRANT CHOCOLATE TORTE, DARK AND DAMP

One 9-inch cake, creating 8 to 10 slices

With its full chocolate presence, this engaging, easy-to-bake cake is one that highlights top-quality bittersweet chocolate, for there are an abounding 11 ounces of it in the batter, making it appropriately sludgy. Yet the end result is, as the title proposes, charming. The seed scrapings from a vanilla bean and almost a full tablespoon of vanilla extract further uplift the batter. Serve slices of the torte casually, with a puff or two of whipped cream, or doll it up with Bittersweet Chocolate Plate Sauce (page 390). A rush of Chocolate Fudge Sauce (page 376) would be marvelous, too.

DARK CHOCOLATE BATTER

11 ounces bittersweet chocolate, chopped

1 ounce unsweetened chocolate, chopped

12 tablespoons (1½ sticks) unsalted butter, cut into chunks

⅔ cup plus 2 tablespoons superfine sugar

Large pinch of salt

5 large eggs, separated

2¾ teaspoons vanilla extract

Seeds scraped from a small split vanilla bean

6 tablespoons bleached cake flour

⅛ teaspoon cream of tartar

Confectioners' sugar, for sifting on top of the baked cake

PREHEAT THE OVEN TO 350 DEGREES F. Lightly butter the inside of a 9-inch springform pan (2¾ inches deep).

MIX THE BATTER Place the chopped bittersweet chocolate, chopped unsweetened chocolate, and butter in a large saucepan. Set over low heat to let the chocolate and butter melt down slowly. Blend well. Add the sugar and stir slowly for 1 minute. As the sugar is integrated in the chocolate-butter mixture, the mixture will thin out—OK. Remove from the heat. As the mixture cools, whisk it now and again, until smooth. Cool to tepid. Stir in the salt.

Place the egg yolks in a large mixing bowl; whisk to combine. Blend in the vanilla extract and vanilla bean seeds. Whisk in about ¾ cup of the chocolate mixture, then blend in the rest. Sift the flour over the chocolate mixture and whisk it in.

In a large mixing bowl, whip the egg whites until just beginning to swell. Add the cream of tartar and continue whipping until moderately firm (not stiff) peaks are formed. Stir 4 large spoonfuls of the egg whites into the chocolate mixture to lighten it, then fold in the remaining whites. The batter will be somewhat thick and muddy.

Scrape the batter into the prepared pan. Gently smooth the top with a rubber spatula.

BAKE AND COOL THE TORTE Bake the torte in the preheated oven for 30 to 35 minutes, or until gently set throughout. Begin checking the torte at 28 minutes. Do not overbake. It will rise with an uneven surface—OK—and as it cools, will settle a bit—also OK.

Open the hinge on the side of the pan and remove the outer ring, allowing the torte to stand on the circular metal base. Sift a little confectioners' sugar on top of the torte and serve, cut into pie-shaped slices.

Bake-and-serve within 2 days

STUDY Almost any bittersweet chocolate in the range of 60% to 70% cocoa would be ideal to use in this cake, notably Scharffen Berger Bittersweet 70% cocoa; Valrhona Le Noir Gastronomie Chocolat Noir Bittersweet Chocolate 61% cocoa; or, Lindt Excellence 70% Cocoa Extra Fine Dark Chocolate.

THE TWOSOME OF HOT CHOCOLATE AND MARSHMALLOWS—the creamy fullness of chocolate-in-a-cup with a plump marshmallow lingering on top—is an alluring match. The combination will warm you and lift your mood. Hot chocolate is simply a matter of combining ingredients and heating them, but a cup crowned with a homemade marshmallow, well, just imagine how sensational that is. The emphasis here is *homemade,* as these marshmallows are thick, joyous, and so good that you'd be inclined to eat them just as I do: straight out of hand, like big, imposing bonbons.

HOT BITTERSWEET CHOCOLATE

*C*ocoa powder mixed to a light paste with hot water and bittersweet chocolate brings depth to this rich liquid beverage. A homemade marshmallow, creamy and touched with vanilla extract, caps it off. And there are times when I don't know which is better: the soothing hot chocolate or the melty marshmallow gliding over it.

2½ teaspoons unsweetened alkalized cocoa powder

2 tablespoons hot water

2 ounces bittersweet chocolate, chopped

1 teaspoon granulated sugar

¾ cup plus 2 tablespoons whole milk

3 tablespoons heavy cream (optional)

⅛ teaspoon vanilla extract

TOPPING (OPTIONAL)

1 Pillowy Cocoa-Dusted Vanilla Marshmallow (page 460) or

1 Ultra-Creamy Deep-Dish Vanilla Marshmallow (page 463)

Mix the cocoa powder and hot water in a ramekin, then scrape into a small, heavy saucepan. Add the chopped chocolate, sugar, and milk.

Place the saucepan over low heat to completely melt the bittersweet chocolate, stirring frequently. Add the heavy cream (if you are using it), increase the heat to moderately high, and whisk rapidly until the mixture is well-combined, smooth, and hot, with small bubbles appearing around the edges of the pan. Do not allow it to reach a rapid simmer.

Remove the saucepan from the heat, whisk in the vanilla extract, and pour into a large cup. Float a marshmallow on top, if you wish, and serve immediately.

STUDY The heavy cream, while optional, adds a rounded, creamy edge to the hot chocolate.

My favorite bittersweet chocolates to use for making hot chocolate are Valrhona Extra Amer Bittersweet 61% Cacao; Michel Cluizel Ilha Toma 65% cocoa; Lindt Excellence 70% Cocoa Extra Fine; Valrhona 64% semisweet couverture; or, Scharffen Berger Semisweet 62% cocoa.

My favorite cocoa powders to use for making hot chocolate are Valrhona Gastronomie 100% Cacao; Droste; Dean & Deluca Bensdorp Cocoa; or, Schokinag Special Edition developed exclusively with Schokinag by the Chocolate Masters of Christopher Norman Chocolates.

HOT WHITE CHOCOLATE

*T*his ivory-colored version of hot bittersweet chocolate is gentle and delightful, and as intense as its bittersweet cousin. Poured into a generously sized cup and crowned with a creamy marshmallow, hot white chocolate is one of my favorite late-night desserts. Sweet dreams.

2 ounces white chocolate, chopped

¾ cup plus 2 tablespoons whole milk

¼ cup heavy cream

¼ teaspoon vanilla extract

TOPPING (OPTIONAL)

1 Ultra-Creamy Deep-Dish Vanilla Marshmallow
(page 463)

Place the white chocolate, milk, and heavy cream in a small, heavy saucepan. Set the saucepan over low heat to completely melt the white chocolate, stirring frequently. Increase the heat to moderate and whisk rapidly until the mixture is well-combined, smooth, and hot, with very small bubbles appearing around the edges of the sauce. Do not allow the mixture to simmer.

Remove the saucepan from the heat and whisk in the vanilla extract. Pour into a large cup. Float a marshmallow on top, if you wish, and serve immediately.

STUDY A superb white chocolate to use in this hot drink is Valrhona Ivoire White Chocolate pistoles. A dash of vanilla bean paste (⅛ teaspoon) can replace the vanilla extract for a deeper finish that accentuates the taste of the white chocolate.

The presence of heavy cream in this drink—and I admit that this is extravagant—builds the luscious taste of good white chocolate. If you wish, make it with whole milk entirely, but realize that you'll be missing the flavor-heightening experience heavy cream conveys.

*T*he most authentic bundle of marshmallows would be made from the root of a plant so aptly called—what else?—the marshmallow plant (*Althaea officinalis*). Thankfully, a contemporary cook can make marshmallows from softened gelatine and a dense corn syrup–sugar mixture. My marshmallows are flavored with vanilla extract. Adding vanilla bean seeds or vanilla bean paste is a delicious option. The freshly made marshmallow mixture (like the one for Ultra-Creamy Deep-Dish Vanilla Marshmallows on page 463) is a sticky, pull-y one, and its creation requires a certain amount of patience, a heavy-duty freestanding electric mixer, and a sense of humor. It is important to read the entire recipe before you begin so that you know what to expect along the way.

Unlike commercial marshmallows, this regal confection does not readily dissolve in hot liquid. Rather, it slowly (*very* slowly, in fact) melts down into a luscious, creamy puddle. This attribute may be disconcerting to children. Although they are perfectly suited to slipping right on the top of a steamy cup of hot chocolate, I also use homemade marshmallows with abandon for flavoring other hot drinks (such as white hot chocolate) and for layering—playfully—within pudding and mousse mixtures (for the latter, dice the marshmallows and use them sparingly, for they are sweet and rich).

VANILLA-SCENTED MARSHMALLOW MIXTURE

Confectioners' sugar, for coating the pan and spatulas

3 envelopes plain unflavored gelatine

⅓ cup plus 3 tablespoons cold water

1⅓ cups plus 2 tablespoons granulated sugar

1⅛ cups (1 cup plus 2 tablespoons) light corn syrup

Large pinch of salt

9 tablespoons cold water

4 teaspoons vanilla extract

Seeds scraped from ½ small split vanilla bean or 1 teaspoon vanilla bean paste (optional)

CONFECTIONERS' SUGAR-COCOA MIXTURE FOR DUSTING THE MARSHMALLOWS

1½ cups confectioners' sugar sifted with 2 tablespoons unsweetened alkalized cocoa powder and whisked well to blend

PREPARE THE BAKING PAN Place about ½ cup of confectioners' sugar in an 8 by 8 by 2-inch baking pan; coat the bottom and sides with it (the sugar will stick in patches). Leave the remaining confectioners' sugar in the pan; it will form an uneven layer on the bottom—OK.

MAKE THE MARSHMALLOWS Place the gelatine in the large bowl of a heavy-duty freestanding electric mixer. Pour the ⅓ cup plus 3 tablespoons water over and let stand for 15 minutes. Put the whisk attachment in place.

While the gelatine is softening, place the granulated sugar, the corn syrup, the salt, and the 9 tablespoons water in a heavy, medium-size saucepan (preferably stainless steel–lined copper or enameled cast iron). Cover and place over moderately low heat to dissolve the sugar; stir the contents slowly (not actively) two or three times.

Uncover the saucepan, increase the heat to high, and insert a candy thermometer at the side. Make sure that the thermometer does not touch the bottom of the pan or the reading will be inaccurate.

Bring the syrup to a boil and boil until it reaches 248 to 250 degrees F. Do not stir the syrup as it is boiling. *Watchpoint: Never allow the hot syrup to come in contact with your skin at any time during the process of making marshmallows and protect your hands at all times when handling the saucepan and syrup.* Immediately and carefully remove the thermometer. Set the mixer on low speed and slowly pour the syrup into the softened gelatine. Increase the speed to moderate and beat until combined, about 1 minute. Increase the speed to high and beat the mixture for 3 minutes. Reduce the speed to low, add the vanilla extract (and optional vanilla bean seeds or vanilla bean paste), and continue beating on the high speed for 10 minutes longer. The mixture will turn opaque and very thick. It will look quite creamy.

TRANSFER THE MIXTURE TO THE BAKING PAN This is the tricky part—to quickly scrape the marshmallow mixture from the mixing bowl into the baking pan. Coat a sturdy spatula with confectioners' sugar and *quickly* (speed is essential here) scrape the marshmallow mixture from the beater and out of the bowl into the prepared pan.

Spread the marshmallow mixture into an even layer, using the spatula dipped in confectioners' sugar. Finally, sprinkle a little more confectioners' sugar around the edges of the pan, right up against where the marshmallow cake meets the sides of the pan.

"CURE" AND CUT THE MARSHMALLOWS Let the large marshmallow cake stand in the pan, uncovered, at room temperature for at least 6 hours (and up to 8 hours) to set and cure. Lift the whole marshmallow cake out of the pan with two spatulas (it will be flexible), score into 9 squares with a chef's knife, and cut it into sections. Coating the sides of the knife with confectioners' sugar will help with the sticking. Lightly coat the cut sides in the confectioners' sugar–cocoa powder mixture. Store, in a single layer, in an airtight container.

Freshly made, the marshmallows keep for 5 days to 1 week.

STYLE Marshmallows in pretty shapes can be made by cutting the large cake with a cookie cutter. To do so, prepare and use a 9 by 9 by 2-inch pan (rather than an 8-inch square pan); the marshmallow cake won't be as thick, which is better for cutting into shapes. Invert the cake onto a cutting board dusted with confectioners' sugar, then cut into shapes with a cookie cutter dipped in confectioners' sugar.

For plain marshmallows, omit the final confectioners' sugar–cocoa coating. Instead, coat the cut sides of the marshmallows in confectioners' sugar alone (without the cocoa powder addition).

For thinner marshmallows, use a 9 by 9 by 2-inch baking pan.

STUDY Do not double the recipe as the marshmallows won't be as texturally consistent.

Do not attempt making the marshmallows with any equipment of lesser power than a heavy-duty free-standing mixer. Do not use a hand mixer, no matter its power.

The ingredients should be measured meticulously to create marshmallows with the most luxurious texture.

I use Knox gelatine to make the marshmallows and the results are always consistent.

Marshmallows made in a hot or humid kitchen or on a rainy day may be stickier and/or denser (and still delicious).

Make sure that all pans and utensils that come in contact with the marshmallow mixture are grease-free; a lingering film of oil or butter will impair the texture of the finished sweet.

A HOMEMADE MARSHMALLOW IS A POWERFUL THING.

My recipes for homemade marshmallows, especially the Ultra-Creamy Deep-Dish Vanilla Marshmallows on page 463, have created a frenzy of marshmallow-lovers. It started innocently enough many years ago, during late winter and again in the spring when I wanted to make pretty pastel marshmallows to heap in a candy dish and offer along with slices of my birthday cake (for someone who dotes on sweets, cake is never quite enough), and to have for Easter, cut into the shapes of little chicks and bunnies or into angelic *petit four*-size cushions. Friends ate them faster than I could turn batches into baking pans to set. There wasn't even enough time to cut them into whimsical shapes, and there I was supplying most of my immediate world with packages of them to be consumed like candy, and probably as dessert. Cooks begged me for the recipe, and those that did not own a heavy-duty mixer thought about leaving the

Marshmallows without end

house immediately to buy one, with the express goal of mixing up their own stash of the confection—once able to secure the recipe.

At last, the two basic formulas for making marshmallows are revealed. In terms of texture, you will find them, as defined by a food-obsessed friend, nougat-like (a good description), and thoroughly scented with vanilla. You can dust the sticky cut sides with grated bittersweet chocolate, cocoa powder, or fine sanding sugar, tint them any color imaginable, or just have them plain.

I have reason to believe that marshmallows keep quite well in a tightly sealed container, although I can't seem to hold onto them long enough to tell without someone sweet-talking me out of a few.

ULTRA-CREAMY DEEP-DISH VANILLA MARSHMALLOWS

9 marshmallows

*T*his is a denser version of the classic, cushiony marshmallows on page 460. Using less gelatine and beating the mixture for a shorter period of time makes a panful of snowy marshmallows. Almost too good to float on a cup of hot chocolate, these marshmallows are like candy.

CREAMY MARSHMALLOW MIXTURE

Confectioners' sugar, for coating the pan and spatulas

2 envelopes plain unflavored gelatine

⅓ cup plus 3 tablespoons cold water

1⅓ cups plus 2 tablespoons granulated sugar

1 cup plus 3 tablespoons light corn syrup

Large pinch of salt

9 tablespoons cold water

4 teaspoons vanilla extract

Seeds scraped from ½ small split vanilla bean or 1 teaspoon vanilla bean paste (optional)

PREPARE THE BAKING PAN Place about ⅓ cup of confectioners' sugar in a 7 by 7 by 2-inch baking pan; coat the bottom and sides with it (the sugar will stick in patches). Leave the remaining confectioners' sugar in the pan; it will form an uneven layer—OK.

MAKE THE MARSHMALLOWS Place the gelatine in the large bowl of a heavy-duty freestanding electric mixer. Pour the ⅓ cup plus 3 tablespoons water over and let stand for 15 minutes. Put the whisk attachment in place.

While the gelatine is softening, place the granulated sugar, the corn syrup, the salt, and the 9 tablespoons water in a heavy, medium-size saucepan (preferably stainless steel–lined copper or enameled cast iron). Cover and place over moderately low heat to dissolve the sugar; stir the contents slowly (not actively) two or three times. Uncover the saucepan, increase the heat to high, and insert a candy thermometer at the side. Make sure that

the thermometer does not touch the bottom of the pan, or the reading will be inaccurate.

Bring the syrup to a boil and boil until it reaches 248 to 250 degrees F. Do not stir the syrup as it is boiling. *Watchpoint: Never allow the hot syrup to come in contact with your skin at any time during the process of making marshmallows and protect your hands at all times when handling the saucepan and syrup.* Immediately and carefully remove the thermometer. Set the mixer on low speed and slowly pour the syrup into the softened gelatine. Increase the speed to moderate and beat until combined, about 1 minute. Increase the speed to high and beat the mixture for 2 minutes. Reduce the speed to low, add the vanilla extract and optional vanilla bean seeds or vanilla bean paste, and beat for 1 minute. Increase the speed to high and beat for 8 minutes longer. The mixture will turn opaque and look creamy.

TRANSFER THE MIXTURE TO THE BAKING PAN Coat a sturdy spatula with confectioners' sugar and quickly scrape the marshmallow mixture off the beater and out of the bowl into the prepared pan.

Quickly spread the marshmallow mixture into an even layer, using a spatula dipped in confectioners' sugar. Finally, sprinkle a little more confectioners' sugar around the edges of the pan, right up against where the marshmallow cake meets the sides of the pan.

"CURE" AND CUT THE MARSHMALLOWS Let the large marshmallow cake stand in the pan, uncovered, at room temperature for at least 6 hours (and up to 8 hours) to set

and cure. Lift the whole marshmallow cake out of the pan with two spatulas (it will be flexible), score into 9 squares with a chef's knife, and cut it into sections. Coating the sides of the knife with confectioners' sugar will help with the sticking. Lightly coat the cut sides of the marshmal- lows in confectioners' sugar. Store, in a single layer, in an airtight container.

Freshly made, the marshmallows keep for 5 days to 1 week.

STYLE To tint marshmallows, have the chosen color of paste or gel color at hand (see page 51 for paste and soft gel food colors). Pretty shades to tint marshmallows, from the Cake Craft line of paste colors, include Salmon Pink, Apricot, Fuchsia Pink, Peach, Pink, and Buttercup. Squeeze a dot of color onto the tip of a clean toothpick or dip the tip into the paste color. Sink the toothpick into the marshmallow mixture when adding the vanilla extract (and optional vanilla bean seeds or vanilla bean paste), twirl to embed the color, remove it, and beat for 1 minute. Continue with the next step, beating the mixture for 8 minutes, but after 4 minutes, judge the color of the marshmallow mixture to determine if you should add a speck more of the food color. To add more color, add a little paste or gel color to the tip of a clean toothpick, stop the mixer, sink the toothpick in the mixture, twirl, and remove it. Continue beating for the remaining 4 minutes.

STUDY I use Knox gelatine to make the marshmallows and the results are always consistent.

Do not double the recipe as the marshmallows won't be as texturally consistent.

Do not attempt making the marshmallows with any equipment of lesser power than a heavy-duty free- standing mixer. Do not use a hand mixer, no matter its power.

Marshmallows made in a hot or humid kitchen or on a rainy day will be denser and stickier, but no less delicious.

Make sure that all pans and utensils that come in contact with the marshmallow mixture are grease- free; a lingering film of oil or butter will impair the texture of the finished sweet.

CHOCOLATE–CHOCOLATE CHIP MARSHMALLOWS

9 large marshmallows

*A*ren't these fun, with miniature chips dotting the puffy chocolate-tinged marshmallows?

1 recipe Pillowy Cocoa-Dusted Vanilla Marshmallows (page 460)

1¼ cups miniature semisweet chocolate chips, divided into ¾ cup and ½ cup amounts

Confectioners' sugar, for coating the baking pan and spatulas

½ cup miniature semisweet chocolate chips

Make the marshmallow mixture as directed in the recipe for Pillowy Cocoa-Dusted Vanilla Marshmallows (page 460) up through adding the vanilla extract: Along with the vanilla extract add ¾ cup chocolate chips and beat on high speed for 8 minutes (the chips will melt down in the marshmallow mixture and turn it a light brown color). Beat 2 minutes longer (total beating on high speed: 10 minutes). When the beating time is up, add the ½ cup chocolate chips and beat for 1 minute to combine.

Turn the marshmallow mixture into the pan as directed in the recipe. Immediately sprinkle the remaining ½ cup chocolate chips on top.

Let the marshmallow mixture stand in the pan for 8 hours, uncovered, before unmolding, cutting, and dusting with the confectioners' sugar and cocoa (or simply confectioners' sugar alone, if you wish), as directed in the recipe. Store, in a single layer, in an airtight container.

Freshly made, the marshmallows keep for 5 days to 1 week.

STUDY This recipe produces softer, slightly stickier marshmallows because the chips melt down in the mixture, causing it to soften more and expand less.

Do not double the recipe as the marshmallows won't be as texturally consistent.

Do not attempt making the marshmallows with any equipment of lesser power than a heavy-duty freestanding mixer. Do not use a hand mixer, no matter its power.

Storing and freezing chocolate baked goods

FRESHLY BAKED COOKIES, cakes, muffins, and scones should be stored in containers with tight-fitting lids at room temperature (or in the refrigerator as noted in certain recipes) and served within the recommended storage time in order to preserve their best taste and texture. It is preferable to store moist drop cookies and bar cookies in a container no more than two layers deep to keep them looking good and appetizing. Place sheets of food-safe greaseproof paper, parchment paper, or waxed paper between the layers for protection.

Freezing dough or fully baked sweets is an easy way to have all or part of the recipe finished in advance. Many quick breads, such as muffins or scones, can be frozen and reheated successfully, as long as an icing, drizzle, or glaze has not been applied. Streusel-topped muffins and scones freeze very well. Many dense chocolate bar cookies or tortes made with melted chocolate and melted butter (like brownies, mud squares, and fudgy one-layer cakes) also take well to freezing once baked. I am passionate about serving layer cakes and most butter cakes freshly baked, so I do not recommend freezer storage for these items. Depending on their structure, a few coffee cakes can be frozen and reheated without blemishing their taste and texture. Unbaked blocks or logs of cookie dough can be frozen successfully, and I encourage you to keep a favorite recipe or two in the freezer.

The following chart has been compiled after several years of baking, freezing, and defrosting the sweets in *ChocolateChocolate*. Those that tasted every bit as fresh and appealing when thawed and warmed, and the doughs that took well to freezing, appear here.

Frozen cookie dough logs must be thawed in the refrigerator in their wrappings; it's also preferable to defrost breads, bar cookies, muffins, and scones in the refrigerator *in their wrappings,* for this is the best way to preserve their texture, especially in warm weather or in a hot kitchen. To reheat coffee cakes (whole, in sections, or in squares), muffins, and scones, remove the wrappings and bundle the slices, squares, or individual pastries in a sheet of aluminum foil, leaving a wide gap at the top to prevent steaming, slide onto a baking sheet, and warm in a preheated oven. *(Note: Remember that all toffee and chocolate chip or chunk–based baked goods should be served cool, not hot. They are warmed only to be refreshed.)*

RECIPE CATEGORY AND RECIPE	FORM AND OPTIMUM FREEZER STORAGE TIME	REHEATING TEMPERATURE AND TIMETABLE
FAVORITE CHOCOLATE CHIP COOKIES (PAGE 138)	unbaked dough 2 months	—
SOFT CHOCOLATE CHUNK COOKIES (PAGE 141)	unbaked dough 2 months	—
DARK CHOCOLATE–CHOCOLATE CHUNK COOKIES (PAGE 142)	unbaked dough 1 month	—
PEANUT BUTTER–CHOCOLATE CHUNK COOKIES (PAGE 149)	unbaked dough 6 weeks	—
TOFFEE BUTTER BRITTLE CRISPS (PAGE 175)	unbaked dough 1 month	—
COCONUT–CHOCOLATE CHIP TURTLE COOKIES (PAGE 348)	unbaked dough 6 weeks defrost, bake, then top	—
BITTERSWEET CHOCOLATE–OATMEAL–DRIED CHERRY COOKIES (PAGE 379)	unbaked dough 6 weeks	—
DOUBLE CHOCOLATE–COCONUT–PECAN COOKIES (PAGE 394)	unbaked dough 6 weeks	—
DOUBLE CHOCOLATE–COCONUT HEAVENS (PAGE 397)	unbaked dough 6 weeks	—
DARK AND WHITE CHOCOLATE COOKIES (PAGE 419)	unbaked dough 1 month	—
BITTERSWEET CHOCOLATE–OATMEAL COOKIES WITH MACADAMIA NUTS (PAGE 428)	unbaked dough 6 weeks	—
BUTTERSCOTCH CHOCOLATE CHIP COOKIES (PAGE 431)	unbaked dough 6 weeks	—
CHOCOLATE CHIP SAND COOKIES (PAGE 425)	unbaked dough 1 month	—
HOMESTYLE CHOCOLATE CHIP–OATMEAL COOKIES (PAGE 435)	unbaked dough 6 weeks	—
CANDYLIKE BUTTERSCOTCH BRITTLE CHIP COOKIES (PAGE 432)	unbaked dough 6 weeks	—

RECIPE CATEGORY AND RECIPE	FORM AND OPTIMUM FREEZER STORAGE TIME	REHEATING TEMPERATURE AND TIMETABLE
CHOCOLATE-TOPPED VANILLA COOKIES (PAGE 439)	unbaked dough 1 month defrost, bake, then top	—
MUDSLIDES (PAGE 453)	unbaked dough 1 month	—

Cookies (molded or hand-formed)

CHOCOLATE CRESCENTS (PAGE 343)	unbaked 1 month freeze in logs for easy forming	—
CHOCOLATE-PECAN BUTTER CRESCENTS (PAGE 344)	unbaked 1 month freeze in logs for easy forming	—
CHOCOLATE CHIP BUTTER BALLS (PAGE 329)	unbaked 1 month freeze in logs for easy forming	—

Muffins

GIANT CHOCOLATE CHIP MUFFINS (PAGE 156)	baked 1 month	350 degree F. oven 10 minutes
GIANT CHOCOLATE CHIP COFFEE CAKE MUFFINS (PAGE 250)	baked 1 month	350 degree F. oven 10 minutes

Yeast-risen Sweet Rolls, Coffee Cakes, and Buns

CHOCOLATE SWIRLS (PAGE 209)	baked, without icing 1 month	350 degree F. oven 10 to 12 minutes to refresh, then apply icing when warm

RECIPE CATEGORY AND RECIPE	FORM AND OPTIMUM FREEZER STORAGE TIME	REHEATING TEMPERATURE AND TIMETABLE
CHOCOLATE CHIP CRUMB BUNS (PAGE 213)	baked 1 month	350 degree F. oven 10 minutes
CHOCOLATE CHIP PANETTONE (PAGE 219)	baked, without flavoring wash 3 weeks	reheat whole 325 degree F. oven 15 minutes, then apply flavoring wash
CHOCOLATE CHIP PILLOWS (PAGE 221)	baked 1 month	350 degree F. oven 10 minutes
VANILLA BABAS WITH BITTERSWEET CHOCOLATE CHUNK CREAM (PAGE 225)	baked, without soaking syrup and filling 1 month	350 degree F. oven 10 minutes, then moisten with syrup, and fill when tepid

Sources

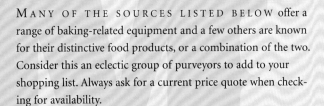

MANY OF THE SOURCES LISTED BELOW offer a range of baking-related equipment and a few others are known for their distinctive food products, or a combination of the two. Consider this an eclectic group of purveyors to add to your shopping list. Always ask for a current price quote when checking for availability.

AMERICAN SPOON FOODS, INC.

P.O. Box 566
Petoskey, Michigan 49770-0566
TEL.: Order toll-free 888-735-6700 or 231-347-9030;
CUSTOMER SERVICE: 800-222-5886
FAX: 800-647-2512 or 231-347-2512
WEBSITE: www.spoon.com

American Spoon Foods, Inc. carries a complete line of fruit-oriented pantry products and condiments. For using in chocolate-based sweets, the following items are worth noting: Chocolate-Covered Dried Red Tart Cherries; Fruit Perfect Cherries; Fruit Perfect Black Cherries; Sour Cherry Preserves; Cherry Marmalade; Red Raspberry Preserves; Apricot Preserves; Apricot Butter; Dried Red Tart Cherries; No Sugar Dried Red Tart Cherries; Dried Cranberries; Red Raspberry Preserves; Apricot Spoon Fruit; and Sour Cherry Spoon Fruit.

THE BAKER'S CATALOGUE
KING ARTHUR FLOUR

P.O. Box 876
Norwich, Vermont 05055-0876
TEL.: 800-827-6836 Monday through Friday 8:30 a.m. to 8:00 p.m., Saturday 9:00 a.m. to 5:00 p.m., Sunday 11:00 a.m. to 4:00 p.m.
FAX: 800-343-3002
BAKER'S HOTLINE: 802-649-3717, Monday through Friday, 9:00 a.m.–5:00 p.m. Eastern Standard Time
WEBSITE: www.bakerscatalogue.com

The Baker's Catalogue is a source for baking supplies and baking-related products, including measuring equipment; the Thermapen digital thermometer; baking pans; cooling racks; cutters; chocolates and cocoa powders, including Dutch-Process Black Cocoa powder and *Pain au Chocolat* sticks; vanilla-based products; sprinkles; specialty flours; and sugars, including Snow White Non-Melting Sugar, sparkling sugars, and sanding sugars.

BRIDGE KITCHENWARE CORPORATION

214 East 52nd Street
New York, New York 10022
TEL.: 212-688-4220
FAX: 212-758-5387
STORE HOURS: Monday through Friday 9:00 a.m. to 5:30 p.m., Saturday 10:00 a.m. to 4:40 p.m. Eastern Standard Time.
WEBSITE: www.bridgekitchenware.com

Bridge Kitchenware is a source for high-quality baking tools, including sifters and dredgers; measuring equipment; bench knives; pastry blenders; cake pans; muffin pans; tart pans; pastry cutter sets; baking sheets; spoons and spatulas; rolling pins; pastry brushes; pastry bags and tips; cooling racks, and other fine supplies.

A COOK'S WARES

211 37th Street
Beaver Falls, Pennsylvania 15010-2103
TEL: Orders, toll free, any time, any day: 800-915-9788
FAX: 800-916-2886
Information and inquiries: 724-846-9490 Monday through Friday 8:00 to 5:00, Saturday 9:00 to 1:00 Eastern Standard Time
WEBSITE: www.cookswares.com

A Cook's Wares stocks appliances (such as freestanding mixers), bakeware (such as muffin pans, jelly-roll and cake pans, dough scrapers and rolling pins, and pastry decorating equipment), cutlery; ovenproof porcelain; and a full range of utensils (including stainless steel shakers, tongs, ladles, whisks, spoons, measuring cups and spoons, mixing bowls, graters, and spatulas).

LA CUISINE—THE COOK'S RESOURCE

323 Cameron Street
Alexandria, Virginia 22314
Tel.: 703-836-4435
Fax: 703-836-8925
USA and Canada: 800-521-1176
Website: www.lacuisineus.com

The staff of La Cuisine is well-informed about every detail of the highly edited classic equipment and food-oriented products sold in this charming store. La Cuisine is a top source for fine bakeware, including madeleine plaques; baba molds; tart and cake pans; tart rings; petite (and charmingly doll-size) individual baking molds; baking sheets of all kinds; wooden spoons, flat paddles, and heat-resistant spatulas; pastry bags and tips; baking mats; and a range of knives. The store also stocks an exemplary selection of quality chocolates and cocoa powders; magnificent whole candied violets; flavoring extracts; nut pastes and nut flours; and decorations for pastries and cakes. The selection of copper, both tin and stainless steel-lined, is superb.

DEAN & DELUCA

New York City: 560 Broadway, New York, New York 10012
Tel.: 212-226-6800
Washington, D.C.: 3276 M Street, Northwest
Washington, D.C. 20007
Tel.: 202-342-2500
Catalog Center (Wichita, Kansas): 316-838-1255
Customer service: 800-221-7714
Website: www.deandeluca.com

In addition to prepared savory foods, baked goods, a full range of pantry items, and seasonal produce, Dean & Deluca stocks a variety of baking staples, including flours; baking sugars (including Arctic Snow Powdered Sugar); premium butters; bar and block chocolates; and a large range of packaged candies.

ENSTROM'S

Enstrom's Almond Toffee
P.O. Box 1088
Grand Junction, Colorado 81502-1088
Tel.: in Grand Junction 970-242-1655
Mail order tel.: 800-367-8766
Fax: 970-245-7727
Website: www.enstrom.com

Enstrom's almond toffee, available in various pound weights, is, quite simply, gorgeous—as candy or in baked goods. The block toffee slabs can be chopped into bits or chunks and used in recipes calling for this ingredient.

FRAN'S CAKE AND CANDY SUPPLIES

10396 Willard Way
Fairfax, Virginia 22030
Tel.: 703-352-1471
Monday through Saturday 10:00 a.m. to 6:00 p.m.

Fran Wheat's decorating and baking supply store offers a wealth of cake pans (standard and specialty square, round, and tube pans, as well as many decorative pans and molds [including the Wilton Mini Wonder Mold pan]); cake decorating equipment (including pastry bags and tips, plus an array of paste food colors); piping gel; a large range of sprinkles, non-pareils, and sanding sugars; decorative cupcake paper cases and picks; and icing spatulas, offset spatulas, and pastry brushes. Ms. Wheat, a talented cake baker and decorator in her own right, is a wellspring of information for the largess of decorating supplies that she sells.

KITCHEN ARTS & LETTERS

Nach Waxman, proprietor
1435 Lexington Avenue
New York, New York 10128
TEL.: 212-876-5550
FAX: 212-876-3584
E-MAIL: kalstaff@arc.com
Monday 1:00 p.m. to 6:00 p.m.; Tuesday through Friday 10:00
a.m. to 6:30 p.m.; Saturday 11:00 a.m. to 6:00 p.m.
Mail order available; annotated listing of new arrivals available
by e-mail (listings are produced 3 times each year)

Nach Waxman is impassioned about the literature of food. His
extensive inventory of books—with an impressive section on
baking, desserts, and chocolate—is all-encompassing to include
cookbooks and wine-related books, volumes on kitchen
antiques, technical and scientific works, and publications related
to the sociology and anthropology of food. Kitchen Arts &
Letters will customize lists for individuals seeking information
about specific areas of concentration.

NEW YORK CAKE AND BAKING DISTRIBUTOR

56 West 22nd Street
New York, New York 10010
TEL.: 212-675-CAKE; 800-94-CAKE-9, 10:00 a.m. to 5:00 p.m.
Eastern Standard Time
FAX: 212-675-7099
WEBSITE: www.nycakesupplies.com

New York Cake and Baking Distributor, a store firmly commit-
ted to the baker, stocks bakeware and decorating supplies of all
types and styles, including cake pans in a range of shapes and
depths; tart pans; muffin pans; cookie cutters; cooling racks;
rolling pins (including the nylon variety); individual baking
molds; sifters, strainers, and measuring equipment (including
nonstick measuring spoons); whisks and spatulas; and pastry
(decorating) bags, tips, and paste colors.

PENZEYS SPICES CATALOG OF SEASONINGS

19300 West Janacek Court
P.O. Box 924
Brookfield, Wisconsin 53008-0924
TEL.: to order toll free 800-741-7787
TEL.: 262-785-7676
FAX: 262-785-7678
8:00 a.m. to 5:00 p.m. Monday through Friday; 9:00 a.m. to 3:00
p.m. Saturday Central Time
WEBSITE: www.penzeys.com

Penzeys carries a full range of spices and extracts. Of particular
interest to chocolate-baking are the pure single and double-
strength vanilla extracts; whole vanilla beans; and pure almond
extract.

PRÉVIN INCORPORATED

2044 Rittenhouse Square
Philadelphia, Pennsylvania 19103
TEL.: 215-985-1996
FAX: 215-985-0323

Prévin offers a prime assortment of spoons and tongs; pastry
spatulas and cutters; dough scrapers; pastry bags and tips;
rolling pins; baking sheets; and baking molds and Bundt pans,
in addition to other baking accessories and supplies.

J.B. PRINCE COMPANY, INC.

36 East 31st Street, 11th Floor
New York, New York 10016
TEL.: 212-683-3553; 800-473-0577; phone orders 9:00 a.m. to
5:00 p.m. Eastern Standard Time
FAX: 212-683-4488
TELEPHONE ORDERS: Monday through Friday 9:00 a.m. to 5:00
p.m., Eastern Standard Time

J.B. Prince offers a fine selection of cutlery and bakeware,
including pastry bags, tips and brushes; cutters; cooling racks;
spoons and spatulas; superbly crafted serrated knives; fluted tart
pans, madeleine pans, cake pans (including extra deep tube
pans), and sheet pans; whisks and tongs; strainers; and an array
of specialty tools.

SUR LA TABLE

P.O. Box 34707
Seattle, Washington 98124-1707
TEL.: 800-243-0852 (24 hours a day)
FAX: 206-682-1026
DEDICATED CUSTOMER ORDERS: 866-328-5412 (Monday through Friday 6:00 a.m. to 6:00 p.m.; Saturday and Sunday 8:00 a.m. to 4:30 p.m. Pacific Standard Time)
WEBSITE: www.surlatable.com

Sur La Table carries knives, cookie cutters, freestanding electric mixers, pastry and decorating equipment, cake pans and molds, and a range of chocolate-specific materials for the baker.

TUPPERWARE

TEL.: for area distributor 1-888-TUPWARE
WEBSITE: for consultant www.my.tupperware.com
WEBSITE: www.tupperware.com

Tupperware storage containers are ideal for keeping cakes, cupcakes, soft drop cookies, all kinds of brownies, moist tortes, and soft-textured sweet yeasted buns and rolls. The base of the "Rectangular Cake Taker" has two useful sides: one side functions as a base for a 13 by 9-inch cake, and the other has 18 round indentations for standard-size cupcakes—very handy. Other items, such as the "Round Cake Taker," "Round Pie Taker" (which I also use for storing moist bar cookies and marshmallows), and the entire range of freezer, refrigerator, and pantry containers will organize your baking life nicely.

WILLIAMS-SONOMA, INC.

Mail Order Department
P.O. Box 7456
San Francisco, California 94120-7456
TEL.: 800-541-2233
FAX: 702-363-2541
TEL.: customer service 800-541-1262; weekdays 7:00 a.m. to 5:00 p.m., Saturdays 8:00 a.m. to 4:30 p.m. Pacific Standard Time
WEBSITE: www.williams-sonoma.com

Williams-Sonoma carries baking items such as cocoa powder and chocolate; vanilla extract, vanilla bean paste, and vanilla beans; top-quality almond extract; cookie and cake decorating equipment and supplies; electric mixers; measuring equipment; mixing bowls; strainers; knives; baking pans; tart, muffin and cake pans; spatulas; and a selection of premium boxed cookies and candies.

WILTON INDUSTRIES, INC.

2440 W. 75th Street
Woodridge, Illinois 60517-0750
TEL.: 800-794-5866
FAX: 888-824-9520
WEBSITE: www.wilton.com

The Wilton *Cake Decorating!* Yearbook (produced annually) is a valuable guide to cake decorating and specialty baking equipment. It is a resource for supplies, including Cake Release; nonstick cooling racks; pastry bags, tips, and couplers; icing spatulas; piping gel; and paste food colors. The Decorating Tips Guide is an important section devoted to showing the reader/baker what the various tips look like and the designs they make (each with a representative, corresponding squirt of icing).

THE INTERNATIONAL CAKE EXPLORATION SOCIETÉ

PMB 166
1740 44th Street SW
Wyoming, Michigan 49509-4249
WEBSITE: www.ices.org

This society spreads the sweet word on the art form of sugar. Its expansive membership works in the exacting world of cake decorating and sugar art. The annual meeting brings together industry professionals, including master craftsmen and craftswomen, authors, renowned teachers in the field, and manufacturers. Along with ICES, an excellent resource for learning about the art of cake decorating can be found in American Cake Decorating (www.gracemcnamarainc.com).

Bibliography

THE FOLLOWING LIST OF BOOKS has been chosen as a resource guide to baking in particular and to culinary techniques in general. Many feature appealing chocolate-based sweets, and some center on chocolate alone. The periodical mentioned at the close of the main bibliography, *Gastronomica: The Journal of Food and Culture,* is a distinguished source for important culinary literature. Good food writing makes delicious reading and this collection will likely have you leaping out of your chair to search the pantry and refrigerator for ingredients.

BOOKS

Allison, Sonia. *The English Biscuit and Cookie Cookbook.* New York: St. Martin's Press, 1983.

Alston, Elizabeth. *Biscuits and Scones.* New York: Clarkson N. Potter, 1988.

———. *Muffins.* New York: Clarkson N. Potter, 1985.

———. *Tea Breads and Coffee Cakes.* New York: HarperCollins Publishers, 1991.

Amendola, Joseph, and Donald Lundberg. *Understanding Baking.* New York: Van Nostrand Reinhold, 1992.

Appel, Jennifer, and Allysa Torey. *The Magnolia Bakery Cookbook.* New York: Simon & Schuster, 1999.

Appel, Jennifer. *The Buttercup Bakeshop Cookbook.* New York: Simon & Schuster, 2001.

Baggett, Nancy. *The International Chocolate Cookbook.* New York: Stewart, Tabori & Chang, 1991.

———. *The International Cookie Cookbook.* New York: Stewart, Tabori & Chang, 1993.

The Baker's Dozen, Inc. *The Baker's Dozen Cookbook,* ed. Rick Rodgers. New York: William Morrow, 2001.

Barrett, James, and Wendy Smith Born. *The Metropolitan Bakery Cookbook.* Emmaus, PA: Rodale, 2003.

Beard, James. *Beard on Bread.* New York: Alfred A. Knopf, 1973.

———. *James Beard's American Cookery.* Boston: Little, Brown and Company, 1972.

Beranbaum, Rose Levy. *The Bread Bible.* New York: W. W. Norton & Company, 2003.

———. *The Cake Bible.* New York: William Morrow and Company, 1988.

———. *The Pie and Pastry Bible.* New York: Scribner, 1998.

Bergin, Mary, and Judy Gethers. *Spago Desserts.* New York: Random House, 1994.

———. *Spago Chocolate.* New York: Random House, 1999.

Berl, Christine. *The Classic Art of Viennese Pastry.* New York: Van Nostrand Reinhold, 1998.

Bernachon, Maurice and Jean-Jacques. *A Passion for Chocolate.* trans. Rose Levy Beranbaum. New York: William Morrow and Company, 1989.

Bertolli, Paul, with Alice Waters. *Chez Panisse Cooking.* New York: Random House, 1988.

Bigelow, Fran, with Helene Siegel. *Pure Chocolate.* New York: Broadway Books, 2004.

Bilheux, Roland, and Alain Escoffier. *Petits Fours, Chocolate, Frozen Desserts, and Sugar Work,* vol. 3 of *Professional French Pastry Series.* Under direction of Pierre Michalet; trans. Rhona Lauvand and James Peterson. Paris: Compagnie Internationale de Consultation Education et Media and New York: Van Nostrand Reinhold, 1988.

Bloom, Carole. *All About Chocolate.* New York: Macmillan, 1998.

———. *Truffles, Candies & Confections.* Berkeley, CA: Ten Speed Press, 2004.

Bodger, Lorraine. *Chocolate Cookies.* New York: St. Martin's Griffin, 1998.

Boyle, Tish. *Diner Desserts.* San Francisco: Chronicle Books, 2000.

———. *The Good Cookie.* Hoboken, NJ: John Wiley & Sons, 2002.

———, and Timothy Moriarty. *Chocolate Passion.* New York: John Wiley & Sons, 2000.

———, and Timothy Moriarty. *Grand Finales: A Neoclassic View of Plated Desserts.* New York: John Wiley & Sons, 2000.

Brachman, Wayne Harley. *Cakes and Cowpokes.* New York: William Morrow and Company, 1995.

Bradshaw, Lindsay John. *The Ultimate Book of Royal Icing.* London: Merehurst, 1992.

Braker, Flo. *Sweet Miniatures.* New York: William Morrow and Company, 1991.

———. *The Simple Art of Perfect Baking,* Updated and Revised. Shelburne, VT: Chapters Publishing Ltd., 1992, 1985.

Braun, Margaret. *Cakewalk.* New York: Rizzoli International Publications, 2001.

Brody, Lora. *Chocolate.* San Francisco: Weldon Owen for Time-Life Books, 1993.

Brooks, Cindy. *Cindy's Itty Bitty Baking Book.* New York: Hearst Books, 1995.

Butts, Diana Collingwood, and Carol V. Wright. *Sugarbakers' Cookie Cutter Cookbook.* New York: Simon & Schuster, 1997.

Buys, Alain, and Jean-Luc Decluzeau. *Decorating with a Paper Cone,* trans. Anne Sterling. Paris: Cicem S.A. and New York: John Wiley & Sons, 1996.

Byrn, Anne. *Chocolate from the Cake Mix Doctor.* New York: Workman Publishing Company, 2001.

———. *The Cake Mix Doctor.* New York: Workman Publishing Company, 1999.

Clayton, Bernard, Jr. *Bernard Clayton's New Complete Book of Breads.* New York: Simon and Schuster, 1973, 1987.

———. *The Breads of France.* Indianapolis: Bobbs-Merrill Company, 1978.

———. *The Complete Book of Pastry Sweet and Savory.* New York: Simon & Schuster, 1981, first Fireside edition, 1984.

Coady, Chantal. *Real Chocolate.* New York: Rizzoli, 2003.

Corriher, Shirley O. *CookWise.* New York: William Morrow and Company, 1997.

Crocker, Betty. *Betty Crocker's Cooky Book,* facsimile ed. New York: Hungry Minds, 2002.

Cullen, Peggy. *Caramel.* San Francisco: Chronicle Books, 2003.

Cunningham, Marion. *The Fanny Farmer Baking Book.* New York: Alfred A. Knopf, 1984.

Daley, Regan. *In the Sweet Kitchen.* New York: Artisan, 2001.

Dannenberg, Linda. *French Tarts.* New York: Artisan, 1997.

Desaulniers, Marcel. *Death by Chocolate.* New York: Rizzoli International Publications, 1992.

———. recipes with Jon Pierre Peavey. *Desserts to Die For.* New York: Simon & Schuster, 1995.

———. recipes with Brett Bailey and Kelly Bailey. *Celebrate with Chocolate.* New York: William Morrow, 2002.

Dodge, Abigail Johnson. *The Weekend Baker.* New York: W. W. Norton & Company, 2004.

Dodge, Jim, with Elaine Ratner. *The American Baker.* New York: Simon and Schuster, 1987.

———. *Baking with Jim Dodge.* New York: Simon & Schuster, 1991.

Elbert, Virginie and George. *Dolci*. New York: Simon and Schuster,1987.

Farrell-Kingsley, Kathy. *Chocolate Cakes*. New York: Hyperion, 1993.

Flatt, Letty Halloran. *Chocolate Snowball and Other Fabulous Pastries from Deer Valley*. Helena, MT: Falcon Publishing, 1999.

Fleming, Claudia, with Melissa Clark. *The Last Course*. New York: Random House, 2001.

Fobel, Jim. *Jim Fobel's Old-Fashioned Baking Book*. New York: Ballantine Books, 1987.

Friberg, Bo. *The Professional Pastry Chef*, Third Edition. NewYork: Van Nostrand Reinhold, 1996.

———, with Amy Kemp Friberg. *The Professional Pastry Chef*, Fourth Edition. New York: John Wiley & Sons, 2002.

Galli, Franco. *The Il Fornaio Baking Book*. San Francisco: Chronicle Books, 1993.

Gand, Gail, and Julia Moskin. *Gale Gand's Just a Bite*. New York: Clarkson Potter Publishers, 2001.

Gisslen, Wayne. *Professional Baking*. New York: John Wiley & Sons, 1985.

Glezer, Maggie. *Artisan Baking Across America*. New York: Artisan, 2000.

González, Elaine. *The Art of Chocolate*. San Francisco: Chronicle Books, 1998.

Gourley, Robbin. *Cakewalk*. New York: Doubleday, 1994.

Gourmet, Editors of. *Gourmet's Best Desserts*. New York: Condé Nast Books, 1987.

Greenspan, Dorie. *Baking with Julia*. New York: William Morrow and Company, 1996.

———. *Paris Sweets*. New York: Broadway Books, 2002.

———. *Sweet Times*. New York: William Morrow and Company, 1991.

Greenstein, George. *Secrets of a Jewish Baker*. Freedom, CA: The Crossing Press, 1993.

Grunes, Barbara, and Phyllis Magida. *Chocolate Classics*. Chicago: Contemporary Books, 1993.

Hadda, Ceri. *Coffee Cakes*. New York: Simon & Schuster, 1992.

———. *Cupcakes*. New York: Simon & Schuster, 1995.

Halberstadt. Piet. *The Illustrated Cookie*. New York: Macmillan, 1994.

Hansen, Kaye, and Liv Hansen. *The Whimsical Bakehouse*. New York: Clarkson Potter Publishers, 2002.

Healy, Bruce, with Paul Bugat. *The French Cookie Cookbook*. New York: William Morrow and Company, 1994.

———. *Mastering the Art of French Pastry*. New York: Barron's, 1984.

———. *The Art of the Cake*. New York: William Morrow and Company, 1999.

Heatter, Maida. *Maida Heatter's Book of Great American Desserts*. New York: Alfred A. Knopf, 1983.

———. *Maida Heatter's Book of Great Chocolate Desserts*. New York: Random House, 1995.

———. *Maida Heatter's Book of Great Desserts*. New York: Alfred A. Knopf, 1974.

Hensperger, Beth. *Beth's Basic Bread Book*. San Francisco: Chronicle Books, 1999.

———. *Beth Hensperger's Bread Made Easy*. Berkeley, CA: Ten Speed Press, 2000.

———. *Bread for Breakfast*. Berkeley, CA: Ten Speed Press, 2001.

———. *The Art of Quick Breads*. San Francisco: Chronicle Books, 1994.

Hermé, Pierre, and Dorie Greenspan. *Desserts by Pierre Hermé*. Boston: Little, Brown and Company, 1998.

———. *Chocolate Desserts by Pierre Hermé.* Boston: Little, Brown and Company, 2001.

Hewitt, Mary-Jo. *The Biscuit Basket Lady.* New York: Hearst Books, 1995.

Johnson, Jann. *The Art of the Cookie.* San Francisco: Chronicle Books, 1994.

Jones, Judith and Evan. *The Book of Bread.* New York: Harper & Row Publishers, 1982.

Kennedy, Teresa. *American Pie.* New York: Workman Publishing Company, 1984.

Klivans, Elinor. *Bake and Freeze Chocolate Desserts.* New York: Broadway Books, 1997.

———. *Bake and Freeze Desserts.* New York: William Morrow and Company, 1994.

Knipe, Judy and Barbara Marks. *The Christmas Cookie Book.* New York: Ballantine Books, 1990.

Kosoff, Susan. *Good Old-Fashioned Cakes.* New York: St. Martin's Press, 1989.

Kunz, Gray, and Peter Kaminsky. *The Elements of Taste.* Boston: Little, Brown and Company, 2001.

Laver, Norma. *The Art of Sugarcraft Piping.* London: Merehurst Press, 1986.

Leach, Richard. *Sweet Seasons.* New York: John Wiley & Sons, 2001.

Lebovitz, David. *Room for Dessert.* New York: HarperCollins Publishers, 1999.

———. *Ripe for Dessert.* New York: HarperCollins Publishers, 2003.

Lenôtre, Gaston, revised and adapted by Philip and Mary Hyman. *Lenôtre's Desserts and Pastries.* Woodbury, NY: Barron's Educational Series, Inc. (English language edition), 1977.

Levy, Faye. *Dessert Sensations Fresh from France.* New York: Dutton, 1990.

———. *Sensational Chocolate.* Los Angeles: HPBooks, 1992.

Linxe, Robert, with Michèle Carles. *La Maison du Chocolat.* New York: Rizzoli, 2000.

Lopez, Ruth. *Chocolate: The Nature of Indulgence.* New York: Harry N. Abrams, 2002.

Luchetti, Emily. *Four-Star Desserts.* New York: HarperCollins Publishers, 1996.

———. *A Passion for Desserts.* San Francisco: Chronicle Books, 2003.

———. *Stars Desserts.* New York: HarperCollins Publishers, 1991.

Mackie, Leslie, with Andrew Cleary. *Leslie Mackie's Macrina Bakery & Café Cookbook.* Seattle: Sasquatch Books, 2003.

MacLauchlan, Andrew. *New Classic Desserts.* New York: Van Nostrand Reinhold, 1995.

Maher, Barbara. *Classic Cakes and Cookies.* New York: Pantheon Books, 1986.

Malgieri, Nick. *Chocolate.* New York: HarperCollins Publishers, 1998.

———. *Cookies Unlimited.* New York: HarperCollins Publishers, 2000.

———. *Great Italian Desserts.* Boston: Little, Brown and Company, 1990.

———. *How to Bake.* New York: HarperCollins Publishers, 1995.

———. *Nick Malgieri's Perfect Pastry.* New York: Macmillan Publishing Company, 1989.

———. *Perfect Cakes.* New York: HarperCollins Publishers, 2002.

McGee, Harold. *On Food and Cooking.* New York: Charles Scribner's Sons, 1984.

———, and Andrew Moore. *Afternoon Delights.* San Francisco: Chronicle Books, 2001.

Medrich, Alice. *Alice Medrich's Cookies and Brownies.* New York: Warner Books, 1999.

———. *Bittersweet.* New York: Artisan, 2003.

———. *Chocolate and the Art of Low-Fat Desserts.* New York: Warner Books, 1994.

———. *Cocolat.* New York: Warner Books, 1990.

———. *A Year in Chocolate.* New York: Warner Books, 2001.

Mentesana, Frank, and Jerome Audureau with Carolynn Carreño. *Once Upon a Tart.* New York: Alfred A. Knopf, 2003.

Moore, Marilyn, M. *The Wooden Spoon Bread Book.* New York: The Atlantic Monthly Press, 1987.

Neal, Bill. *Biscuits, Spoonbread, and Sweet Potato Pie.* New York: Alfred A. Knopf, 1996.

Ojakangas, Beatrice. *The Great Scandinavian Baking Book.* Boston: Little, Brown & Company, 1988.

Ortiz, Gayle and Joe, with Louisa Beers. *The Village Baker's Wife.* Berkeley, CA: Ten Speed Press, 1997.

———, Joe. *The Village Baker.* Berkeley, CA: Ten Speed Press, 1993.

Patent, Greg. *Baking in America.* Boston and New York: Houghton Mifflin, 2002.

Payard, François, with Tim Moriarty and Tish Boyle. *Simply Sensational Desserts.* New York: Broadway Books, 1999.

Peck, Paula. *The Art of Fine Baking.* New York: Simon and Schuster, 1961.

Peery, Susan Mahnke. *The Wellesley Cookie Exchange Cookbook.* New York: Simon & Schuster, 1986.

Pépin, Jacques. *La Methode.* New York: Times Books, 1979.

———. *La Technique.* New York: Pocket Books, 1976.

Peters, Colette. *Cakes to Dream On.* Hoboken: John Wiley & Sons, 2004.

Petzke, Karl, and Sara Slavin. *Chocolate: A Sweet Indulgence.* San Francisco: Chronicle Books, 1997.

Presilla, Maricel E. *The New Taste of Chocolate: A Cultural and Natural History of Cacao with Recipes.* Berkeley, CA: Ten Speed Press, 2001.

Purdy, Susan G. *A Piece of Cake.* New York: Atheneum, 1989.

Rabinovich, Adriana. *The Little Red Barn Baking Book.* New York: Clarkson Potter Publishers, 2002.

Reich, Lilly Joss. *The Viennese Pastry Cookbook.* New York: Collier Books, 1970.

Reinhart, Peter. *Crust and Crumb.* Berkeley, CA: Ten Speed Press, 1998.

———. *The Bread Baker's Apprentice.* Berkeley, CA: Ten Speed Press, 2001.

Robbins, Maria. *Baking for Christmas.* New York: St. Martin's Griffin, 1995.

———. *Chocolate for Christmas.* New York: St. Martin's Griffin, 1996.

Robbins, Maria Polushkin. Editor. *Blue Ribbon Cookies.* New York: St. Martin's Press, 1988.

Rodgers, Rick. *Kaffeehaus.* New York: Clarkson Potter Publishers, 2002.

Rosenberg, Judy, with Nan Levinson. *Rosie's Bakery All-Butter, Fresh Cream, Sugar-Packed, No-Holds-Barred Baking Book.* New York: Workman Publishing Company, 1991.

———. *Rosie's Bakery Chocolate-Packed, Jam-Filled, Butter-Rich, No-Holds-Barred Cookie Book.* New York: Workman Publishing Company, 1996.

Roux, Michel and Albert. *The Roux Brothers on Patisserie.* New York: Prentice Hall Press, 1986.

Rubin, Maury. *Book of Tarts.* New York: William Morrow and Company, 1995.

Rushing, Lilith, and Ruth Voss. *The Cake Cook Book.* Philadelphia: Chilton Books, 1965.

Sanchez, Maria Bruscino. *Sweet Maria's Cake Kitchen.* New York: St. Martin's Griffin, 1998.

———. *Sweet Maria's Cookie Jar.* New York: St. Martin's Griffin, 2002.

———. *Sweet Maria's Italian Cookie Tray.* New York: St. Martin's Griffin, 1997.

Sax, Richard. *Classic Home Desserts.* Shelburne, VT: Chapters Publishing, Ltd., 1994.

———. *The Cookie Lover's Cookbook.* New York: Harper & Row, 1986.

Scherber, Amy, and Toy Kim Dupree. *Amy's Bread.* William Morrow and Company, 1996.

Schinz, Marina. *The Book of Sweets.* New York: Harry N. Abrams, 1994.

Schulz, Philip Stephen. *As American as Apple Pie.* New York: Simon and Schuster, 1990.

Scicolone, Michele. *La Dolce Vita.* New York: William Morrow and Company, 1993.

Shere, Lindsey Remolif. *Chez Panisse Desserts.* New York: Random House, 1985.

Silverton, Nancy, with Heidi Yorkshire. *Desserts by Nancy Silverton.* New York: Harper & Row, 1986.

———, with Laurie Ochoa. *Nancy Silverton's Breads from the La Brea Bakery.* New York: Villard Books, 1996.

Simmons, Marie. *A to Z Bar Cookies.* Shelburne, VT: Chapters Publishing, Ltd., 1994.

Standard, Stella. *Our Daily Bread.* New York: Funk and Wagnalls, 1970.

Thompson, Sylvia. *The Birthday Cake Book.* San Francisco: Chronicle Books, 1993.

Truax, Carol, Editor. *Ladies' Home Journal Dessert Cookbook.* Garden City: Nelson Doubleday & Company, 1964.

Urvater, Michele. *Chocolate Cake.* New York: Broadway Books, 2001.

Van Cleave, Jill. *Icing the Cake.* Chicago: Contemporary Books, 1990.

Vincent, Kerry. *Romantic Wedding Cakes.* London: Merehurst, 2001.

Walter, Carole. *Great Cakes.* New York: Ballantine Books, 1991.

———. *Great Cookies.* New York: Clarkson Potter Publishers, 2003.

Warren, Ann, with Joan Lilly. *The Cupcake Café Cookbook.* New York: Doubleday, 1998.

Weinstein, Bruce. *The Ultimate Brownie Book.* New York: William Morrow & Company, 2002.

Weinstock, Sylvia, with Kate Manchester. *Sweet Celebrations.* New York: Simon & Schuster, 1999.

Welch, Adrienne. *Sweet Seduction.* New York: Harper & Row, 1984.

Wilkerson, Arnold, Patricia Henly, and Michael Deraney, with Evie Righter. *The Little Pie Company of the Big Apple Pies and Other Dessert Favorites.* New York: HarperPerennial, 1993.

Willan, Anne. *Anne Willan's Look and Cook Chocolate Desserts.* New York: Dorling Kindersley, 1992.

———. *La Varenne Practique.* New York: Crown Publishers, 1989.

Wilson, Dede. *A Baker's Field Guide to Chocolate Chip Cookies.* Boston: The Harvard Common Press, 2004.

———. *A Baker's Field Guide to Christmas Cookies.* Boston: The Harvard Common Press, 2003.

Witty, Helen. *Mrs. Witty's Monster Cookies.* New York: Workman Publishing Company, 1983.

Wolke, Robert L. *What Einstein Told His Cook: Kitchen Science Explained.* New York: W. W. Norton & Company, 2002.

Yard, Sherry. *The Secrets of Baking.* Boston: Houghton Mifflin Company, 2003.

Yockelson, Lisa. *Baking by Flavor.* New York: John Wiley & Sons, 2002.

Zipe, Bruce. *Bruce's Bakery Cookbook.* New York: Clarkson Potter Publishers, 2000.

Zisman, Honey and Larry. *The 47 Best Chocolate Chip Cookies in the World.* New York: St. Martin's Press, 1983.

———. *57 More of the Best Chocolate Chip Cookies in the World.* New York: St. Martin's Griffin, 1997.

———. *Chocolate Fantasies.* New York: Pocket Books, 1988.

PERIODICALS

Yockelson, Lisa. "Brownies: A Memoir." *Gastronomica: The Journal of Food and Culture.* Berkeley: University of California Press, Winter 2002, Volume 2, Number 1, 84–88.

———. "The Gentle Rise of (Real) Cake." *Gastronomica: The Journal of Food and Culture.* Berkeley: University of California Press, Summer 2004, Volume 4, Number 3, 75–77.

PAGE II:
So beautiful. This Rose Petal Bar 54% Cacao from Byrne & Carlson Chocolatier*Confectioner is nestled in linen to showcase its figure, style, and luxury

PAGE XVI:
The Pansy Bar 54% Cacao from Byrne & Carlson Chocolatier* Confectioner is a charming chocolate nibble

PAGE 4:
Scharffen Berger Cacao Nibs are the essence of chocolate itself

PAGE 7: *upper left*
Chunks of Valrhona White Gastronomie Chocolat Blanc would boldly distinguish any dark chocolate batter

PAGE 7: *upper right*
A longstanding favorite and enduring staple of an American childhood, Nestle's Chocolate Chips are ready to tumble right into a cookie dough

PAGE 7: *bottom right*
Deeply chocolate, cut into craggy pieces or melted, Valrhona Le Noir Amer Chocolat Noir Dark Bittersweet Chocolate 71% Cacao is an indulgent way to make a sweet sing with flavor

PAGE 7: *bottom left*
Scharffen Berger 70% Cacao Dark Chocolate Bittersweet Bar is deluxe and complex

PAGE 10: *upper left*
Eclats de Cacao Michel Cluizel Cocoa Bean Pieces Coated with Dark Chocolate become a sweet and dramatic accessory to the rounded edge of a tart or an iced torte

PAGE 10: *upper right*
Creamy and lavish, premium milk chocolate from Schokinag by the Chocolate Masters of Christopher Norman Chocolate, Ltd., Special Edition Milk Chocolate Bar 38% cacao, adds depth to a drop cookie dough or press-in-the-pan shortbread

PAGE 10: *bottom right*
Zing! Dr. Peter's Chocolate-Covered Peppermint Crunch (Jo's Candies), crushed into bits and fragments, is a favorite ingredient for dark chocolate drop cookies or deep chocolate brownies

PAGE 10: *bottom left*
Valrhona Cocoa Pate Extra 100% Unsweetened Chocolate is potent and complex

PAGE 15: *upper left*
Not-to-be-missed candy, Enstrom's Almond Toffee is buttery-divine: be indulgent and make chunks of it your secret ingredient in a brownie batter

PAGE 15: *upper right*
Using classic American candy bars—Heath, Milky Way Midnight, Reese's Peanut Butter Cups, Zagnut, Mounds, Skor, and Snicker's among them—in all kinds of baking adds great dimension and wonderful, old-fashioned flavor

PAGE 15: *bottom right*
What fun! Beautiful—and so long—India Tree Chocolate Vermicelli Decoratifs to sprinkle on anything lavishly frosted

PAGE 15: *bottom left*
Roll and tuck Pain au Chocolat Sticks (from King Arthur Flour, The Baker's Catalogue) into a yeast dough for a chocolate surprise

PAGE 42:
Queen Guinevere Cake Flour (from King Arthur Flour, The Baker's Catalogue) makes the lightest cakes, gorgeous and impressive

PAGE 45:
Plugrá and Celles sur Belle butter, catching a glimmer of the morning light, await creaming into a suave, sugary mixture for a batter or dough

PAGE 50: *upper left*
Sweetness: India Tree Caster Sugar, India Tree Fondant & Icing Powdered Cane Sugar, and India Tree Golden Baker's Sugar

PAGE 50: *upper right*
Rich blocks of premium butter

PAGE 50: *bottom right*
BIA Organic Marzipan (from BIA Stramondo, produced and packed by Stramondo, Sicily, Imported Exclusively by Purely Organic, Ltd., Fairfield, IA) adds a moist, nutty edge and rounded almond bouquet to a fudgy chocolate cake or pan of bar cookies

PAGE 50: *bottom left*
Star Kay White's Chocolate Extract is luminous in a glass cruet

PAGE 53:
Baker's delight—a radiant mound of cocoa powder

PAGE 58: *upper left*
Chocolate Chip and Nut "Gravel" makes a deliciously bumpy and craggy topping or filling

PAGE 58: *upper right*
Fleur de Sel Caramels (from Crossings, Importers of Specialty French Food) are a great flavor boost and contrast to chocolate

PAGE 58: *bottom right*
Vanilla—in the form of Zeron Double Intensity Pure Veracruz Vanilla Extract, Pure Bourbon Vanilla Powder from Madagascar, and homemade Essence of Vanilla Granulated Sugar—releases a fragrant and rounded aroma to nearly anything baked with chocolate

PAGE 58: *bottom left*
Chocolate Liqueur and Sugar Wash, ready to brush on a warm butter cake, adds a crackly, high-flavor coating

PAGE 61:
Simply stated, these Aracuana eggs (from Highfield Dairy and Farm in Fulton County, PA) are exquisite in color, taste, and texture

Index